W9-AOB-601

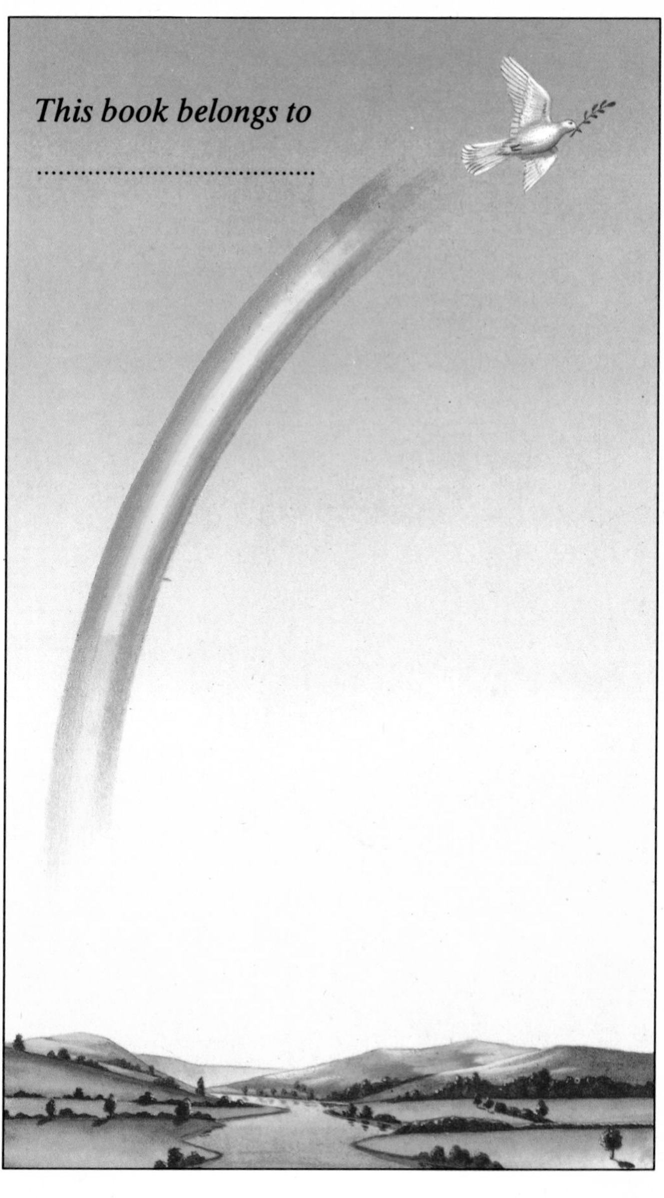

This book belongs to
....

COLLINS BIBLE HANDBOOK

COLLINS BIBLE HANDBOOK

by Jacques Musset

translated by Sarah Thomas and Penny Stanley-Baker

Collins Liturgical Publications
8 Grafton Street, London W1X 3LA

Harper & Row
Icehouse One – 401
151 Union Street, San Francisco, CA 94111-1299

Collins Liturgical in Canada
Novalis, Box 9700, Terminal
375 Rideau St, Ottawa, Ontario K1G 4B4

Collins Dove
PO Box 316, Blackburn, Victoria 3130

Collins Liturgical New Zealand
PO Box 1, Auckland

First published in two parts as *Le Livre de la Bible: L'Ancien Testament,* © Editions Gallimard 1985, and *Le Livre de la Bible: Le Nouveau Testament,* © Editions Gallimard 1987.

First published in English, 1988

ISBN 0 00 599134 X

Typeset by Swains (Glasgow) Limited
Printed in Italy

Old Testament Table of Contents

THE CHARACTERS

THE STORY

New Testament Table of Contents

Symbols of Christ. **The anchor**: hope; **the lamb**: Christ, the sacrificial victim; **the cross**: redemption; **the tree of life**; **alpha and omega**: the beginning and end of all things;

JESUS THE MESSIAH

THE FIRST CHRISTIANS

the pelican: feeds its young on its own flesh; **the vine**: Jesus; **chrism**: first two Greek letters of Christ; **the fish**: in Greek, Jesus Christ, son of God, saviour.

A guide to some of the different versions of the Bible

Details of the history of the Bible and the first translation into English are given on pages 20-25. This is a guide to some of the well known versions currently in use.

King James Version (Authorised Version)

The most widely used version of the Bible, conforming to the edition of 1611 which was a translation from the Greek and Hebrew texts commissioned by King James I of Great Britain.

Revised Standard Version

This is a widely used modern translation of the Bible, authorised in 1937 by the International Council for Religious Education. It was first published in 1952. It incorporates the advances of modern biblical scholarship both in improved textual readings and improved understanding of biblical Hebrew and New Testament Greek. The New Testament was further revised in 1952. The **Common Bible** includes the Apocrypha/Deuterocanonical books and is a translation accepted by all major denominations.

Good News Bible (Today's English Version)

This is the version used in the *Collins Bible Handbook*. This version seeks to express the true meaning of the text in language accepted as standard by English-speaking people everywhere. It was first published in 1976.

New English Bible

This was prepared by a Joint Committee formed in 1946 by the Methodist, Baptist and Congregational Churches of the United Kingdom, along with the Churches of England and Scotland. The complete New English Bible was first published in 1970.

The Jerusalem Bible

This translation is fairly widely used, particularly by Roman

Catholics. It is noted for the beauty of its English. First published in 1966, a revised edition was published in 1985.

New American Bible

The first American translation of the complete Bible from the original languages into English. First published 1960.

New International Version (NIV)

Over 100 scholars worked directly from the Hebrew, Aramaic and Greek texts. The New Testament was first published in 1973 and the complete Bible in 1978.

The New Testament by William Barclay

A translation that seeks, in the writer's own words, 'to make the New Testament intelligible to the man who is not a technical scholar', and which does not need 'a commentary to explain it'. Reflects the author's excellent reputation among biblical scholars. Written in simple, clear and graceful English. First published in 1968.

COLLINS BIBLE HANDBOOK

Old Testament

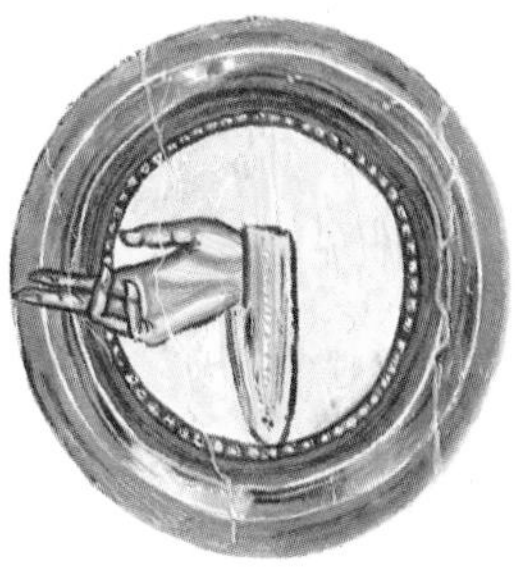

A book that never grows old

The earliest surviving fragments of the Bible are the Dead Sea Scrolls, which are about two thousand years old. The handwritten leather scrolls, preserved in sealed jars, were only discovered in 1947 at Qum'ran near the Dead Sea.

In the Middle Ages monks copied out the Bible on to parchments.

No other book in the world is as widely read as the Bible. For the last two thousand years people have been copying, printing and translating it into different languages.

The Bible is the story of two great world religions: Judaism and Christianity. The Jews are descended from a small nation called Israel. The Bible records the history of Israel from the

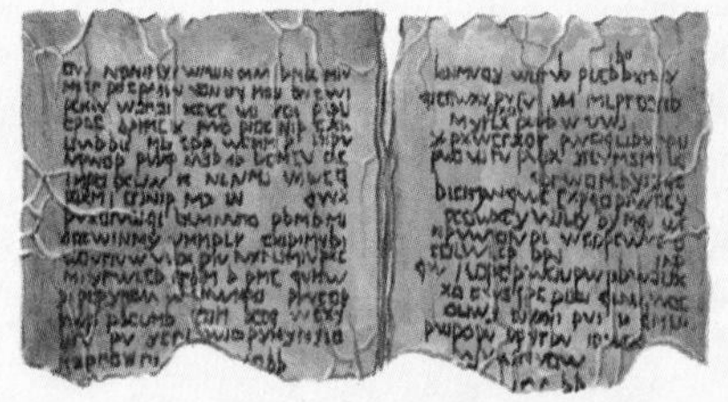

year 1800 B.C. to 50 B.C. Christians are the followers of a Jew called Jesus who lived two thousand years ago.

The book Christians call 'The Bible' is bigger than that which the Jews call by the same name. The latter comprises only the Old Testament (or 'Covenant'), whereas the Christian Bible also includes the New Testament which is all about Jesus and his followers, the first Christians.

In the first half of this book we will be talking about the Old Testament, and in the second half we consider the New Testament.

You don't have to be a Jew or a Christian to find the Bible interesting. The Bible has something to say to each of us. Generations of poets, painters, sculptors, writers and philosophers have found inspiration in its pages.

The Qumran caves where the Dead Sea Scrolls were found.

Old and New Testament

The word testament comes from the Latin *testamentum* meaning an agreement or 'covenant'. This was a solemn and binding contract, with conditions on both sides. Christians believe the Old Testament to be the first agreement or Covenant made between God and the people of Israel. The New Testament is the New Covenant made by God with all people through Jesus Christ.

Page from the first printed version of the Bible, the Gutenberg Bible (about 1450).

In 1980, a total of 10 million Bibles were sold in 275 different languages.

1 Jewish Bible: Old Testament only.
2 Christian Bible: Old and New Testaments.

A collection of books

Books of the Old Testament in alphabetical order of abbreviation:

Amos	Amos
Bar	Baruch
1 Chr	1 Chronicles
2 Chr	2 Chronicles
Dan	Daniel
Deut	Deuteronomy
Ecc	Ecclesiastes
1 Esd	1 Esdras
2 Esd	2 Esdras
Esth	Esther
Ex	Exodus
Ezek	Ezekiel
Ezra	Ezra
Gen	Genesis
Hab	Habbakuk
Hag	Haggai
Hos	Hosea
Is	Isaiah
Jer	Jeremiah
Job	Job
Joel	Joel
Jon	Jonah
Josh	Joshua
Judg	Judges
Jdt	Judith
1 Kgs	1 Kings
2 Kgs	2 Kings
Lam	Lamentations
Lev	Leviticus
1 Macc	1 Maccabees
2 Macc	2 Maccabees
Mal	Malachi
Mic	Micah
Nah	Nahum
Neh	Nehemiah
Num	Numbers
Obad	Obadiah
Prov	Proverbs
Ps	Psalms
Ruth	Ruth
1 Sam	1 Samuel
2 Sam	2 Samuel
Sir	Sirach
Song	Song of Songs
Ws	Wisdom
Zech	Zechariah
Zeph	Zephaniah

The word 'Bible' comes from the Greek *ta biblia*, meaning 'books'.

This is just what the Bible is – a collection of some forty books, written in Hebrew over a period of a thousand years.

Traditionally they were divided into three separate categories: the Law (or Torah), the Prophets, the Scriptures.

Page from the Book of Job (11th c.)

At the end of the first century A.D., the Jews in Palestine declared the list of thirty-nine books complete. These Hebrew texts make up the Jewish Bible, still in use today.

At the same time, the Jews in Egypt drew up a separate list which included several books written in Greek.

Nowadays Protestant Christians use only those Old Testament books on the Palestine Jews' list, whereas Roman Catholics use the Egyptian Jew's extended version of the Old Testament.

The roof of the Book Sanctuary in Jerusalem where the Dead Sea Scrolls are kept.

The first translation of the Bible into English

The first complete translation of the Bible into English was the work of John Wycliffe. The official version of the Bible was in Latin until the sixteenth century when the first English Bibles were used in churches. There are now a great many modern translations and versions of the Bible to choose from; the version used in this book is the *Good News Bible.*

Finding your way around the Bible; chapter and verse

Originally the books were not divided into chapters and verses. Stephen Langton, an English bishop, first thought of dividing each book into chapters in the 13th century. Three hundred years later a French printer, Robert Estienne, broke up the text into verses of one or two sentences each.

The chapters and verses are numbered. Whenever a passage from the Bible is quoted, the name of the book (in abbreviated form) is given first, followed by the chapter and the verse. This is what is called a text reference. So **Ex 3.2-6** means Book of Exodus, chapter 3, verses 2 to 6.

Torah Scroll (the Law)

This is the order of books in most Bibles. Catholic Bibles include those in Group 5, the Apocrypha. These were originally part of the Greek Septuagint Bible (see p. 258). They are interspersed amongst the other Old Testament books.

1 The Law
2 History
3 Poetry and Wisdom Literature
4 The Prophets
5 The Apocrypha (Deuterocanonical Books)

The Bible in history

3200 B.C. Cyclades civilisation

3100 Sumerians invent cuneiform writing

3000 Stonehenge (England)

2600 Pyramids

2500-2000 Early Minoan civilisation

About 1250 The Exodus

The Tablets of the Law

1250 The Trojan War

1210 Joshua. Fall of Jericho

926 Kingdom split in two: Israel – North Judah – South

776 First Olympic games
850-750 Poetry of Homer

753 Rome founded
750-700 Prophets, Amos, Hosea, Isaiah

772 Samaria falls to Assyrians, Hebrews deported from Northern kingdom
700 Nineveh, Assyrian ca
612 Fall of Nineveh, Babylonian rule

462-429 Golden Age of Athens. Pericles, Socrates, the Parthenon

445 Nehemiah, governor of Judaea. Rebuilding of walls of Jerusalem

334-23 Rise to power of Alexander the Great. Collapse of Persian empire Greek domination of Near East
290 Library of Alexandria

Why do the nations plan rebellion?
Why do people make their useless plots?
Ps 2.1

t 1800 ham	**1800** First Assyrian Empire **1750** Babylonian Empire	**1700** Jacob's family move to Egypt	**1650-1300** Hebrews slaves in Egypt **1380** Akhenaton (1st monotheistic cult)	**About 1300** Moses

200-1010 :onfederation of 2 tribes of rael. Judges **170** Samson	**1010** Death of Saul, 1st King of Israel	**1010-970** David, 2nd King	**969-959** Building of temple under Solomon	Queen of Sheba **932** Rebellion of Northern tribes

86 Nebuchadnezzar estroys Jerusalem **86-536** Exile in abylon. Prophet zekiel	**515** Rebuilding of the Temple	**490 and 480** Greeks conquer Persians at Marathon and Salamis

18 Hannibal rosses the Alps. unic wars	**167** Persecution of Jews by Antiochus. Maccabean revolt **149** Carthage destroyed by Romans	**59-49** Gallic wars **30** Death of Anthony and Cleopatra. Egypt under Roman rule	**6** A.D. Judaea a Roman province

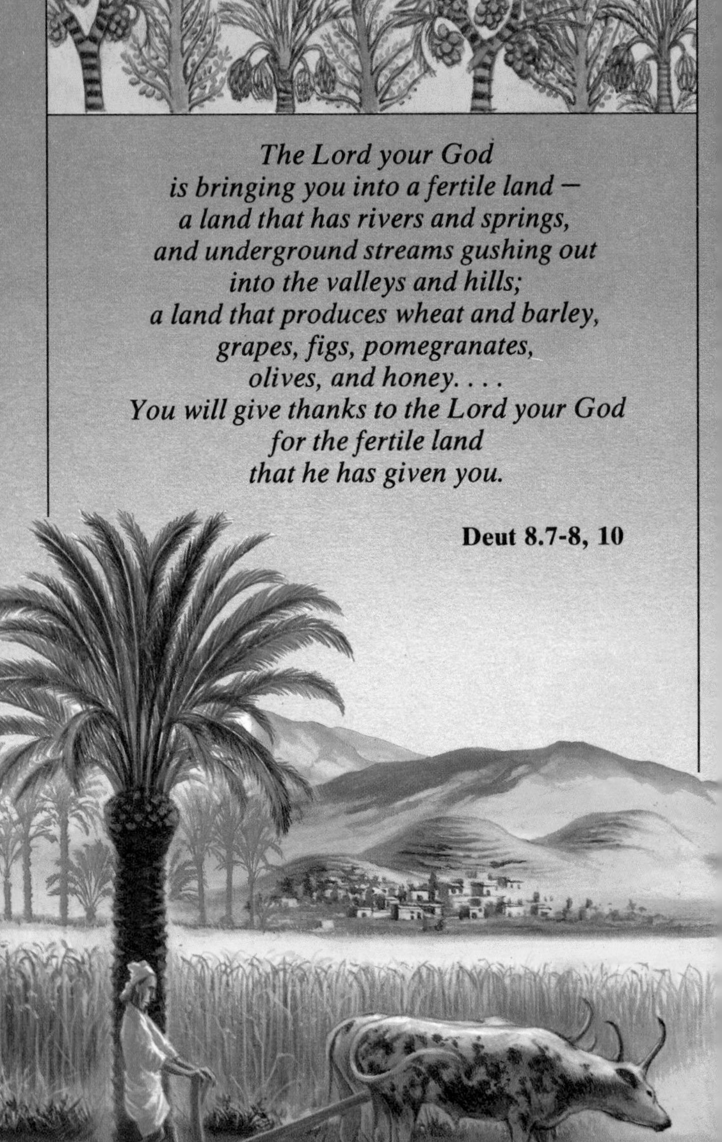

The Lord your God
is bringing you into a fertile land —
a land that has rivers and springs,
and underground streams gushing out
into the valleys and hills;
a land that produces wheat and barley,
grapes, figs, pomegranates,
olives, and honey. . . .
You will give thanks to the Lord your God
for the fertile land
that he has given you.

Deut 8.7-8, 10

THE SETTING

The Bible lands

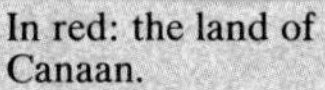

In red: the land of Canaan.

MEDITERRANEAN SEA

PHOENICIA

CANAAN

Jerusalem

MOAB

EDOM

Nile Delta

Memphis

Sinai desert

EGYPT

Nile

RED SEA

Thebes

The lands the Bible speaks of lay in the very centre of the vast region we call the Middle East. To the West, on the River Nile, there was Egypt with its Pharaohs and Pyramids. To the East, on the Tigris and the Euphrates, were Assyria and Babylonia with their fertile plains and hanging gardens.

The land of Canaan, the land of the Israelites, was sandwiched between the mighty empires to the East and West of it. There could be no communication between them, be it peaceful or otherwise, without passing through Canaan. This is why, in the course of its history, Israel was constantly involved in the affairs of its powerful neighbours.

But Canaan was by no means the only small country in the region. Among its many neighbours were Phoenicia, Syria, Bashan, Ammon and Moab, the home of the Philistines.

The land of Canaan

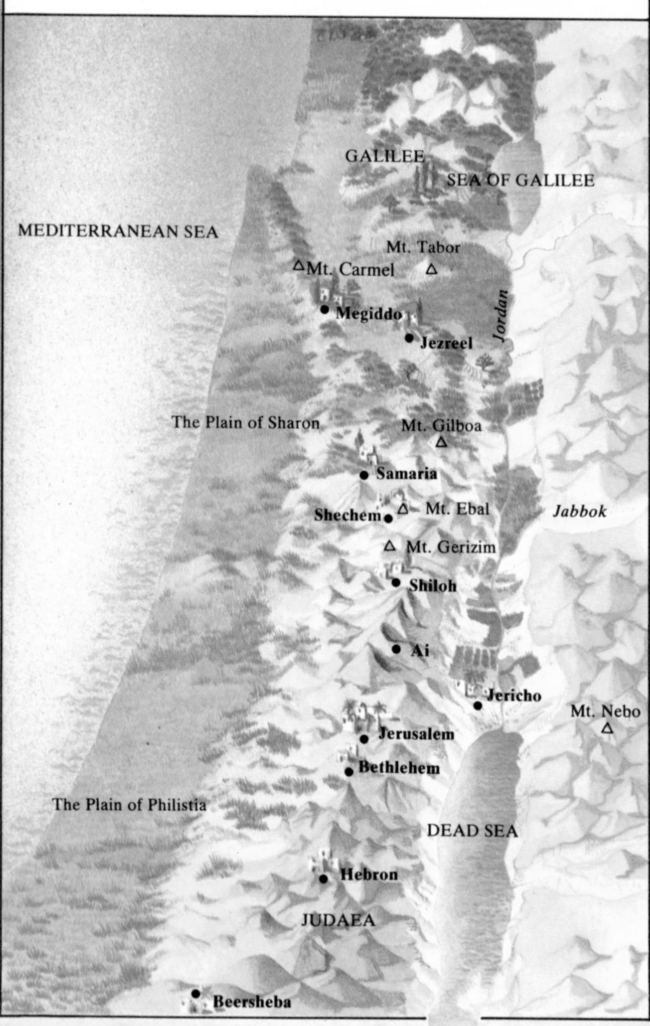

Jerusalem
Jericho
Mediterranean Sea
Dead Sea
Sea level
Jordan

West-East cross-section of the land of Canaan

The land of Canaan can be divided into three strips, running North to South:
– a very narrow coastal plain, running the length of the Mediterranean
– a central mountain range with peaks rising to 1200 m (3900 ft), made up of plateaux (Galilee), and hills (Samaria, Judaea), dotted with small plains
– the remarkable valley of the River Jordan, which lies almost completely beneath sea level. The Jordan rises in Mt. Hermon 200 m (660 ft) above sea level, flows through the Sea of Galilee (-212 m/695 ft) and out into the Dead Sea (-392 m/1290 ft). It was in this land, which had been the home of the Canaanites for over two thousand years, that the Bible people eventually settled.

This Canaanite vase is a caricature of a typical Canaanite face

Over a period of twelve centuries the land of Canaan was known successively as:
– the Promised Land
– the land of Israel
After the kingdom split in two:
– the kingdom of Israel, the Northern kingdom (see p. 206)
– the kingdom of Judah, the Southern kingdom (see p. 220)
After the Exile:
– Galilee (the far North)
– Samaria (the centre)
– Judaea (the South)
– Palestine, the name it was given by the Greeks and Romans.

Many names, one people
In the course of 1200 years the Bible people were known:
- *first* as **Hebrews**, before they settled in Canaan in about 1235 B.C.
- *later* as **Israelites**, from the time they settled in Canaan until the Exile 1235-586 B.C.)
- *finally* as **Jews**, from the return from Exile in 536 B.C. onwards.

The climate

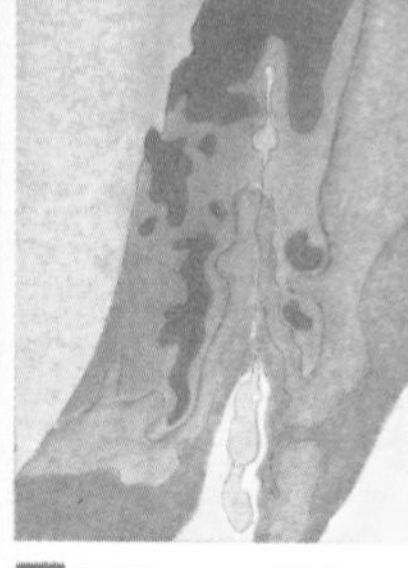

	1000 mm	39 ins
	800	32
	600	24
	400	16
	200	8
	100	4

Annual rainfall

Israel's climate is one of extremes. In winter, it can be snowing in Jerusalem while Jericho, only 25 km (15 miles) away but 1000 m (3280 ft) lower in altitude, is basking in tropical heat. There can also be huge variations in temperature from one year to the next. In years of torrential rain the desert may burst into bloom, but years of drought and famine may follow.

Rain

Winter is the rainy season. It usually begins to rain about mid-September and goes on raining almost continuously until the beginning of April. December and January are the wettest months. Altitude has a lot to do with rainfall. When the Westerly rain-bearing winds hit the mountains, they shed their load of rain. This is why the Galilean mountains in the North get twice as much rain as the coastal plain. The further South you go towards the Negev desert and the Sinai peninsula, the drier it is.

Who has ever caught the wind in his hand?
Or wrapped up water in a piece of cloth?
Or fixed the boundaries of the earth?
Who is he, if you know? Who is his son? **Prov 30.4**

Dew

This condensation which occurs at night when the temperature drops is crucial in coastal areas, where rain is scarce. In some places, dew accounts for almost a quarter of the humidity; it is vital in the cultivation of crops.

Winds

The West wind is a cool wind. It blows in off the sea, bringing welcome relief from the heat in summer, and rain in winter. The East wind is a hot, dry wind. It blows across from the desert. It was a strong East wind that drove the Red Sea back when the Hebrews were fleeing from Egypt (**Ex 14.21**).

Temperature

In the summer the temperature can be 40°C (104°F) in the Dead Sea and less than 0°C (32°F) in the mountains of Upper Galilee. Generally speaking, however, winters are cool and damp, summers long, hot and dry. On an average summer's day on the coast or in the hills of Judaea, the temperature will be about 23°C (73°F).

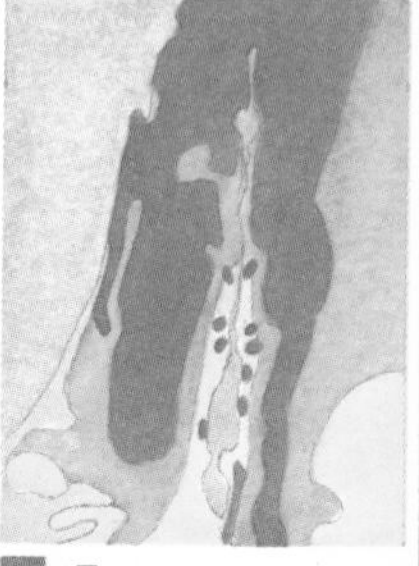

Forest
Scrub and grassland
Desert
Sand dunes
Oasis

Vegetation in biblical times.

'Wind, breath, spirit'
In the Bible, the wind, the act of breathing, the spirit of God and the spirit of mankind are all expressed in the one word: *Ruah*.

The desert

Remember how the Lord your God led you on this long journey through the desert these past forty years, sending hardships to test you, so that he might know what you intended to do and whether you would obey his commands.
Deut 8.2

The desert is the geographical and historical setting for the Bible. It was in the desert that the Hebrews first became aware that they were no longer individual tribes, but one people.

Judah is in mourning;
its cities are dying,
its people lie on the ground in sorrow,
and Jerusalem cries out for help.
The rich people send their servants for water;
they go to the cisterns,
but find no water;
they come back with their jars empty.
Discouraged and confused,
they hide their faces.
Because there is no rain
and the ground is dried up,
the farmers are sick at heart;
they hide their faces.
In the field the mother deer
abandons her new-born fawn
because there is no grass.
The wild donkeys stand on the hill-tops
and pant for breath like jackals;
their eyesight fails them
because they have no food.
Jer 14.2-6

Vast areas of desert surrounded Canaan on all sides. The Promised Land was like a garden in the midst of a wilderness.
In **Gen 2**, the universe is a barren desert before God creates Adam and the Garden of Eden.

The inhabited areas of this part of the East were tiny islands lost in a vast wilderness of desert and scrub land. The Bible lands, fertile areas along the banks of the Nile, the Mediterranean coast and the plains watered by the Tigris and the Euphrates, were known as the Fertile Crescent. Beyond them lay a desolate wasteland of sand, stone, salt and flint.

I cry out to you, Lord, because the pastures and trees are dried up, as though a fire had burnt them.

Joel 1.19

Consider the sheer number of deserts: the Ethiopian desert, the Egyptian desert, the Sinai deserts of Etam, Param, Zin and Sin, the Arabian desert, the Negev desert, the steppes of Moab and Syria. In these regions fertile land was scarce indeed.

The desert was a constant threat to the land of Israel. Where the soil is made of porous limestone rock, water is quickly absorbed and collects in underwater pockets or rivers, which can easily dry up in drought conditions. Hence there was always a danger that fertile land would become dry and barren.

They did not care
about me, even though
I rescued them from
Egypt and led them
through the wilderness:
a land of deserts
and sand-dunes, a dry
and dangerous land,
where no one lives
and no one will even
travel. **Jer 2.6**

He found them
wandering through
the desert,
a desolate, wind-swept
wilderness.
He protected them and
cared for them as he
would protect himself.
Deut 32.10

The mountains

Mountains were special places – a bridge between heaven and earth.
On the plains people constructed special man-made mountains (called ziggurats in Mesopotamia) so that their gods could visit them.

The land of Israel was full of mountains and hills, and neighbouring nations thought of the Israelites as mountain people. In many religions mountains were sacred places where gods and humans met. In the Bible one of the first names for God is *El Shaddai*, 'God of the mountain'.

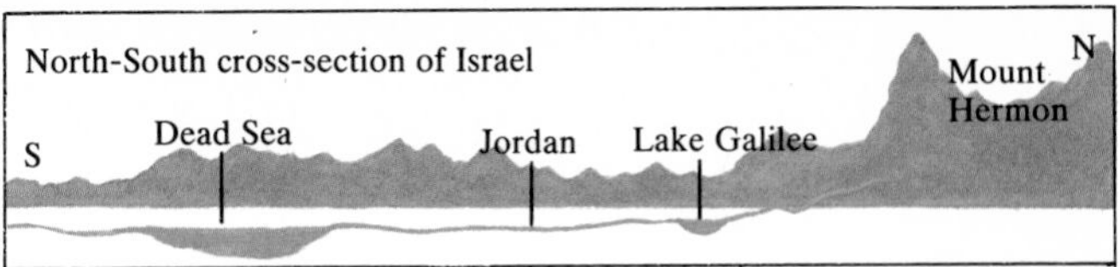

North-South cross-section of Israel

Two mountains in particular are the setting for significant events in the Bible: the mountain of God in the Sinai desert and Mount Sion.

The mountain of God

It was on Mount Sinai, in the course of their long and weary march through the wilderness, that God gave the Hebrews the Ten Commandments (see p. 174). It was to Mount Sinai that the prophet Elijah, in danger of his life, fled to speak with God (see p. 208).

Mount Sion

This is the hill on which the city of Jerusalem and Solomon's temple were built (see p. 86). Pilgrims making their way up to Jerusalem used to sing the *Songs of Ascents* (**Ps 120-134**).

The pyramids of ancient Egypt represented small mountains where the dead would rest at peace under the protection of the gods.

Mt. Horeb, the Mountain of God, in the Sinai peninsula.

Water and rivers

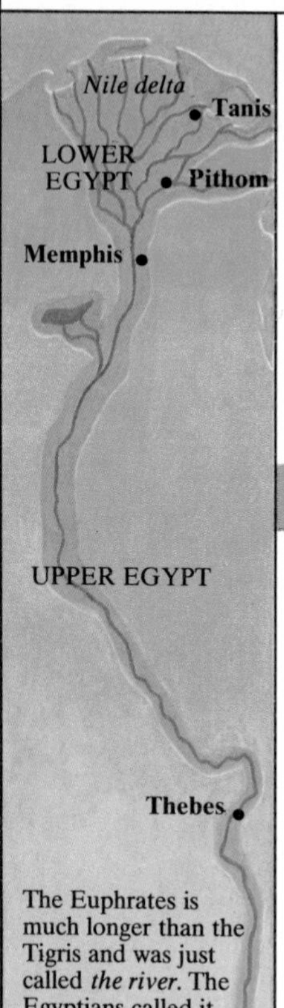

The Euphrates is much longer than the Tigris and was just called *the river*. The Egyptians called it *the river which flows the other way* (to the Nile).

In areas of desert and barren scrub, all forms of life are dependent on water. This may take the form of a river, as in Egypt, or rainfall, which in Israel is sufficient to irrigate the fields and replenish springs and wells.

The rivers

In Egypt, where rain is scarce, the river **Nile** is a lifeline. This water, as the Bible tells us, is the water *beneath the earth* (**Gen 7.11**), as distinct from the water that falls from the sky.

The Nile from February to March

The Nile from August to September

It does actually rain on the Nile, but only in the far South on the Abyssinian plains. This rain is what causes the river to flood each year. Rich deposits of fertile silt are left where the river overflows its banks.

Of all the land in Egypt only 3.5% is under cultivation. This tiny percentage has to support 99.5% of the population.

The **Tigris** and the **Euphrates** were as vital to Mesopotamia as the Nile was to Egypt. Their flooding both irrigated and fertilised the soil. Unfortunately, they did not flood with the same measured regularity as the Nile. Tales of catastrophic flooding and the devas-

A desert well with a shaduf – the mechanism used for raising the water.

tation it brought in its wake probably gave rise to the Bible story of the flood.

Wells

Deep well-shafts, dug painstakingly through the porous limestone to reach the precious water beneath, are further evidence of the struggle for survival in an arid land. A well was more than just a life-giving oasis, it was also a meeting place where nomadic tribes might exchange news, trade their wares or even hope to find a wife or husband. Wells were an integral part of social life and customs.

Desert downpours

Torrential rain sometimes falls in these areas with such force that the ground cannot absorb it. Vast torrents of water pour off the slopes and into the valleys. Within minutes the winding roads through the valleys are awash beneath four or five metres of water (13 to 16 ft).

Water-bearers

You show your care for the land by sending rain; . . . you send abundant rain on the ploughed fields and soak them with water; you soften the soil with showers and cause the young plants to grow. . . . Everything shouts and sings for joy. **Ps 65.9-13**

Small craft on the Nile, from an Egyptian mural

The three seas

Leviathan encircling the town of Hebron. Leviathan is the Bible name for a huge sea monster which could take the shape of a sea serpent, crocodile or whale.

He churns up the sea like boiling water and makes it bubble like a pot of oil. He leaves a shining path behind him and turns the sea to white foam.
Job 41.31-32

1 Egyptian galley
2 Merchant ship from King Solomon's fleet

The Mediterranean

The Bible people were not seafarers. Far from it! Firstly, the coast-line of Israel was too straight to offer any natural protection in the form of harbours; secondly, their neighbours to the South and North, the Egyptians and the Phoenicians, were extremely skilled sailors and they had no desire to enter into competition with them.

The Israelites' forefathers had been herdsmen and nomads. They were land-lovers, who feared the sea and all the dangers that went with it – not least the invading armies of their warlike, sea-faring neighbours.

The Dead Sea

This sea is also known as the Salt Sea, the Sea of the Akabah (or Plain) or the Asphaltic Pool. The Dead Sea is quite unique. It lies in a deep depression

392 metres (1290 ft) below the level of the Mediterranean. Evaporation is so intense that the sea is about four times more salt than other seas; so that you float in it but swimming is almost impossible and there is no life in its waters. Minerals such as magnesium and sodium chlorides, bitumen and sulphur are extracted from it.

Solidified masses of salt on the Dead Sea coast.

Fisherman. From a 13th c. B.C. fresco

The Sea of Galilee

This sea, which is also known as the Sea of Chinnareth, the Tiberian Sea or Lake Gennesaret, is, in contrast to the Dead Sea, very much alive. It is a freshwater lake which provides plentiful supplies of drinking water and fish.

Some sailed over the ocean in ships, earning their living on the seas. They saw what the Lord can do, his wonderful acts on the seas. **Ps 107.23-24**

3 Philistine warship
4 Phoenician galley

The universe

The Babylonians imagined the world to be a hollow mountain resting on the sea.

Human beings are naturally curious. They want to understand the reason for things being as they are. One of the first questions people asked themselves in ancient times was: 'What sort of a world are we living in? . . . Why does some water fall from the sky and some spring up from underground? How do the sun and the stars stay up in the sky? Why does the earth sometimes quake?' Each nation came up with different answers to these questions and formed its opinion of the world accordingly.

The Egyptians portrayed the earth as a god, Keb. He lies outstretched while Nout, goddess of the sky, bends over him. The god of the air supports Nout's arched body. Sun and moon travel up and down it.

According to an ancient Indian belief, the earth would shake when the elephants moved.

The people of the Bible saw the world as a flat, round disk surrounded by seas and resting on pillars which were suspended in a void. The sky was an arched dome. From it hung lamps to light the world – the sun, moon and stars. The sun was known as the great

The foundations of the earth belong to the Lord; on them he has built the world.
1 Sam 2.8

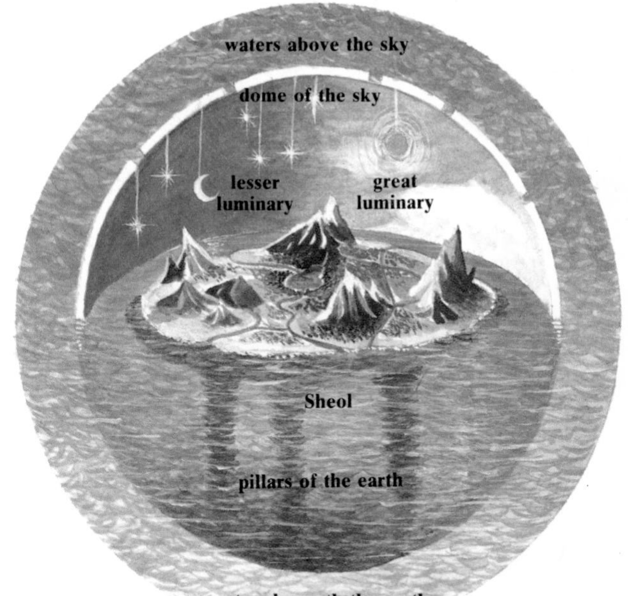

This is how the Hebrews saw the universe

luminary, the moon the lesser luminary. The dome of the sky held up the upper waters of the earth. In the dome were holes which God could shut or open at random. When opened, the waters above the sky would fall as rain. When shut, there would be drought. Deep in the very depths of the earth was *Sheol*, the resting place of the dead.

All the outlets of the vast body of water beneath the earth burst open, all the floodgates of the sky were opened.
Gen 7.11

Trees

Oak
Is 1.30

Poplar
Gen 30.37

Cedar
1 Kgs 6.18

Walnut

Acacia
Ex 25.13

Terebinth

I have come down among the almond-trees
to see the young plants in the valley,
to see the new leaves on the vines and the
blossoms on the pomegranate trees. **Song 6.11**

Apple tree
Song 2.3

Almond tree
Jer 1.11

Almond

Pomegranate tree
Song 7.12

Pomegranate

Palm tree
Song 7.8

Date

Plants

Flax
Josh 2.6

Rye grass
Is 28.25 *AV*

Cumin
Is 28.27

The poppy, from which 'gall' is extracted

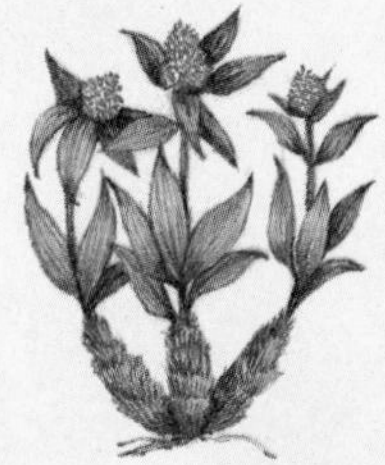

Nard
Song 4.13

Wormwood (the bitter plant)
Prov 5.4

Rose

Narcissus

Anemone

Myrtle
Neh 8.15
Castor-oil plant
Mustard
Fennel
Anethum
Hyssop
Ex 12.22
Thistle, thorn
Gen 3.18
Coriander
Ex 16.31 *AV*
Papyrus

The vine

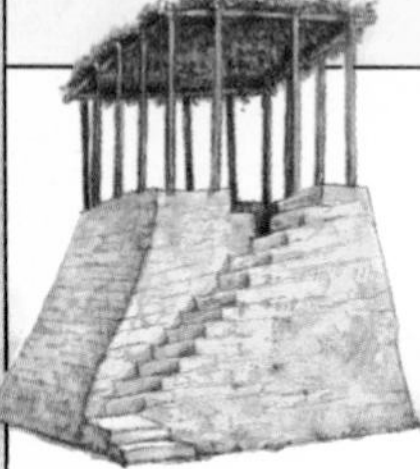

Watch-tower

Catch the foxes, the little foxes, before they ruin our vineyard in bloom. **Song 2.15**

In Bible times a vine was a treasured possession. The owner would go to great lengths to make sure it flourished. He would choose a sunny slope for it, dig the ground carefully, prune the young vine shoots as they came up, and then build a wall around the vine to protect it. Nearby he would build a watch-tower so that he could keep an eye out for thieving foxes or robbers.

In the autumn the grapes were harvested and pressed underfoot in a stone wine-press. This was an occasion for celebration.

Wine makes people merry and is

Vines were usually trained to grow up high trellises.
A shady spot for a mid-day snooze.

therefore a symbol of joy and festivity. However, the prophets and wise men in the Bible uttered many dire warnings about the effects of too much wine.

Don't let wine tempt you, even though it is rich red, though it sparkles in the cup and it goes down smoothly. The next morning you will feel as if you had been bitten by a poisonous snake. Weird sights will appear before your eyes and you will not be able to think or speak clearly. **Prov 23.31-33**

In the Bible Israel is often compared to a vine which the Lord tends with infinite care and devotion. Alas, all too often the Lord's efforts are in vain – the grapes are sour!

Picking and treading the grapes (Egyptian painting)

Listen while I sing you this song, a song of my friend and his vineyard: My friend had a vineyard on a very fertile hill. He dug the soil and cleared it of stones; he planted the finest vines. He built a tower to guard them, dug a pit for treading the grapes. He waited for the grapes to ripen, but every grape was sour. **Is 5.1-2**

Grapes were eaten raw or dried and made into cakes.

They all went out into their vineyards and picked the grapes, made wine from them, and held a festival. **Judg 9.27**

The olive tree

Olive picking: the trees were beaten with sticks to make the olives fall. (Greek vase)

I grew tall . . . like beautiful olive-trees in the fields. . . . Come to me, all you that want me, and eat your fill of my fruit.
Sir 24.13-19

Olive trees and fig trees were, next to the vine, the most common fruit-bearing trees in the land of Israel.

Olive trees, with their gnarled trunks and shiny silvery leaves, grew all over the place. The olives were picked in the autumn and pressed to extract the oil. Olive oil was used in a variety of ways: as fuel for lamps, for cooking, as a healing salve for a wound, and as a soothing body ointment. Olive oil was the oil used to anoint kings. In the Bible the olive tree is a symbol of strength and vigour.

But I am like an olive-tree growing in the house of God; I trust in his constant love for ever and ever. **Ps 52.8**

The abundance of fruit on the tree is a reminder of God's bounty and goodness.

Happy are those who obey the Lord, who live by his commands. . . . your sons will be like young olive-trees round your table. **Ps 128.1, 3**

The fig tree

Fig trees, with their thick leafy branches, provided welcome shade in a hot country, a cool resting place where families and friends might gather in the heat of the noon-day sun. This is why in the Bible the fig tree is a symbol of peace, well-being and companionship.

As long as he lived, the people throughout Judah and Israel lived in safety, each family with its own grapevines and fig-trees. **1 Kgs 4.25**

Fig trees will grow even in very stony ground provided there is some moisture. Fresh figs are deliciously juicy. Dried figs keep well.

Then Isaiah told the King's attendants to put on his boil a paste made of figs, and he would get well.

2 Kgs 20.7

Barley and corn

Goad

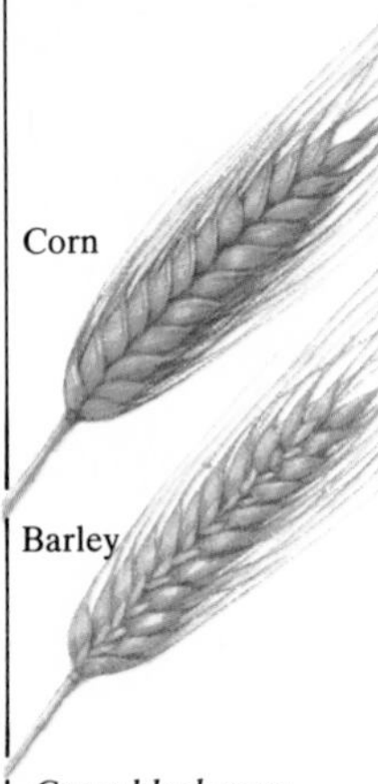

There were two main cereals from which people in Biblical times made their bread: barley and corn. Barley, being the cheaper of the two, was what the poor ate.

Ploughing and sowing

Ploughing was done in October, the rainy season, when the earth was soft. The farmer used a wooden plough with an iron ploughshare, drawn by oxen or donkeys. He held the handle of the plough in one hand, and a pointed wooden goad, with which to drive the animals pulling the plough, in the other. Once the earth had been turned, the farmer simply scattered the seed over the ground by hand.

Can a black man change the colour of his skin, or a leopard remove its spots? If they could, then you that do nothing but evil could learn to do what is right. The Lord will scatter you like straw that is blown away by the desert wind.
Jer 13.23-24

Harvest

Barley was harvested in April, corn in May or June. A good crop might yield as

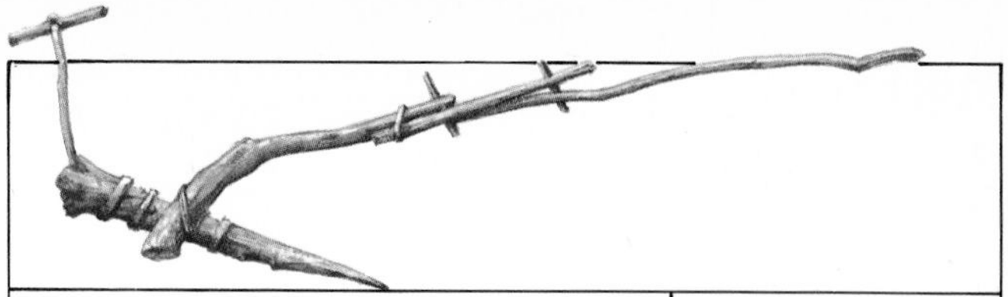

much as 100 to 400 kg (220-880 lbs) for every kilo of seed sown. But drought, desert winds or flocks of hungry birds could spoil the crop. Harvest was always a festive time. Once all the grain was gathered in, the people offered the first fruits of the harvest to God as part of their harvest celebrations.

Threshing

In Bible times the grain was separated from the ear of corn (threshed) using oxen, which pulled weighted sleds over the harvested crop. This was done on the village threshing floor. Winnowers then separated the grain from the husk by tossing it into the air from big winnowing baskets. The grain, being heavier, fell to the ground while the chaff was blown away. The left-overs or 'tailings' were used as animal fodder.

Early plough, made entirely of wood.

Sickle. Iron was first used for making agricultural tools in the 10th c. B.C.

Harvest, from an Egyptian painting. These men are sifting the grain with scoops to get rid of the last of the chaff.

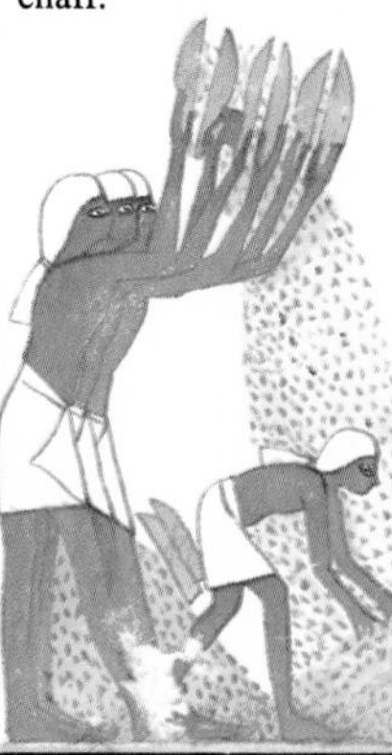

Sheep and goats

The Lord is my shepherd; I have everything I need. He lets me rest in fields of green grass and leads me to quiet pools of fresh water.
Ps 23.1-2

Their many flocks of sheep and goats were one of the Bible people's most precious possessions. During the day the flocks grazed on the hills; at night they were rounded up into little dry-stone pens with low walls. The sheep and goats provided not only meat, wool and leather, but also milk and butter, cream and cheese. Sheep-shearing took place in the spring and was a festive occasion.

Both sheep and goats were frequently offered as sacrifices to God.

The Bible compares the people of Israel to a flock of sheep and goats, with God as their shepherd. The Lord is a good shepherd, whose loving care for the flock knows no bounds. Unfortunately, as the Bible points out, many of the people's leaders were bad shepherds.

The shepherds of Israel

The Lord spoke to me. 'Mortal man,' he said, 'denounce the rulers of Israel. . . . You are doomed, you shepherds of Israel! You take care of yourselves, but never tend the sheep.

You drink the milk, wear clothes made from the wool, and kill and eat the finest sheep. But you never tend the sheep. You have not taken care of the weak ones, healed those that are sick, bandaged those that are hurt, brought back those that wandered off, or looked for those that were lost. Instead you treated them cruelly. Because the sheep had no shepherd, they were scattered, and wild animals killed and ate them.' **Ezek 34.1-5**

The Good Shepherd

'I, the Sovereign Lord, tell you that I myself will look for the sheep and take care of them in the same way as a shepherd takes care of his sheep that were scattered and brought together again.' **Ezek 34.11-12**

'I will look for those that are lost, bring back those that wander off, bandage those that are hurt, and heal those that are sick; but those that are fat and strong I will destroy, because I am a shepherd who does what is right.' **Ezek 34.16**

'You, my sheep, the flock that I feed, are my people, and I am your God,' says the Sovereign Lord. **Ezek 34.31**

Donkeys

So Moses took his wife and his sons, put them on a donkey, and set out with them for Egypt, carrying the stick that God had told him to take.
Ex 4.20

In Bible times donkeys were much loved domestic animals. They were larger and stronger than our present-day donkeys, and had more energy. In those days a donkey was expected to walk all day with a rider on its back, and to trot for hours on end. Being sturdy and sure-footed, a donkey could outstrip a horse on an uphill slope or on rough ground.

Under the donkey's well-padded saddle went a folded blanket, and over the top a brightly coloured carpet. Its bridle was embroidered and hung with tassels or even little bells.

Donkeys were extremely useful beasts. Even the rich and people in high office rode them. They were used for ploughing and threshing. They were

also beasts of burden for carrying heavy loads. The name of the load a donkey was capable of carrying became a unit of measure: the homer.

Camels are capable of carrying heavy loads long distances. (see **Gen 24.10, 37.25**)

Whereas in the Bible the horse is a symbol of power, the donkey is a symbol of peace. It is on a donkey, not on a horse, that Zechariah foresees the future King entering Jerusalem.

Rejoice, rejoice, people of Zion! Shout for joy, you people of Jerusalem! Look! your king is coming to you! He comes triumphant and victorious, but humble and riding on a donkey – on a colt, the foal of a donkey. **Zech 9.9-10**

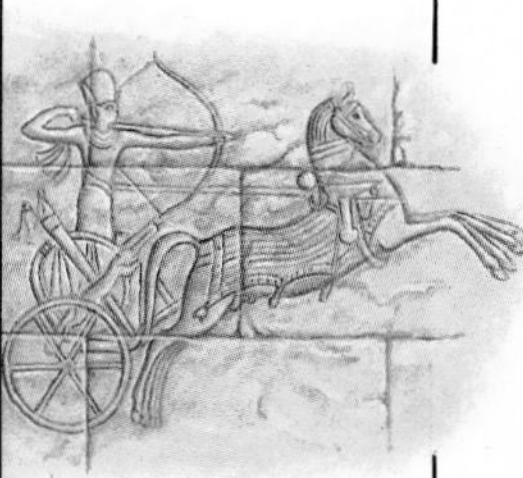

Egyptian war chariot

The rights of the donkey

If you happen to see your enemy's cow or donkey running loose, take it back to him. If his donkey has fallen under its load, help him get the donkey to its feet again; don't just walk off. **Ex 23.4-5**

From an Egyptian mural (19th c. B.C.)

The rights of the ox

Do not muzzle an ox when you are using it to thresh corn. **Deut 25.4**

Birds

Owl

Crow

Dove

Sparrow

Peacock

In the Psalms, men and women of the Bible frequently compare themselves to birds they know.

The owl
I am like a wild bird in the desert,
like an owl in abandoned ruins.
I lie awake;
I am like a lonely bird on a house-top.
Ps 102.6-7

The dove
I wish I had wings, like a dove. I would fly away and find rest. **Ps 55.6**

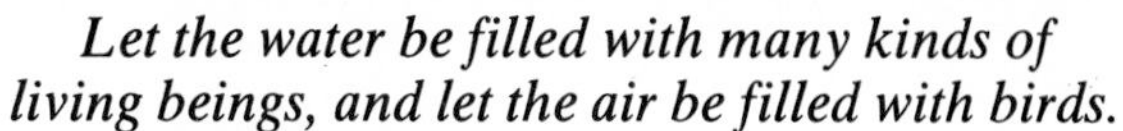

Let the water be filled with many kinds of living beings, and let the air be filled with birds.
Gen 1.20

Eagle

Turtle dove

Stork

Swallow

The eagle
Praise the Lord, my soul!
All my being, praise his holy name!
Praise the Lord, my soul,
and do not forget how kind he is.
He forgives all my sins
and heals all my diseases.
He keeps me from the grave
and blesses me with love and mercy.
He fills my life with good things,
so that I stay young and strong like an eagle.
Ps 103.1-5

The stork
The cedars of Lebanon get plenty of rain —
the Lord's own trees, which he planted.
There the birds build their nests;
the storks nest in the fir-trees.
The wild goats live in the high mountains,
and the badgers hide in the cliffs.
Ps 104.16-18

Wild animals

Bear
Amos 5.19

Wolf
Is 11.6

Hare
Job 9.22

Leopard
Jer 13.23

Fox
Judg 15.4

Harmless animals

Hares and **gazelles** grazed in the forests and scrub lands of the Bible countries. Deer, ibex and chamois made their home higher up in the mountains.

Dangerous animals

Lions roamed wild in the forests and thickets of Jordan. The lion was the strongest of all the wild animals in Israel, and a threat to livestock and travellers alike. In the Bible the lion is usually a symbol of strength and courage in the face of danger.

Rock-badger
Deut 14.7

Gazelle
Song 2.89

There were **bears** in the mountains and forests of Israel. They fed chiefly on fruit, honey, roots and eggs, but would attack sheep when food was scarce. A mother bear separated from her cubs was extremely dangerous.

Shepherds also had to watch out for **wolves**, which were quick to pounce on any stray animal. Wolves are symbols of fierceness and cruelty in the Bible.

The **fox** and the **jackal** lay up during the day and hunted at night. Both were fond of fruit, particularly grapes, and could wreak havoc in a vineyard. The fox hunted alone, jackals in packs. They ate carrion, the carcasses of dead animals.

The **snake** is a symbol of cunning; slithering furtively towards its unsuspecting prey, to strike with deadly accuracy.

In Bible times it was forbidden to eat **hares** or **rock-badgers**. Although they 'chewed the cud', they did not have cloven hoofs and were therefore unclean – that is, not fit to eat.

Jackal
Is 43.20

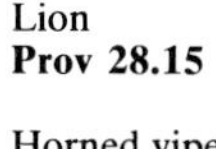

Lion
Prov 28.15

Horned viper
Is 59.5

Insects

Bees

Wild bees make their homes in the cracks of rocks, in hollow trees, and even in the carcasses of dead animals. From early on the Israelites began to keep bees for their honey. The hives were thick clay pipes. There were stoppers with holes in at either end, so that the bees could fly in and out. The hives were stacked up in piles and covered with earth and greenery to protect them from the sun. When the time came to collect the honey, the stoppers were removed and the honeycombs extracted with an iron hook. The honey made in Israel was strongly scented and it was used to sweeten food. The beeswax was used to make candles.

Beehives

Ants

This is what the Bible has to say about these hardworking creatures:

Lazy people should learn a lesson from the way ants live. They have no leader, chief, or ruler, but they store up their food during the summer, getting ready for winter. How long is the lazy man going to lie in bed? When is he ever going to get up?
Prov 6.6-9

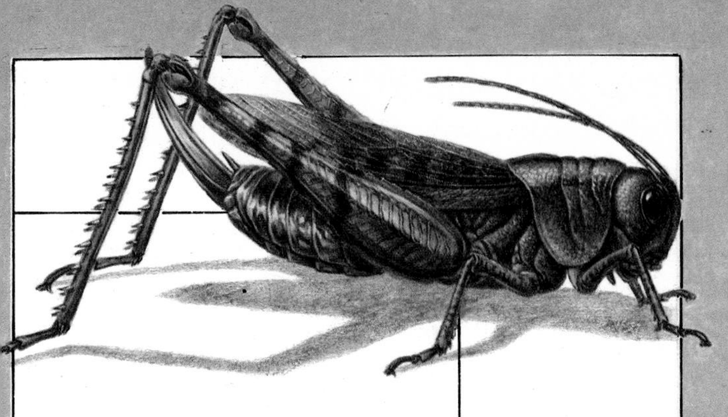

Locusts

These were all too plentiful in Israel. Locusts feed on all forms of vegetation, plants and trees. They descend in huge clouds, eating everything in sight and devastating the crops – a farmer's nightmare. The Bible tells how swarms of locusts and flies, sent by God, descended on Egypt before Pharaoh decided to set the Hebrews free.

Flies

The Lord sent great swarms of flies into the king's palace and the houses of his officials. **Ex 8.24**

Fleas

Even this tiny insect, which bites so viciously and is so hard to catch, gets a mention in the Bible. King Saul was jealous of David, one of his most brilliant warriors, and wanted to kill him.
David kept escaping. One day, he cried out to Saul from a safe distance, 'Look what you are chasing! . . . a flea!'
1 Sam 24.15 (adapted)

The calendar

	Hebrew months	
January	Sebat	
February	Adar	Late rains
March	Nisan	
April	Iyyar	
May	Sivan	
June	Tammuz	
July	Ab	Summer heat
August	Elul	
September	Tishri	
October	Marchesvan	First rains
November	Kislev	
December	Tebet	Rainy season

On that day, take some of the best fruit from your trees, take palm branches and the branches of leafy trees, and begin a religious festival to honour the Lord your God.
Lev 23.40

Work in the fields	Festivals	
Winter figs		
Pulling flax	13-14: Purim	
Barley harvest	14: Passover	
Corn harvest	Feast of Weeks *or* Pentecost	
Vine tending		

Summer fruit		
Olive harvest		
Ploughing	9: New Year 10: Atonement 15: Tabernacles	
Grain planting		
When you harvest your fields, do not cut the corn at the edges of the fields, and do not go back to cut the ears of corn that were left; leave them for poor people and foreigners. **Lev 23.22**	25: Feast of Lights	

Houses

Then they made a cover for the Tent out of eleven pieces of cloth made of goats' hair. . . .

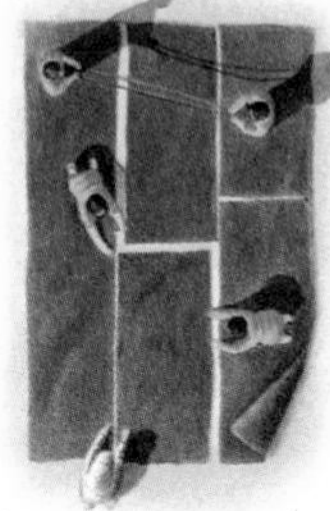

They sewed five of them together in one set and the other six in another set.
Ex 36.14, 16

In Hebrew the word for house also means family. The house was where the family spent most of its time.

In a country where it was hot and dry for much of the year, houses were designed to keep out the heat.

They were built on rock foundations. The walls were made of cob, a mixture of clay and straw, or brick, and less often in stone. An outside staircase led on to a flat roof made of interwoven branches and clay. Here the family would sleep in the summer or rest in the cool of the evening. To keep the house cool, there were very few windows and those there were were small. This meant the house was dark inside. An oil lamp was kept burning night and day to give light. The floor was often just earth.

Rich man's house

Above the entrance hung the *Mezuzah*, a tube containing a piece of parchment on which the Great Commandment was written: *'Israel, remember this! The Lord – and the Lord alone – is our God. Love the Lord your God with all your heart, with all your soul, and with all your strength.'* **Deut 6.4**

Poor families lived in the one room. They ate and slept on rush mats at one end of the room, while the other end was used to store earthenware jars, grinding stones and other utensils.

Rich families had bigger houses with several rooms giving on to a central courtyard. They might even have had an upper storey. Rich people had beds and tables.

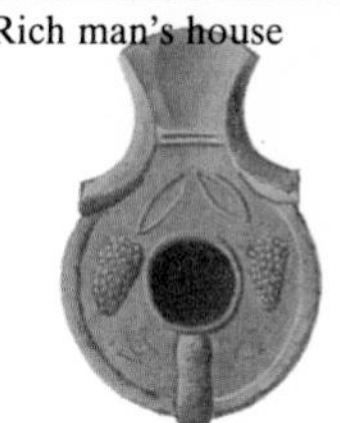

Oil lamp

Bread chest

Poor man's house

Food

Terracotta statue dating from the 8th c. B.C. of a woman kneading dough for bread in a trough.

Two main meals were eaten in the course of the day: one at midday, the other at sundown, plus a small breakfast of a piece of bread and a few olives.

In the days of their desert forefathers, the Hebrews' food was plain and simple: lentils, beans, roasted corn, milk and cheese, grilled meat. They ate from a communal bowl, squatting on the ground. After they settled in Canaan,

Baking bread

Abraham hurried into the tent and said to Sarah, 'Quick, take a sack of your best flour, and bake some bread'.

Gen 18.6

however, things changed. The prophet Amos protested indignantly at the feasting that went on in the houses of the rich:

How terrible it will be for you that stretch out on your luxurious couches, feasting on veal and lamb! You like to compose songs as David did, and play them on harps. You drink wine by the bowlful and use the finest perfumes, but you do not mourn over the ruin of Israel.

Amos 6.4-6

Salt

Salt was an important element not only in the diet, but also in the social and religious life of Israel. It was used to season and preserve food. It was added to animal fodder. New-born babies were rubbed in salt. Sacrifices were sprinkled with salt and it was a symbol of permanence in the signing of treaties, known as Covenants of Salt. The Dead Sea was an inexhaustible source of salt.

Earthenware pots and jars

Grinding stone for grain

Animals, clean and unclean

The Bible makes a distinction between things which are 'clean', and may be eaten, and those which are 'unclean' and should not be eaten under any circumstances.

Egyptian butchers at work (2150 B.C.)

Grasshoppers were eaten fried, boiled or dried. They were also ground into flour and baked into a nutritious bread.

Permitted clean animals

Here is a short list of the animals the children of Israel were allowed to eat, as set out in Chapter 11 of Leviticus:

– the hung meat of any animal that has divided hoofs and chews the cud, such as beef and mutton
– any kind of fish that has fins and scales
– any birds not listed as unclean
– hopping insects of the grasshopper family.

The Lord gave Moses and Aaron the following regulations for the people of Israel.

Lev 11.1

Forbidden unclean animals

Here are some of the unclean animals which they were forbidden to eat:

– any meat-eating animals; these can be a source of infection in a hot climate, and their meat spoils fast

– pork, which often carries parasites if not well-cooked

– all vermin and birds of prey

– all shell-fish, which even nowadays can cause food-poisoning

– finally, rats, moles and different types of lizards, chameleons and frogs.

. . . anything living in the water that does not have fins and scales must not be eaten. **Lv 11.12**

Eating horsemeat or pork is against the Jewish religion.

Clothes

Sheep-shearing

Carding

Spinning

Flax flower

Clothes were mostly made of wool or goats' hair. Only the rich could afford linen or silk. Cotton was first introduced in the 6th c. B.C.

Different coloured dyes were made from plants, roots, nuts and shellfish. The Hebrew people wore long shirts: knee-length for the men, ankle-length for women. Round the waist they wore a cloth belt, into which the shirt could be tucked when walking or working. Coins could be slipped into the folds of

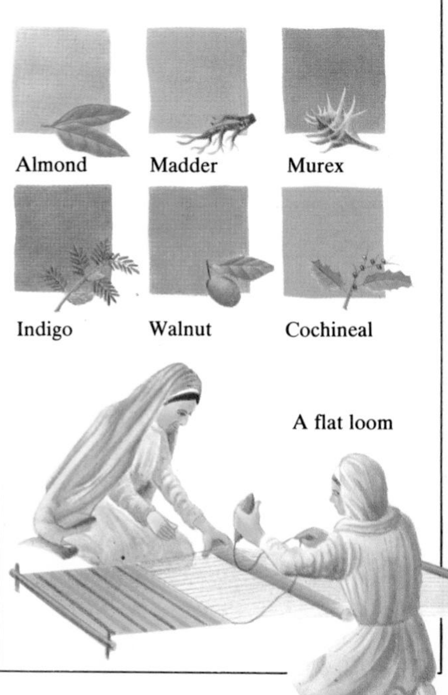

A flat loom

the belt for safe-keeping.

Over the tunic went a coat. This was a long strip of material with holes for head and arms.

Both men and women covered their heads. They used a length of material which was either wound into a turban or simply held in place by means of a cord tied around the head.

Hebrew nomads (Egyptian painting 2nd millenium B.C.)

Gold cloak fastening. Persian

Sandals

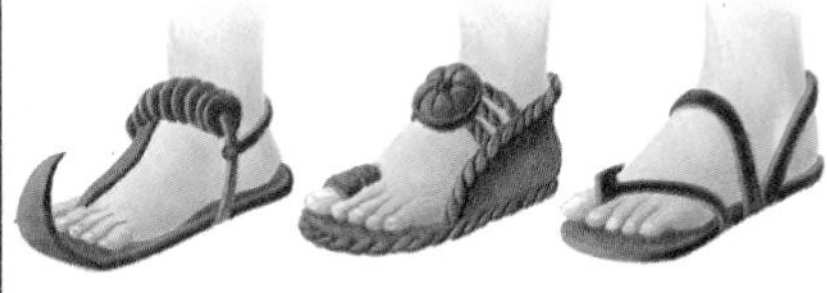

Egyptian Babylonian Greek

Tunics Robe

To make a robe using a small loom, strips of cloth were placed

one on top of the other as shown and sewn together along the seams.

Money

Double silver shekel. King of Persia in his chariot (4th c. B.C.)

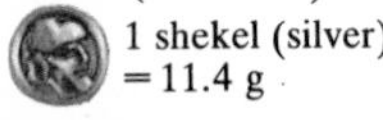

1 shekel (silver) = 11.4 g

1 mina (silver) = 571 g = 50 shekels

1 talent (gold) = 34 kg = 60 minas

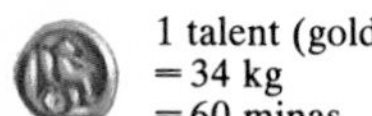

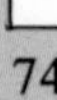

Money only came into existence in Israel in the 7th c. B.C. Up until then people simply exchanged one type of goods for another: be it goats, sheep, jewellery, wood or food. This method of buying and selling was known as barter.

Gradually, precious metals – gold, silver and copper – began to be used for payment. As time went on, their value was determined by their weight. This explains why some coins bear the same name as certain measures of weight.

Coins were adopted for convenience sake. It was easier to carry a purse than a pile of things for barter!

Interest-free loans

If you lend money to any of my people who are poor, do not act like a moneylender and require him to pay interest. **Ex 22.25**

Compensation money

If the bull kills a male or female slave, its owner shall pay the owner of the slave thirty pieces of silver, and the bull shall be stoned to death. **Ex 21.32**

Weights

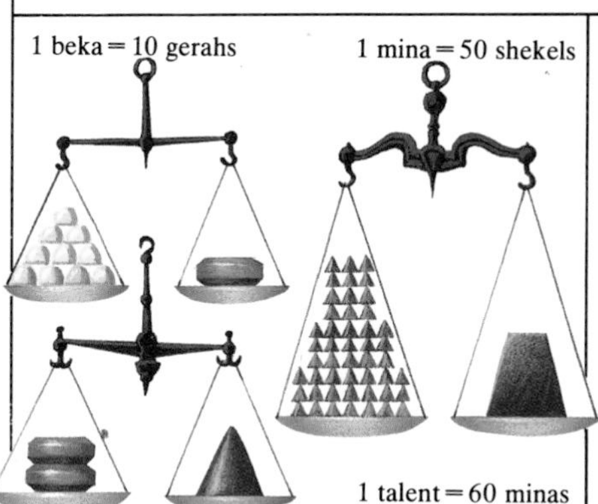

1 beka = 10 gerahs

1 mina = 50 shekels

1 talent = 60 minas

1 shekel = 2 bekas

1 talent = 30 kg = 66 lbs

1 gerah = 0.5 g = 0.018 ounces

Listen to this, you that trample on the needy. . . . You say to yourselves, '. . . When will the Sabbath end, so that we can start selling again? Then we can overcharge, use false measures, and tamper with the scales to cheat our customers.' **Amos 8.4-6**

Hebrew stone weights (7th-6th c. B.C.)

Assyrian weight in the shape of a lion, weighing two thirds of a mina.

Measures of length

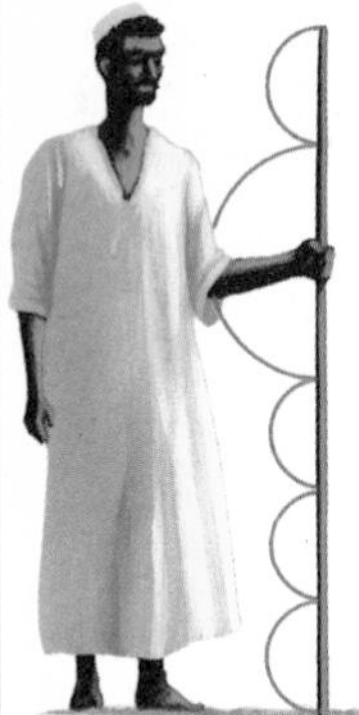

The rod
=6 cubits
=12 spans
=36 palms
=144 fingers

The measures of length are based on the dimensions of the human body.

Finger (or digit) = 1.9 centimetres (0.75″) (a finger's breadth)
Palm = 7.5 centimetres (3″) (a hand's breadth, measured across the palm)
Span = 22.5 centimetres (9″) (the breadth of the hand with fingers outstretched, from the end of the thumb to the end of the little finger)

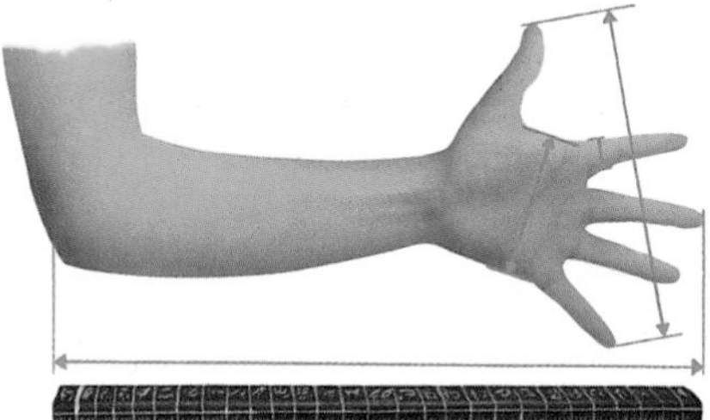

Egyptian rule

Cubit = 45 centimetres (17.5″) (from the elbow to the end of the middle finger)

Water was used to make sure foundations were laid level.

Measures of capacity

1 bath = 23 litres
= 5 gallons

10 baths = 1 homer
(or donkey-load)
=230 litres
=50 gal (IMP)*

Liquid measures

There were different measures of volume for liquids (oil and wine), and solids (corn, barley). These measures were named after the appropriate container for the quantity involved.

*1 gal (IMP)= 1.2 gal (US)

5 ephahs = 1 lethech

1 ephah

10 ephahs = 1 homer

Dry measures

Do not cheat anyone by using false measures of length, weight, or quantity. Use honest scales, honest weights, and honest measures.
Lev 19.35-36

Festivals

The annual festivals were times of solemn assembly and joyful celebration.

The Passover or Feast of Unleavened Bread which began in April, was a solemn reminder of how God spared the Hebrews on the eve of their flight from Egypt. Families celebrated Passover with a special meal at which a roasted Paschal lamb and unleavened bread were served in memory of that fateful night when there was no time to let the bread rise.

The Feast of Harvest, or Feast of Weeks, at the end of May, seven weeks or fifty days after Passover. Also called Pentecost (from the Greek word for fifty days). The people thanked God for the grain harvest and for the Law given to Moses in the wilderness.

The Feast of Trumpets in mid September, was also the Festival of the New Year. This day commemorated the creation of mankind. It was a solemn day of remembrance, which preceded a ten day period of reflection and repentance, terminating in the Day of Atonement.

The Day of Atonement (Yom Kippur), late September. The people asked God's forgiveness for their sins. A goat was chosen to carry the people's sins symbolically into the desert (hence the expression 'scapegoat').

The Feast of Tabernacles, early October, was a feast of thanksgiving for the fruit and wine harvest, during which the people lived in tents like their forefathers in the wilderness.

Feast of the Purification of the Temple, early December. This feast recalls the day in 165 B.C. when the temple of God, which the Syrians had defiled, was restored to the Jews and reconsecrated for use following the Maccabean revolt.

Festivals began with blowing the *shophar*, (ram's horn).

Feast of Purim, early March. This celebrated the story of Esther. Haman ordered lots to be drawn (Purim means 'lots') to decide the day the Jews were to be massacred (p. 266). On the festival the book of Esther was read aloud and presents exchanged.

Musical instruments

The Sea of Galilee is shaped like a lyre. Another name for it is the Sea of Chinnereth, meaning 'lyre'.

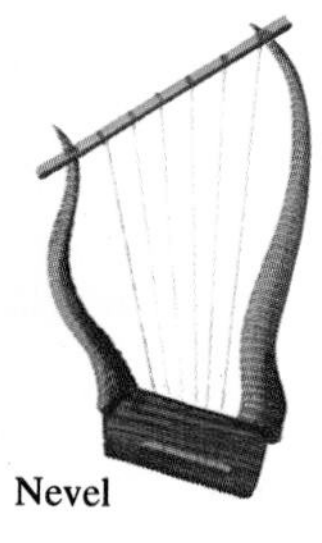

Nevel

Kinnor

Assyrian musician

Egyptian harp

Music and dance played an important part in religious ceremonies. People sang solo and also in unison.

Praise God in his Temple! . . .
Praise him with trumpets.
Praise him with harps and lyres.
Praise him with drums and dancing.
Praise him with harps and flutes.
Praise him with cymbals.
Praise him with loud cymbals.
Ps 150.1-5

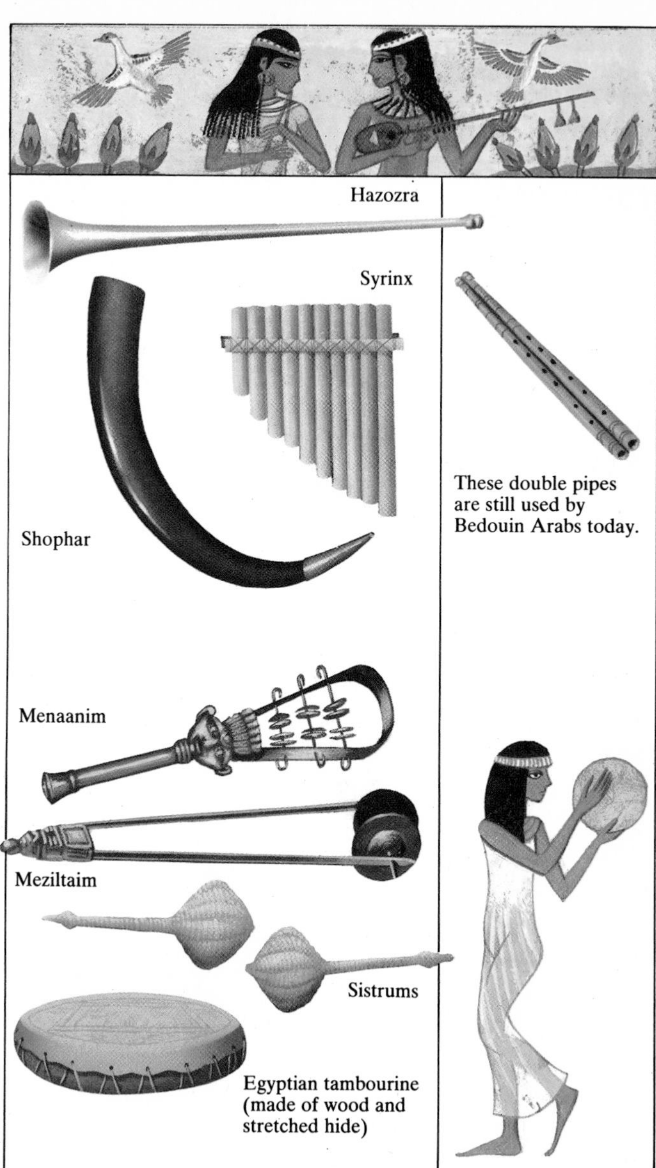
Hazozra
Syrinx
Shophar
These double pipes are still used by Bedouin Arabs today.
Menaanim
Meziltaim
Sistrums
Egyptian tambourine (made of wood and stretched hide)

The Sabbath

A sabbath service in the synagogue
The people sat while a passage from the scriptures was read aloud from the pulpit by one of the readers. They stood, facing Jerusalem, to pray. Once the service was over, the scrolls on which the scriptures were written were returned to the special chest in which they were kept.

All work ceased on the Sabbath, the seventh day of the week. The Sabbath began on Friday night and ended on Saturday night.

You have six days in which to do your work, but the seventh day is a day of rest dedicated to me. On that day no one is to work – neither you, your children, your slaves, your animals, nor the foreigners who live in your country. Your slaves must rest just as you do. Remember that you were slaves in Egypt and that I, the Lord your God, rescued you by my great power and strength. That is why I command you to observe the Sabbath. **Deut 5.13-16**

Observe the Sabbath and keep it holy, as I, the Lord your God, have commanded you.

Deut 5.12

The Sabbath was a day of celebration and prayer, when families put on their best clothes and enjoyed the meals and cakes prepared the day before.

Reading from the Torah. Public readings from the Torah go right back to the time of the prophet Ezra, who in 444 or 445 B.C. assembled the people for a solemn reading of 'the Book'.

The Synagogue

The synagogue was a special house where Jewish people met to study the Bible and pray. The temple in Jerusalem was the centre of Israel's religious life, where people came to worship God, to offer sacrifices and to obtain pardon. However, from the 6th

The Sabbath meal (14th century German engravings)

century B.C. onwards, people began to make a habit of meeting on the Sabbath to study the scriptures and pray together. Soon this custom was being practised throughout the land, and even in Jerusalem. The synagogue was run by a group of elders. They elected from amongst themselves a chief elder whose duty it was to organise the service and appoint people to say the prayers and interpret the scriptures which had been read aloud.

The sabbatical year
Every seventh year the land was rested. Each field was left in turn to lie fallow and whatever grew there was given to the poor.

Jerusalem

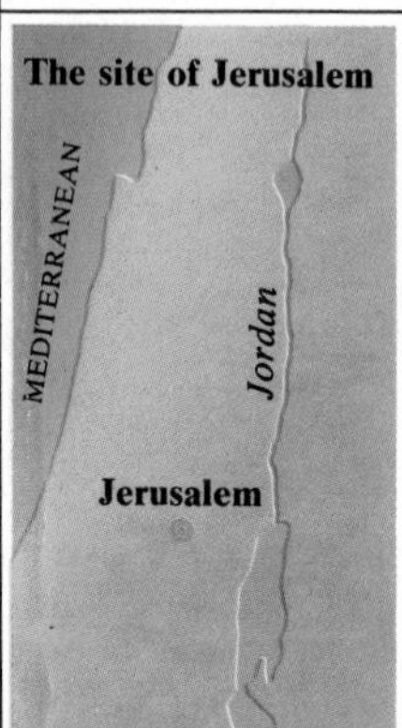

Jerusalem means 'the town of peace'. It was a little town perched on a hill when King David proclaimed it the capital of his kingdom. His son, Solomon, added many beautiful buildings and built a wall around the town. His great masterpiece was the temple which stood next to his palace.

King Hezekiah made sure the inhabitants would never die of thirst in a siege. He had a tunnel dug to carry water from the Spring of Gihon outside the city walls to the Pool of Siloam within the city.

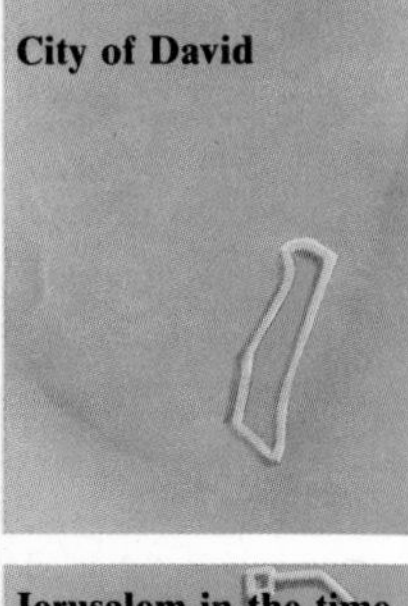

Jerusalem in the time of the kings

Temple

City of Solomon

City of David

Spring of Gihon

Pool of Siloam

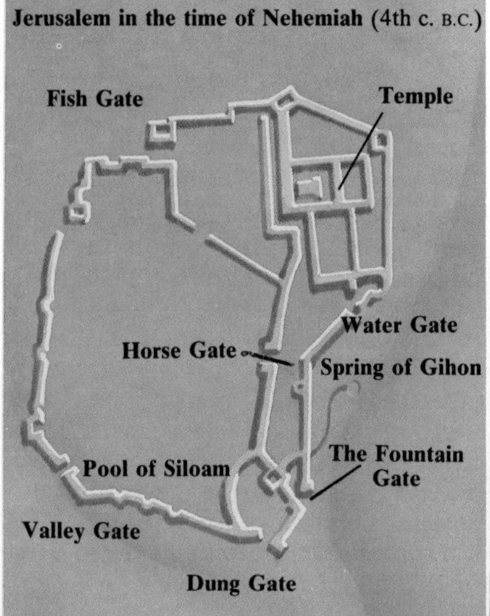

May I never be able to play the harp again if I forget you, Jerusalem!
Ps 137.6

The population of Jerusalem was quite small. Many of the inhabitants were employed in the running and maintenance of the temple. However, at the Feasts of Passover and Harvest the streets would be filled with bustling crowds of pilgrims coming from far and wide.

In 586 B.C. King Nebuchadnezzar captured the town and set fire to it. Many of its most prominent citizens were deported to Babylonia. Fifty years later they returned from exile. In time and with difficulty, both town and temple were rebuilt. The new temple could not match the splendour of Solomon's. New walls and gates were built in record time to protect the people from attack.

Jerusalem is still the meeting point for Jews the world over, the true home of their religion.

I was glad when they said to me,
'Let us go to the Lord's house.'
And now we are here, standing inside the gates of Jerusalem!
Jerusalem is a city restored in beautiful order and harmony.
This is where the tribes come, the tribes of Israel,
to give thanks to the Lord according to his command.
Here the kings of Israel
sat to judge their people.
Ps 122.1-5

The Temple

The temple of God stood in the heart of Jerusalem. For the people it was the dwelling place of God, just as the Tabernacle had been in the desert.

Prayers were said in the temple each day and on the great annual Feast days. People brought offerings: fruits of the harvest, cattle, sheep or goats, and these were burnt on the altar.

Terracotta model of a Moabite temple (9th c. B.C.). Its two pillars recall the giant free-standing columns of Solomon's temple.

Three successive temples

- The first was built by King Solomon in the 10th c. B.C. (see p. 202). Four centuries later, in 587 B.C., it was destroyed by Nebuchadnezzar, King of Babylon.
- A second temple was rebuilt in 515 B.C. (see p. 236)
- in 20 B.C. King Herod the Great began to construct a third temple. It was completed 80 years later, only to be destroyed in its turn by the Romans in 70 A.D. (See p. 310)

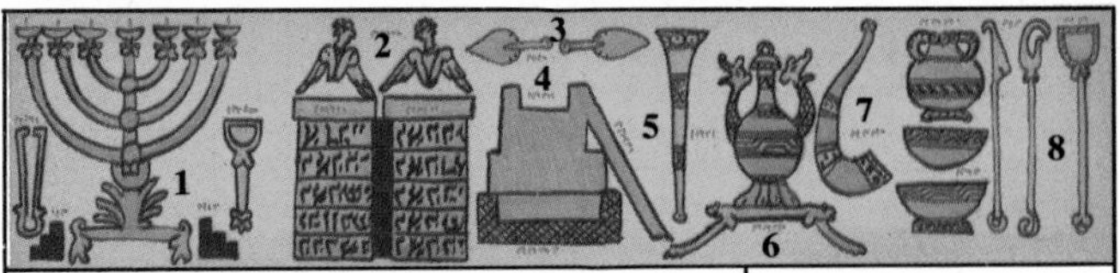

These offerings were called sacrifices. The faithful offered their most treasured possessions to God as a gift and as a sign of their devotion.

Then in the presence of the people Solomon went and stood in front of the altar, where he raised his arms and prayed. **1 Kgs 8.22**

1 Entry porch
2 Storage chambers
3 The 'holy' place
4 Holy of Holies
5 Altar
6 Sea of bronze

5

6

Used in the Temple

1 Menorah (seven-branch candlestick) and its accessories: tongs, snuffers, and steps
2 The Tablets of the Law
3 Incense shovel
4 Altar for burnt offerings
5 Silver trumpet
6 Water jar
7 Shophar
8 Sacrificial instruments: ash bowls, sprinklers, scrapers, tongs

Different types of sacrifice

- **Burnt offerings:** whether vegetable or animal these were burned in their entirety on the altar, as a sign of total dedication to God.
- **Peace offerings** were gifts shared in a spirit of communion with God. A part of every peace offering was burned on the altar, while the rest was shared between the priest and the people offering the sacrifice.
- **Sin offerings** were ritual sacrifices offered at major festivals like Yom Kippur (see p. 79).

No less than 2,400 people are named in the Old Testament. It tells us how they came into the world, how they grew up and how they met their death.
We read of them at work and at rest, at prayer and at war, at home and on the move. We learn about their loves, their hatreds, the battles they fought, their deeds – both good and bad. We share in their laughter and in their tears. They are very different, and yet all are human like ourselves – each with a part to play in the story which is theirs.

You and Aaron
are to take a census
of the people of Israel
by clans and families.
List the names
of all the men
twenty years old or older
who are fit for
military service.
Num 1.2-3

THE CHARACTERS

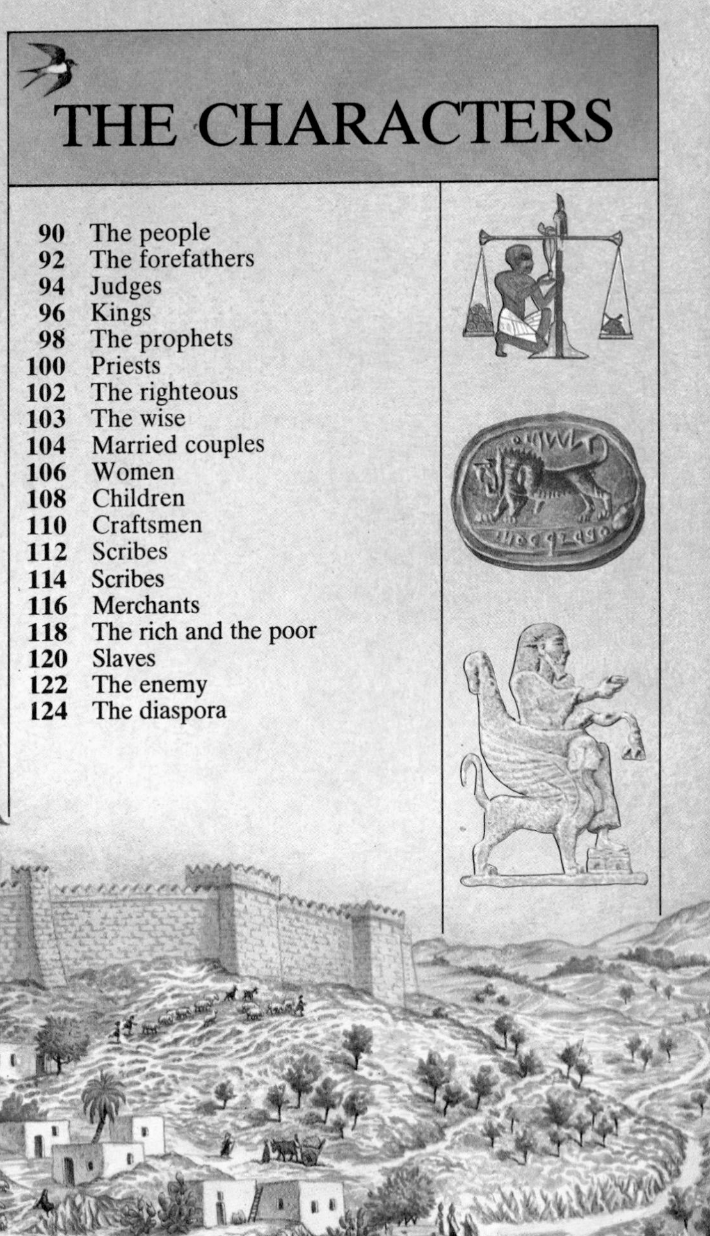

The people

Israel considered itself different from other nations. Had not the one true God, Creator of Heaven and Earth, chosen Israel to make God's presence known to other nations?

The God Israel worshipped was a loving, caring God who had freed the people from slavery in Egypt and made a covenant with them in the wilderness – an unbreakable covenant. The Law that God gave the people of Israel was based on righteousness and brotherly love. God gave the people a land of their own and ruled them first by means of appointed leaders or Judges and then by Kings. God sent prophets to guide them, wise people to educate them.

The Hebrews

The word means: one who has passed over, a passer-by. The children of Israel were known as Hebrews while they were still nomadic tent-dwellers, before they settled in the land of Canaan in about 1235-1210 B.C.

Israel

El is one of the names used to describe the power of God. Israel means 'May God contend, may God rule'.

Israel was the name given to Jacob. Later it became the name of the people who were his descendants, the 'children of Israel'. In 930 B.C., when David's kingdom was split in two, the Northern kingdom (capital, Samaria) kept the

*Do not be afraid, my people!
You know that from ancient times until now I have predicted all that would happen, and you are my witnesses.
Is there any other god?
Is there some powerful god I never heard of?* **Is 44.8**

name Israel, while the Southern kingdom (capital Jerusalem) became known as Judah.

The Jews

The word means to praise or celebrate. It was originally the name of a member of the tribe of Judah, or any inhabitant of Judah. After the return from exile in 536 B.C., the name was used of the nation as a whole.

'The Lord did not love you and choose you because you outnumbered other peoples; you were the smallest nation on earth. But the Lord loved you and wanted to keep the promise that he made to your ancestors. That is why he saved you by his great might and set you free from slavery to the king of Egypt.'
Deut 7.7-8

The forefathers

In order to trace their descent from these famous ancestors, the people of the Old Testament went to great lengths to keep family records. A family tree is a list of all the people in a family, past and present, from the earliest (the roots) to the last in line (the top branches). There are several such family trees in the Bible.

The founder members or patriarchs were Abraham, Isaac, Jacob and the twelve sons of Jacob – the ancestors of the twelve tribes of Israel.

Then there were the great figures who left their mark on the history of the people: Moses, David, Solomon. . . . and finally, the fathers from whom each separate family was descended.

'I will renew the covenant that I made with their ancestors when I showed all the nations my power by bringing my people out of Egypt, in order that I, the Lord, might be their God.' **Lev 26.45**

King David's family tree. This shows how he was descended from the patriarch Abraham, as set out in **1 Chr 2.1-15**.

DAVID

Jesse

Obed

Boaz

Salmon

Nahshon

mminadab

Ram

Caleb

hmeel

Hezron

Hamul

Shelah

Perez

Zerah

Judah

Zebulon

Issachar

Dan

Naphtali

Manasseh

JACOB

Joseph

Ephraim

Rebecca

ISAAC

Benjamin

Sarah

agar

ABRAHAM

Judges

Then the Lord gave the Israelites leaders who saved them from the raiders. **Judg 2.16**

In Hebrew the word to judge does not just mean to administer justice, but also to rule or command. The Judges were leaders, men of action (save for one woman, Deborah) who delivered their tribe or nation from foreign powers in times of crisis.

At that time Israel was not a united nation but twelve separate, independent tribes scattered across the country. Each tribe was divided into clans and elected its own ruling elders.

Whenever one of the tribes was threatened by another nation, someone of exceptional courage and daring within the tribe was elected as leader.

The story of Samson
(Read **Judg 13-16**)
The Judge Samson is the hero of one of the most well-known Bible stories. Samson was renowned for his strength. Single-handed he killed 1,000 Philistines. He up-rooted the gates of the city of Gaza and carried them on his shoulders all the way to the top of a hill.

He set foxes carrying fire in the corn.

Samson's weapon was a donkey's jaw-bone.

Delilah persuaded Samson to tell her the secret of his strength. She betrayed him.

Samson's enemies got Delilah to cut Samson's hair. His strength left him. He was captured and blinded. But he was to have his revenge.

Samson carried off the gates ot Gaza.

He destroyed the Philistine temple.

This champion of the people was called a Judge. It was his (or her) job to gather an army together and lead the people to victory.

Once the particular crisis was over, some of the Judges continued to be national or local rulers, others returned home and carried on life as before.

You can read about the exploits of these national heroes, or saviours, as they are also called, in the *Book of Judges* and the *first Book of Samuel.* The most famous of them were Deborah, Gideon, Jephthah, Samson and Samuel.

Philistine warriors

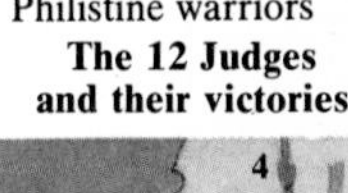

The 12 Judges and their victories

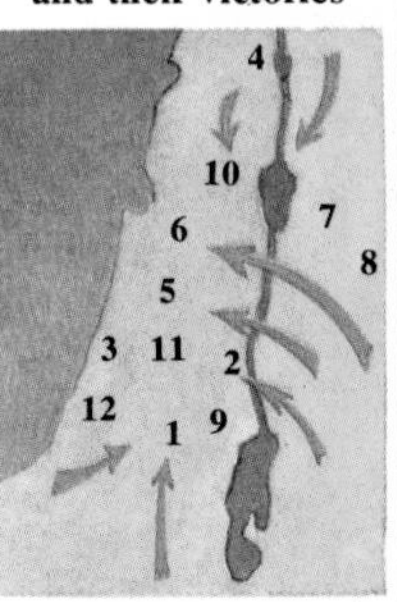

1 **Othniel** of Judah (**Judg 3.9**) over the Mesopotamians.
2 **Ehud** of Benjamin (**Judg 3.15**) over the Moabites.
3 **Shamgar** (**Judg 3.31**) over the Philistines.
4 **Deborah** and **Barak** of Naphtali (**Judg 4.4-6**) over the Canaanites.
5 **Gideon** of Manasseh (**Judg 6.11**) over the Midianites and the Amalekites.
6 **Tola** of Issachar (**Judg 10.1**)
7 **Jair** of Gilead (**Judg 10.3**)
8 **Jephthah** of Gilead (**Judg 11.11**) over the Ammonites.
9 **Ibzan** of Bethlehem (**Judg 12.8**)
10 **Elon** of Zebulon (**Judg 12.11**)
11 **Abdon** of Ephraim (**Judg 12.13**)
12 **Samson** of Dan (**Judg 15.20**) over the Philistines.

Kings

Seal of Jeroboam II.

King of Israel, 8th c. B.C.

Many of the countries round Israel had kings long before Israel. *Below*, from left to right:
Seth I, Pharaoh, 13th c. B.C.
Hiram, King of Byblos, 11th c. B.C.
Melishipak II, King of Babylonia, 12th c. B.C.

Around the year 1000 B.C. the tribes of Israel were under heavy attack from their powerful enemies, the Philistines. They decided their only hope of survival was to form a central government. What they needed, they said, was a king to rule them.

Many people viewed this change with deep misgivings. Hitherto God had been the only king they needed. If a king was appointed, some people might turn away from God and worship the king instead – as they did in other countries. Besides, a king might make unfair demands on his subjects.

After much deliberation, the first king of Israel was appointed. This was Saul. After him came David. The kings of Israel were not like other kings. They were never regarded as divine, nor did they rule in God's place, but on God's behalf. It was their duty to serve the people and to administer justice and

Kings will be like fathers to you;
queens will be like mothers.
Is 49.23

maintain peace. They were subject to God's law like everyone else. Many kings fell far short of these expectations.

When the last king's rule came to an end in 586 B.C., the people began to dream of another king, a king of justice and peace, whom God would one day send to rule over the chosen people and over all nations.

The Messiah

In Hebrew Messiah means 'anointed with oil'. Oil was poured over the king's head at his consecration. In this sense each king was a Messiah. After the disappearance of the monarchy in the 6th c. B.C., the word came to mean the future king, a descendant of David, who would establish God's reign on earth. Jews still await the coming of the Messiah. For Christians, Christ is the Messiah.

A king's promise
I will get rid of
anyone who whispers
evil things about
someone else;
I will not tolerate
a man who is proud
and arrogant.
I will approve of
those who are
faithful to God and
will let them live in
my palace.
Ps 101.5-6

The prophets

Baal, the Canaanite god of fertility

Idols, and idol worship
The Israelites constantly fell into the trap of worshipping idols or statues of their own creation (such as the Golden Calf) or foreign gods (Baal). The prophets fought hard to stop them worshipping idols.

The prophets were men of faith with a particular calling. It was through them that God spoke to the people in times of crisis. The prophets were from all walks of life: peasants, aristocrats and priests. Many of them covered huge distances in the pursuit of their calling.

The Lord said to me, 'I chose you before I gave you life, and before you were born I selected you to be a prophet to the nations.' **Jer 1.4-5**

Then the Lord stretched out his hand, touched my lips, and said to me, 'Listen, I am giving you the words you must speak.' **Jer 1.9-10**

The prophet pointed an accusing finger at people who piously offered sacrifices while breaking the Law or exploiting the poor. He spoke out against people who put their faith in wealth and weapons, led a life of luxury, or worshipped idols. No one was spared, not even the King. He warned the people that misfortune would befall them unless they mended their ways. He

urged them to turn away from their idols and to worship the one true God.

Whenever the people were disheartened or beginning to lose faith in the face of some great ordeal, the prophet would comfort them and remind them of God's promises.

Prophets did not just use words; sometimes they acted out the message to make it clearer. Isaiah walked naked through the streets of Jerusalem to warn the people how dangerous an alliance with Egypt was. Jeremiah carried a wooden ox yoke on his shoulders as a sign that the people should submit to Nebuchadnezzar.

The prophets' messages were not always well-received. The truth they had to tell was not always what people wanted to hear. They were often mocked or persecuted. It was a lonely and often dispiriting way of life.

A third of the Bible is made up of writings by the Prophets. The most famous of them are Elijah, Amos, Hosea, Jeremiah and Ezekiel.

Sacrificing to an idol

Prophets used images and actions to get their message across.

Branch of an almond-tree **Jer 1.11-12**

Boiling pot **Jer 1.13**

Broken clay jar
Jer 19.1-13

Priests

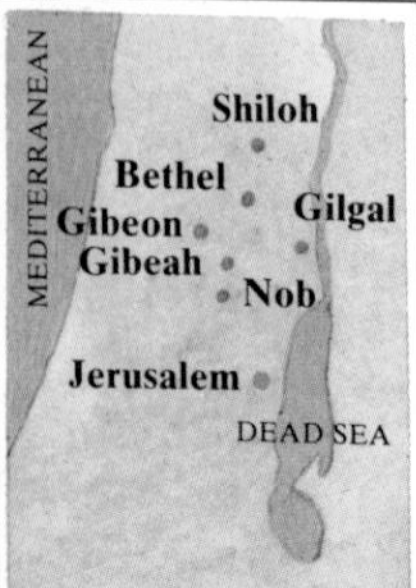

These were the chief sanctuaries up until the 7th c. B.C.

The High Priest: the 12 precious stones on his breastplate represented the 12 tribes of Israel.

In the days of the patriarchs there were no priests. Fathers were responsible for their family's spiritual welfare. It was they who said prayers, offered sacrifices and instructed the family in the ways of God.

After the signing of the Covenant on Mount Sinai, the Tabernacle became the symbol of God's presence in the midst of the people. The Tabernacle and the Ark were entrusted to Aaron and his sons. They were the first priests. It was their duty to instruct the Hebrews in the Law, to lead them in worship and to offer sacrifices.

Only members of the tribe of Levi could be priests. This tribe did not own any land, and relied entirely on the other tribes for food. In the 7th c. B.C. all the priests from the different sanctuaries were brought to serve in the temple in Jerusalem. Jerusalem became the religious centre of Israel.

The high priests and chief priests conducted the services. Priests served in the temple for only two weeks of the year. The rest of the time they spent in their own homes or villages.

Time and time again the prophets accused the priests of worshipping idols, earning money by dishonest means or making free with goods offered in sacrifice.

After the return from Exile there were no kings or prophets to guide the people. For a while this role fell to the priests.

The Tabernacle of the Covenant in the desert; early temple

A harvest offering: the first sheaf and first loaves

When you harvest your corn, take the first sheaf, the first-fruits of your harvest, to the priest. The priest shall present it to the Lord. You shall also sacrifice a male lamb that has no defects. Seven weeks later you are to bring two loaves of bread and present them to the Lord as a special gift. These are the Lord's first-fruits. Furthermore, you shall present seven lambs, one bull, two rams, all without defect. The priest shall present the bread with the two lambs as a special gift to the Lord for the priests. These offerings are holy.

(From **Lev 23.10-20**)

Priest

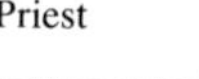

Priest's sceptre

Daily offerings

Every day for all time to come, sacrifice on the altar two one-year-old lambs. Sacrifice one of the lambs in the morning and the other in the evening.
Ex 29.38-39

Incense-burner

The righteous

The righteous will flourish like palm trees. **Ps 92.13**

Cedar of Lebanon **Ps 92.13**

The righteous were good people who tried to lead upright, honest lives and to keep God's commandments. They were not deceived by idols, wealth or power, but continued to trust in God alone, and in God's word. The righteous struggled to put their beliefs into practice day by day. As a result they were persecuted and rejected by those who betrayed the Covenant.

A good man's words are wise, and he is always fair. He keeps the law of his God in his heart and he never departs from it. A wicked man watches a good man and tries to kill him; but the Lord will not abandon him to his enemy's power or let him be condemned when he is on trial. **Ps 37.30-33**

They are like the trees that grow beside a stream . . . **Ps 1.3**

The wise

Every nation has its wise men and women – people of great learning, with a thirst for truth. They ponder the fundamental questions we all ask ourselves about life and human nature: 'Why was I born? Why must I die? Why do people fight wars?' and they try to provide some answers.

There were wise men and women at every stage in Israel's history, from the time of the desert nomads onwards. Their wisdom was not just a question of

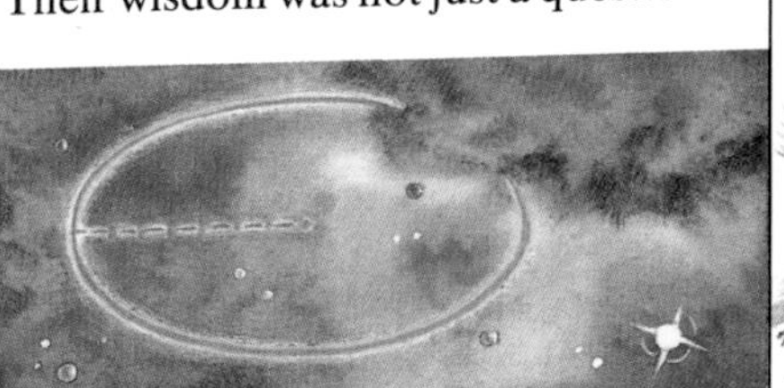

knowledge, but of faith. Their thinking was done in the light of that faith.

Many of the books in the Bible were written by wise men: Proverbs, the Book of Job, Ecclesiastes.

The benefits of wisdom

I am Wisdom, I am better than jewels;
nothing you want can compare with me.
I am Wisdom, and I have insight;
I have knowledge and sound judgement.
To honour the Lord is to hate evil;
I hate pride and arrogance, evil ways and false words. **Prov 8.11-13**

Sure-footed as a deer
Ps 18.33-34

Small, but very very clever
Prov 30.24-25

The stars in the sky
Job 9.9

The bear
Prov 17.12

An honest person is as brave as a lion. **Prov 28.1**

Married couples

It was very rare for people not to marry in Israel. In the days of the patriarchs a man often had more than one wife. Polygamy was permitted by law. Gradually, under the influence of the prophets, monogamy (one husband, one wife) became more frequent.

Couples married very young. The minimum age for a girl was twelve, for a boy thirteen.

Marriages were generally arranged by the parents, but many of the Old Testament marriages were, nonetheless, love matches: Abraham and Sarah, Isaac and Rebecca, Jacob and Rachel, Boaz and Ruth. The law discouraged people from marrying foreigners, but the Book of Ruth (see p. 248) seems to question the strictness of this rule.

The wedding ceremony

Before a young couple married, they had to be formally betrothed. A solemn betrothal ceremony was held during which a contract was drawn up in the presence of two witnesses. The parents of the bridegroom-to-be paid the parents of the bride a large sum of money, called in Hebrew the *mohar* or bride price. From that moment the bride was legally her husband's property, his *beoula*. He was her owner, or *baal*. It was customary for the bride's father to hand over some or all of the bride price to his daughter, possibly together with some slaves from his household to serve her.

Persian miniature (16th c. A.D.)

The wedding took place a year later, generally after the harvest.

On the evening of the appointed day the bridegroom, wearing a special crown, made his way to the bride's house, escorted by his family and friends. There the couple received a blessing from the bride's parents. Then the bride, wearing her finest clothes, was solemnly escorted to the bridegroom's house by the assembled wedding guests. This torchlight procession was a ritual symbolising the girl's entry into her husband's family.

The celebrations and the wedding feast sometimes lasted a full week or more.

Then Raguel called his daughter. When she came in, he took her by the hand and gave her to Tobias with the blessing, 'Take her to be your wife according to the teachings in the Law of Moses. Take her safely with you to your father's house. May the God of heaven give you a happy life together.' Raguel asked his wife to bring him a blank scroll so that he could write out the agreement. . . . After the ceremony they began the meal. . . . Edna made up the bed as Raguel had told her. Then she took Sarah into the room with her, and Sarah began to cry. But Edna wiped away her tears and said, 'Don't worry, Sarah. I'm sure the Lord of heaven will make you happy this time and not sad'.

Tob 7.13-18

The levirate law
This was the law whereby a widow, whose husband died without leaving her a son, married her husband's brother. She thus remained in her husband's family.

How hard it is to find a capable wife! She is worth far more than jewels!
Her husband puts his confidence in her, and he will never be poor.
As long as she lives, she does him good and never harm.
She keeps herself busy making wool and linen cloth.
She brings home food from out-of-the-way places, as merchant ships do.
She gets up before daylight to prepare food for her family and to tell her servant-girls what to do.
She looks at land and buys it, and with money she has earned she plants a vineyard.

Prov 31.10-16

Women

Hittite idol of the third millenium representing the goddess of fertility

Women did not share the same privileges and responsibilities as men in Biblical times, although they were considered equal in other ways. A married woman was legally her husband's property. Any important decisions were taken on her behalf by her husband. She was responsible for the running of the house and the bringing up of children.

Egyptian collar from the time of Moses

A woman was not allowed to appear in court. Her husband could divorce her, but she could not divorce him. However, there were laws protecting women. If a woman was childless, she could offer her maidservant to her husband and raise their children as her own.

Egyptian beauty aids: combs, mirror, hairpins, jars of make-up

Some famous Old Testament women

Bathsheba (daughter of plenty) 11th c. B.C., David's favourite wife, mother of King Solomon. **(2 Sam 11-12)**

Deborah (the bee) 12th c. B.C., prophetess and Judge. **(Judges 4-5)**

Esther (the star) a young Jewess, who became the Persian King Xerxes' Queen. She successfully foiled Haman's plot to massacre the Jews. **(Esther)**

Eve (life) the first woman in the world. **(Genesis 2-3)**

A festive scene in ancient Egypt (13th c. B.C.)

Hagar (the Egyptian girl) 18th c. B.C., Sarah's maid, who bore Abraham a son, Ishmael. **(Gen 16; 21.9-21)**

Hannah (grace) 11th c. B.C., mother of Samuel. **(1 Sam 1-2)**

Judith (the Jewess) the brave heroine who saved her people from Nebuchadnezzar. **(Judith)**

Spoon for make-up

Myriam (the lady) 13th c. B.C., Moses' sister. **(Exodus 15.19-21)**

Rachel (the ewe) Jacob's favourite wife, mother of Joseph and Benjamin. **(Gen 24)**

Ruth (the friend) 12th c. B.C, a foreigner from the land of Moab, wife of Boaz. **(Ruth)**

Sarah (the princess) wife of Abraham, mother of Isaac, their much-longed for son. **(Gen 12; 18.9-15)**

Amongst her many other domestic duties a woman was expected to grind barley and corn, bake bread, prepare food, fetch water from the well, spin and weave wool.

Children

Every child was regarded as a gift from God. The birth of a child was a cause for rejoicing.

Birth

At birth, the baby was bathed in water, salt was rubbed into its skin to make it firm and the child was then closely wrapped in swaddling clothes.

The child was given a name with a particular meaning, e.g.: Esther, star; Naomi, my pleasantness; Benjamin, son of the right hand (the right was the place of honour); David, the beloved.

The child was also called by the father's name, e.g.: Benjamin, son of Jacob. . . .

Toy from the ancient city of Susa, dating from the third millenium B.C.

Boys were circumcised when they were eight days old. All children were breast-fed for the first two or three years of their lives.

Unlike its neighbours, where this practice spread, Israel did not have child sacrifice. A statue of the Canaanites god, Moloch, to whom many children were sacrificed.

Education

There were no synagogues until the 6th c. B.C., so the children's education took place in the home. Parents taught their children a trade or craft. They also taught them the Law of Moses and the meaning of the different religious festivals. Later, children went to the synagogue to learn to read and write, and to study history, geography, arith-

metic and the prayers that were part of the religious services.

The Bar Mitzvah

Circumcision

This was the removal of the foreskin, the piece of skin covering the end of a boy's penis. Circumcision was practised in several other countries at the time, including Ethiopia and Egypt. However, from the time of the Exile it was considered to be the outward sign of God's covenant with Israel, which distinguished Jews from other peoples.

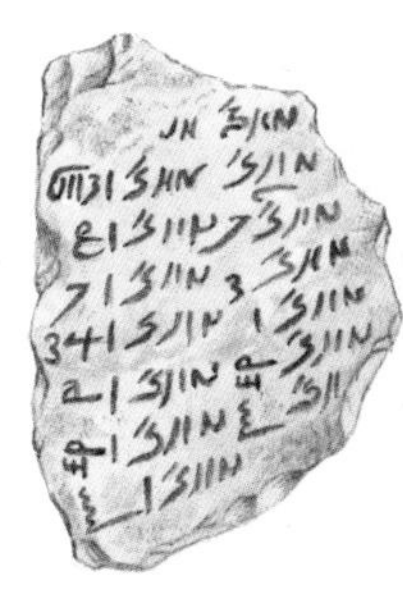

Schoolboy's exercise: Conjugating the verb 'to speak' in an ancient Egyptian script.

Bar Mitzvah

Bar Mitzvah was a ritual celebration which marked the end of a boy's childhood. On the day after his 13th birthday, a boy became Bar Mitzvah – a son of the Law. He was allowed to read the Law in the synagogue on the Sabbath.

Children's games

Craftsmen

The carpenter used a bow drill to make holes in the wood.

The carpenter

Carpenters worked with wood in every shape and form. They were woodcutters, coach-builders, cabinet-makers and sculptors all rolled into one. More especially they would decorate the interiors of rich men's houses, make and repair furniture and agricultural implements (ploughs, pitch-forks, threshing sleds).

Their tools were an axe, adze, hammer,

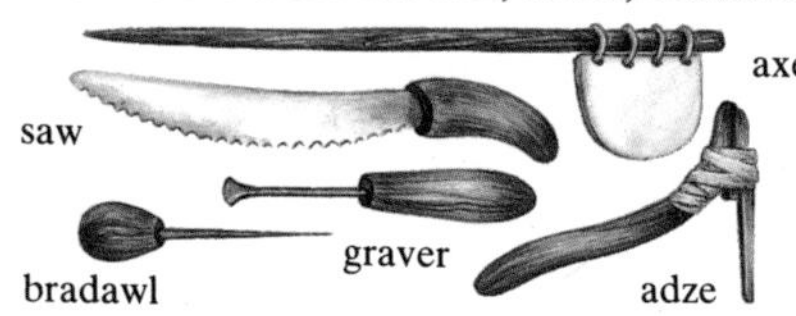

saw, small hand-saw, chalkline, pencil, chisel and a pair of compasses.

The mason

Masons quarried and fashioned stone. They hollowed out tombs and wine vats in the rock and built houses for the rich. The tools they used were: sledgehammer, saw, plumbline, ruler, chalkline. Bricks were made of clay and earth mixed with straw, which was pressed into rectangular moulds and left to dry in the sun.

Brick-making

The artist and the craftsman. . . .
take great pains to produce a lifelike image,
and will work far into the night to finish the work.
Sir 38.27

Potters

All sorts of things were made in clay: earthenware jars for storing scrolls and parchments, jugs, writing tablets, toys, kitchen utensils (jugs, bowls, dishes, lamps).

It is the same with the potter, sitting at his wheel and turning it with his feet, always concentrating on his work, concerned with how many objects he can produce. He works his clay with his feet until he can shape it with his hands.
Sir 38.29-30

The potter first trampled the clay underfoot to make it malleable. He then placed it on a wheel which he turned with his hand or with a pedal. The objects were then dried, glazed and fired in an oven. This last operation was a particularly delicate one: the temperature and firing time varied according to the type of clay and it took skill and experience to get it right.

Trying to teach a fool
is like gluing
a broken pot
together again.
Sir 22.7

Egyptian craftsmen in the third millenium B.C. used a primitive sort of wheel for making pots.

As time went on, more sophisticated wheels made the potter's task easier.

Pots ready for decoration and firing.

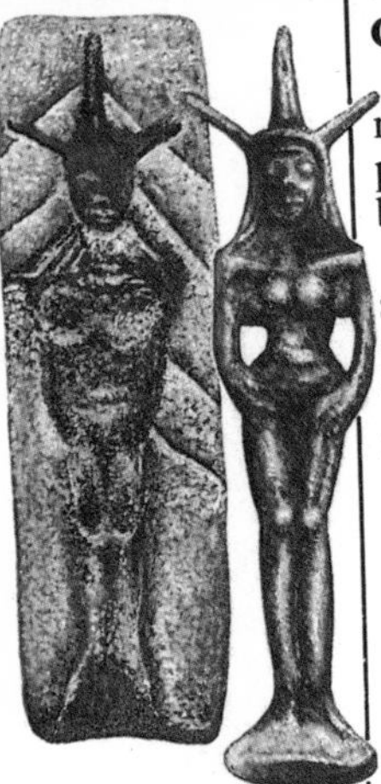

Bronze statue and its mould.

Goldsmiths

Goldsmiths made jewellery, using not only gold but also silver, ivory, precious stones, mother of pearl and bronze.

They also made seals out of precious stones and metals. A seal left a personalised imprint on wax or clay which was like a signature on a document.

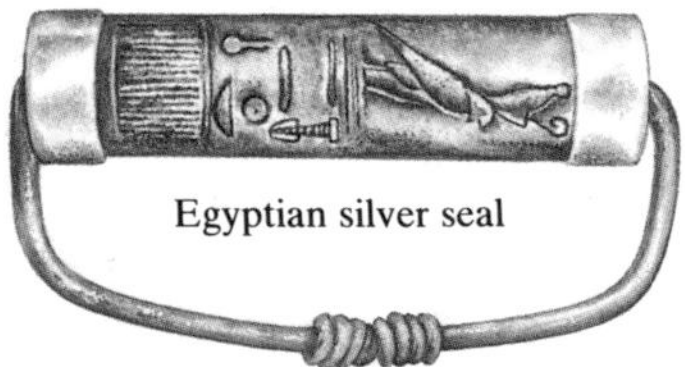

Egyptian silver seal

Now send me a man with skill in engraving, in working gold, silver, bronze, and iron, and in making blue, purple and red cloth. **2 Chr 2.6-7**

Sickle

Meat fork

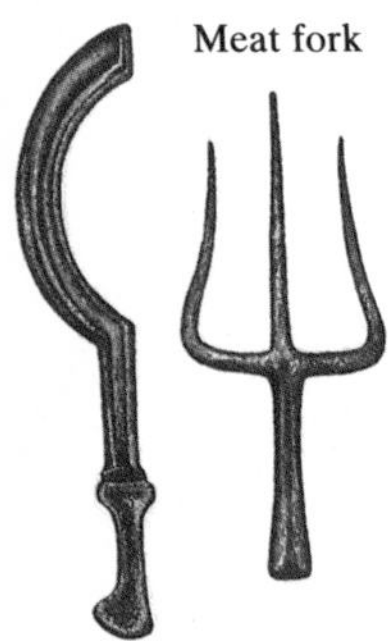

Tools began to be made in iron in about 1000 B.C.

Blacksmiths

The blacksmith made the objects used in religious ceremonies, weapons, and later, kitchen utensils. The metals he worked with were iron and bronze, which was an alloy of copper and tin.

His tools were the hammer, the anvil and bellows. The first blacksmiths made their appearance in Israel during the reign of David and Solomon. They adopted techniques used by the

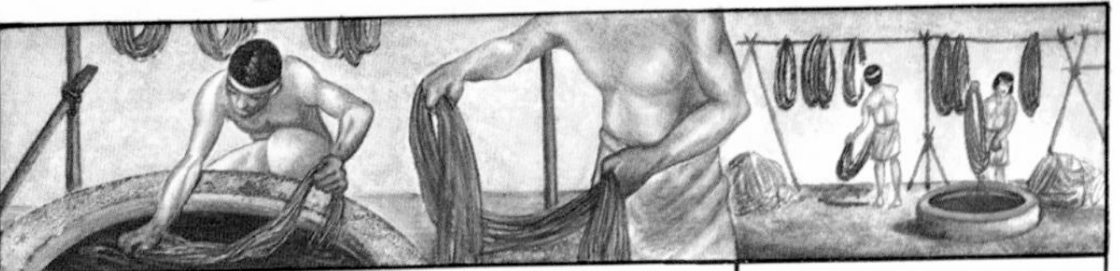

Dyeing

Canaanites and Philistines. Copper was mined in the Sinai peninsula, and iron from South of the Dead Sea.

Dyers

It was the dyer's job to dye materials and skins. The most beautiful colours were the purples made from the plant, red antimony, and the murex mollusc, a type of shellfish.

Weavers

Most families still wove the cloth for the clothes they wore at home. More elaborate clothes for special occasions, such as the Temple priests' robes, were made by the weaver.

Tanners (or leather-dressers)

Sheep and goatskins were left to steep in water. They were then dried, before being tanned and dressed. From the skins tanners made leather bottles for wine, water or milk, seats to sit on, coats and tunics, leather straps, sandals, belts and parchment.

Fullers

Fullers were the people who cleaned the animal skins. They washed them in water and trod them underfoot to get out all the grease before spreading them out to dry. The smell was so strong that tanners and fullers had to work outside the town or village.

A basket made of strips of papyrus.

Another type of basket probably made of palm fronds.

A tanner dressing a skin with a special scraping tool.

Scribes

Making papyrus

Thin strips were cut from the papyrus stem.

The strips were arranged in layers.

covered with a cloth, pounded with a mallet,

and pressed with a heavy stone.

The first schools only came into being in the 6th c. B.C. Before this, only a small minority of people knew how to read and write. If they wanted to write a letter, do their accounts, or draw up a bill of sale, they called on the scribe.

There were scribes at the royal court from the days of Kings David and Solomon onwards (10th c. B.C.). The scribes recorded in writing the major events in the life of the King and his realm. They also began to draw up a history of the people of Israel and their origins, based on the old traditional tales that had been handed down by word of mouth.

After the Exile (4th c. B.C.) the scribes began to teach children to read and write in the synagogue, using the holy scriptures.

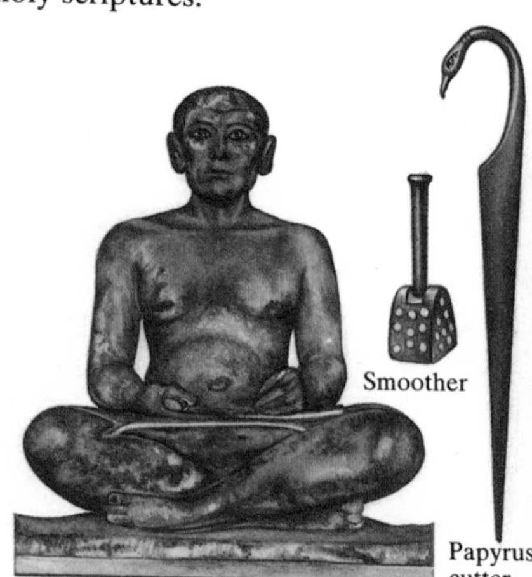

Hieroglyphics on papyrus

The invention of writing

Writing was invented in Babylonia and Egypt in about 5,000 B.C. At first the individual letters or signs looked more like a series of pictures of well-known objects. There were between 800 and 1,000 of them. Very few people knew how to write.

The alphabet

The alphabet was invented in Phoenicia in the 16th c. B.C. It was revolutionary: each sign now represented a sound, rather than an object. This meant only about 30 signs – far less than before – were needed. The alphabet was easy to learn; anybody could learn to write. All alphabets are based on that of Phoenicia.

Phoenician alphabet (10th c. B.C.)	Hebrew alphabet	
𐤀	א	aleph
𐤁	בּ	beth
𐤂	גּ	gimel
𐤃	דּ	daleth
𐤄	ה	he
𐤅	ו	waw
𐤆	ז	zayin
𐤇	ח	heth
𐤈	ט	teth
𐤉	י	yod
𐤊	כּ	kaph
𐤋	ל	lamed
𐤌	מ	mem
𐤍	נ	nun
𐤎	ס	samekh
𐤏	ע	ayin
𐤐	פּ	pe
𐤑	צ	tsadhe
𐤒	ק	qoph
𐤓	ר	resh
𐤔	שׁ	shin
𐤕	תּ	taw

Books were made by attaching sheets of papyrus or parchment together until one had a roll up to 40 m (130 ft) long.

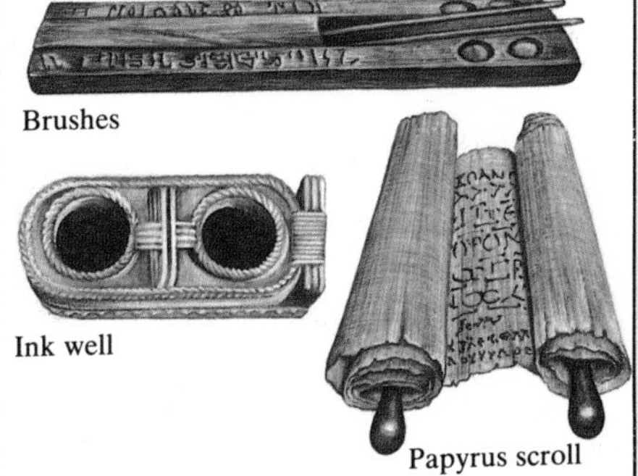

Brushes

Ink well

Papyrus scroll

Merchants

So when you sell land to your fellow-Israelite or buy land from him, do not deal unfairly.
Lev 25.14

Israel lay at the cross-roads of the major trade routes between Asia Minor, Egypt, Arabia and Mesopotamia. However, despite this key geographical position, Israel does not seem to have

had a particular aptitude for trade and commerce. An early form of banking already existed in Mesopotamia, but there was no such system in Israel.

The Phoenicians and the merchants of Tyre dominated international trade. Their ships called at all the Mediterranean ports, where they established colonies. They even ventured as far as England, as it now is, and, via the Red Sea, the East coast of Africa.

It was by making alliances with their powerful neighbours that the kings of

Egyptian merchant

Israel finally succeeded in developing trade with other countries.

With the aid of the Phoenicians, King Solomon (967 to 928 B.C.) built a fleet of merchant ships. This merchant navy enabled him to trade with Africa and Arabia. Solomon imported large numbers of horses from Cilicia (modern Turkey) and chariots from Egypt, which he then sold to Syria.

Later, another king, Jehoshaphat (King of Judah, 870-848 B.C.) also made an alliance with the Phoenicians, but his fleet came to grief at sea.

King Ahab (King of Israel, 874-853 B.C.) opened up trade with Damascus.

Israel imported:
tin, lead, silver, copper, wood, linen, purple dye, spices, gold.

Israel exported:
oil, cereals, fruit, nuts, aromatic gums, myrrh, wool, woven goods.

The great trade routes over land and by sea

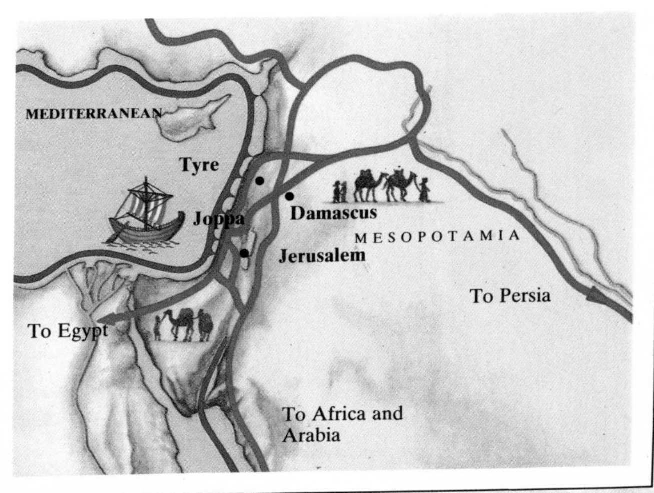

The rich and the poor

In the time of the monarchy (10th c. B.C.), certain privileged people benefited at the expense of others from Israel's

developing trade with neighbouring countries. The prophets criticised the unscrupulous attitude of the wealthy.

The rich as seen by the prophets

The rich accumulated property, land and material possessions to the exclusion of everyone else, said the prophets.

They were dishonest in their dealings; they weighted the scales in their favour, and bribed the magistrates.

They filled their many houses with fine things by robbing the poor.

They started drinking early in the morning and went on carousing late into the night. They feasted and drank to the sound of harp, tambourine and flute.

The women were haughty. They walked with their noses in the air, taking

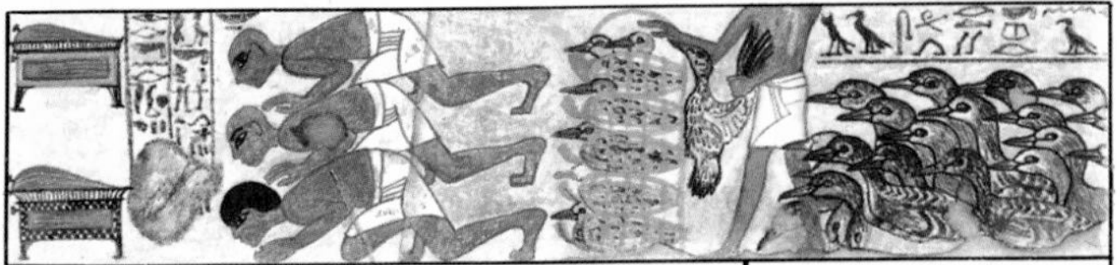

dainty little steps which made the bracelets on their ankles jingle.

The poor as seen by the prophets

The prophets deplored the injustice of this state of affairs. It was an affront to their God who intended the land of Israel to be shared equally by all.

The rich trampled on the poor. They robbed them of their livelihood by taking their vineyards and fields from them.

The poor were forced to buy goods of poor quality at high prices and to live in hovels.

In order to survive, some people sold themselves into slavery.

Agricultural labourers were not paid on time.

The poor would not get a hearing in court.

(From **Amos** and **Isaiah**, 8th c. B.C.)

Taxes: farmers had to hand over a portion of their produce as payment.

Inscribed on this clay tablet (about 2100 B.C.), is the quantity of oil paid to a workman as wages.

Slaves

Egyptian slaves making mud bricks

Slavery existed throughout the Middle Eastern countries. There were fewer slaves in Israel than in other countries, and they were better treated.

Slaves were either prisoners of war, or foreigners purchased as slaves at the slave markets in Phoenicia. An Israelite found guilty of stealing money, or unable to pay a debt, might become a slave for a limited time. There were certain laws protecting slaves from cruelty at the hands of their owners.

If a man takes a stick and beats his slave, whether male or female, and the slave dies on the spot, the man is to be punished. **Ex 21.20**

Prisoners-of-war being led into captivity by the Assyrians

If a man hits his male or female slave in the eye so that he loses the use of it, he is to free the slave as payment for the eye. **Ex 21.26**

Slaves were entitled to a day off on the Sabbath. If a slave was badly treated, he could run away. Run-away slaves were automatically granted asylum.

Foreign slaves were slaves for life,. whereas Israelite slaves were freed after six years' service.

If a fellow-Israelite, man or woman, sells himself to you as a slave, you are to release him after he has served you for six years. . . . When you set him free, do not send him away empty handed. Give to him generously from what the Lord has blessed you with – sheep, corn, and wine. Remember that you were slaves in Egypt and the Lord your God set you free. **Deut 15.12-15**

Most of the great monuments of Antiquity were the work of slaves, prisoners of war or bad debtors. Solomon used slave labour to construct the many roads, buildings and ramparts of Jerusalem.

The enemy

Persian archers

The enemy was never far off. Israel was a small nation and an easy target. From the time of the Exodus onwards Israel had constantly to contend with attacks from foreign armies. Sometimes when threatened, the Israelites attacked first, but they were by no means always victorious in battle.

O God, do not keep silent; do not be still, do not be quiet!
Look! Your enemies are in revolt, and those who hate you are rebelling.
They are making secret plans against your people; they are plotting against those you protect.
'Come,' they say, 'let us destroy their nation, so that Israel will be forgotten for ever.'
Ps 83.1-4

In the 13th c. the greatest threat to Israel's survival was Egypt. In the 11th-12th c. the main enemies were the

smaller nations in and around Canaan. The warlike Philistines were the most dangerous as they had chariots and iron weapons. The Hebrews had only wood, bronze and leather weapons and no chariots. Horse-drawn chariots only came in Solomon's reign.

From the 8th-6th c. the 'major powers' (Assyria, Babylonia, Egypt) were fighting for supremacy of the entire region. By the 2nd c. Syria was the main enemy. The Syrian king persecuted the Jews for their religious beliefs.

Cover their faces with shame, O Lord, and make them acknowledge your power. May they be defeated and terrified for ever; may they die in complete disgrace. May they know that you alone are the Lord, supreme ruler over all the earth. **Ps 83.16-18**

Jehu paying tribute to the Assyrian king

The Assyrian soldiers were experts with slings.
They could hurl missiles from the depths of a nearby valley right over the ramparts of a fortified town.

Armies used battering rams on city gates and walls.

The diaspora

The dispersion of the Jews from the 6th c. B.C.

Diaspora means 'scattered abroad'. It is the word used to describe those Jews living outside Israel at the beginning of the 6th c. B.C. They were the descendants of exiles and traders who had emigrated.

These Jewish immigrants often formed sizeable communities abroad. They built synagogues where they could meet to pray and study the Law. They remained deeply faithful to the religion and land of their ancestors, making annual pilgrimages to Jerusalem for the major religious festivals.

I will bring war on you and scatter you in foreign lands.
Lev 26.33

I scattered my people, but I will gather them.
Jer 31.10

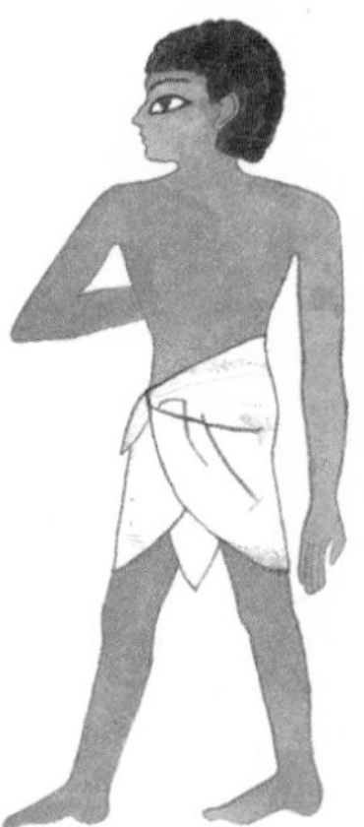

Egyptian

Some of them began to translate the Scriptures into the language of their adopted homeland. Thus men and women from all over the world, who had never heard of the God of Israel, learned about the Jewish religion. Foreigners who converted to Judaism were called proselytes.

By the time the Roman Emperor Augustus came to power in the 1st c. B.C., there were as many as seven or eight million Jews living outside Israel as part of the diaspora, compared to a mere half million in Israel itself.

Persian

THE STORY

Listen, my people, to my teaching,
and pay attention to what I say.
I am going to use wise sayings
and explain mysteries from the past,
things we have heard and known,
things that our fathers told us.
We will not keep them from our children;
we will tell the next generation
about the Lord's power and his great deeds
and the wonderful things he has done.

Ps 78.1-4

Major landmarks in the history of Israel

18th-15th c. B.C.	The forefathers: Abraham, Isaac, Jacob, Joseph. Captivity in Egypt.
13th c.	Moses: Pharaoh frees Hebrews; flight from Egypt. Crossing of the Sinai desert.
	Conquest and occupation of Canaan.
12th c.	Judges defend the tribes of Israel.
11th c.	Beginning of the monarchy: Saul, David.
10th c.	King Solomon. Kingdom divided in two: Israel (north), Judah (South).
9th c.	The prophets Elijah and Elishah.
8th c.	The prophets Amos, Hosea, Isaiah. Fall of the kingdom of Israel (722).
7th c.	The prophet Jeremiah.
6th c.	Fall of the kingdom of Judah and destruction of Jerusalem. Deportation and exile in Babylon (586). Return from exile (536) and rebuilding of Jerusalem.
5th c.	Jews under Persian rule.
4th c.	Jews under Greek rule.
3rd c.	Translation of the Bible into Greek in Alexandria.
2nd c.	Persecution of the Jews under King Antiochus of Syria.
1st c.	Jews under Roman rule.

A constant reminder

The Old Testament is the history of a small nation from its beginnings in the 18th c. B.C. right up to the 1st c. B.C. The history of Israel encompasses nearly eighteen centuries and the rise to power of no less than six ancient empires: Egypt, Assyria, Babylonia, Persia, Greece and Rome. One by one these mighty empires fell, but Israel survived. Throughout all the ups and downs and twists of fortune that mark their history, the Bible people are sustained by a belief that is fundamental to the Jewish faith: namely that God is faithful to the promises made to them in the Covenant and will never desert them.

Do not be afraid — I will save you. I have called you by name — you are mine. When you pass through deep waters, I will be with you; your troubles will not overwhelm you. When you pass through fire, you will not be burnt; the hard trials that come will not hurt you. For I am the Lord your God, the holy God of Israel, who saves you. . . .

Do not be afraid — I am with you! From the distant east and the farthest west, I will bring your people home. I will tell the north to let them go and the south not to hold them back. Let my people return from distant lands, from every part of the world. They are my own people, and I created them to bring me glory. **Is 43.1-7**

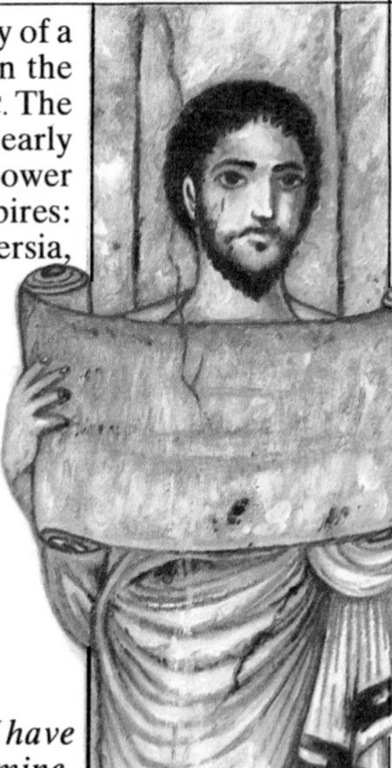

The sacred texts, the origins of a long tradition.

A nation of writers

Cuneiform script

The Old Testament was written over a period of ten centuries. So it is not the work of one author but of a great number of different authors, most of whom are unknown. The earliest of these were recording events and experiences going right back in time, which had been handed down orally from one generation to the next.

The oral tradition

In the days of the forefathers, everything to do with the history and origin of the people, the Law, the proverbs and prayers, was handed down by word of mouth and added to as time went by.

The Old Testament books are a great mixture: there are historical accounts (such as the Book of Kings), legends and tales (Jonah), poems (Song of Songs), prayers (the Psalms), and religious teaching (Proverbs). The style in which each book is written reflects the outlook and background of the author.

A collection assembled later by scholars

The order in which the books of the Old Testament appear today is not the order in which they were originally written. For example, the first chapter of the Bible was written in the 6th c. B.C., the second chapter four centuries later. The Book of Jonah dates from the 4th c. B.C. Yet it precedes the book of the prophet Micah, which belongs to the 8th c. B.C. This is because the books of

Remember these commands and cherish them. . . .
Teach them to your children.
Talk about them when you are at home and when you are away,
when you are resting and when you are working.
Deut 11.18-20

the Old Testament were eventually divided into three major categories: the Law, the Prophets and the Scriptures.

The thread that binds them together

Some of the books in the Bible are actually several books rolled into one. For example, both Exodus and Genesis are made up of a series of texts written at different times and in different places. The Book of Isaiah is the work of three successive authors: chapters 1-39 were written in the 8th c. B.C., chapters 40-56 in the 6th c. B.C., chapters 57-66 in the 5th c. B.C.

Although the books of the Bible are different, endlessly corrected and re-written over time, there is nonetheless one thing which they all have in common: each in its own way is an expression of the faith of the people of Israel.

From hieroglyphics to

Aramaic and Hebrew . . .

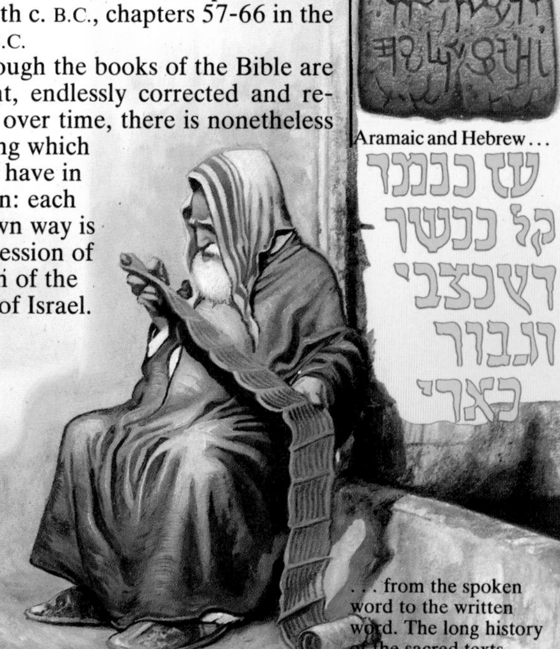

. . . from the spoken word to the written word. The long history of the sacred texts.

The creation of the world

(Read *Genesis 1*)

The 15th century A.D. Italian painter Giovanni di Paolo portrays the creation of the world as the work of God's hand, as described in the Bible.

The Old Testament begins with two separate accounts of the Creation (*Gen 1 and 2*), which were written at completely different times. The first account is the more recent (6th c. B.C.), the second dates from the 10th c. B.C.

These first chapters are a great poem to the glory of God the Creator. They are not intended to explain how the world was made or how mankind came into being. The Bible leaves scientific truth to the scientists. What the Bible does in its own poetic language is to remind us that all creation is a gift – a gift to us from God, intended for our pleasure and enjoyment.

In the beginning, when God created the universe, the earth was formless and desolate. The raging ocean that covered everything was engulfed in total darkness, and the power of God was moving over the water. **Gen 1.1-2**

The first biblical account of the Creation includes elements from a Babylonian legend of the 12th c. B.C. In both accounts the creation represents a victory of earth over water, the separation of darkness from light, of heights from depths, of land from sea. In the Babylonian poem many different gods fight each other for supremacy: the sun and the moon are gods. Men and women are created to serve these gods as slaves.

In the biblical poem there is only one God, and God is good; the sun and the moon are lamps to light the earth; men and women are created for their own good and ultimate happiness.

God stretched out
the northern sky and
hung the earth in
empty space.
It is God who fills
the clouds with water
and keeps them from
bursting with the
weight.
He hides the full
moon behind a cloud.
Job 26.7-10

The creation day by day

(Read *Genesis 1, 2, 3-4*)

Over the centuries a great variety of names were invented to describe the nature of God, many of which found their way into the pages of the Bible. The Jewish name, Yahweh, from the verb 'to be' in Hebrew, means 'the God who is actively present.' This name was considered too holy to speak. It was written YHWH; four consonants which were unpronounceable. They were known as the Sacred Tetragammaton. Other names were used: Elohim, the Most High, Adonai. The word Jehovah is derived from the vowels in Adonai and the consonants YHWH.

Then God commanded, 'Let there be light' – and light appeared. God was pleased with what he saw . . . and he named the light 'Day' and the darkness 'Night'. Evening passed and morning came – that was the first day. Then God commanded, 'Let there be a dome to divide the water and to keep it in two separate places' – and it was done. . . . He named the dome 'Sky'. Evening passed and morning came – that was the second day.

Then God commanded, 'Let the water below the sky come together in one place, so that the land will appear' – and it was done. He named the land 'Earth', and the water which had come together he named 'Sea'. And God was pleased with what he saw. Then he commanded, 'Let the earth produce all kinds of plants, those that bear grain and those that bear fruit' – and it was done. God was pleased with what he saw. Evening passed and morning came – that was the third day.

Gen 1.3-13

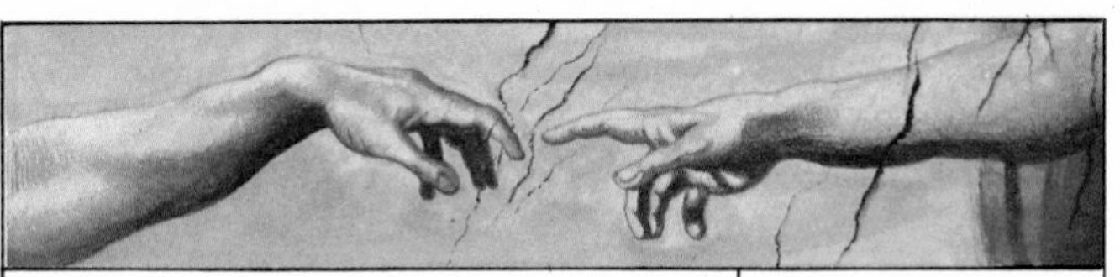

Then God commanded, 'Let lights appear in the sky to separate day from night and to show the time when days, years and religious festivals begin' – and it was done. . . . And God was pleased with what he saw.

Then God commanded, 'Let the water be filled with many kinds of living beings, and let the air be filled with birds. . . . He told the creatures to reproduce . . . and the birds to increase in number. . . . Fifth day.

Then God commanded, 'Let the earth produce all kinds of animal life: . . . and it was done.

Then God said, 'And now we will make human beings; they will be like us and resemble us. . . . He created them male and female. . . .

God looked at everything he had made, and he was very pleased. . . . sixth day. . . . the seventh day God . . . stopped working. He blessed the seventh day and set it apart as a special day.' . **Gen 1.14 . . . 2.3**

The touch of God's hand brings Adam to life. The Creation story inspired some of the finest frescoes ever painted by Michaelangelo (15th c. A.D.).

When these traditions were gathered into one account, the different names for God survived. That is why there are so many names for God in this book.

Adam and Eve

(Read *Genesis 2*)

The garden of Eden where Adam and Eve lived was a sort of paradise where

all sorts of beautiful flowers, fruit and trees grew.

God had just made heaven and earth. *But there were no plants on the earth, nor had any seeds sprouted because God had not sent any rain, and there was no one to cultivate the land. Water came up from beneath the surface of the earth and watered the ground.*

Then God formed a man out of soil and *breathed life-giving breath into his nostrils. The man began to live.*

Then God planted a garden in Eden . . . and there he put the man he had formed.

God gave the man this great garden to cultivate and guard. *You may eat the fruit of any tree in the garden except the tree that gives knowledge of what is good and what is bad.* If you eat the fruit of that tree, *you will die.*

The tree was the tree of knowledge. Adam was forbidden to eat the fruit because the fruit was wisdom. All wisdom belongs to God. It cannot be stolen from God, but must be received from God as a gift.

God said, *'It is not good for the man to live alone. I will make a suitable companion to help him.'* God took some soil and formed all the animals and all the birds, and brought them for the man to see. *The man named all the birds and all the animals but not one of them was a suitable companion to help him.*

God made the man fall into a deep sleep. He took one of the man's ribs and fashioned a woman out of it. He presented the woman to the man, who said, *'At last, here is one of my own kind – Bone taken from my bone, and flesh from my flesh. "Woman" is her name because she was taken out of man.'* **Gen 2.23**

The man and the woman were happy. They had faith in God and they trusted one another. Both went naked.

The name Adam means fashioned out 'of earth'. Eve means 'life'. The Hebrew name for Adam is Ish, for Eve Ishshah. The similarity between the two words shows how close the man and woman are.

The tempting by the serpent

(Read *Genesis 3*)

Serpents were both respected and feared in the ancient world. They were seen both as a source of evil and a source of good. In the Bible story of the Creation, the serpent is the personification of evil.

This episode follows the account of the creation of Adam and Eve. The tempting of Eve by the serpent is a symbolic answer to the question of how evil came into the world. Mankind has been instrumental in introducing evil, but is not entirely responsible for its existence in the world.

Of all the animals in God's garden, the serpent was the most cunning. One day the serpent asked Eve, *'Did God really tell you not to eat fruit from any tree in the garden?' 'We may eat the fruit of any tree in the garden,' the woman answered, 'except the tree in the middle of it. . . . If we do, we will die.' The snake replied, 'That's not true; you will not die. God said that, because he knows that when you eat it you will be like God and know what is good and what is bad.'*

Gen 3.1-5

Eve was tempted by the forbidden fruit on the beautiful tree. She took some of it and ate it. Then she gave some to Adam to eat. They were immediately aware of their nakedness, and covered themselves with fig leaves in shame.

God called, *'Where are you?'* Adam came out of hiding. *'I was afraid and hid from you.'* God asked the woman, *'Why did you do this?'* She replied, *'The snake tricked me into eating it.'*

God said to the snake, *'You will be punished. . . . From now on you will crawl on your belly, and you will have to eat dust as long as you live. I will make you and the woman hate each other; her offspring and yours will always be enemies. Her offspring will crush your head, and you will bite their heel.'*

And he said to the woman, 'I will increase your trouble in pregnancy and your pain in giving birth. . . .' And he said to the man, . . . 'Because of what you have done, the ground will be under a curse. . . . You will have to work hard . . . to make the soil produce anything.'

Gen 3.14-19

You will have to work
hard all your life to
make it produce enough
food for you.
It will produce
weeds and thorns,
and you will have to
eat wild plants.

Gen 3.17-19

Cain and Abel

(Read *Genesis 4*)

'Tit for Tat'
The law of retaliation, the Talion Law, which seems to prescribe vengeance, actually prevented it from deteriorating into uncontrolled violence by defining precisely what form it should take.

The story of Cain and Abel, written in the 10th c. B.C., is about murder and violence between individuals and nations. The author points out that to kill someone is always a crime. Anyone who gives in to fear, jealousy or hatred may end up committing murder. Revenge only leads to more violence.

Cain's jealousy

Adam and Eve had two sons. The oldest, Cain, was a farmer who looked after the land. Abel was a shepherd, who watched over his sheep.

One day, Cain brought some of his harvest and offered it to the Lord. Abel brought the first-born lamb from his flock as an offering. God accepted Abel's offering but rejected Cain's.

These 11th c. A.D. ivory figures show how God rejected Cain's offering. It was Cain's resentment that made him seek revenge by murdering his brother Abel.

Cain was furious and scowled in anger. God said to Cain, *'Why are you angry? . . . If you had done the right thing, you would be smiling; but because you have done evil, sin is crouching at your door. It wants to rule you, but you must overcome it.'*

But Cain took his brother Abel out into the fields and killed him.

Condemned to wander homeless

The Lord asked Cain, *'Where is your brother Abel?' He answered, 'I don't know. Am I supposed to take care of my brother?' Then the Lord said, 'Why have you done this terrible thing? Your brother's blood is crying out to me from the ground, like a voice calling for revenge. You are placed under a curse and can no longer farm the soil. It has soaked up your brother's blood. . . . you will be a homeless wanderer on the earth.'*

And Cain said to the Lord, '. . . anyone who finds me will kill me.' But the Lord answered, 'No. If anyone kills you, seven lives will be taken in revenge.' So the Lord put a mark on Cain to warn anyone who met him not to kill him. And Cain went away from the Lord's presence and lived in a land called 'Wandering', east of Eden.

The punishment shall be life for life, eye for eye, tooth for tooth, hand for hand, foot for foot, burn for burn, wound for wound, bruise for bruise. **Ex 21.23-25**

Noah's ark

(Read *Genesis 6-9*)

Floods were frequent occurrences in ancient times; the memory of them lingered on amongst the people of the East. The flood in the Bible story had a particular meaning. It was God's way of punishing mankind for all sorts of wickedness. But by saving Noah, his family, and the animals, God was giving mankind a fresh start. The rainbow was a symbol of this new covenant between God and God's people.

God saw that there was no end to mankind's wickedness and violence, nor to the evil in people's hearts.

He said, *'I will wipe out these people I have created, and also the animals and the birds, because I am sorry that I made any of them.'* Only Noah found grace in

God's eyes because he was a righteous man. God said to Noah, *'I have decided to put an end to all mankind. I will destroy them completely. . . . Build a boat for yourself out of good timber; make rooms in it and cover it with tar inside and out. Make it 133 m (436 ft) long, 22 m (72 ft) wide, and 13 m (42 ft) high. Make a roof for the boat. . . . Build*

it with three decks and put a door in the side. I am going to send a flood on the earth to destroy every living being. Everything on earth will die, but I will make a covenant with you. Go into the boat with your wife, your sons, and their wives. Take into the boat with you a male and female of every kind of animal and . . . bird, in order to keep them alive. Take along all kinds of food. . . .

Noah did as God commanded. Everyone went into the ark, and the Lord shut the door behind them.

The rain began to fall. The water began to rise, until the ark was afloat and drifted away. Still the water rose.

Every living being on earth died. The only ones left were Noah and those with him in the ark.

The rain ceased, and the water began to go down. After 150 days the ark came to rest on Mount Ararat. Noah sent out a dove to see if there was any dry land. The dove returned with a fresh olive leaf in its beak. Not long afterwards the ground was dry. Noah and his family left the ark, followed by the animals in groups according to their species.

Mount Ararat in Turkey is 5,165 m (16,950 ft) high.

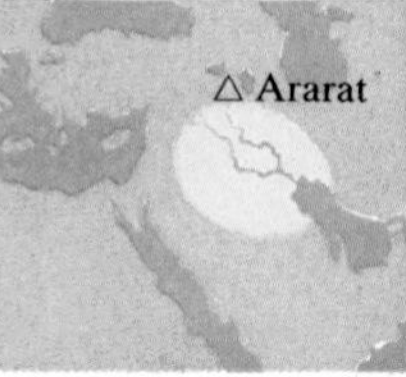

According to the story, Noah's ark came to rest on the top of the mountain.

The olive leaf which the dove brought back was a sign that the water had gone down.

The Tower of Babel

(Read *Genesis 11*)

This is just the beginning of what they are going to do. Soon they will be able to do anything they want.

Gen 11.6

After the flood people the world over spoke the same language and used the same words. *As they wandered about in the East, they came to a plain in Babylonia and settled there. They said to one another, 'Let's make bricks and bake them hard. . . . Now let's build a city with a tower that reaches the sky, so that we can make a name for ourselves and not be scattered all over the earth.'*

Gen 11.3-4

Then the Lord came down to see the city and the tower the men were building, and he said: *'Now then, these are all one people and they speak one language. . . . Soon they will be able to do anything they want! Let us go down and mix up their language so that they will not understand one another.'*

Gen 11.6-7

So the Lord scattered the people far and wide across the earth and they stopped building the city. The city was called Babylon, which means 'mixed up', because it was there that the Lord mixed up the language of the people and scattered them all over the earth. (The name Babylon sounds like the Hebrew word for 'mixed up', *bavel.*)

Babylon

On the left: an artist's impression of the Tower of Babel. From a painting by Bruegel.

The Tower of Babel was a symbol of mankind's foolishness in trying to rival God in greatness. This huge unfinished tower or 'ziggurat' stood in the heart of Babylon. At the top of the many-tiered building was a temple. Stairways led from one level to the next.

Abraham

(Read *Genesis 11-12*)

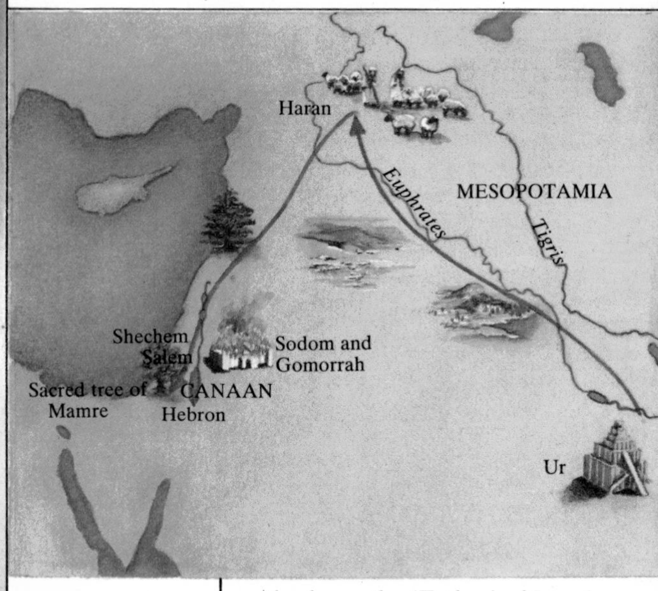

Abraham's journey

The biblical accounts of Abraham's life were written centuries after the events took place (10th-6th c. B.C.).

Abraham, the 'Father' of Israel, was one of the desert nomads who moved from one grazing ground to another across vast areas of the Middle East between the years 1800 and 1500 B.C.

Abraham came from Ur in Chaldea (Mesopotamia), he moved to Haran with his wife Sarah and his nephew Lot. Abraham was rich and owned huge flocks.

The Ur Standard
Sumerian mosaic of the 3rd millenium B.C.

However, his wife Sarah was childless. They were both old and had given up hope of ever having children.

One day the Lord said to Abraham, *'Leave your country, your relatives, and your father's home, and go to a land that I am going to show you. I will give you many descendants, and they will become a great nation. I will bless you and make your name famous, so that you will be a blessing. I will bless those who bless you. But I will curse those who curse you. And through you I will bless all the nations.'* **Gen 12.1-3**

By now Abraham was 75 years old, but he nonetheless left Haran and started out for the land of Canaan, taking Sarah, Lot, their slaves, their flocks and all their possessions with him.

They travelled through Canaan until they came to the sacred tree of Moreh. The Lord appeared to Abraham and said to him, '*This is the country I am going to give your descendants.*' Abraham built an altar there.

After that he moved on south to the hill-country and set up camp between Bethel and Ai.

Then he moved on south towards the Negev desert. There were many surprises still in store for him. . . .

Abraham is often referred to as 'the father of many nations' because of his many descendants, both real and spiritual. This illustration is from the 12th century Souvigny Bible.

The birth of Isaac

(Read *Genesis 18 and 21*)

Then the Lord asked Abraham, 'Why did Sarah laugh and say, "Can I really have a child when I am so old?" Is anything too hard for the Lord? As I said, nine months from now I will return, and Sarah will have a son.' **Gen 18.13-14**

God had promised Abraham that he would be the father of a great nation. Yet years went by and still Abraham had no children.

Sarah decided that as she herself was unable to have children, her slave-girl Hagar should bear Abraham a child instead. In those days this custom was common. Abraham agreed. Not long afterwards Hagar bore Abraham a son, whose name was Ishmael.

God had not forgotten his promise to Abraham. In the heat of the mid-day sun, when Abraham was sitting at the entrance to his tent under the sacred tree of Mamre, the Lord appeared to him.

He looked up to see three men standing not far off. He ran out to meet them, bowing low, and said, *'Sirs, please do not pass by my home without stopping; . . . Let me bring you some water . . . to wash your feet; you can rest here beneath this tree.'*

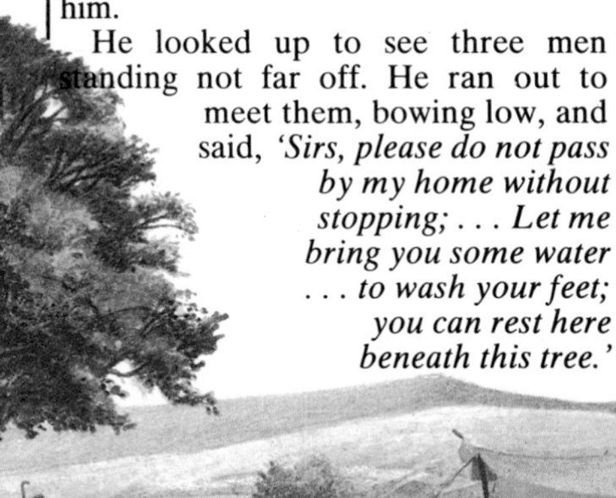

Nine months from now I will come back, and your wife Sarah will have a son.

Gen 18.10

Abraham hurried into the tent and said to Sarah, *'Quick, take a sack of your best flour, and bake some bread.' Then he ran to the herd and picked out a calf that was tender and fat, and gave it to a servant, who hurried to get it ready. . . . Then he set the food before them and served them himself while they ate.*

Then they asked him, 'Where is your wife Sarah?' 'She is there in the tent,' he answered. One of them said, 'Nine months from now I will come back, and your wife Sarah will have a son.'

Sarah had been listening at the door of the tent. She could not believe her ears. She and her husband were old and had passed the age of child-bearing. Sarah laughed to herself, and wondered how she could possibly have a child at her age.

Sarah did become pregnant and gave birth to a son Isaac, which means *One laughs.*

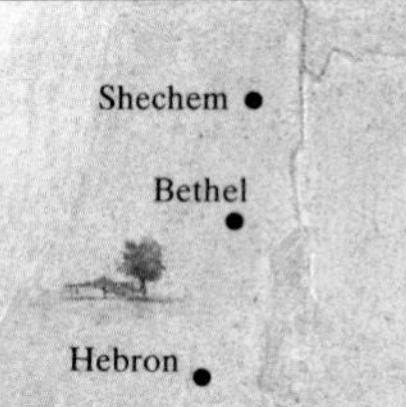

Chief resting places on Abraham's journey to Canaan

Mother and child from the time of Abraham. Statue from the tombs of Beni Hassan in Egypt.

Nomads' tent

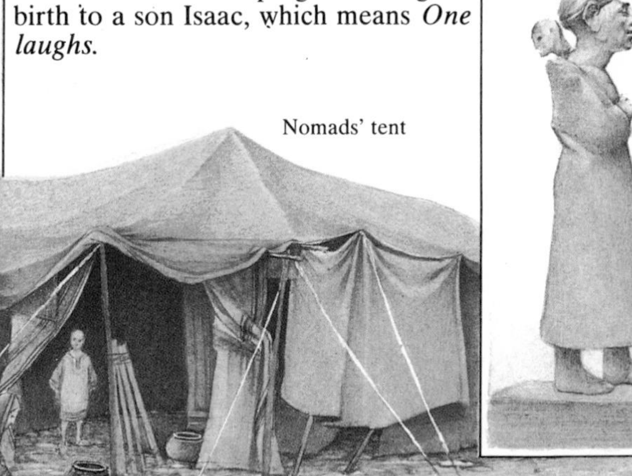

Ishmael is sent away

(Read *Genesis 21*)

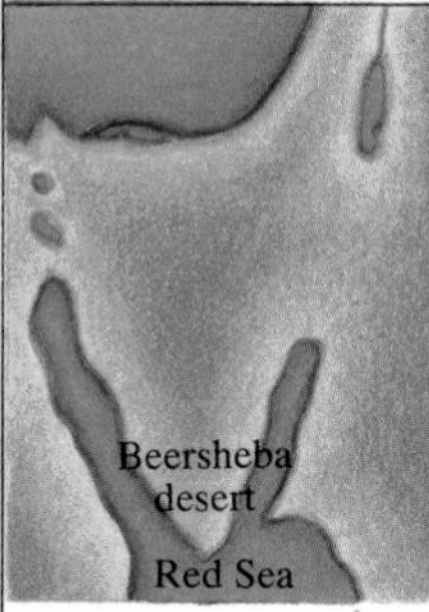

Beersheba lies in the heart of the Negeb desert. It was here that the Lord came to Hagar and Ishmael's aid.

After Ishmael's birth there was trouble between Sarah and Hagar. Sarah was jealous and Hagar proud. Things became worse after Isaac's birth.

When Isaac was three years old, Abraham gave a great feast to celebrate the weaning of his son. Sarah thought Ishmael was making fun of Isaac. She said, *'Send this slave-girl and her son away. The son of this woman must not get any part of your wealth, which my son Isaac should inherit.'* This troubled Abraham very much, because Ishmael was also his son. But God said to Abraham, *'Don't be worried.... Do whatever Sarah tells you, because it is through Isaac that you will have the descendants I have promised. I will also give many children to the son of the slave-girl, so that they will become a nation. He too is your son.'*

Early the next morning Abraham

gave Hagar some food and a leather bag full of water.

Then he sent her away with her son. Hagar set off and wandered for days in the wilderness of Beersheba. When the water was all gone, she left the child under the shade of a bush and sat down some way off, not wanting to see the child die. She wept bitterly. The angel of God called to Hagar from heaven, *'What are you troubled about, Hagar? Don't be afraid. God has heard the boy crying. Get up, go and pick him up, and comfort him. I will make a great nation out of his descendants.'*

Then God opened Hagar's eyes and she saw a well. She went and filled the leather bag with water from the well and gave some to the boy.

God took care of Ishmael. He became a great hunter, living in the wilderness of Paran, married to an Egyptian.

This Assyrian bas-relief from the first millenium B.C. depicts a hunting scene. Hunting was an important activity in those days.

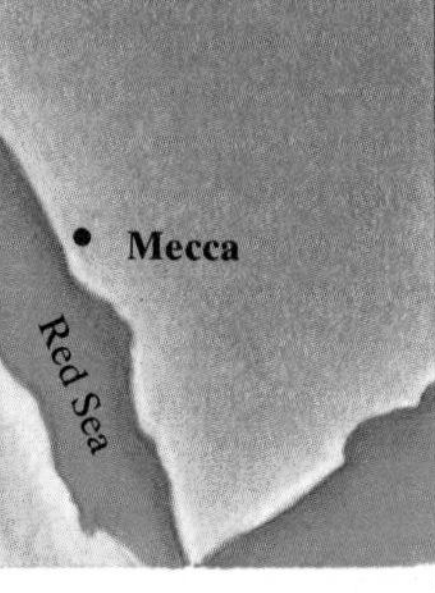

Arabia, which became Ishmael's home. Mecca is the holy city of Islam.

Ishmael, ancestor of the Arab people?
According to the Koran, the sacred book of Islam, the Arabs are descended from Ishmael as the Jews are from Isaac. Islam, the religion of the Muslim people, originated in Arabia. Its founder, Mohammed, the author of the Koran, had a great respect for Abraham.

Abraham offers Isaac as a sacrifice

(Read *Genesis 22*)

God had kept his promise. Despite everything, Abraham and Sarah now had a son, Isaac. Future generations would surely follow. But now suddenly everything was once more put in question.

Abraham and Isaac make their way to the appointed place, carrying the wood, the fire and the knife for the sacrifice. (13th c. Danish Psalter.)

Some time later God tested Abraham: *'Take your son . . . Isaac, whom you love so much, and go to the land of Moriah. There, on a mountain . . . offer him as a sacrifice to me.'*

Early the next morning Abraham cut some wood for the sacrifice, loaded his donkey, and took Isaac and two servants with him. . . . 'Stay here with the donkey. The boy and I will go over there and worship, and then we will come back to you.'

Abraham made Isaac carry the wood for the sacrifice, and he himself carried a knife and live coals for starting the fire. As they walked along together, Isaac said, 'Father! . . . I see that you have the coals and the wood, but where is the lamb for the sacrifice?' Abraham answered, 'God will provide one.'

When they reached the mountain, Abraham built an altar and arranged the wood on it. *He tied up his son and placed him on the altar, on top of the wood. Then he picked up the knife to kill him. But the angel of the Lord called to him. 'Abraham, Abraham! . . . Don't hurt the boy or do anything to him. . . . Now I know that you honour and obey God, because you have not kept back your only son from me.' Abraham looked around and saw a ram caught in a bush by its horns. He offered it as a burnt offering instead of his son. Abraham*

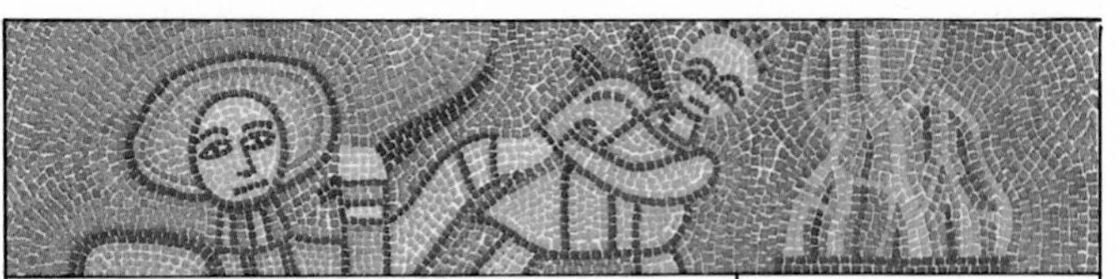

named that place 'The Lord provides.'
The angel spoke to him again, *'I will give you as many descendants as there are stars in the sky.'* **Gen 22.16-17**

Mosaic from the 6th c. A.D.

Mount Moriah was the place appointed by God for the sacrifice. It is supposed to have been one of the hills on which Jerusalem now stands.

The Bible and child-sacrifice

It was customary, in dire circumstances, to sacrifice first-born children to the local deities or Baals in the land of Canaan. In this story God refuses to allow Abraham to sacrifice his son – a sure sign that child-sacrifice was not pleasing to the God of the Bible.

In this dramatic story Abraham's faith in the Lord is tested to the utmost. It remains firm. Abraham's supreme trust in God was an example for generations to come.

Abraham is on the point of killing Isaac when the angel of the Lord stops him. He finds a ram with its horns caught in a bush and offers this in sacrifice instead.

Jacob's ladder

(Read *Genesis 28*)

Isaac married Rebecca. They had twin sons, Esau and Jacob. Esau, the firstborn, should normally have been Isaac's heir, but Jacob was very cunning. He deceived his old, blind father into giving him the blessing intended for his brother. Esau hated Jacob and planned to kill him, but Jacob fled to the land of Haran, where his uncle Laban lived.

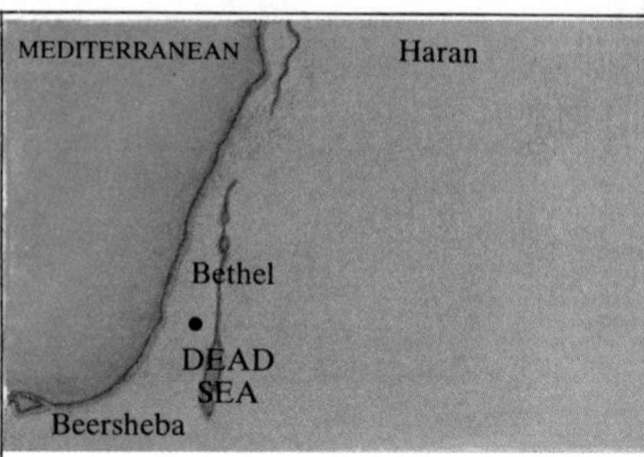

Jacob's journey

Fleeing from his brother Esau's wrath, Jacob set out for Haran, where Laban, his mother's brother, lived. Towards sunset he came on a holy place named Louz, which means almond (tree), and camped there for the night.

He dreamt that he saw a stairway reaching from earth to heaven, with angels going up and coming down on it. And there was the Lord standing beside him. 'I am the Lord, the God of Abraham and Isaac,' he said. 'I will give to you and to your descendants this land on which you are lying. They will be as numerous as the specks of dust on the earth. They will extend their territory in all directions, and through you and your

descendants I will bless all the nations. Remember, I will be with you and protect you wherever you go, and I will bring you back to this land. I will not leave you until I have done all that I have promised you.' Jacob woke up and said, 'The Lord is here! He is in this place, and I didn't know it!' He was afraid and said, 'What a terrifying place this is! It must be the house of God; it must be the gate that opens into heaven.'

Jacob got up . . . took the stone that was under his head, and set it up as a memorial. Then he poured olive-oil on it to dedicate it to God. He named the place Bethel.*

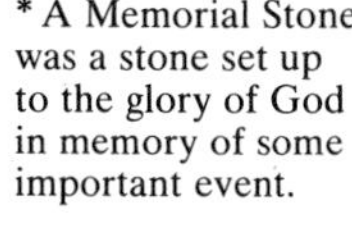

* A Memorial Stone was a stone set up to the glory of God in memory of some important event.

Jacob's dream from a 14th c. manuscript. The ladder is the link between heaven and earth, between God and mankind.

Jacob in Laban's land

(Read *Genesis 29-33*)

The twelve sons of Jacob were the ancestors of the twelve tribes of Israel.
Reuben (Leah's son)
Simeon (Leah's son)
Levi (Leah's son)
Judah (Leah's son)
Dan (son of Rachel's slave-girl, Bilhah)
Naphtali (Bilhah's son)
Gad (son of Leah's slave-girl, Zilpah)
Asher (Zilpah's son)
Issachar (Leah's son)
Zebulun (Leah's son)
Joseph (Rachel's son)
Benjamin (Rachel's son)

At his uncle Laban's home, Jacob became a shepherd in charge of all the sheep. Jacob fell in love with Rachel, Laban's daughter, *'I will work seven years for you if you will let me marry Rachel.'* But when the seven years were up, Laban tricked Jacob and gave him his eldest daughter, Leah, in marriage. He promised to give Rachel as well if he would work another seven years.

Jacob had eleven children by his two wives and their slave-girls. He longed to return home to the land of Canaan. *Then the Lord said to him, 'Go back to the land of your fathers and to your relatives. I will be with you.'* But Laban did not want to let him go. Jacob left secretly taking with him his wives and children and the flocks that were his. Laban and his kinsmen overtook him. Instead of confronting each other, they decided to come to an agreement. Laban said to Jacob, *'I am ready to make an agreement with you. Let us*

make a pile of stones to remind us of our agreement.' So Jacob took a stone and set it up as a memorial. He told his men to gather some rocks and pile them up. Then they ate a meal beside the pile of rocks. Laban named it Jegar Sahadutha (which means 'a pile to remind us' in Aramaic) *while Jacob named it Galeed* (which means the same in Hebrew). **Gen 31.44-48**. *Laban said to Jacob, 'This pile of rocks will be a reminder to both of us.'* **Gen 31.48**

The pile of stones and the memorial stone were to remind Laban and Jacob of the solemn agreement they had made, with God as their witness.

Jacob went on his way, a worried man. 'What would happen when he met his brother Esau? Did Esau still bear him a grudge? Would he try to kill him?'

When news came that Esau was on his way with four hundred men, Jacob assumed his brother meant to destroy them all. Then an idea came to him. He would send a party on ahead with presents for Esau: whole herds of goats, ewes, milk camels, cows, bulls, and donkeys.

As soon as Jacob saw Esau he went forward, bowing low as a token of respect. But Esau ran to meet him, threw his arms round him and embraced him. They both wept. Esau had forgiven Jacob. They parted friends.

Some time later, Jacob's beloved wife Rachel died while giving birth to Benjamin, the last of their sons.

This alabaster statue shows what was considered in the Hellenistic period (3rd to 1st c. B.C.) to be the ideal in feminine beauty.

Rachel was shapely and beautiful. Jacob was in love with Rachel. **Gen 29.17-18**

I will never go beyond this pile to attack you and you must never go beyond it or beyond this memorial stone to attack me. **Gen 31.52**

Jacob wrestles with the angel of the Lord

(Read *Genesis 32*)

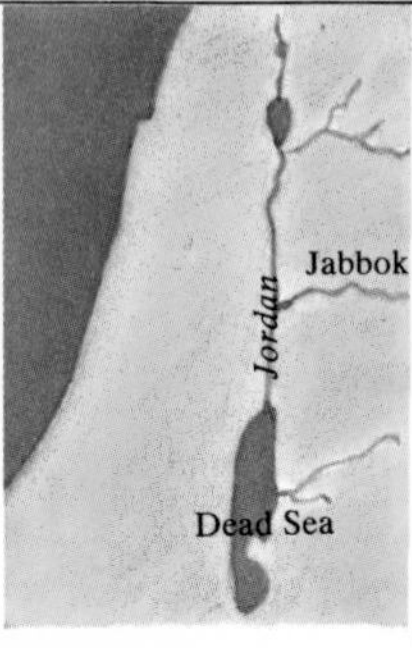

Jacob's wrestling bout is a symbol of all struggles – be they with God, with ourselves, or for the survival of mankind. From a 13th c. Byzantine painting (Yugoslavian).

Jacob was on his way home after the many years spent working for his uncle Laban. The night before he met his brother Esau, Jacob sent his two wives and eleven children on ahead, across the river Jabbok, while he stayed behind alone.

He wrestled all night with a mysterious being. Just before daybreak, *when the man saw that he was not winning . . ., he struck Jacob on the hip and it was thrown out of joint. The man said, 'Let me go; daylight is coming.' 'I won't, unless you bless me,' Jacob answered.*

'What is your name?' the man asked. 'Jacob,' he answered. The man said, 'Your name will no longer be Jacob. You have struggled with God and with

To give a blessing is to wish or to cause another person to thrive. In the Bible it is God who gives blessings. God's promises are always kept. Blessings usually included health, long life and many children.

Jacob stayed behind alone. Then a man came and wrestled with him until just before daybreak.
Gen 32.24

men, and you have won; so your name will be Israel.'

Jacob said, 'Now tell me your name.' But he answered, 'Why do you want to know my name?' Then he blessed Jacob.

Jacob said, 'I have seen God face to face, and I am still alive.' So he named the place Peniel.

The Bible states repeatedly that it is impossible to see God and live – a reminder of the immeasurable difference between God and mankind. In this respect, Jacob's experience was unique.

Names Giving one's name meant making oneself known, entrusting one's identity to someone else. Likewise, to know someone's name was to exercise a certain power over that person. Jacob was given a new name, and with it a new identity. Note that the angel of God refused to give his name.

Joseph is sold into captivity

(Read *Genesis 37-42*)

1 Joseph, the victim of his brothers' jealousy, is sold to a caravan of merchants who take him to Egypt.

Joseph was Jacob's eleventh son and the apple of his father's eye. His mother was Jacob's much loved wife, Rachel. Joseph's jealous brothers wanted to kill him, but Reuben, the eldest, dissuaded them. Instead they sold Joseph to some passing merchants and Joseph was taken into Egypt as a slave. The brothers led Jacob to believe that Joseph had been eaten by wild beasts. Jacob was heartbroken.

2 The brothers in turn make their way to Egypt. This time it is they who are at Joseph's mercy.

The merchants sold Joseph to Potiphar, one of Pharaoh's trusted officers. Joseph was barely twenty, but so able and upright that Potiphar soon made him his personal servant and put him in charge of his entire household.

However, Potiphar's wife falsely accused Joseph of making advances to her. Joseph was flung into prison.

Amongst his fellow-prisoners were two members of Pharaoh's household. Joseph, who knew how to interpret people's dreams, predicted their future. In due course Pharaoh himself needed someone to interpret a dream of his. Joseph was sent for. Pharaoh said to Joseph, *'I have had a dream, and no one can explain it. I have been told that you can interpret dreams.' Joseph answered, 'I cannot, Your Majesty, but*

Joseph was sold to Potiphar, an Egyptian officer

The seven fat cows (Egyptian fresco)

God will give a favourable interpretation.' **Gen 41.15-16**

Pharaoh told him that in his dream he had seen seven fat cows eaten up by seven lean cows, and seven full ears of corn swallowed up by seven thin ones. Joseph explained that seven years of great plenty would be followed by seven years of drought and famine. Pharaoh and his people must therefore stock up against the lean years to come.

Pharaoh appointed Joseph governor over all Egypt. He organised the collection and storing of huge supplies of grain in Pharaoh's vast storehouses. *The famine grew worse and spread over the whole country, so Joseph opened all the storehouses and sold corn to the Egyptians. People came to Egypt from all over the world to buy corn from Joseph, because the famine was severe everywhere.* **Gen 42.56-57**

A gold ring engraved with the royal seal, like the one given to Joseph by Pharaoh.

Fragment from an Egyptian book of dreams with their interpretations, probably from Joseph's time.

This model was discovered in an Egyptian tomb. It shows corn being stored in one of Pharaoh's granaries.

Joseph saves his brothers' lives

(Read *Genesis 42; 44; 47*)

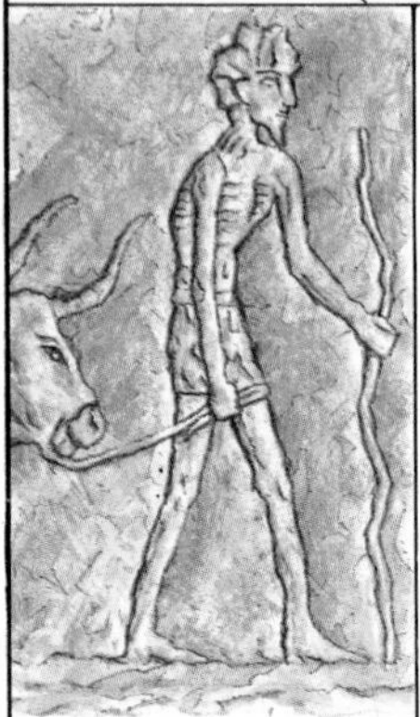

The severity of the famine which swept the land is reflected in the painfully thin figure of the nomad in this Egyptian bas-relief.

The famine that followed the years of plenty spread to other countries nearby. Jacob sent his sons to Egypt to buy corn, but kept his youngest son, Benjamin, by him. Joseph recognised his brothers, but not they him. He was deeply moved, but hid his feelings, accusing them fiercely of being spies, *'You are spies; you have come to find out where our country is weak.' . . . 'We are not spies, sir, we are honest men . . . sons of the same man . . . the youngest is now with our father.'*

Joseph insisted that one brother stayed behind as a hostage while the others fetched their youngest brother to him.

Joseph's brothers set out, laden with sacks of corn, leaving Simeon in prison in Egypt.

At first Jacob refused to let Benjamin go. However, he finally gave in and despatched his sons once more to the governor of Egypt, bearing gifts.

When they arrived in Egypt the second time, the brothers were royally received at Joseph's table. When Joseph set eyes on Benjamin, he was once again deeply moved. Finally he could contain himself no longer, and, sobbing aloud, made himself known to his brothers.

Joseph then sent for his father, Jacob, who went to live with his sons in Egypt. *Then Joseph settled his father and his brothers in Egypt, giving them property in the best of the land near the city of Rameses, as the king had commanded.*
Gen 47.11

Joseph's brothers came bearing gifts for the governor of Egypt.

All foreigners were made to bow low before high-ranking Egyptian officials (Egyptian bas-relief from Memphis). Joseph's brothers bowed low before him, as he had once dreamed they would.

Moses strikes a blow for freedom

(Read *Exodus 1-2*)

The Pharaoh, Rameses II, forced the Hebrews into slavery. They were ill-treated and beaten.

The descendants of Jacob were still living in Egypt in the 13th c. B.C., when a new king came to power who saw these numerous foreigners as a possible threat to his own authority. He began to persecute the Hebrew people, forcing them to work as slaves in the building of two new cities, Pithom and Rameses. It was gruelling work and the Egyptian overseers were merciless. Worse still, in order to check the ever increasing numbers of Hebrews, Pharaoh ordered every newborn Hebrew baby boy to be thrown into the Nile.

Moses' mother succeeded in hiding her son for three months. Then, fearing the Egyptians would find him, she placed the baby in a basket and hid it amongst the tall grasses growing along the Nile. Moses' elder sister stood guard nearby to see what would happen.

Pharaoh's daughter came down to the river with her servants to bathe. She saw

Egyptian painting (6th c. B.C.)

the basket and took pity on the little baby she found crying inside it.

Moses' sister asked if she should fetch a Hebrew woman to act as wet-nurse. Pharaoh's daughter agreed. Moses' sister then fetched her own mother. Thus it was Moses' own mother who nursed him until he was weaned.

After this, Moses was returned to Pharaoh's daughter and raised as her adopted son. *'I pulled him out of the water, so I name him Moses,'* she said.

Moses was a grown man before he discovered how cruelly his fellow-Hebrews were being treated. One day his anger got the better of him and he killed an Egyptian overseer who was beating a Hebrew slave to death. Pharaoh ordered Moses to be put to death. Moses fled to the land of Midian.

There he married Zipporah, the priest of Midian's daughter, and tended his father-in-law's flocks.

Jacob's descendants provided the labour force for the Pharaoh's many buildings.

Moses' mother put her baby in a watertight basket made of rushes sealed with pitch, which she hid on the banks of the Nile.

The burning bush

(Read *Exodus 3*)

Moses and the burning bush from a 14th century miniature.

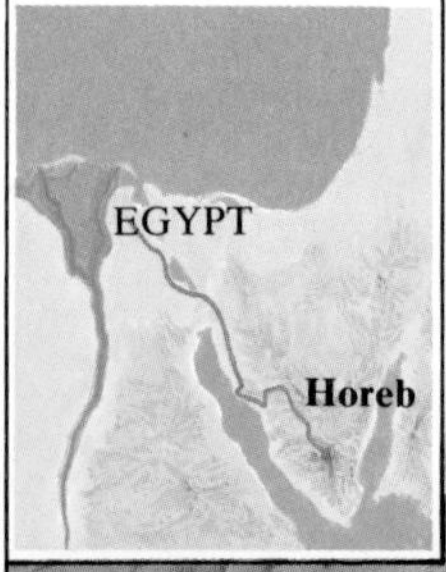

Moses' journey from Egypt to the desert of Horeb

One day Moses was leading his father-in-law's flocks across the desert to Sinai, the holy mountain. *There the angel of the Lord appeared to him as a flame coming from the middle of a bush. Moses saw that the bush was on fire but that it was not burning up. 'This is*

יהוה

strange,' he thought. 'Why isn't the bush burning up? I will go closer and see.' When the Lord saw that Moses was coming closer, he called to him from the middle of the bush and said, 'Moses! Moses!' He answered, 'Yes, here I am.' God said, 'Do not come any closer. . . . I am . . . the God of Abraham, Isaac, and Jacob.' So Moses covered his face, because he was afraid to look at God.

Then the Lord said, 'I have seen how cruelly my people are being treated in Egypt; I have heard them cry out to be rescued from their slave-drivers . . . so I have come down to rescue them from the Egyptians and to bring them out of Egypt to a spacious land, one which is rich and fertile. . . . Now I am sending you to the king of Egypt so that you can lead my people out of his country.' But Moses said to God, 'I am nobody. How can I go to the king and bring the Israelites out of Egypt?' God said, 'I am who I am. This is what you must say to them: 'The one who is called I AM has sent me to you. . . . This is what all future generations are to call me.'

Yahweh in Hebrew. The letters are read from right to left. Only the four consonants of God's name are recorded in the Bible: Y H W H.
The name comes from the verb 'to be'. There are three possible interpretations:

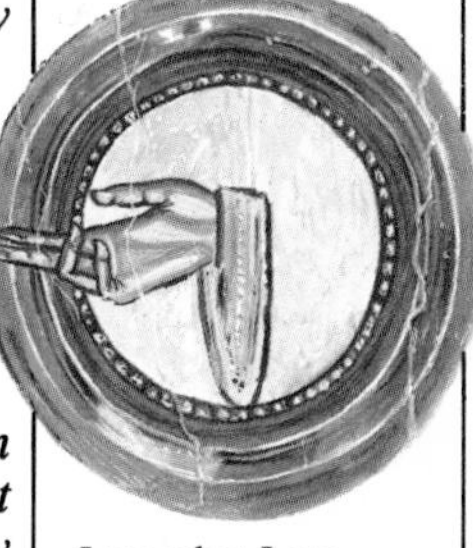

- I am what I am (divine, mysterious)
- I am that that is (a living god, as opposed to an idol)
- I will be what I will be (the nature of God is made manifest in what God does for us).

The Flight from Egypt

(Read *Exodus 4, 7-12*)

God ordered Moses to go with his brother Aaron to ask Pharaoh to set the Hebrews free. God gave Moses the power to change his stick into a snake, and then back into a stick again.

After a prolonged exile in the land of Midian, Moses returned to Egypt. The Pharaoh who had tried to have him killed was dead. The Hebrews were still living in forced slavery.

Pharaoh's stubborness

Moses and his brother Aaron asked Pharaoh to let their people go out into the desert so that they might offer sacrifices to their God. Pharaoh refused. He accused Moses of encouraging the people to neglect their work, and he made their working conditions even more intolerable. The Hebrew people begged Moses not to approach Pharaoh again for fear still more hardships would be inflicted on them. However, Moses did not give up. He went back to the king again, demanding that he set the people free. Pharaoh stubbornly refused to do so, whereupon God brought a series of plagues on the land of Egypt.

The ten plagues of Egypt

The waters of the Nile were turned into blood; the country was over-run with frogs, gnats and flies; a terrible disease struck all the animals dead; the people were covered in boils; all the crops were ruined – first by hailstorms, then by locusts; for three whole days the land of Egypt was plunged in darkness.

Still Pharaoh refused to let the people go. The last plague was the most terrible of all. God killed the eldest son in every Egyptian family, including Pharaoh's own son. At this, Pharaoh relented, *'Get out, you and your Israelites! Go and worship the Lord as you asked. Take your sheep, goats and cattle, and leave. Also pray a blessing for me.'*

Ex 12.31-33

The Hebrews left Egypt in great haste, rejoicing. They were free at last. God had kept the promise made to them.

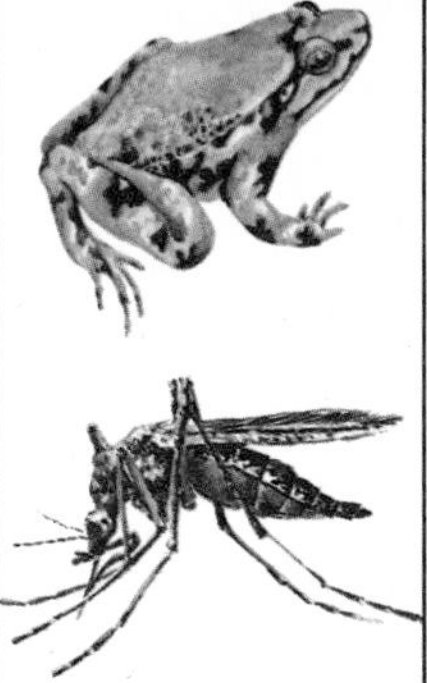

The story of the ten plagues of Egypt is a symbol of the conflict between Pharaoh and God. A powerful man is forced into submission by an all-powerful God.

The crossing of the Red Sea

(Read *Exodus 14-15*)

No one really knows what happened at the crossing of the Red Sea. The account we read in the Bible was actually drawn up in the 4th c. B.C. It was based on two or three previous texts, which are all slightly different. The meaning behind the incident is more important than the details. The Hebrews saw their miraculous last minute escape from the advancing Egyptian army as further proof of God's saving grace.

The Hebrews thought they had escaped from Pharaoh's clutches for once and for all. However, when Pharaoh and his officials realised that they had lost their entire Hebrew work force, they said, '*What have we done? We have let the Israelites escape, and we have lost them as our slaves!' The king got his war chariot and his army ready. He set out with all his chariots, including the six hundred finest, commanded by their officers.* **Ex 14.5-7**

The Hebrews, meanwhile, were camped by the Red Sea. When they saw the king and his army approaching they were panic-stricken at the sight of so many charioteers, and they began to wish they had never come. Moses reassured them and urged them to put their trust in the Lord.

Egyptian bas-relief. Pharaoh riding his chariot at the head of his army.

Moses then held out his hand over the sea, and the Lord drove the sea back with a strong east wind. It blew all night. . . . The water divided and the Hebrews walked across the sea on dry land with walls of water on either side.

The Egyptians pursued them and went after them into the sea with all their horses, chariots, and drivers. There they stuck in the mud. *The Lord said to Moses, 'Hold out your hand over the sea, and the water will come back over the Egyptians and their chariots and drivers.' So Moses held out his hand over the sea, and at daybreak the water returned to its normal level. . . . The water returned and covered the chariots, the drivers and all the Egyptian army that had followed the Israelites into the sea; not one of them was left. But the Israelites walked through the sea on dry ground with walls of water on both sides. On that day the Lord saved the people of Israel from the Egyptians, and the Israelites saw them lying dead on the seashore. When the Israelites saw the great power with which the Lord had defeated the Egyptians, they stood in awe of the Lord; and they had faith in the Lord and in his servant Moses.*

Ex 14.26-31

Rejoicing, the people began to sing:

The Lord is my strong defender;
he is the one who has saved me.
He is my God, and I will praise him.

Ex 15.2

Probable site of the crossing of the Red Sea

Lift up your stick and hold it out over the sea. The water will divide, and the Israelites will be able to walk through the sea on dry ground.

Ex 14.16

The desert wanderings

(Read *Exodus 16; Numbers 20*)

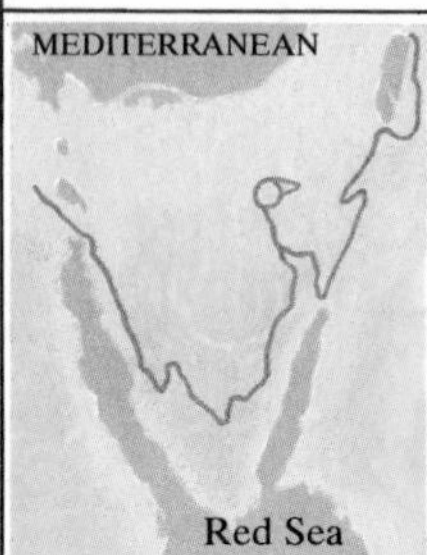

The route taken by the children of Israel in their desert wanderings

Quails: the smallest of all migratory birds. The flocks of quails they encountered on their way provided the Hebrews with the food God had promised them.

The children of Israel were to spend forty years wandering in the desert before they reached the promised land of Canaan.

Now that they were at last safe from Pharaoh, the Hebrews were confronted with dangers of another sort. Ahead of them lay the desert, where water would be scarce and food hard to find – a desert where people died of hunger and thirst. Yet the way to Canaan, the land of their forefathers, lay across that desert.

Once the excitement of leaving Egypt was over, there were a hundred and one practical everyday problems to be resolved – such as finding food and water, sorting out differences of opinion, discontent or loss of morale:

We wish that the Lord had killed us in Egypt. There we could at least sit down and eat meat and as much other food as we wanted. But you have brought us out into this desert to starve us all to death.

Ex 16.3

The Lord was not deaf to their complaints.

In the evening a large flock of quails flew in, enough to cover the camp, and in the morning there was dew all round the camp. When the dew evaporated, there was something thin and flaky on the surface of the desert. It was as delicate as frost. When the Israelites saw it, they didn't know what it was and asked each other, 'What is it?' Moses said to them, 'This is the food that the Lord has given you to eat.'

Ex 16.13-15

They said, *'Give us water to drink.'. . . Moses prayed earnestly to the Lord and said, 'What can I do with these people? They are almost ready to stone me.' The Lord said to Moses, 'Take some of the leaders of Israel with you, and go on ahead of the people. Take along the stick with which you struck the Nile. I will stand before you on a rock at Mount Sinai. Strike the rock, and water will come out of it for the people to drink.' Moses did so in the presence of the leaders of Israel.*

Ex 17.2, 4-6

A seven-branched candelabra. Round it stand representatives of the twelve tribes of Israel.

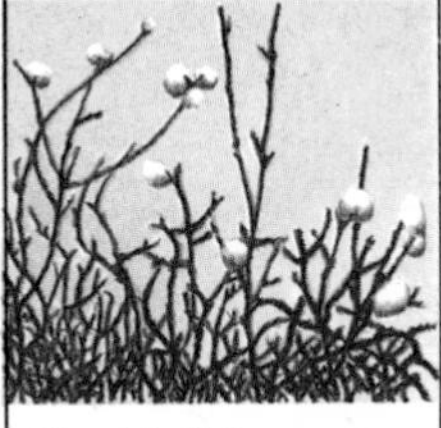

The thin flaky substance which the Hebrews collected and ate was Manna. It tasted 'like biscuits made with honey'.

The Covenant and the Golden Calf

(Read *Exodus 19; 24; 32-34*)

Do not make for yourselves images of anything in heaven or on earth. **Ex 20.4**

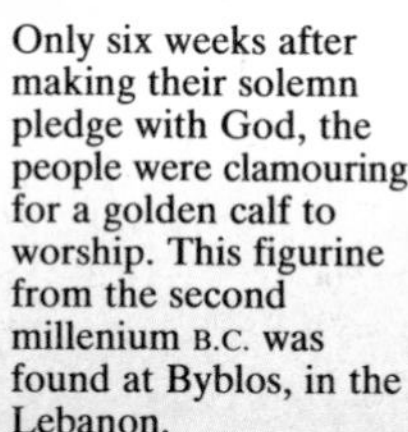

Only six weeks after making their solemn pledge with God, the people were clamouring for a golden calf to worship. This figurine from the second millenium B.C. was found at Byblos, in the Lebanon.

Three months after leaving Egypt, the children of Israel arrived at the foot of Mount Sinai. Moses went up the mountain to meet with God. In the midst of thunder, lightning and smoke God gave Moses the ten commandments. These were the basis of the covenant made between God and the people. A feast was held at the foot of the mountain to celebrate the sealing of the covenant.

Moses wrote down all the Lord's commands. Early the next morning he built an altar at the foot of the mountain and set up twelve stones, one for each of the twelve tribes of Israel. Then he sent young men, and they burnt sacrifices to the Lord and sacrificed some cattle as fellowship-offerings. Moses took half the blood of the animals and put it in bowls; and the other half he threw against the altar. Then he took the book of the covenant, in which the Lord's

commands were written, and read it aloud to the people. They said, 'We will obey the Lord and do everything that he has commanded.' **Ex 24.4-7**

Moses went back up the mountain and stayed there a further forty days. God gave him the stone tablets with the Law written on them. Meanwhile, the children of Israel, seeing no sign of Moses, made a gold statue of a calf and proclaimed it to be their god. They built an altar and made burnt offerings to their golden idol. Moses came down from the mountain to find the people dancing in front of this golden calf. The people had broken the first commandment: 'Worship no God but me.' In his fury Moses hurled the stone tablets to the ground where they shattered. He took the golden calf, melted it down and ground it into fine dust. Then he sought out and punished the chief wrongdoers.

Aaron, Moses' brother, performing his duties as High Priest of Israel.

Moses takes the tables of the Law given to him by God on Mount Sinai, and presents them to the assembled people. (13th c. miniature.)

The Law of the Covenant

(Read *Exodus 20-23; Deuteronomy 6*)

Moses carrying the tablets of the Law (Byzantine painting)

The Great Commandment

Love the Lord your God with all your heart, with all your soul, and with all your strength. **Deut 6.5**

The ten commandments

Worship no God but me.
Do not make images or bow down to any idol.
Do not use my name for evil purposes.
Observe the Sabbath and keep it holy.
Respect your father and mother.
Do not commit murder.
Do not commit adultery.
Do not steal.
Do not accuse anyone falsely.
Do not desire another man's house; do not desire his wife, his slaves, his cattle, his donkeys, or anything else that he owns. **Ex 20.3-17**

A carving, hewn out of stone, depicting the Ark of the Covenant. Found in Capernaum, 4th c. B.C.

People of Israel, listen to all the laws that I am giving you today. Learn them and be sure that you obey them.

Deut 5.1

The law-codes of the Covenant

Do not cheat a poor and needy hired servant, whether he is a fellow-Israelite or a foreigner living in one of your towns. Each day before sunset pay him for that day's work. **Deut 24.14-15**

If you take someone's cloak as a pledge that he will pay you, you must give it back to him before the sun sets. **Ex 22.26**

Do not follow the majority when they do wrong or when they give evidence that perverts justice. **Ex 23.2**

If a man takes a stick and beats his slave, whether male or female, and the slave dies on the spot, the man is to be punished. **Ex 21.20**

Do not ill-treat any widow or orphan. If you do, I, the Lord, will answer them when they cry out to me for help, and I will be angry and kill you in war. **Ex 22.22-24**

When you gather your crops and fail to bring in some of the corn that you have cut, do not go back for it; it is to be left for the foreigners, orphans, and widows. **Deut 24.19**

The Ark of the Covenant was a rectangular chest made of acacia wood, covered with gold. It was carried by means of long poles. The Ark contained the two stone tablets on which the ten commandments were written. It was a sign of God's presence amongst the chosen people. The Ark accompanied them on all their travels until they finally reached Canaan safely.

Settlers in Canaan

(Read *Numbers 13; Joshua 1; 6; 11; 23*)

Joshua takes Moses' place
Moses was to die without ever setting foot in the land of Canaan. Joshua was appointed by God to be his successor. The *Book of Joshua* records the many events that occurred during the Hebrews' conquest and occupation of Canaan. The account was written two centuries after the events it describes. The authors of the *Book of Joshua* did not intend it to be an accurate historical record, but rather a testimony to Joshua's faithfulness to the Law of Moses, and a reaffirmation of God's continuing presence amongst the Israelites.

Forty years after their escape from Egypt, the children of Israel finally reached Canaan, the Promised Land, only to find it occupied. The rich, fertile plains were inhabited by herdsmen, farmers and craftsmen who kept a watchful eye on the surrounding countryside from their strongholds in the hills.

At first the Israelites established themselves in the arid hill country. Some of their encounters with the Canaanites were peaceful, but many a fierce battle was fought before the land became theirs.

In the North, the children of Israel came across distant relatives who were eager to accept the Law of the Covenant. Joshua gathered all the people together at Shechem, where the solemn promises made in the Covenant were renewed. The people then dispersed to their allotted territories.

Joshua divided the land from North to South amongst the twelve tribes of Israel. Each tribe was named after one of the twelve sons of Jacob, the grandson of Abraham.

The Israelites had been nomads. When they settled in Canaan, their way of life changed. They became farmers and craftsmen, adopting many of the customs and the skills of the Canaanites. They were tempted too to worship the Canaanite gods, Baal and Asherah.

Shortly before his death Joshua warned the Israelites to be on their guard: . . . *you will not associate with these peoples left among you or speak the names of their gods or use those names in taking vows or worship those gods or bow down to them. Instead be faithful to the Lord, as you have been till now.* **Josh 23.7-9**

The fall of Jericho, as seen by a 15th century Italian artist. (Bronze bas-relief.)

Sent by Moses to explore the land of Canaan, his spies . . . *cut off a branch which had one branch of grapes on it so heavy that it took two men to carry it on a pole between them.* **Num 13.23**

Joseph's descendants felling trees, on Joshua's advice, in order to increase their share of land.

Demarcation of the boundaries between the tribes.

The Lord showed [Moses] the whole land: the territory of Gilead . . . Naphtali . . . Ephraim and Manasseh . . . and the plain that reaches from Zoar to Jericho, the city of palm-trees. Then the Lord said to Moses, 'This is the land that I promised Abraham, Isaac, and Jacob I would give to their descendants. I have let you see it, but I will not let you go there.' **Deut 34.1-5**

Symbols of the twelve tribes

Reuben Simeon Ephraim

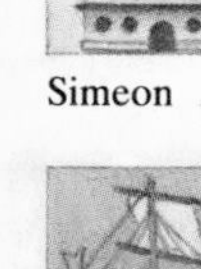

Judah Zebulun Issachar

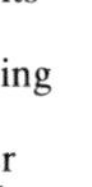

Naphtali Dan Gad

Manasseh Benjamin Asher

Lots were drawn and the land was divided up between the twelve tribes of Israel.
Each tribe had its emblem.
Reuben: the rising sun
Simeon: a tower
Ephraim: a bull
Judah: a lion cub
Zebulun: a ship
Issachar: a lean donkey
Naphtali: a doe
Dan: a serpent
Gad: a tent
Manasseh: a palm tree
Benjamin: a wolf
Asher: an olive tree

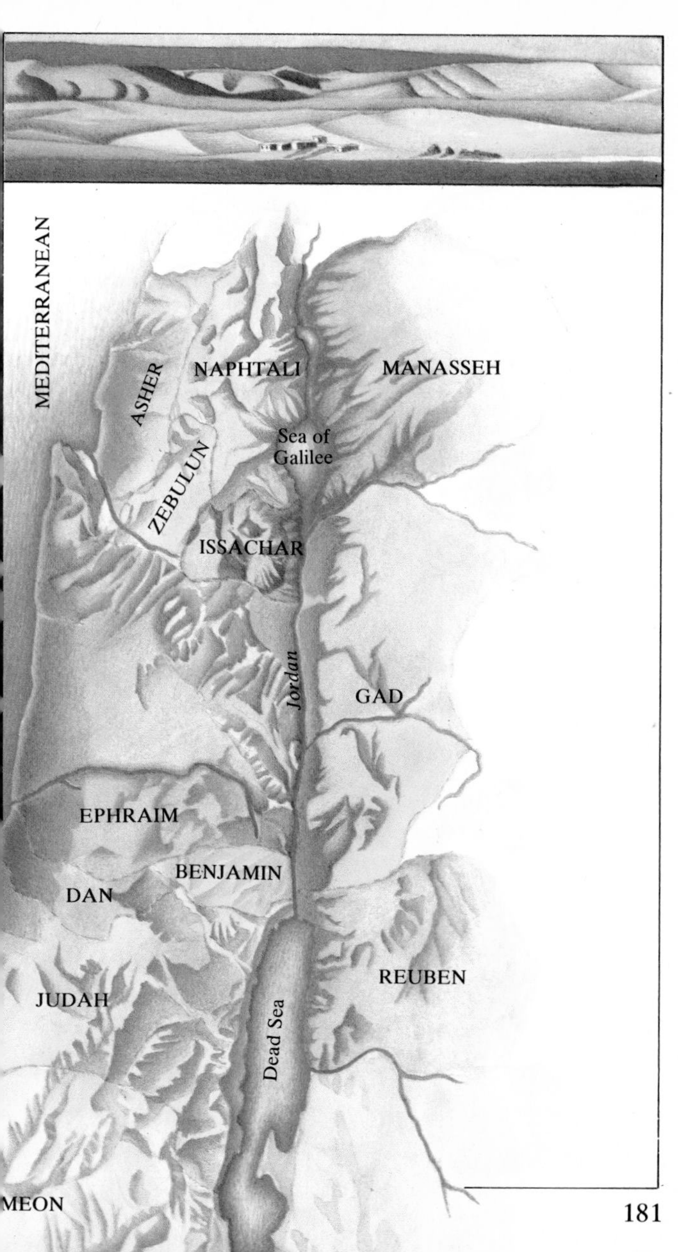
MEDITERRANEAN
ASHER
NAPHTALI
MANASSEH
Sea of
Galilee
ZEBULUN
ISSACHAR
Jordan
GAD
EPHRAIM
BENJAMIN
DAN
REUBEN
JUDAH
Dead Sea
MEON

Gideon

(Read *Judges 6*)

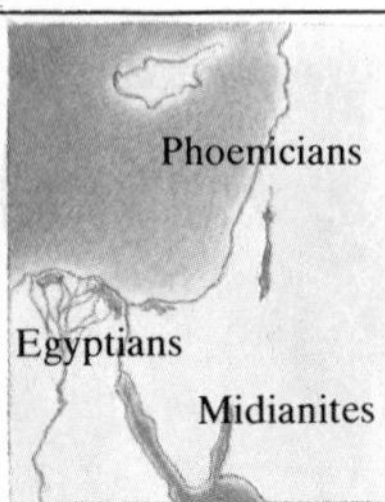

The Midianites were Bedouin nomads who travelled great distances with their caravans of camels, plundering and raiding as they went. They were threatening to drive the Israelites from their homes when Gideon defeated them at a place called the Spring of Harod.

They would come with their livestock and tents, as thick as locusts. They and their camels were too many to count.
Judg 6.5-6

Each tribe was independent and self-governing. But there was a mutual agreement between the tribes that if one was attacked, the others would go to its aid. In the case of enemy attack, the tribes united under the leadership of one outstandingly brave man or woman. This person was known in the Bible as a Judge. This is the story of Gideon, a famous Judge of the tribe of Manasseh.

The Midianites were marauding Bedouin Arabs who kept on harassing the Israelites. Whenever a fresh crop was sown or ready to harvest, they would launch a raid, wrecking the crop and carrying off all the livestock so that the Israelites were left with nothing.

One day the angel of the Lord came and sat under the shade of the oak tree that grew near Gideon's house.

The Midianites kept setting fire to their crops.

Gideon was threshing wheat secretly in a winepress, where the dreaded Midianites would not see him. *The Lord's angel appeared to him there and said, 'The Lord is with you, brave and mighty man!' Gideon said to him, 'If I may ask, sir, why has all this happened to us if the Lord is with us? What about all the wonderful things that our fathers told us the Lord used to do – how he brought them out of Egypt? The Lord has abandoned us and left us to the mercy of the Midianites.' Then the Lord ordered him, 'Go with all your great strength and rescue Israel from the Midianites. I myself am sending you.'*

In this 15th century miniature, Gideon is depicted as a knight in armour. The Judges were national heroes and heroines chosen by God to save the people in times of danger. Amongst the most well-known are Deborah, Jephthah and Abimelech.

The thorn bush king

(Read *Judges 9*)

Like the proud, self-satisfied king in this 15th century Spanish miniature, Abimelech ruled his people by force.

One of Gideon's sons was extremely ambitious and brutal. This was Abimelech. He managed to get himself elected king by certain members of his tribe against the will of the rest. He was so determined to have things entirely his own way that he massacred all his brothers, except for the youngest one, Jotham, who ran away and hid.

An anti-monarchist tale

On hearing that Abimelech had been made king, Jotham went and stood on top of Mount Gerizim where he told this parable concerning the new, bloodthirsty and ruthless king: *Once upon a time the trees got together to choose a king for themselves. They said to the olive-tree, 'Be our king.' The olive-tree answered, 'In order to govern you, I would have to stop producing my oil, which is used to honour gods and men.' Then the trees said to the fig-tree, 'You come and be our king.' But the fig-*

Besieging a city

tree answered, 'In order to govern you, I would have to stop producing my good sweet fruit.' So the trees then said to the grapevine, 'You come and be our king.' But the vine answered, 'In order to govern you, I would have to stop producing my wine, that makes gods and men happy.' So then all the trees said to the thorn-bush. 'You come and be our king.' The thorn-bush answered, 'If you really want to make me your king, then come and take shelter in my shade.' **Judg 9.8.15**. Having told this tale, Jotham then fled for fear of his life.

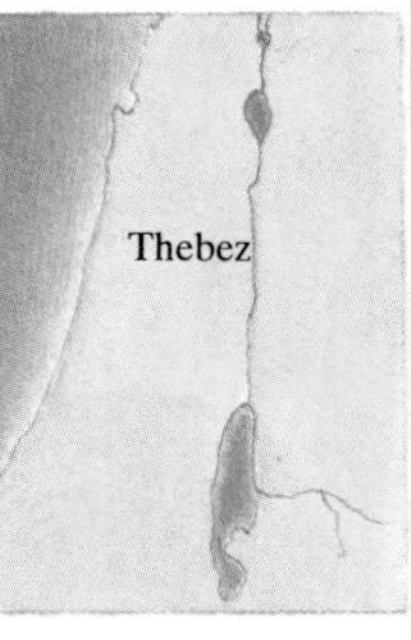

Abimelech was killed by an old woman who dropped a mill-stone on his head during the siege of Thebez – a fittingly violent end for such a violent man.

A fitting end for a tyrant

In time the inhabitants of Shechem rebelled against Abimelech. He crushed their attempted uprising with devastating brutality, but finally, after three years in power, he was killed whilst laying siege to the nearby city of Thebez.

Samuel

(Read *1 Samuel 1*)

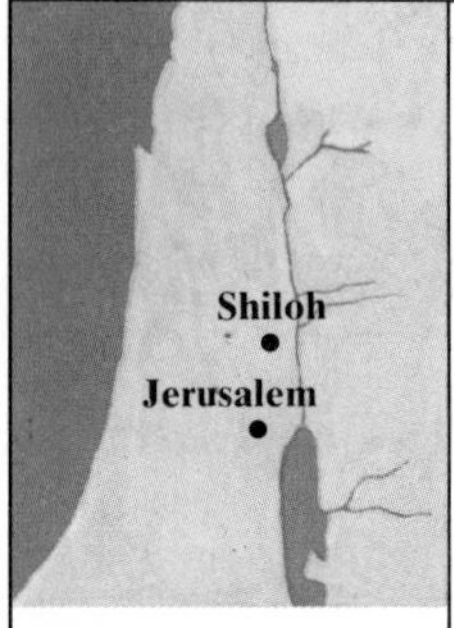

The town of Shiloh is 30 km (18 miles) north of Jerusalem.

A man called Elkanah and his wife Hannah lived in the town of Ramah in the hill country of Ephraim. Hannah was sad because she had no children. Whenever they went up to the sanctuary at Shiloh, the others would all be eating, drinking and making merry while Hannah wept and refused to eat. *Her husband Elkanah would ask her, 'Hannah, why are you crying? Why won't you eat? Why are you always so sad? Don't I mean more to you than ten sons?'*

One day, when they had finished their meal in the sanctuary, Hannah got up, crying bitterly as she prayed to the Lord. She continued to pray silently for a long time. Only her lips were moving. Eli, the priest, who was watching her, thought she must be drunk and said to her: *'Stop making a drunken show of yourself! Stop your drinking and sober up!' 'No, I'm not drunk, sir,' she answered. 'I am desperate, and I have been praying, pouring out my troubles to the Lord. Don't think I am a worthless woman. I have been praying like this because I'm so miserable.' 'Go in peace,' Eli said, 'and may the God of Israel give you what you have asked him for.'*

Hannah went away. She ate some food and was no longer sad. When she returned home, Hannah became pregnant and gave birth to a son, whom she named Samuel, which means 'asked of the Lord'.

So it was that she became pregnant and gave birth to a son. She named him Samuel.

1 Sam 1.20

Hannah prayed this prayer of thanksgiving to the Lord:

'The Lord has filled my heart with joy;
how happy I am because of what he has done!
I laugh at my enemies; how joyful I am because God has helped me!

The bows of strong soldiers are broken,
but the weak grow strong.
The people who were once well fed
now hire themselves out to get food,

but the hungry are no more.
The childless wife has borne seven children,
but the mother of many is left with none.

He lifts the poor from the dust and raises
the needy from their misery.
He makes them companions of princes
and puts them in places of honour.
The foundations of the earth belong to the Lord;
on them he has built the world.

He protects the lives of his faithful people,
but the wicked disappear
in darkness.'

Elkanah, Samuel's father, went up to the temple at Shiloh each year to worship and offer sacrifices to the Lord. This would have been in the autumn, at the time of the fruit and olive harvest.

King Saul

(Read *1 Samuel 8-10*)

Saul's campaigns

In Samuel's time the people of Israel were in danger of being wiped out by the Philistines, a fierce warlike people who had settled along the Mediterranean coast and were trying to take over the Promised Land. The Philistines were renowned for their cruelty in battle and the devastation they left behind them.

The tribes of Israel were in no position to withstand attack from such a powerful adversary. What they needed was one person to rule the whole country. Surely Israel ought to have a king like other nations?

When they weren't waging war, kings went hunting. Here we see the Assyrian king Ashurbanipal (7th c. B.C.) engaged in his favourite sport.

Should Israel have a king?

Opinion was divided. Samuel was the first to warn the Israelites of the possible consequences. *'This is how your king will treat you,'* Samuel explained. *'He will make soldiers of your sons; some of them will serve in his war chariots, others in his cavalry, and others will run before his chariots. . . . Your sons will*

So then, appoint a king to rule over us,
so that we will have a king, as other countries have.
1 Sam 8.5

have to plough his fields, harvest his crops, and make his weapons and the equipment for his chariots. Your daughters will have to make perfumes for him and work as his cooks and his bakers. He will take your best fields, vineyards, and olive-groves, and give them to his officials. He will take a tenth of your corn and of your grapes for his court officers and other officials. He will take your servants and your best cattle and donkeys, and make them work for him. He will take a tenth of your flocks. And you yourselves will become his slaves.' **1 Sam 8.11-17**

Crowns have been symbols of royalty since ancient times. This bronze crown probably dates from 3000 B.C.

Saul is appointed king

Samuel's warnings went unheard. The people insisted on having a king to lead them like other nations. Samuel summoned the tribes together at Mizpah. *'Very well, then, gather yourselves before the Lord by tribes and clans.' Then Samuel made each tribe come forward and the Lord picked the tribe of Benjamin. Then Samuel made the families of the tribe of Benjamin come forward, and the family of Matri was picked out. Then the men of the family of Matri came forward, and Saul son of Kish was picked out. . . . . They could see that he was a head taller than anyone else. Samuel said to the people, 'Here is the man the Lord has chosen! There is no one else among us like him.' All the people shouted, 'Long live the king!'* **1 Sam 10.19-24**

Once the King of Israel was anointed in the name of Yahweh, he was considered to be God's representative on earth, but not divine. (Gilt-embossed Saint-Gall Psalter.)

David and Goliath

(Read *1 Samuel 17*)

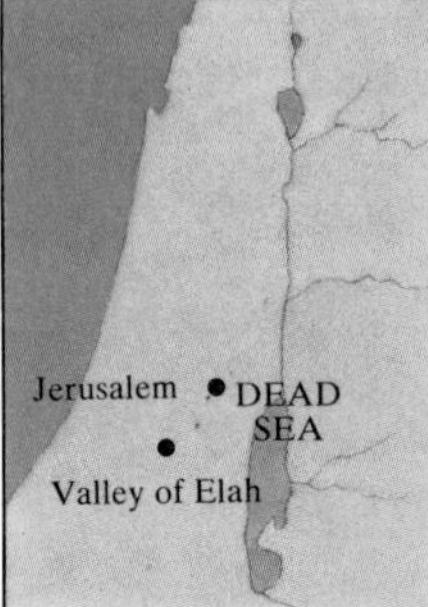

The valley of Elah where David fought Goliath.

This stone carving of a warrior armed with a sling is from Upper Mesopotamia and dates from the time of David.

Saul and his army repeatedly defeated the Philistines in battle. Amongst Saul's soldiers was one whose courage and daring endeared him to the people. This was David. Tales of his strength were told in every town and village. Slaying the mighty Goliath was one of his first triumphs.

Saul's army and the army of the Philistines were drawn up facing each

other. From out of the Philistine ranks there stepped a giant of a man, named Goliath. His armour weighed almost sixty kg (130 lb), and the iron head of his spear seven (15 lb). He bellowed a challenge: *'Choose one of your men to fight. If he wins and kills me, we will be your slaves; but if I win and kill him, you will be our slaves.'* Saul and his men were terrified by this monster of a man.

David decided to take up this challenge. Saul protested, *'You are just a boy and he has been a soldier all his life'*. David replied that, as a shepherd, he had killed lions and bears that attacked his father's sheep. *'The Lord*

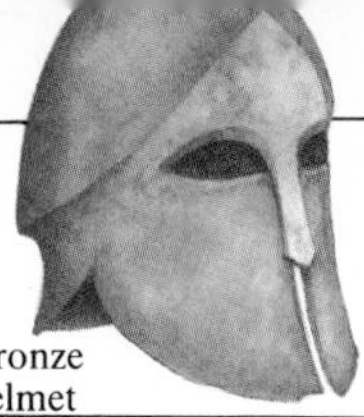

Bronze helmet

Two-edged dagger

Tip of a spear

has saved me from lions and bears; he will save me from this Philistine.

Saul gave David his own armour to wear; he put his helmet on David's head and strapped his sword to his belt. David found the armour hampered his movements. He took it off, picked up his shepherd's stick, chose five smooth stones from the stream and, catapult in hand, went out to meet Goliath.

The Philistine began hurling abuse at David, but David simply retorted, *'You are coming against me with sword, spear, and javelin, but I come against you in the name of the Lord Almighty, the God of the Israelite armies, which you have defied.'*

David put a stone in his catapult and took aim. The stone hit Goliath in the middle of the forehead. He fell to the ground. David took the giant's sword and.cut off his head. Whereupon the Philistines turned and fled, with Saul's army in hot pursuit.

David and Goliath (13th century miniature)

Saul's jealousy

(Read *1 Samuel 18; 19; 26; 2 Samuel 1*)

David: king, musician, and psalm-writer, from an illustration in the Citeaux Bible, 12th century.

David's victories made him increasingly popular both with the people and at the king's court. Jonathan, one of Saul's sons, became his close friend. Saul's daughter Michal fell in love with David and became his wife. All over the country, people sang his praises; *'Saul has killed thousands, but David tens of thousands.'*

Saul became very jealous of all the attention David was getting. He tried on several occasions to kill him.

One day, while David was playing the harp nearby, Saul hurled a spear at him, hoping to pin him to the wall. But David was too quick for him.

Saul sent soldiers by night to kill David while he was asleep. But Michal heard about the plot and helped David to escape out of a window.

David fled to his home near Bethlehem and hid in the mountains. His friends joined him and together they fought off the Philistines and desert raiders.

David bore no grudge against Saul, but Saul continued to pursue him relentlessly.

One night David entered Saul's camp unseen. He took the king's spear and his water jug. From the top of a hill on the other side of the valley, David brandished the spear and the jar in full view of the horrified commander of Saul's army, *'Abner . . . why aren't you protecting your master, the king?' he cried. 'Look, where is the king's spear? Where is the water jar that was beside his head?'*

Saul was overcome with shame when he discovered that David had spared his life. He promised not to harm him again, and begged him to return. But David refused, and returned instead to the mountains.

Some years later Saul and Jonathan were killed during a battle against the Philistines. David mourned them both in a lament which he ordered the people of Judah to learn (**2 Sam 1.19-27**).

King Saul's Israelite soldiers paying homage to their king.

A figure of an ancient warrior from Ras-Shamra in Syria, probably dating from the second millenium B.C.

King David

(Read *2 Samuel 5-6*)

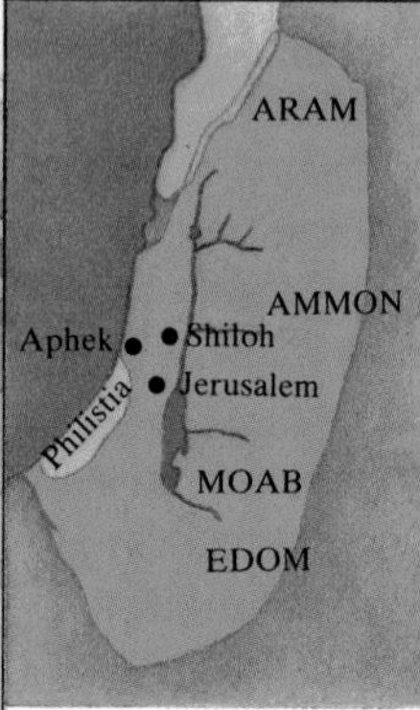

David's kingdom

The Philistines succeeded in capturing the Ark of the Covenant at Aphek. However, David finally defeated them and drove them out of his kingdom.

When Saul died David was proclaimed king of his own tribe, the tribe of Judah. Seven years later the other tribes asked him to be their king. He was now king over all the tribes of Israel. For the first time the country was united under one leader.

David took Jerusalem, a fortified hill-town strategically placed in the middle of the kingdom, and made it the capital of Israel. He named it the City of David and built himself a palace within its walls.

The Philistines, alarmed at how powerful David had become, launched two further attacks, but David finally succeeded in driving them out of his kingdom for good.

David decided to make Jerusalem the religious capital of his kingdom. He had the Ark of the Covenant, which had been at Shiloh until then, brought to Jerusalem. A great celebration was organised in honour of the occasion. *Then he offered sacrifices and fellowship-offerings to the Lord. When he had finished offering the sacrifices, he blessed the people in the name of the Lord Almighty and distributed food to them all. He gave each man and woman in Israel a loaf of bread, a piece of roasted meat, and some raisins. Then everyone went home.* **2 Sam 6.17-19**

David made plans to build a temple to house the Ark. But the prophet Nathan told him, *'You are not the one to build a temple'*. . . for the Lord. *'You will*

The hill of Jerusalem

always have descendants, and I will make your kingdom last for ever.'

Henceforth God was closely allied to the line of David. The king was the living proof of God's presence in the midst of the chosen people.

Within the space of a few years David had consolidated and enlarged his empire. He subdued the neighbouring kingdoms of Ammon, Moab, Edom and Aram. Within the extended boundaries of his realm he devised a form of government whereby law and justice could be effectively administered.

Aphek
Shiloh
Ekron
Obed-edom
Jerusalem
Ashdod
Beth-shemesh
Gath

In this mediaeval miniature King David is accompanying the Ark to its final resting place in Jerusalem, the religious centre of the kingdom. Music emphasises the solemnity and joy of the occasion. David himself leads the procession playing the psaltery, a type of zither.

David sins and repents

(Read *2 Samuel 11-12*)

One day, late in the afternoon, David got up from his nap and went to the palace roof. As he walked about up there, he saw a woman having a bath. She was very beautiful. . . . David sent messengers to fetch her. **2 Sam 11.2-4**

Much is said in the Bible about the good things David did, but his misdeeds also get a mention. In particular we hear about the crime he committed against Uriah, one of his best officers. David had fallen in love with Bathsheba, Uriah's wife. He had Uriah killed in battle so that he could make Bathsheba his wife. God was not pleased with David.

The prophet Nathan was sent by God to David. This was the tale he told: *There were two men who lived in the same town; one was rich and the other poor. The rich man had many cattle and sheep, while the poor man had only one*

This miniature from Our Lady's Book of Hours (15th c. A.D.) shows King David gazing intently at the young woman, Bathsheba, bathing in the heat of the day. She does not know she is being observed, still less that her beauty has aroused in the King an overwhelming passion.

lamb, which he had bought. He took care of it, and it grew up in his home with his children. He would feed it with some of his own food, let it drink from his cup, and hold it in his lap. The lamb was like a daughter to him.

One day a visitor arrived at the rich man's home. The rich man didn't want to kill one of his own animals to prepare a meal for him; instead he took the poor man's lamb and cooked a meal for his guest.

David was furious when he heard this and said to Nathan, *'I swear by the living Lord that the man who did this ought to die! For having done such a cruel thing, he must pay back four times as much as he took.'*

'You are that man,' Nathan said to David. 'And this is what the Lord God of Israel says: "I made you king of Israel. . . . If this had not been enough, I would have given you twice as much. Why, then, have you disobeyed my commands? Why did you do this evil thing? You had Uriah killed in battle; . . . and then you took his wife!"' 'I have sinned against the Lord,' David said. Nathan replied, 'The Lord forgives you; you will not die. But because you have shown such contempt for the Lord in doing this, your child will die.'

David and Bathsheba's first son did indeed die. A second son was born to them, whose name was Solomon and who succeeded David.

David takes Uriah's wife and then has Uriah killed in battle – like the rich man in Nathan's story who took his poor neighbour's only ewe-lamb.

Even the king is subject to the law: 'Do not kill'. Having sinned, David humbly asks God's forgiveness – like this praying figure of a man (Assyrian-Babylonian).

Solomon, king of kings

(Read *1 Kings 9 and 11*)

This miniature from the Bible of Citeaux (12th century) illustrates the quality for which Solomon is best-known – his sense of justice. He did also bring immense wealth and prosperity to his country.

David's son Solomon succeeded him as King. Israel was by now at peace with its neighbours. Solomon was able to consolidate his father's kingdom, bringing it material wealth and renown.

He undertook an ambitious building programme. He enlarged the city of Jerusalem, building not only several palaces but above all a magnificent temple to house the Ark of the Covenant (page 177). In other major cities he built fortifications, palaces, store-houses and stables for his war horses. He developed trade with other countries. From the king of Tyre he bought timber in exchange for oil and wheat. He imported horses from Asia, to sell to other countries. He established a merchant fleet in the Red Sea, which brought back gold and precious stones from Arabia and Africa. He set up an industry to smelt copper and iron ore.

Solomon reorganised the government of the country. He divided his kingdom into twelve districts and appointed a prefect in charge of each area.

Outside Israel, Solomon was respected not only for the power and prosperity he brought to the country, but also for his great wisdom. However, he did have shortcomings. His ambitious projects cost his people dear in labour and in taxes. He also had a great number of foreign wives whose heathen gods he began to worship,

thereby breaking the sacred Law.

It was during Solomon's reign that the many Hebrew oral traditions were first systematically collected and written down. These were the first written records of the Bible.

During his reign Solomon established a flourishing ocean-going merchant fleet. (Bas-relief showing shipping of timber.)

Solomon traded in horses and chariots. He added a horse and chariot division to the standing army.

According to the Bible, 'no less than five thousand litres of fine flour, ten thousand litres of meal, ten stall-fed cattle, twenty pasture-fed cattle and a hundred sheep, besides deer, gazelles, roebucks and poultry,' were required each day in the way of supplies at Solomon's court.

The wisdom of Solomon

(Read *1 Kings 3, 10*)

Solomon showed much wisdom and insight in judging difficult cases, such as the case of the two mothers arguing over the baby, that the Queen of Sheba herself decided to put his wisdom to the test. She came to Solomon's court laden with presents in order to ask the king a series of testing questions.

The Old Testament is full of praise for Solomon's wisdom. He was undoubtedly a man of great learning, but he also had an understanding of human nature and a strong sense of justice.

One day two women were brought before the king. One said, *'Your Majesty, this woman and I live in the same house, and I gave birth to a baby boy at home while she was there. Two days after my child was born she also gave birth to a baby boy. Then one night she accidentally rolled over on her baby and smothered it. The next morning, when I woke up and was going to feed my baby, I saw that it was dead. I looked at it more closely and saw that it was not my child.' But the other woman said, 'No! the living child is mine, and the dead one is yours!' The first woman answered, 'No! The dead child is yours and the living one is mine!' Then King Solomon . . . sent for a sword, and when it was brought, he said, 'Cut the living child in two and give each woman half of it.' The real mother, her heart full of love for her son, said to the king, 'Please, Your Majesty, don't kill the*

Solomon pronouncing judgement

child! Give it to her!' But the other woman said, 'Don't give it to either of us; go ahead and cut it in two.' Then Solomon said, 'Don't kill the child! Give it to the first woman – she is its real mother.' **1 Kgs 3.16-27**

The Queen of Sheba had heard tell of Solomon's wisdom. She was eager to test his knowledge by asking him a series of difficult riddles. She arrived in Jerusalem with a large number of attendants and camels laden with spices, precious stones and gold. She put her carefully prepared questions to Solomon, but he answered them all.

The queen was amazed at the extent of Solomon's wisdom, and she was impressed by the splendour of his palace, by the meals served at his table and by his retinue of servants. She said to Solomon, *'What I heard in my own country about you and your wisdom is true! But I couldn't believe it until I had come and seen it all for myself. But I didn't hear even half of it. . . . Praise the Lord your God! He has shown how pleased he is with you by making you king of Israel.'* **1 Kgs 10.1-10**

Solomon's temple

(Read *1 Kings 5*)

The temple took seven and a half years to build. Thousands of Israelites were conscripted to build it.

The temple was built on a huge platform (7) 150 m (490 ft) long and 100 m (330 ft) wide. The design of the temple was based on Egyptian and Syrian models. It consisted of a Porch (1), and two main rooms: the Holy Place (2) and the Holy of Holies (4). On either side were store-rooms (3). Only priests could enter the Holy Place. In the Holy of Holies stood the Ark of the Covenant (page 177). This darkened room was thought to be God's dwelling-place. Only the high priest (page 100)

5 The great altar for burnt offerings

6 The Sea of Bronze

Water was carried to the Sea of Bronze by means of a smaller basin mounted on wheels

Solomon prays while the temple is built. (From a 15th century miniature.)

I will live among my people Israel in this Temple that you are building, and I will never abandon them.
1 Kgs 6.13

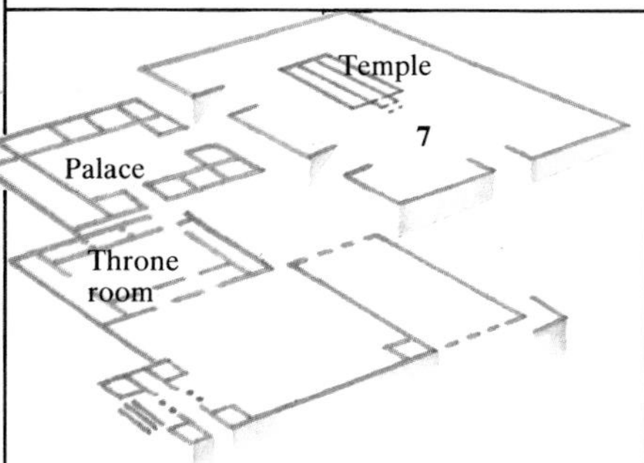

The temple and the palace

ever entered the Holy of Holies, and then only once a year at the Feast of Yom Kippur.

In front of the temple stood the altar (5), 10 m (33 ft) long and 4.50 m (15 ft) high, where burnt offerings (page 87) were made. Here too was the 'Sea of Bronze' (6), a huge brass vessel which held 40,000 l (8800 gal, 10,600 gal (US)) of water where the priests washed their hands and feet in ritual purification.

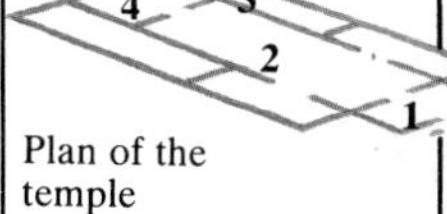

Plan of the temple

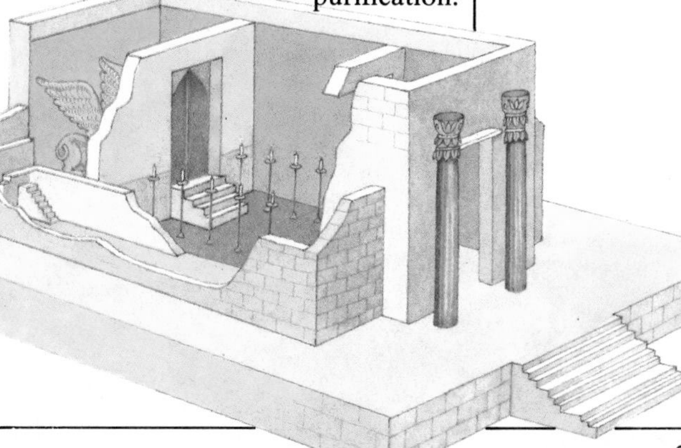

David's kingdom is divided

(Read *1 Kings 11-12*)

Rehoboam, Solomon's son, refused to listen to the people's demands for easier working and living conditions. As a result, David's kingdom was split in two.

Solomon was succeeded by his son Rehoboam. The Northern tribes, remembering the hardships imposed on them by Solomon, went to the new king, saying, *'Your father Solomon treated us harshly and placed heavy burdens on us. If you make these burdens lighter and make life easier for us, we will be your loyal subjects.'* **1 Kgs 12.4**

Rehoboam refused to listen. He decided to deal even more severely with the people. *'My father placed heavy burdens on you; I will make them even heavier. He beat you with a whip; I'll flog you with a horsewhip!'* At this the Northern tribes rebelled and declared their independence. Only Judah remained loyal to the king.

The tribes of the North and South, which David had succeeded in uniting, were now split into two separate kingdoms. The Northern kingdom, known as Israel, had Samaria as its capital; the Southern kingdom, Judah, had Jerusalem as its capital.

The rift between these twin nations, which shared the same religion and ancestry, was never to close.

As foreseen by the prophet

Some years before Solomon's death, a man of the northern tribes, Jeroboam, led a rebellion against the King. One day he met the prophet Ahijah on the road from Jerusalem. Ahijah removed the new robe he was wearing and tore it into twelve pieces, saying to Jeroboam,

Many of the building materials required in Solomon's plans to fortify and embellish the city of Jerusalem were imported from abroad, like these cedar trunks.

'Take ten pieces for yourself, because the Lord, the God of Israel, says to you, "I am going to take the kingdom away from Solomon, and I will give you ten tribes. Solomon will keep one tribe, for the sake of my servant David and for the sake of Jerusalem, the city I have chosen to be my own from the whole land of Israel. I am going to do this because Solomon has rejected me and has worshipped foreign gods. . . . Solomon has disobeyed me; he has done wrong, and has not kept my laws and commands as his father David did."'

1 Kgs 11.31-33

Forced labour

In order to carry out his ambitious building programme, Solomon had to commandeer a regular army of forced labourers: no less than 30,000 men were sent to the Lebanon in shifts of 10,000 men a month, to fell and transport the cedar required. At the same time a team of 150,000 men were employed in quarrying and transporting the stone.

When Solomon died, Jeroboam became king of the Northern kingdom, the new Israel.

Solomon's lavish building projects meant more forced labour for his subjects.

The Northern Kingdom

(Read *1 and 2 Kings*)

Hazael, the Assyrian king, held Jerusalem to ransom.

The kings of Israel
Jeroboam I 933-911
Nadab 911-910
Baasha 910-887
Elah 887-886
Omri 886-875
Ahab 875-853
Ahaziah 853-852
Joram 852-841
Jehu 841-820
Jehoahaz 820-803
Jehoash 803-787
Jeroboam II 787-747
Zechariah 747
Shallum 747-746
Menahem 746-737
Pekahiah 736-735
Pekah 735-732
Hosea 732-722

On the right, the righteous worship God while the wicked bow before foreign idols.

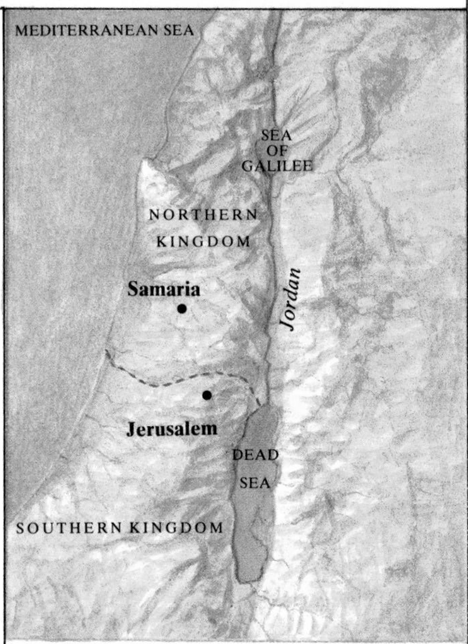

The Northern kingdom of Israel lasted just over 200 years (930-722 B.C.). They were turbulent years, during which seven of the nineteen kings were assassinated. There were seven uprisings and a succession of wars against the kings of Judah, Aram and Assyria.

Idolatry was a constant temptation in a time of unrest. The people were for ever turning to new gods in the hope that they would bring them victory in battle. *Ahab, son of Omri, became king of Israel. . . . He sinned against the lord more than any of his predecessors. It*

They made themselves impure by their actions and were unfaithful to God.
Psalm 106.39

was not enough for him to sin like King Jeroboam; he went further and married Jezebel, the daughter of King Ethbaal of Sidon, and worshipped Baal. He built a temple to Baal in Samaria, made an altar for him, and put it in the temple.
1 Kgs 16.30-32

The gods and goddesses of the Canaanites appeared to have much to offer. They were supposed to guarantee the fertility of agriculture, animals and mankind.

Rich people who had made their fortunes in trade and commerce acquired land and property at the expense of the poor, cheating and robbing them of what little they had. As the gap in wealth widened, the number of poor people increased.

Two idols
Horned figure of Baal found in Ras Shamra.

Syrian deity of 2nd mill. B.C.

Elijah, the greatest of all the prophets

(Read *1 Kings 16-17*)

He drank water from the brook, and ravens brought him bread and meat every morning and every evening.

1 Kgs 17.6

By the year 870 B.C. Israel was steeped in idolatry. King Ahab, influenced by his wife Jezebel (daughter of the pagan king of Tyre), had begun to worship the Phoenician gods Asherah and Baal.

Ahab's behaviour provoked the wrath of the prophet Elijah, *'In the name of the Lord, the living God of Israel, whom I serve, I tell you that there will be no dew or rain for the next two or three years until I say so.'*

Then the Lord said to Elijah, 'Leave this place and go east and hide yourself near the brook of Cherith, east of the Jordan. The brook will supply you with water to drink, and I have commanded ravens to bring you food there.'

Elijah was appointed by God to punish the king for his impiety. He was able to command the forces of nature. He lived a long time in the desert clad only in a leather loin-cloth and a cloak made of animal skins, as John the Baptist was to do after him.

Elijah was one of the greatest of the Old Testament prophets. At the end of his life his companion, Elisha, witnessed his ascension into heaven.

Lord God Almighty, I have always served you — you alone. But the people of Israel have broken their covenant with you, torn down your altars.
1 Kgs 19.10

A 17th century Greek icon showing Elijah going up to heaven in a fiery chariot.

They kept talking as they walked on; then suddenly a chariot of fire pulled by horses of fire came between them, and Elijah was taken up to heaven by a whirlwind. **2 Kgs 2.11**

Elijah performed many miracles in the course of his life. The end of his life was itself a miracle.

Judgement by fire

(Read *1 Kings 18*)

The prophets of Baal invoked the power of their Phoenician god in vain on Mount Carmel.

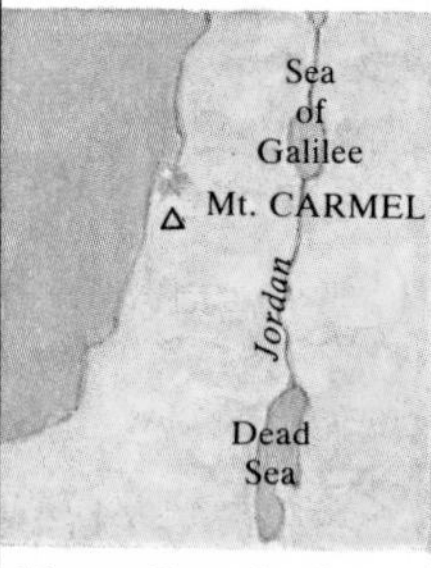

Mount Carmel, where Elijah summoned the prophets of Baal to a contest between their gods and his.

In the third year of the drought, the Lord said to Elija, *'Go and present yourself to King Ahab, and I will send rain.'* . . . When Ahab saw Elijah, he said, *'So there you are — the worst troublemaker in Israel!' 'I'm not the troublemaker,' Elijah answered. 'You are — you and your father. You are disobeying the Lord's commands and worshipping the idols of Baal. Now order all the people of Israel to meet me at Mount Carmel. Bring along the four hundred and fifty prophets of Baal and the four hundred prophets of the goddess Asherah who are supported by Queen Jezebel.'* **1 Kgs 18.17-19**

Baal is deaf to their entreaties

Elijah asked for two bulls to be brought. The prophets of Baal were to take one and prepare it for sacrifice, but without lighting the fire beneath it. Elijah would do the same with the second bull. They were to call on their god, and he on his. The one who answered by sending fire would be the true God.

Elijah asked the prophets of Baal to begin. All morning they prayed and danced around the altar. But no answer came. At noon, Elijah began to taunt them, saying, *'Pray louder! He is a god. Maybe he is day-dreaming or relieving himself, or perhaps he's gone on a journey! Or maybe he's sleeping, and you've got to wake him up!'*

1 Kgs 18.27

So the prophets prayed louder and cut themselves with knives and daggers, according to their ritual, until blood flowed . . . but no answer came, not a sound was heard. **1 Kgs 18.28-29**

A bull was the finest animal offering that could be made in the way of a sacrifice.

The Lord sends down fire

Elijah now began to build an altar to the Lord and set his bull on it. He prayed, *'O Lord, the God of Abraham, Isaac and Jacob, prove now that you are the God of Israel and that I am your servant and have done all this at your command. Answer me, Lord, answer me, so that this people will know that you, the Lord, are God, and that you are bringing them back to yourself.'*

1 Kgs 18.36-37

At once, the Lord sent down fire and it burnt up the sacrifice. The people fell to the ground, exclaiming, *'The Lord is God; the Lord alone is God.'*

1 Kgs 18.39

In the Bible God's presence is often manifested through fire.

Elijah gives judgement

(Read *1 Kings 21-22*)

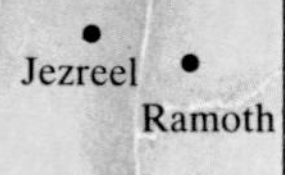

Near King Ahab's palace in Jezreel there was a vineyard which he coveted. He asked Naboth, the owner, to give it to him in exchange for a better vineyard, or to sell it for a fair price.

But Naboth refused. He could not part with land inherited from his ancestors.

The King was very angry. He lay down on his bed to sulk, and refused to eat. When Jezebel, his wife, found out what was wrong, she told him not to worry. She would make sure he got the vineyard.

Jezebel the wicked

The queen wrote letters in the King's name to the chief officials of the city of Jezreel, asking them to bring a false charge against Naboth. They were to find false witnesses who would accuse him of cursing God and the King; he would be found guilty and stoned to death as was the custom. The officials carried out the queen's orders. Naboth was duly accused, condemned and stoned. Then Jezebel told Ahab that Naboth was dead. The vineyard he coveted was his.

Elijah predicted the punishment God would bring on Ahab for stealing Naboth's vineyard. Ahab died at Ramoth-Gilead fighting the Syrians.

However, when Ahab went to take possession of the vineyard, he found Elijah there. *'After murdering the man, are you taking over his property as well? . . . In the very place that the dogs licked up Naboth's blood they will lick up your blood.'* **1 Kgs 21.19-1**

Elijah's prophecy comes true

Three years later Ahab was mortally wounded in battle. Blood ran down into his chariot. When the chariot was being cleaned in Jezreel, dogs came and licked the King's blood. Some years later, when Jehu, Ahab's former general, took command he ordered the evil Jezebel to be thrown to her death from the windows of her palace at Jezreel.

The prophets were the voice of the King's conscience. Nathan reproached David for having Uriah slain; Elijah reproached Ahab for Naboth's death. The people had looked first to the Judges, then to the Kings of Israel to lead them and to resolve the many social and political problems that beset the realm. From now on the prophets were to be the mouthpiece of God and chief defenders of the people.

By chance, however, a Syrian soldier shot an arrow which struck King Ahab between the joints of his armour. 'I am wounded!' he cried out to his chariot driver. 'Turn round and pull out of the battle!'
While the battle raged on, King Ahab remained propped up in his chariot, facing the Syrians. The blood from his wound ran down and covered the bottom of the chariot, and at evening he died.
1 Kgs 22.34-35

'Let me have your vineyard; it is close to my palace, and I want to use the land as a vegetable garden. I will give you a better vineyard for it, or if you prefer, I will pay you a fair price.' **1 Kgs 21.2**

Amos, the fearless

(Read *Amos 5-8*)

Amos, depicted in an illuminated letter of a 12th century Bible.

A hundred years went by before the voice of another prophet, Amos, was heard in Israel, in about 775-750 B.C. Israel was no longer at war, but the state of affairs within the country had not improved.

The rich lived in luxury, exploiting the poor. They spent their time feasting and enjoying themselves. They also made a great show of religious fervour. Meanwhile the poor, who far outnumbered them, worked hard for low wages, and were down-trodden.

Rich Samarian women are rebuked

'Listen to this, you women of Samaria, who grow fat like the well-fed cows of Bashan, who ill-treat the weak, oppress the poor, and demand that your husbands keep you supplied with liquor! As the Sovereign Lord is holy, he has promised, "The days will come when they will drag you away with hooks; every one of you will be like a fish on a hook."' **Amos 4.1-2**

A young Egyptian slave-girl serving refreshments to a group of Egyptian ladies. This scene recalls the rich women of Samaria that Amos so deplored.

Go to the Lord, and you will live.
If you do not go, he will sweep down like fire
on the people of Israel.

Amos 5.6

Amos attacks religious hypocrisy

'I hate your religious festivals; I cannot stand them! When you bring me burnt-offerings and grain-offerings, I will not accept them; I will not accept the animals you have fattened to bring me as offerings. Stop your noisy songs; I do not want to listen to your harps. Instead, let justice flow like a stream, and righteousness like a river that never goes dry.' **Amos 5.21-24**

Amos was made of the same stuff as Elijah. He was energetic and courageous. The herdsman from the Southern kingdom was not afraid to speak his mind. He was so outspoken in fact, that he was sent back to his native Judah.

Man drinking (1000 B.C.)

The plight of the poor in Amos' time was like that of the Hebrew slaves when in Egypt.

Hosea, the prophet of the love of God

(Read *Hosea 1-4; 2 Kings 15*)

In green, the region known as the Fertile Crescent. This stretched from the Mediterranean in the West to the Persian Gulf in the East. Many of the early episodes in the history of Israel took place in this area.

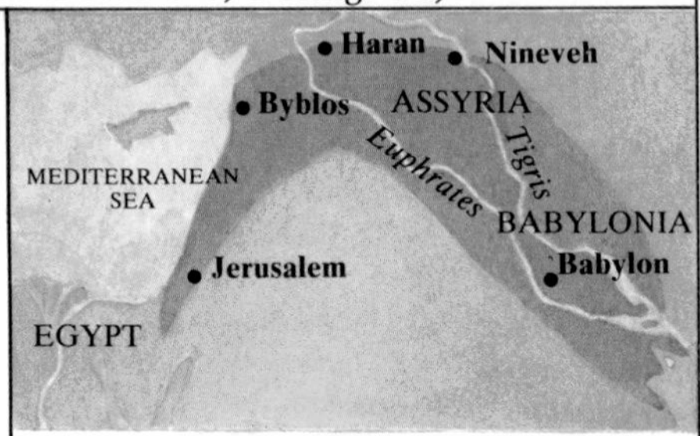

In Samaria, in the space of fifteen years, there were no less than five palace revolutions and four kings assassinated.

Bronze figures of Egyptian gods: behind the sacred bull stands Hathor, goddess of dance, music and happiness.

In about 745 B.C., some ten years after Amos had been sent back to Judah, another prophet appeared. By this time the situation in the Northern kingdom was critical. Idolatry was rife, and, after a succession of violent uprisings all ending in bloodshed, the country was even more open to attack from outside. Meanwhile, Assyria was gathering strength.

Hosea loved his wife but she was unfaithful: she had deserted him in the pursuit of idolatry.

Hosea saw a direct parallel between his own relationship with his wife and that of God with the people of Israel.

Israel was the unfaithful wife. Her people worshipped pagan gods, entered

into dubious alliances with foreign powers, and committed all manner of crimes and atrocities.

They ask for revelations from a piece of wood! A stick tells them what they want to know! They have left me. Like a woman who becomes a prostitute, they have given themselves to other gods.

Hos 4.12

Hosea went on loving his wife in spite of everything, just as God continued to love and care for the people of Israel despite their unfaithfulness.

A day would come when the people would turn to the Lord.

But the time will come when the people of Israel will once again turn to the Lord their God, and to a descendant of David their king. Then they will fear the Lord and will receive his good gifts. **Hos 3.5**

Music played an important part in religious ceremonies. Each of the figures in this contemporary bas-relief is playing an instrument.

I want your constant love, not your animal sacrifices. I would rather have my people know me than burn offerings to me.

Hos 6.6

The ancient civilisations of the Near and Middle East set great store by the love between man and wife, as can be seen in this Sumerian statue carved in gypsum dating from 2,500 B.C.

The end of the Northern Kingdom

(Read *2 Kings 17-18*)

The Assyrian empire at the end of the 8th c. B.C.

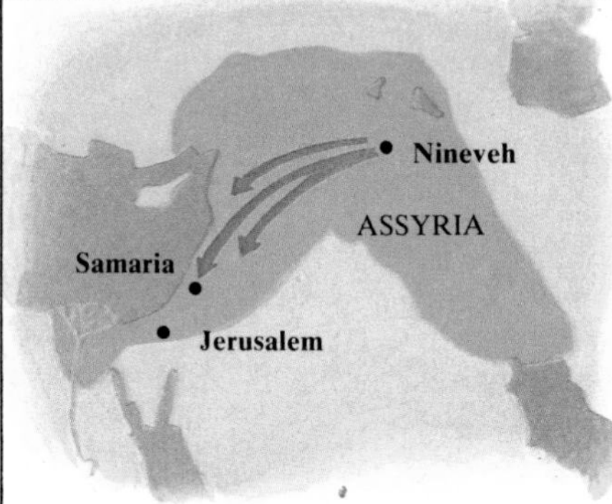

Vanquisher and vanquished

In ancient times when a city was taken by the enemy, the men were either killed, maimed or sold as slaves, while the women and children were taken prisoner. The walls of the city were pulled down, the houses plundered and burned.

However, if a city surrendered without offering any resistance, the enemy contented itself with taking some hostages. and demanding a large sum of tribute money.

By the year 745 Assyria had begun to take over the Middle East. The Assyrians were cruel warriors, equipped with an arsenal of chariots, battering rams and assault towers.

This powerful army was unleashed on the small kingdoms of Syria, Israel and Judah, which had allied themselves with Egypt. One after the other they succumbed to the invading army.

In 732 Syria fell to the Assyrians. Ten years later the Northern kingdom of Israel was under attack. The siege of Samaria, the capital, lasted three whole years. The victorious Assyrians, true to form, plundered and set fire to the city and massacred its inhabitants. As was

They are doomed!
They have left me and rebelled against me.
They will be destroyed.
Hos 7.13

Scene showing prisoners being deported, from a bas-relief in King Ashurbanipal's palace in Nineveh.

the custom, the King of Assyria, Sargon II, deported a number of Israelites and resettled Israel with Assyrian prisoners. In time these foreigners intermarried. It was from them that the people later known as the Samaritans were descended.

The Southern kingdom of Judah was spared by the Assyrians on this occasion because King Ahaz swore allegiance to the Assyrian king. Judah was not destroyed, but it did have to pay a very large sum in tribute. Many of those who escaped from the Northern kingdom made their way to Jerusalem, bringing with them their sacred books and religious customs.

The Assyrian warriors who invaded the kingdom of Israel were renowned for their ruthlessness and skill in battle.

The Southern Kingdom

(Read *Genesis 49*)

A lion, symbol of the kingdom of Judah
Judah is like a lion, killing his victim and returning to his den, stretching out and lying down. No one dares disturb him.
Gen 49.9

The Southern kingdom, Judah, was smaller than Israel. It was drier, less fertile and less prosperous. There were only 300,000 inhabitants in all as against 800,000 in the North. No more than 30,000 of these lived in Jerusalem, the capital.

However, this tiny kingdom was better able to fend off attack from the great Eastern powers than Israel. Judah was more efficiently governed; it had a stable monarchy. In the period between 930 B.C. when it was founded and 587 when Nebuchadnezzar finally destroyed it, there was not a single uprising. Solomon's temple was a great source of national pride to this small and vulnerable nation.

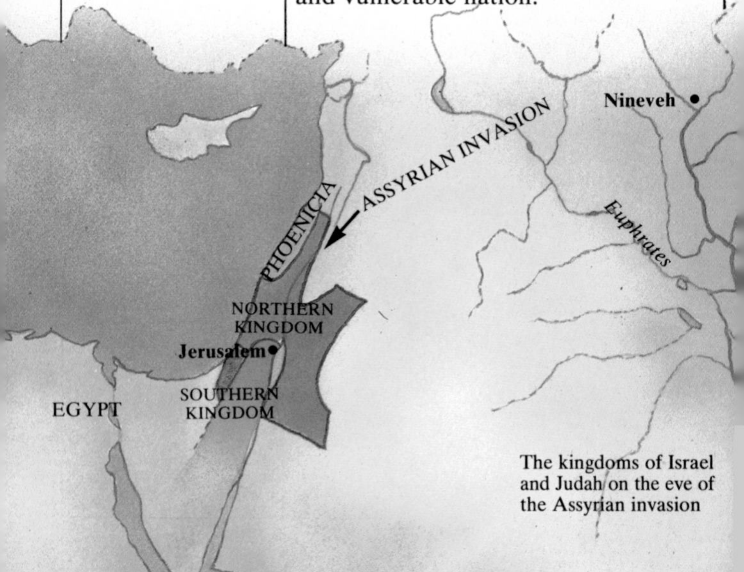

The kingdoms of Israel and Judah on the eve of the Assyrian invasion

Judah will hold the royal sceptre,
and his descendants will always rule.

Gen 49.10

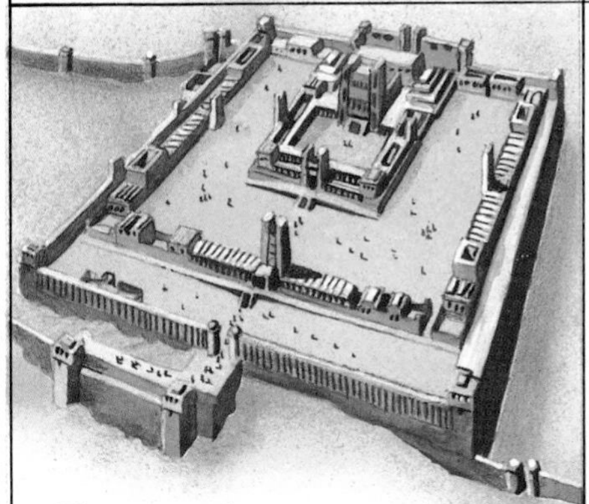

Solomon's temple was regarded as the supreme symbol of God's protecting presence amongst the people. Its destruction was all the more devastating as a result.

There was, however, much injustice in Judah as there was in Israel. As trade developed, a few privileged people grew rich at the expense of the poor. All too often governors and judges turned a blind eye to corruption. Some of the kings of Judah were weak-minded and unscrupulous. They lacked any firm religious conviction and practised idolatry. From time to time the prophets succeeded in stirring the conscience of the sovereign and the people. King Josiah (640-609), for instance, led a determined campaign against idol worship, and his reign was a period of intense religious reform.

From the 8th c. B.C. onwards, Judah was under threat first from Assyria and then from Babylon. In an attempt to maintain their independence the kings of Judah entered into alliances with each of the major powers in turn: Egypt, Assyria and Babylon.

The kings of Judah, descendants of David

Rehoboam 933-916
Abijah 915-913
Asa 912-871
Jehoshaphat 870-846
Yoram 848-841
Ahaziah 841
Athaliah 841-835
Joash 835-796
Amaziah 811-782
Uzziah 781-740
Jotham 740-735
Ahaz 735-716
Hezekiah 716-687
Manasseh 687-642
Amon 642-640
Josiah 640-609
Joahaz 609
Jehoiakim 609-598
Jehoiachin 598-597
Zedekiah 597-587

A prediction

Judah will hold the royal sceptre,
and his descendants will always rule.
Nations will bring him tribute and bow in obedience before him. **Gen 49.10**

Isaiah, prophet of hope

(Read *Isaiah 6-7*)

Jerusalem was under attack on two sides: from the Assyrian armies and from the joint forces of King Rezin and King Pekah.

In the year 745 B.C. the kingdom of Judah was in dire peril. The Assyrians were intent on conquering the Middle East, while King Rezin of Syria and King Pekah of Israel had joined forces to halt the Assyrian advance. The two kings asked King Ahaz of Judah to join them, but he refused. Incensed, King Rezin and King Pekah decided to replace Ahaz with a king of their choosing. They prepared to march on Jerusalem with their joint armies.

The people of Judah were panic-stricken. Was David's dynasty to disappear for ever? Could God have forgotten the promises made to David?

When you die and are buried with your ancestors, I will make one of your sons king and will keep his kingdom strong. . . . I will be his father, and he will be my son. . . . You will always have descendants, and I will make your kingdom last for ever. Your dynasty will never end. **2 Sam 7.12-16**

Isaiah's calling

Isaiah was about thirty years old. Five years previously he had had a vision which had changed his life. He had 'seen' God. The God of the Covenant, whom the people had deserted and betrayed, had appeared to Isaiah in

Those whom the Lord has rescued . . . will reach Jerusalem with gladness, singing and shouting for joy. They will be happy for ever.

Is 35.9-10

God appeared to Isaiah seated on a throne surrounded by a host of angels with six wings, as depicted in this 12th century Greek manuscript. Isaiah was called by God to be a prophet, to make the word of God known to the people.

great splendour and called him, saying, *'Whom shall I send? Who will be our messenger?'* Isaiah had replied unhesitatingly, *'I will go! Send me!'* Since then he had spoken out against all forms of injustice, crime and idolatry.

A message of trust

In the face of the impending invasion, Isaiah declared that Jerusalem had nothing to fear, her enemies would be wiped out, . . . *The Lord is announcing to all the earth: 'Tell the people of Jerusalem that the Lord is coming to save you'. . . . You will be called 'God's Holy People,' 'The People the Lord has Saved.' Jerusalem will be called 'The City That God Loves', 'The City That God Did Not Forsake.'* **Is 62.11-12**

The future Messiah

(Read *Isaiah 11*)

When Jerusalem was under heavy siege from the Assyrians, King Hezekiah sought to come to terms with King Sennacherib, the Assyrian king. This sculpture in the palace of Nineveh shows Hezekiah's envoys being received by Sennacherib.

King Ahaz was a great disappointment to Isaiah. Not only had he allowed idolatry to flourish throughout his kingdom, but he had also turned to the country's chief enemy, Assyria, for help in the crisis. *You have rejected the Lord, the holy*

God of Israel, and have turned your backs on him. **Is 1.4**

The prophet pinned all his hopes on Ahaz' son, the young Hezekiah, or Emmanuel, a symbolic name meaning 'God is with us'. In 716 B.C. Hezekiah came to power, and he undertook some extensive religious reforms. He tore down the pagan sanctuaries and smashed the Canaanite idols.

This Egyptian painting depicts the reign of the future Messiah, a reign of peace and harmony.

However, despite Isaiah's warnings, Hezekiah wavered in his dealings with other countries. He entered into conflicting alliances with the great rival powers and enemy nations of Assyria, Babylonia and Egypt, which put the kingdom of Judah in great danger on more than one occasion.

Hezekiah feared Jerusalem's water supply would be cut off if the Assyrians attacked. He ordered a tunnel to be dug from the Spring of Gihon outside the city walls to a reservoir inside the city. The tunnel was cut through 530 m (1750 ft) of solid limestone.

Messiah and king

King Hezekiah did not live up to Isaiah's expectations. However, the people continued to dream of a future descendant of King David who would be the perfect Messiah and King in the eyes of God.

. . . a new king will arise from among David's descendants. The spirit of the Lord will give him wisdom, and the knowledge and skill to rule his people. He will know the Lord's will and have reverence for him, and find pleasure in obeying him. He will not judge by appearance or hearsay; he will judge the poor fairly and defend the rights of the helpless. At his command the people will be punished, and evil persons will die. He will rule his people with justice and integrity. **Is 11.1-5**

* Isaiah, the father of David, should not be confused with Isaiah the prophet.

Wolves and sheep will live together in peace, and leopards will lie down with young goats. **Is 11.6**

Jeremiah, a much-abused prophet

(Read *Jeremiah 1; 17; 23; 31*)

Just as the almond tree blossoms in spring, so do God's deeds follow God's words.

. . . they are like a vine with no grapes, like a fig-tree with no figs . . .

Jer 8.13

Jeremiah used the image of a yoke to denote enslavement.

Much of Hezekiah's good work was undone by the two ungodly kings who succeeded him. They actively encouraged paganism and the country was in a state of moral and social decline. However, a new era began when the young King Josiah assumed power in 639 B.C. Josiah ordered the destruction of all pagan shrines and forbad idolatry on pain of death. He also campaigned fiercely against the corruption amongst heads of government, judges and priests and he took the over-privileged, the rich and the false prophets to task. His purges met with considerable opposition.

Jeremiah started his mission of prophet in an atmosphere of reform. Unlike Isaiah, Jeremiah was of a nervous disposition, whose acts of violence were undertaken in the name of God. He supported the efforts of King Josiah to give new faith to the people.

The Lord says, 'I will condemn the person who turns away from me and puts his trust in man, in the strength of mortal man. He is like a bush in the desert, which grows in the dry wilderness, on salty ground where nothing else grows. Nothing good ever happens to him.' **Jer 17.5-6**

Everyone, great and small, tries to make money dishonestly; even prophets and priests cheat the people. They act as if my people's wounds were only scratches. 'All is well,' they say, when all is not well. Were they ashamed be-

I will gather the rest of my people from the countries where I have scattered them, and I will bring them back to their homeland.

Jer 23.3

cause they did these disgusting things? No, they were not at all ashamed; they don't even know how to blush. And so they will fall as others have fallen; when I punish them, that will be the end of them. I, the Lord, have spoken.

Jer 6.13-15

The Lord said to me, 'I chose you before I gave you life, and before you were born I selected you to be a prophet to the nations.' I answered, 'Sovereign Lord, I don't know how to speak; I am too young.' But the Lord said to me, 'Do not say that you are too young, but go to the people I send you to, and tell them everything I command you to say. Do not be afraid of them, for I will be with you to protect you. I, the Lord, have spoken!' Then the Lord stretched out his hand, touched my lips, and said to me, 'Listen, I am giving you the words you must speak.'

Jer 1.4-10

Jeremiah laments the fate of Jerusalem. (14th c. A.D. manuscript)

Jeremiah's actions speak louder than words

(Read *Jeremiah 27; 28*)

The exiles leave Judah for Babylon (Bas-relief from Nineveh)

Jeremiah prophesied the eventual destruction of Babylon, which is depicted in this 13th c. A.D. rendering of the Apocalypse. On high, the heavenly kingdom. Below, Babylon in flames.

Worse was still to come. In 606 B.C. Nebuchadnezzar, the mighty king of Babylon, conquered Assyria and proceeded to invade Egypt and her allies. Egypt was defeated and Judah was forced to pay a heavy tribute.

Jeremiah advised King Jehoiakim not to resist the Babylonian giant, for he feared Judah would be crushed. The prophet was accused of being a subversive influence on the people. King Jehoiakim ignored his remonstrations and unwisely rebelled against the Babylonians. Nebuchadnezzar was not slow to respond. In 597 he laid siege to Jerusalem. The city surrendered. Jehoiakim's son Jehoiachin, and many of his advisers were deported to Babylonia.

The new king, Zedekiah, uncle to the former king, also chose to ignore the prophet's warnings. He was busy plotting a rebellion with some of the smaller adjacent states. Jeremiah protested, saying it was madness to try and rebel against such powerful masters. Far better, he insisted, to assume the yoke of oppression bravely, without further bloodshed.

To stress the urgency of his message, Jeremiah appeared before the King with

a wooden yoke tied to his shoulders, saying, *'Submit to the king of Babylonia. Serve him and his people, and you will live.'* **Jer 27.12**

A false prophet, Hananiah, took the yoke off Jeremiah's shoulders and broke it, but Jeremiah returned; saying, *'The Lord has said that you may be able to break a wooden yoke, but he will replace it with an iron yoke.'*

Jer 28.13

Instead of taking Jeremiah's predictions and warnings seriously, the people regarded him as a traitor. He was flung into prison, beaten, shackled, and even lowered down a well.

Once again, events proved him right. In 587 disaster struck. After a prolonged siege Nebuchadnezzar took Jerusalem. The city was burned to the ground. Some of the inhabitants were led away in chains. The kingdom of Judah was no more. Left behind in the ruins of the devastated city, Jeremiah sounded a note of hope. All was not over.

The exiles leave Jerusalem on their way to Babylonia.

Exile in Babylon

(Read *Psalm 137; Jeremiah 39*)

In ancient times it was customary to blind and brand prisoners. A captive of the Assyrian king, Ashurbanipal, receives this treatment.

The destruction of Jerusalem in 587 B.C. was a catastrophe. The city was plundered and burnt to the ground, the walls and temple destroyed. Many of the people were massacred; all the king's sons were put to death.

For many of the nation's leaders, defeat meant exile in Babylonia as it had done for others ten years previously. Amongst those taken prisoner was Zedekiah, the last of the kings of Judah. He was a blind man now, his eyes put out by his captors. Babylon was 1300 km (over 800 miles) from Jerusalem. A long and exhausting journey on foot.

This bull is one of many relief figures executed in glazed tiles decorating the Ishtar gate of Babylon.

In Babylon the prisoners were granted some small degree of freedom. They had to provide the statutory work-force, navvying, building and working the land, but they were allowed to build their own homes, grow their own crops, assemble and worship as they pleased.

By the rivers of Babylon we sat down;
there we wept when we remembered
Zion.
On the willows nearby we hung up our

harps. Those who captured us told us to sing. . . . 'Sing us a song about Zion.' 'How can we sing a song to the Lord in a foreign land?' **Ps 137**

After the fall of Judah, even the most pious exiles were troubled by doubts. The Promised Land had fallen into pagan hands. Did that mean God had turned against the children of Israel? The temple, God's dwelling-place amongst them, lay in ruins. Had God deserted them? The dynasty established by David was at an end. Would the Lord keep his promises now?

Worse still, if Judah had fallen to the Babylonians, perhaps their Babylonian god Marduk was more powerful than the Lord of the Covenant. Perhaps their God was not the one and only God after all?

Deportation scene sculpted on the walls of the palace of Nineveh (7th c. B.C.). The Exile was God's way of punishing the people for their lack of faith, their corrupt ways and their failure to listen to the prophets' warnings.

A model of the city of Babylon as it may have appeared during the reign of Nebuchadnezzar.

Ezekiel, prophet and visionary

(Read *Ezekiel 1; 2; 3; 11; 34; 36; 47*)

The prophet Ezekiel (11th century miniature from the Palatine Bible)

The captives in exile were close to despair. If, as it appeared, their own God had abandoned them, what had they to lose by transferring their allegiance to Marduk, the god of their captors?

Amongst the exiles there was, however, a man of faith who was able to restore the people's trust and confidence. This was Ezekiel, a priest who had been sent to Babylon with the first exiles in 597 B.C. He became the exiled community's prophet.

Ezekiel assured the disillusioned and despairing exiles that their God had not deserted them. He too had travelled the road to Babylonia and shared their plight as an outcast in a foreign land.

The prophet reminded them that during the flight from Egypt and the wandering in the wilderness (page 172) God had appeared to the Israelites in a pillar of cloud. In a series of visions Ezekiel described God's presence amongst them as a cloud arising from the ruins of the burning temple in Jerusalem, and making its way to Babylon. There the cloud had come to rest over the banks of the Euphrates where the exiles had their quarters. When the time came it would return with them in triumph to Jerusalem to take up residence once more in a new temple, which would be raised from the ruins.

Ezekiel's startling prophecies revived the people's faith. Repeatedly he

Each new year a huge procession wound its way through the streets of Babylon. This was in celebration of the many feats of the Babylonian god, Marduk, who was supposed to have created the world.

assured them that the Babylonian god Marduk was nothing but an idol and that their own God was the only true God, the God of Heaven and Earth and all things living. He also foretold, in his famous vision of the dried bones coming to life, the exiles' ultimate return to Israel and the re-birth of the nation of Israel.

I felt the powerful presence of the Lord, and his spirit took me and set me down in a valley where the ground was covered with bones. He led me all round the valley, and I could see that there were very many bones and that they were very dry. He said to me, 'Mortal man, can these bones come back to life?' I replied, 'Sovereign Lord, only you can answer that!'

He said, 'Prophesy to the bones. Tell these dry bones to listen to the word of the Lord.' So I prophesied as I had been told. Breath entered the bodies, and they came to life and stood up. There were enough of them to form an army. God said to me, 'Mortal man, the people of Israel are like these bones. They say that they are dried up, without any hope and with no future. So prophesy to my people Israel and tell them that I, the Sovereign Lord, am going to open their graves. I am going to take them out and bring them back to the land of Israel. When I open the graves where my people are buried and bring them out, they will know that I am the Lord.'

Is 37.1-4, 10-13

Ezekiel's vision of the resurrection of the dry bones (11th century Catalonian Bible)

The god Marduk, chief god of Babylon

The Babylonian gods
Supreme amongst the gods were the sky god, Anu, and his wife Ishtar, goddess of war and love.
Anu's son Enlil, the god of the wind, was the king of the gods.
Enki was master of the earth, of water and wisdom.
Enki's son was Marduk, the god of Babylon.

The return of the exiles

(Read *Ezra 1*)

A Persian (right) and a Mede awaiting an audience with the king. (Bas-relief from Persepolis)

In 538 the mighty and supposedly impregnable city of Babylon fell to Cyrus, King of the Medes and Persians. Cyrus' conquest was welcomed by those living in captivity. Here was a king, who, unlike the Babylonians and the Assyrians, showed remarkable tolerance and understanding towards his new subjects. It was his policy to send captive exiles home to their own countries.

This clay cylinder discovered in Babylon contained a scroll describing the edict issued by Cyrus, granting the exiles their freedom.

In 536 Cyrus issued a decree authorising the Jews to return to Jerusalem and to rebuild the temple. He gave them money and restored to them some of the items stolen from the temple in 587 B.C.

There was great rejoicing at the news. The exiles saw their liberation as a second exodus. A first party of some one hundred and fifty thousand people set forth immediately for Jerusalem. The youngest of them had never set eyes on the Promised Land. *Then the heads of the clans of the tribes of Judah and Benjamin, the priests and Levites, and everyone else whose heart God had moved got ready to go and rebuild the Lord's Temple in Jerusalem. All their*

A Persian coin brought back to Jerusalem by the exiles

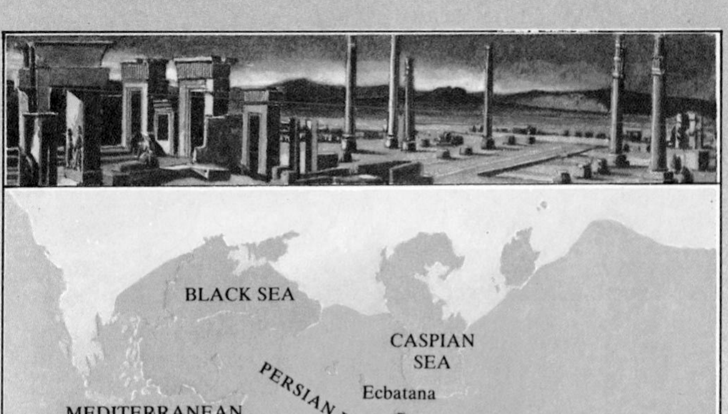

neighbours helped by giving them many things . . . **Ezra 1.5**

Other parties of exiles followed, but a certain number of exiles stayed where they were on Babylonian soil.

When the Lord brought us back to
Jerusalem, it was like a dream!
How we laughed, how we sang for joy!
Then the other nations said about us,
'The Lord did great things for them.' . . .
Lord, make us prosperous again,
just as the rain brings water back to dry
river-beds.
Let those who wept as they sowed their
seed, gather the harvest with joy!
Those who wept as they went out
carrying the seed
will come back singing for joy,
as they bring in the harvest. **Ps 126**

At the top of the page, Persepolis, founded by the Persian king, Darius I.

Cyrus was from distant Anshan. In 550 B.C. he took on the all-powerful Medes and conquered the city of Ecbatana. People were slow to realise what a threat he posed. Within a few years the Persian prince had conquered the vast empire of the Medes and all of Mesopotamia.

The rebuilding of the temple

(Read *Ezra 3-6*)

The Persian king Darius gave the exiles his support.

Two years after their return to Jerusalem the exiles set about rebuilding the temple of God. The Samaritans offered assistance, claiming that they too worshipped the same God. The Jews firmly refused.

Incensed, the Samaritans determined to stop the reconstruction work. They enlisted the support of the Persian governor of Samaria, and work on the temple stopped for fifteen years.

Distress and difficulties

Despondency spread amongst the repatriated exiles. They were beset on all sides by difficulties of one sort or another. Accommodation and funds were scarce, the drought was severe and crops poor.

Then the people of Israel — the priests, the Levites, and all the others who had returned from exile — joyfully dedicated the temple.

Ezra 6.16

In 520 the people were once more stirred into action by two prophets, Haggai and Zechariah, and by the arrival of a second party of returning exiles, the bearers of good news. The new Persian king, Darius, had once more authorised the rebuilding of the temple and would provide funds for its completion. *This is to be done so that they can offer sacrifices that are acceptable to the God of Heaven. . . .* Work on the temple began again and it was completed in the year 515 B.C.

The dedication of the temple

The second temple had none of the splendour and magnificence of Solomon's temple, but it was nonetheless a symbol of the Jewish people's return to the land of their forefathers. The dedication of the temple was celebrated at the Passover by the exiles and all who were still true to their faith.

The sacrifices were eaten by all the Israelites who had returned from exile and by all those who had given up the pagan ways of the other people who were living in the land and who had come to worship the Lord God of Israel. For seven days they joyfully celebrated the Festival of Unleavened Bread. They were full of joy because the Lord had made the emperor of Assyria favourable to them, so that he supported them in their work of rebuilding the Temple of the God of Israel.

Ezra 6.21-22

The Samaritans were descended from colonists settled by the Assyrians in Samaria after the fall of the Northern kingdom in the 8th c. B.C. They worshipped the God of Israel, but still retained certain non-Jewish rituals associated with their former religion.

Rebuilding the walls of Jerusalem

(Read *Nehemiah 2-4*)

In 445 B.C., very nearly a hundred years after the return from exile, much of Jerusalem still lay in ruins: an impenetrable mass of rubble. The city walls needed rebuilding, but money was scarce and the governor of Samaria was opposed to the scheme.

Nehemiah, a trusted Jewish official at the Persian court, was moved to tears when he heard of the wretched plight of his fellow Jews. After months of fasting and prayer, he asked the Persian king, Artaxerxes, for permission to go to Jerusalem and undertake the rebuilding of the city walls himself.

The king gave Nehemiah the money to carry out the task.

The inhabitants of Jerusalem set to with a will, but were much handicapped in their work by the Samaritans who taunted and threatened them. Nehemiah spurred his fellow citizens on. He organised a twenty-four hour guard to patrol the walls. The men laboured from dawn till dusk, sleeping fully clothed, swords to hand. Finally the Samaritans left them in peace.

The wall and the gates were completed after fifty-two days of gruelling labour. A great celebration began, which was attended by Jews from far and wide.

The dedication of the city walls was celebrated amidst singing and the playing of cymbals, harps and lyres.

Break into shouts of joy, you ruins of Jerusalem! The Lord will rescue his city and comfort his people.
Is 52.9

Poems of the Servant of God

(Read *Isaiah 49, 50, 52 and 53*)

In Hebrew the word which describes the loving tenderness of God is the same as the word for a pregnant woman's womb, which contains the unborn child.
The Hebrew people saw God as both male and female, Father and Mother.

Right hand page: The servant of God in his glory (illustration from a 14th c. French manuscript).

Yahweh's people had known the misery of deportation and captivity. This is reflected in the bowed figures of this bas-relief from the palace in Nineveh.

These poems are found in the Book of Isaiah, but they were written long after the return from exile when the people were beset with problems: loss of political freedom and status, mass poverty, a scarcity of prophets. Why was there so much suffering? Had the Lord forgotten the promises made to Abraham and David? An unknown prophet examines these issues in an imaginary three-way conversation between God, the faithful people and the unbelievers.

The people Before I was born, the Lord chose me and appointed me to be his servant. . . . He said to me, 'Israel, you are my servant; because of you, people will praise me.' I said, 'I have worked, but how hopeless it is! I have used up my strength, but have accomplished nothing. Yet I can trust the Lord to defend my cause.'

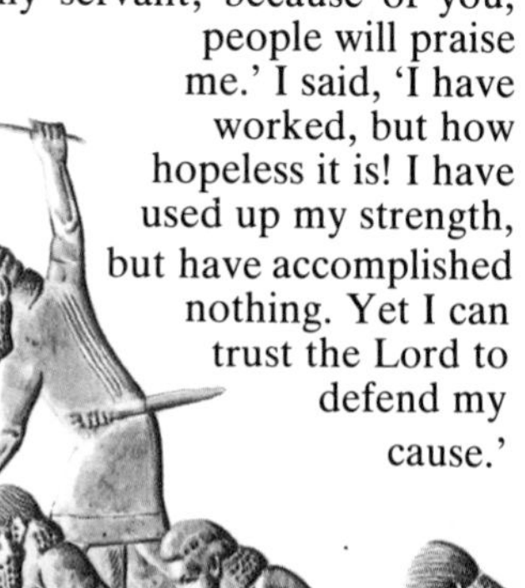

It was the will of the Lord that his servant should grow like a plant taking root in dry ground.

Is 53.2

God Can a woman forget . . . and not love the child she bore? Even if a mother should forget her child, I will never forget you. . . . I have written your name on the palms of my hands.

The people The Lord has given me understanding, and I have not rebelled or turned away from him. I bared my back to those who beat me.

God My servant will succeed in his task; he will be highly honoured. Many people were shocked when they saw him . . . But now many nations will marvel at him, and kings will be speechless with amazement.

The unbelievers Who could have seen the Lord's hand in this? It was the will of the Lord that his servant should grow like a plant taking root in dry ground. He had no dignity or beauty to make us take notice of him. There was nothing attractive about him, nothing that would draw us to him. We despised and rejected him; he endured suffering and pain. But he endured the suffering that should have been ours, the pain that we should have borne. All the while we thought that his suffering was punishment sent by God. We are healed by the punishment he suffered, made whole by the blows he received.

God My devoted servant, with whom I am well pleased, will bear the punishment of many and for his sake I will forgive them. And so I will give him a place of honour, a place among great and powerful men.

The reading of the Law

(Read *Ezra 7-10; Nehemiah 8*)

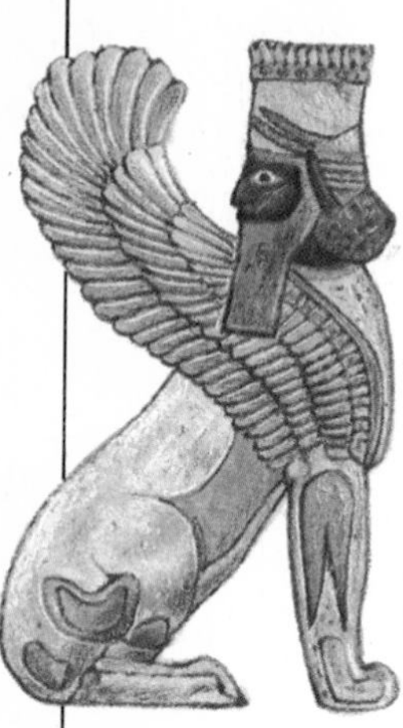

Under Persian rule the Jewish Law was reinstated in Jerusalem

At the beginning of the 4th century B.C. Judaea, the area round Jerusalem, was a Jewish state under Persian rule. Like other Persian colonies it was self-governing with its own laws and customs.

The Persians maintained that the best way of ensuring peace amongst their colonies was to grant them this degree of freedom. Inspectors were sent round to each country in turn to report on local government affairs.

Ezra, priest and scholar

In 398 B.C. King Artaxerxes II appointed a Jewish scribe by the name of Ezra to go to Jerusalem. Ezra was a priest and scholar, well-versed in Jewish Law. He was also a man of authority:

Ezra had devoted his life to studying the Law of the Lord, to practising it, and to teaching all its laws and regulations to the people of Israel.

Ezra 7.10

Ezra was instructed to report on the state of affairs in Jerusalem, and above all, to see how closely the people were following the Law of the Covenant.

To his dismay Ezra discovered that the commandments were not being kept. Idolatry and injustice, the twin evils, were rampant . . . *the people, the priests and the Levites had not kept themselves separate from the people in the neighbouring countries. . . . They were doing the same disgusting things that those people did. Jewish men were*

From the first day of the festival to the last they read a part of God's Law every day. They celebrated for seven days.
Neh 8.18

marrying foreign women, and so God's holy people had become contaminated. The leaders and officials were the chief offenders. **Ezra 9.1-2**

Ezra was swift to take action when he discovered how far the people had strayed from the Mosaic Law. He forbad any more foreign marriages.

He gathered all the Jews together, both young and old, for a public reading of the Law. *So Ezra brought it to the place where the people had gathered – men, women, and the children who were old enough to understand. There in the square by the gate he read the Law to them from dawn until noon, and they all listened attentively.* **Neh 8.2-3**

Ezra then ordered a feast: *So all the people went home and ate and drank joyfully and shared what they had with others, because they understood what had been read to them.* **Neh 8.12**

You, Ezra, using the wisdom which your God has given you . . . **Ezra 7.25**

Teaching of the Law in a Jewish school in the Middle Ages

Jonah and the whale

(Read *Jonah 1-4*)

In the 4th century B.C., after the reforms introduced by Ezra, the Jews were tempted to turn in on themselves. They wanted to avoid all contact or intermarriage with other pagan nations for fear of once again succumbing to idolatry. They soon came to think that God was only concerned with the Jews, and that the rest of the world was not worth bothering about. The story of Jonah has a moral to it. The author gently points out that God loves Jews and heathens alike.

Jonah is thrown into the sea and swallowed by a large fish. (From a 15th century miniature.)

The Lord spoke to Jonah saying, *Go to Nineveh, that great city, and speak out against it; I am aware how wicked its people are.* **Jon 1.2**

Jonah, however, set out in the opposite direction to get away from the Lord.

The Lord sent a raging storm which threatened to destroy the ship and crew. The terrified sailors saw the storm as a punishment and tried to find out what had angered their gods. They discovered that Jonah was to blame. He admitted that he had disobeyed the Lord his God, and insisted they throw him into the sea. The storm was getting worse by the minute. Reluctantly the sailors did as he asked. The storm ceased at once.

The Lord sent a huge fish which swallowed Jonah and three days later spewed him up on the beach.

Once again the Lord asked him to go to Nineveh and to implore the people to change their wicked ways. Jonah began to walk through the city proclaiming aloud as he went, *In forty days Nineveh will be destroyed.* **Jon 3.4**

It took three days to walk through the city of Nineveh. At the end of the first day the people had not only heard God's message, they had already taken it to heart.

The King issued precise instructions: every man, woman and beast must fast and put on sackcloth as a sign of repentance. They must all pray

Then the Lord ordered the fish to spew Jonah up on the beach, and it did.
Jon 2.10

earnestly to God and abstain from sin. Perhaps then God would take pity on them and not punish them.

God saw that the people had genuinely repented of their wicked ways, and decided not to punish them. Jonah was most put out. *So he prayed, 'Lord, didn't I say before I left home that this is just what you would do? That's why I did my best to run away to Spain! I knew that you are a loving and merciful God, always patient, always kind, and always ready to change your mind and not punish. Now, Lord, let me die. I am better off dead than alive.'*
Jon 4.2-3

Jonah stalked out of the city in high dudgeon and sat down all alone. The sun was beating down mercilessly. God made a plant grow up, so that Jonah was sitting in the shade of it. The following day, however, the plant died, and Jonah, faint from the heat of the sun, wished he were dead. But God said to him, *'This plant grew up in one night and disappeared the next; you didn't do anything for it, and you didn't make it grow – yet you feel sorry for it! How much more, then, should I have pity on Nineveh, that great city. After all, it has more than 120,000 innocent children in it, as well as many animals!'*
Jon 4.10-11

The city of Nineveh lay on the East bank of the Tigris.
It was founded five thousand years before Christ. Sennacherib made Nineveh the capital of the vast Assyrian empire. It was destroyed by the Babylonians in 612 B.C.

Job

(Read *Job 1-3; 10; 19; 42*)

The Book of Job dates from the 5th and 6th centuries B.C. It is concerned with the suffering of innocent people. In the Old Testament view, God rewarded the righteous and punished the wicked. Why, then, did God allow innocent people to suffer? The author of the Book of Job examines the problem in the form of a story and a series of poems, and he tries to come up with some answers.

Job, before all his afflictions

Job was a good and upright man who loved God. He was a fortunate man, blessed with many children and large flocks and herds.

One day, Satan, the arch-enemy of mankind, said to God, *'Would Job worship you if he got nothing out of it? . . . You bless everything he does, . . . but now suppose you take away everything he has – he will curse you to your face!'* God agreed to let Satan test Job.

From one day to the next Job lost all he had. His entire herd was stolen, his children were killed when a house fell on top of them, and he himself was covered from top to toe in bleeding sores. Nobody would go near him for fear of being infected. He went and sat all alone near the town rubbish heap,

pitifully scratching at his sores with a piece of broken pottery.

His wife urged him to curse God. Three friends came to visit him. Job protested bitterly to God. Why should he, an innocent man, suffer so? His friends scolded him and accused him of insulting God. Job continued to call on God – who now seemed remote, and unjust.

Finally, God spoke to Job: 'Why do you accuse me unjustly? How could I – I who made the earth in all its beauty and splendour, the very earth you tread – how could I wish mankind ill?'

Job replied, 'I spoke foolishly and in ignorance of things I did not understand. Now I know that you are the friend and not the enemy of all mankind.'

God restored Job to health and prosperity and gave him many more children and possessions and a long life in which to enjoy them.

All his possessions were destroyed or scattered.

Left hand page: Satan asking God's permission to put Job to the test (15th c. Book of Hours).

Three of Job's friends . . . when they heard how much Job had been suffering, . . . decided to go and comfort him.
Job 2.11

Then, after Job had prayed for his three friends, the Lord made him prosperous again and gave him twice as much as he had had before. **Job 42.10**

Ruth
the girl from Moab

(Read *Ruth 1-4*)

French 14th century miniature depicting Ruth and Boaz.

After she had left to go on picking up corn, Boaz ordered the workers, 'Let her pick it up even where the bundles are lying, and don't say anything to stop her.'
Ruth 2.15-16

This delightful tale probably dates from the 4th c. B.C. Marriage to a foreigner was against the law, but a Jewish story-teller points out that King David himself was descended from a foreigner: Ruth, the girl from Moab.

In the time of the Judges there was a famine in Bethlehem. A man called Elimelech and his wife Naomi fled to the country of Moab to escape starvation. Their two sons both married Moabite girls: Orpah and Ruth. First Elimelech and then his two sons died, leaving the women all alone.

Naomi decided to return to Bethlehem. She begged her daughters-in-law to return to their own homes. But Ruth refused to leave Naomi. *'Wherever you go, I will go. Your people will be my people, and your God will be my God.'* **Ruth 1.16-17**

They arrived in Bethlehem at the time of the barley harvest. By law,

foreigners, poor people and widows were allowed to pick up the left-over corn at harvest-time. Ruth went to glean in a field belonging to Boaz, who was, unbeknownst to her, a relative of her dead father-in-law, Elimelech. When he heard who Ruth was, Boaz asked his workers to look after her.

Naomi realised that Boaz could marry Ruth. By Jewish law if a man died childless one of his relatives was obliged to marry his widow in order to provide an heir to carry on the dead man's name. Naomi told Ruth to go to Boaz' field at nightfall and to lie down at his feet once he was asleep.

Ruth did as Naomi had told her. Boaz awoke in the night, startled to find Ruth there, whereupon Ruth asked him if, as a close relative, he would marry her.

Boaz willingly agreed and the couple were married. Their son Obed was the father of Jesse, who was David's father.

Harvest-time in ancient Egypt

At meal-time Boaz said to Ruth, 'Come and have a piece of bread, and dip it in the sauce.' So she sat with the workers, and Boaz passed some roasted grain to her.

Ruth 2.14

13th century miniature

The Psalms

(Read *Psalms 4; 8; 88*)

David is said to have invented special musical instruments to which the Psalms were sung, in order to distinguish them from ordinary hymns. In this 15th century A.D. Italian fresco from a cathedral in Venetia, we can imagine him praising the wonders of creation.

The Psalms are a collection of prayers, used at different times and on different occasions by the people of Israel to express thanksgiving, joy, sorrow, despair and urgent need. They are an expression of the whole range of human experience and of the religious life of Israel – rooted in time and yet timeless.

After the return from Exile a hundred and fifty of these psalms were collected together in a book called the Psalter.

Psalm of praise

O Lord, our Lord, your greatness is seen in all the world! Your praise reaches up to the heavens; . . . When I look at the sky, which you have made, at the moon and the stars, which you set in their places – what is man, that you think of him; mere man, that you care for him? Yet you made him inferior only to yourself; you crowned him with glory and honour. You appointed him ruler over everything you made; you placed him over all creation: sheep and cattle, and the wild animals too; the birds and the fish and the creatures in the seas.

Ps 8

A cry for help

Lord God, my saviour, I cry out all day, and at night I come before you. Hear my prayer; listen to my cry for help! . . .

Lord, I call to you for help; every morning I pray to you. Why do you reject me, Lord? Why do you turn away

from me? Ever since I was young, I have suffered and been near death; I am worn out from the burden of your punishments. Your furious anger crushes me; your terrible attacks destroy me. All day long they surround me like a flood; they close in on me from every side. You have made even my closest friends abandon me, and darkness is my only companion.

Ps 88

When I lie down,
I go to sleep in peace;
you alone, O Lord,
keep me perfectly
safe. **Ps 4.8**

The Song of Songs

(Read *Song of Songs 2; 5; 8*)

This book is a series of poems on the theme of love between a man and a woman. Although attributed to Solomon, the poems were in fact written much later, in the 5th and 6th centuries B.C. They were sung at the Festival of the Passover and at weddings. The Jews regarded the Song of Songs as a symbol of the love between God and the people of Israel.

The Woman
I hear my lover's voice.
He comes running over the mountains,
racing across the hills to me.
My lover is like a gazelle,
like a young stag.
There he stands beside the wall.
He looks in through the window and
glances through the lattice.
My lover speaks to me.

The Man
Come then, my love;
my darling, come with me.
The winter is over;
the rains have stopped;
In the countryside the flowers are in bloom.
This is the time for singing;
the song of the doves is heard in the fields.

Figs are beginning to ripen;
the air is fragrant with
blossoming vines.
Come then, my love;
my darling, come with me.
You are like a dove that hides
in the crevice of a rock.
Let me see your lovely face
and hear your enchanting voice.

Song 2.8-14

The *Song of Songs,* like the love songs of ancient Egypt, are full of images of the countryside in Spring. These images reflect the lovers' feelings for each other.

The Woman

Love is as powerful as death;
passion is as strong as death itself.
It bursts into flame
and burns like a raging fire.
Water cannot put it out;
no flood can drown it.

Song 8.6

Proverbs

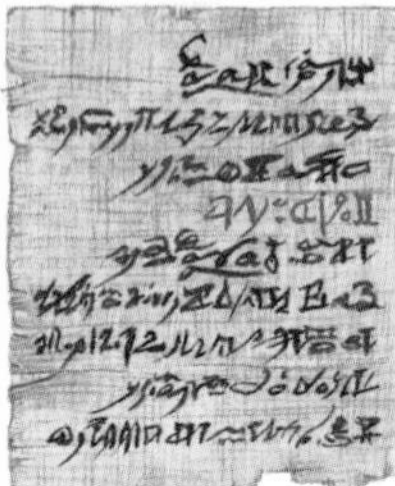

The Teaching of Amenemope was a collection of Egyptian wise sayings similar to the biblical proverbs. (10th c. B.C. papyrus)

The Book of Proverbs was completed after the return from Exile in the 4th and 5th centuries B.C.

It is a collection of wise sayings, a sort of textbook for people of all ages, setting out what is right and wrong. All human wisdom is based on reverence for God and obedience to God's Law. The Proverbs express this in a series of short, sharp phrases and scenes covering every aspect of everyday life: human relationships, work, home, religion, justice.

The meeting of Wisdom and the madman. 13th c. manuscript.

Never get a lazy man to do something for you; he will be as irritating as vinegar on your teeth or smoke in your eyes. **Prov 10.26**

It is better to be patient than powerful. It is better to win control over yourself than over whole cities. **Prov 16.32**

Help your brother and he will protect you like a strong city wall, but if you quarrel with him, he will close his doors to you. **Prov 18.19**

Don't take advantage of the poor just because you can; don't take advantage of those who stand helpless in court. **Prov 22.22**

Beauty in a woman without good judgement is like a gold ring in a pig's snout. **Prov 11.22**

Finally hearing good news from a distant land is like a drink of cold water when you are dry and thirsty. **Prov 25.25**

Getting involved in an argument that is none of your business is like going down the street and grabbing a dog by the ears. **Prov 26.17**

Insincere talk that hides what you are really thinking is like a fine glaze on a cheap clay pot. **Prov 26.23**

Even if you beat a fool until he's half dead, you still can't beat his foolishness out of him. **Prov 27.22**

Rich people always think they are wise, but a poor person who has insight into character knows better. **Prov 28.11**

Egyptian proverb
When a quarrel is brewing, close the doors of your heart on your anger.

Babylonian proverbs
In woman lies the future of man.

A door turns on its hinges, and an idle man turns in his bed.

Whosoever knows how to listen, will know how to speak.

He who has money in plenty may well be happy, but he who has nothing sleeps easy.

A historic turning point

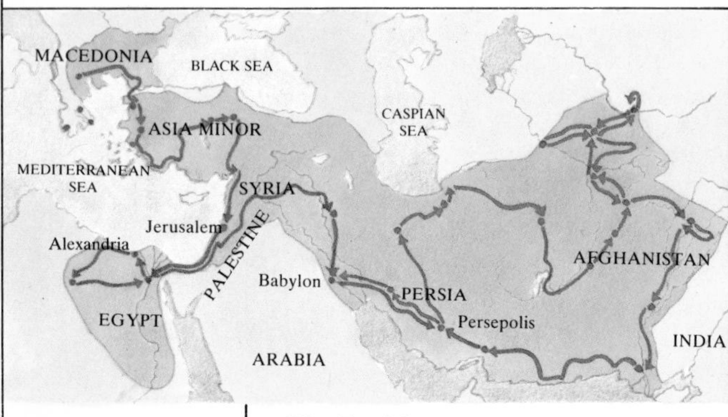

The Greek empire: the route followed by Alexander.

An Alexandrian coin. Alexander the Great's lighthouse was one of the seven wonders of the world.

The Jewish community in Judaea had been living under Persian rule since the return from Exile in 536 B.C.

In 332 B.C. there was a change of ruler. The Macedonian king, Alexander, conquered the entire Persian empire in the space of ten years. He extended it to include Greece, Egypt and India. Wherever he went, Alexander the Great built cities in the Greek style, with theatres, stadiums and baths. The most important of these was the city of Alexandria in Egypt, which was named after him.

Alexander imposed the customs, art, way of thinking, language and religion of the Greek people on the countries that came under his rule. This strong Greek influence revolutionised life within the occupied countries.

Darius III, King of Persia, under attack from Alexander the Great

After Alexander the Great's death, the empire was divided into three separate kingdoms: Egypt, Syria and Greece. Jerusalem and Judaea were merged first with Egypt, and then with Syria.

Many important changes took place amongst the Jewish people during this period. As they grew in number, many began to emigrate to Babylonia, Egypt, Syria, Asia Minor and as far afield as the Black Sea. There they either settled in existing Jewish communities or founded new ones. One of the largest and most thriving communities was Alexandria .

In Jerusalem the Jewish community was divided. Some Jews had adopted the traditions, customs, language and life-style of their Greek masters wholeheartedly, abandoning many of the traditional Jewish customs, such as circumcision. Others, the Hassidim (or faithful), rejected anything non-Jewish as a threat to their faith.

Ill-feeling and tension between these rival factions built up over the years, and came to a head in 170 B.C.

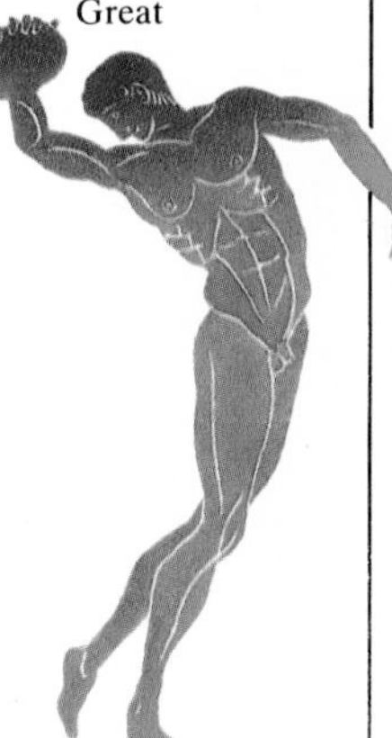

Discus thrower

A Greek hunter returning home with his catch.

Flute player providing entertainment in a Greek household.

Translation of the Bible into Greek

Alexandria in the time of Ptolemy, from a 15th century Florentine miniature.

A young Greek scholar teaching Greek.

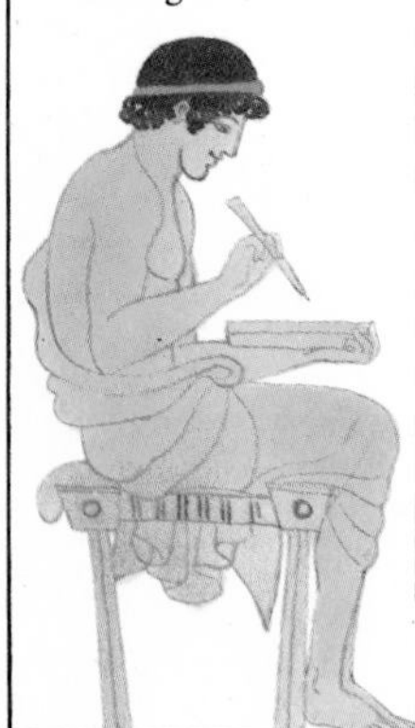

Greek Alphabet

Α	Β	Γ	Δ	Ε	Ζ
Alpha	Beta	Gamma	Delta	Epsilon	Zeta
a	**b**	**g**	**d**	**e, é**	**z**
Η	Θ	Ι	Κ	Λ	Μ
Eta	Theta	Iota	Kappa	Lambda	Mu
è	**th**	**i**	**c, k**	**l**	**m**
Ν	Ξ	Ο	Π	Ρ	Σ
Nu	Xi	Omicron	Pi	Rho	Sigma
n	**x**	**o**	**p**	**r, rh**	**s**
Τ	Υ	Φ	Χ	Ψ	Ω
Tau	Upsilon	Phi	Chi	Psi	Omega
t	**y, u**	**ph**	**kh**	**ps**	**ô**

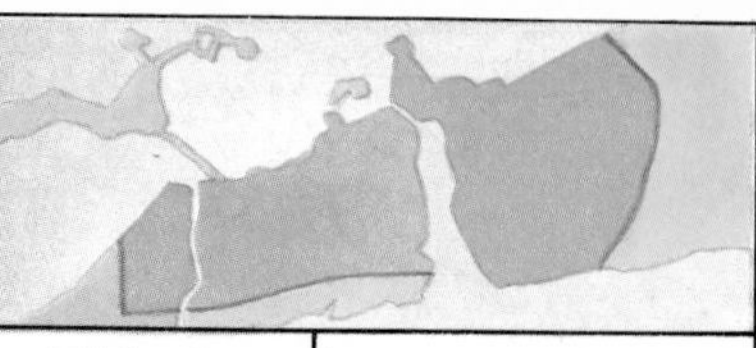

The translation of the Bible from Hebrew into Greek took place in Alexandria between 250 and 150 B.C. By this time there was a pressing need for a Greek version of the Bible amongst the Jews in Alexandria. The majority spoke only Greek, and did not understand Hebrew. There were also increasing numbers of non-Jewish believers who had converted to the Jewish faith. All these people would benefit from a Greek translation of the Scriptures.

However, some Hebrew-speaking Jews in Jerusalem objected. They accused the translators in Alexandria of falsifying the text. In their defence the Jews in Alexandria allowed a rumour, which became known as the letter of Aristeas, to circulate in the year 80 B.C. According to this letter, in the third century B.C., at the request of Ptolemy II, seventy-two Rabbis from Jerusalem had been shut up in separate cells on the island of Poros. They were each given seventy-two days in which to produce a full translation of the Bible. At the end of the allotted time the translations had turned out to be identical. How then could there be any doubt that the translation was authentic, indeed, divinely inspired?

This translation is called the Septuagint (meaning seventy) because of the seventy-two translators and the seventy-two days it took to complete.

The town of Alexandria, the great centre of Hellenistic culture, on the Nile delta.

The Bible's message was a universal one, so it was natural enough for each nation to want its own translation in time. A great many translations were made in the 2nd c. A.D. and the invention of printing by Gutenberg in the 15th century meant copies could be made in large numbers. In 1980 the Bible was translated into 275 languages. The number of copies sold the world over for that year alone exceeded 9 million.

Symbols of the Jewish faith painted in gold on a glass background (from 4th century catacombs).

Persecution under Antiochus

(Read *Maccabees*)

Coin showing head of Antiochus IV Epiphanes (215-163 B.C.)

The Sadducees
They were extremely conservative in religious matters. They were the allies of the Maccabees' descendants, powerful both in politics and religion.

In 167 B.C. Judaea was under Syrian rule. The king of Syria was Antiochus. He was determined to wipe out the Jewish religion altogether. He began attacking certain cherished Jewish practices. He forbad the keeping of the Sabbath and circumcision. He ordered the people to eat pork, and to offer sacrifices to Greek gods.

Antiochus then proceeded to desecrate the temple. He set up a statue of Zeus in the Holy of Holies and held wild pagan celebrations and orgies within the temple walls.

Faced with this persecution, some Jews gave in to the King's demands, some were ready to die for their faith, while others decided to take matters into their own hands. They rose in armed rebellion under the leadership of Judas Maccabeus and his brothers.

In 164 Judas and his men recovered the temple, purified it and consecrated it anew to the worship of God.

Divinities from Greek mythology: the goddess Athena emerges from the skull of Zeus, which Hephaestus, the god of fire and metals, cleaves with an axe.

However, victory was not yet theirs. Judas was killed fighting. It was another two years before his brothers Jonathan and Simon finally succeeded in getting the new Syrian king to sign a peace treaty.

From then on the men who had so bravely defended the Jewish faith began to devote all their time and energy to power-politics. They were appointed high priests and set about conquering neighbouring territory in order to enlarge the province of Judaea.

Many who had supported the brothers during the persecution became disillusioned. Three rival religious groups emerged: the Pharisees, the Essenes and the Sadducees.

In 104 B.C. a descendant of the Maccabees declared himself King, but his dynasty came to an end when the Romans appeared on the scene in 63 B.C.

The Pharisees
The word means 'apart'. Their chief preoccupation was with spiritual matters and observance of the Law.
They reproached the Maccabees' successors for being too involved in politics.

The Essenes
These were extremely devout Pharisees, who withdrew to live in communities in the desert. One of these communities was at Qumran, where the Dead Sea Scrolls were found.

Below:
Athena, the warrior goddess of wisdom, and Poseidon, god of the sea, dispute over Athens.

Hermes

The Book of Daniel

(Read *Daniel 3-4; 7*)

Mene: Numbered
Tekel: Weighed
Parsin: Divided
While King Belshazzar was feasting, a hand appeared and wrote these words in Aramaic on the wall. Only Daniel was able to decipher the message of God, which foretold the end of Belshazzar's reign.

The Book of Daniel was written at the time of the persecution of the Jews under the pagan king Antiochus of Syria (169-164 B.C.). It was intended to restore the people's faith and courage in adversity.

The first part is an account of Daniel's life. As a young boy he was deported in 606. His skill in interpreting dreams earned him a good position at Nebuchadnezzar's court. This was not enough to save him, however, from further trouble. Daniel's three companions were thrown into a blazing furnace for refusing to worship a gold statue set up by Nebuchadnezzar. *Officials of the king gathered to look at the three men, who had not been harmed by the fire. Their hair was not singed, their clothes were not burnt, and there was no smell of smoke on them.*

Dan 3.27

So the king gave orders for Daniel to be arrested and he was thrown into the pit filled with lions.

Dan 6.16

Daniel, whose faith carried him through the very worst ordeals, was an example to the persecuted Jews. (Byzantine mosaic).

The second part of the Book of Daniel is a succession of visions and dreams which foretell the final judgement of God. They constitute an *Apocalypse*– from the Greek, meaning 'an unveiling of what is hidden'. A biblical Apocalypse reveals to believers the true meaning of events.

Daniel's visions contain a message of hope to a nation in need, a nation facing the daily ordeal of enemy occupation and persecution. The language and plentiful symbols give added emphasis to the visions themselves and the message behind them.

The symbols used are closely linked to the traditions of the Jewish religion.

Daniel had a vision of four fantastic beasts, each symbolising one of the four enemy empires which were to suffer defeat before the final judgement. *The power and greatness of all the kingdoms on earth will be given to the people of the Supreme God.*
Dan 7.27

Life after death

The Jewish people did not believe in life after death. When a man or woman died, their life was at an end. They went to Sheol, a sort of dark underground world, a place of dust, silence and forgetfulness.

This was the fate of all people, good or bad. There was no way out of Sheol, no way of communicating from there either with God or with the land of

On the left: a 13th century miniature

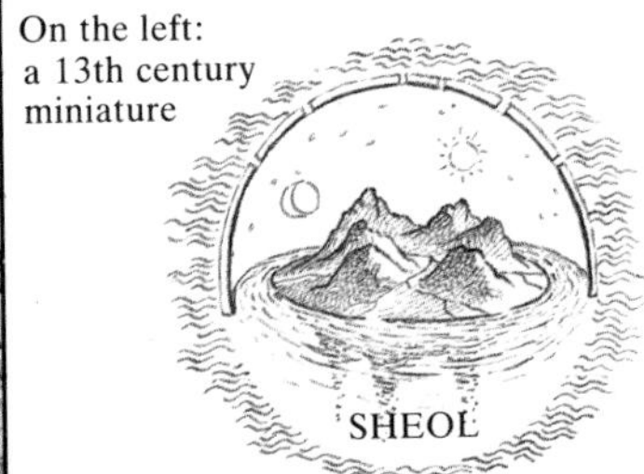

the living. King Hezekiah rejoiced on recovering from an illness, *I thought that in the prime of life I was going to the world of the dead, never to live out my life. I thought that in this world of the living I would never again see the Lord or any living person.* **Is 38.10-11**

During the persecution of the Jews under Antiochus many Jews chose to die a martyr's death rather than renounce their faith. The question the Jews now asked themselves was whether God really would desert those who had suffered martyrdom rather

than renounce their faith. The belief spread amongst the faithful that God would one day raise the righteous from the dead to live for ever with God in heaven. The Book of Daniel, written during the persecution, reflects this hope. *Many of those who have already died will live again: some will enjoy eternal life, and some will suffer eternal disgrace.* **Dan 12.2**

The Old Testament does not say how this will come about. It simply states that God made a covenant with mankind, and being stronger than death, God is faithful to that promise beyond the grave.

For a long time the people of the Old Testament believed that all life came to an end with death. Little by little the idea of life after death, in the form of a physical and spiritual rebirth, emerged. In Egypt, on the other hand, the soul was said to leave the body in the form of a bird at death.

Esther

(Read *Esther 1-10*)

The *Book of Esther* was probably written at the end of the persecution by Antiochus by a Jew from Susa, the former capital of the Persian empire. Judas Maccabeus and his brothers had freed Jerusalem and restored the temple to the Jews. The attempt to destroy the Jews had failed. They had won a resounding victory over the enemy.

Xerxes I, King of the Persian empire and son of Darius I

Xerxes, King of Persia, ruled over an immense empire from India to Ethiopia. Xerxes was looking for a new queen, and he fell in love with Esther, a lovely Jewish girl whom her cousin Mordecai had adopted when her parents died. Shortly afterwards – when Esther was Queen – Mordecai unearthed a plot to assassinate Xerxes. He told Esther and so saved the king's life. Some time later King Xerxes appointed a man named Haman prime minister, Haman demanded that everyone in his service kneel or bow to him. Mordecai refused. As a Jew, he would bow only to God.

Haman was furious, and hearing that Mordecai was a Jew, he decided to have every Jew in the Persian empire killed on the 13th day of the 12th month. In desperation Mordecai asked Esther to approach the king and beg him to save her people. Esther knew that to appear before the king uninvited was to risk death. Xerxes, however, spared Esther and consented to join her and Haman at a banquet. Meanwhile, Haman decided to have Mordecai hanged for refusing to salute him.

That night, the king was unable to sleep. When he asked for the official records to be read, he was reminded that Mordecai had saved his life. At this point Haman came to ask permission to have his enemy Mordecai hanged. Before he could speak, the King said, *There is someone I wish very*

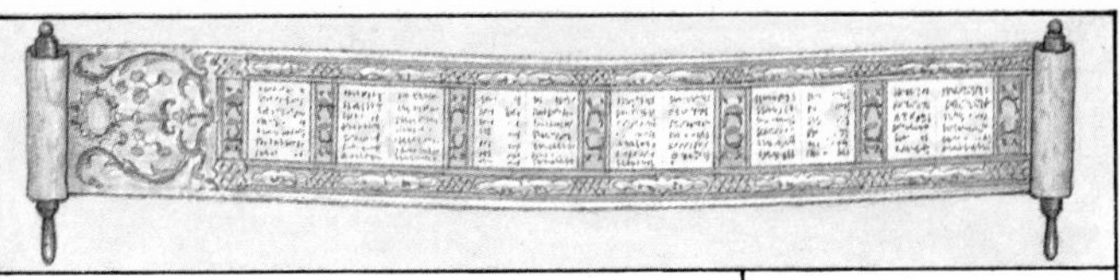

much to honour. What should I do for this man? Haman assumed that the King was referring to him, and told him what form of reward would be appropriate. 'Good!' said the King, 'Do all these things for Mordecai!'

Esther told Xerxes of Haman's plot to exterminate her fellow Jews. Incensed, the King ordered Haman to be hanged on the gallows he had prepared for Mordecai. Mordecai became Prime Minister in his place. The Jews were saved. Thereafter this event was celebrated on the 15th day of the 12th month (Purim) with a reading from the Book of Esther. *These were the days on which the Jews had rid themselves of their enemies; this was a month that had been turned from a time of grief and despair into a time of joy and happiness.* **Esth 9.22**

Parchment of the Book of Esther (17th c.)

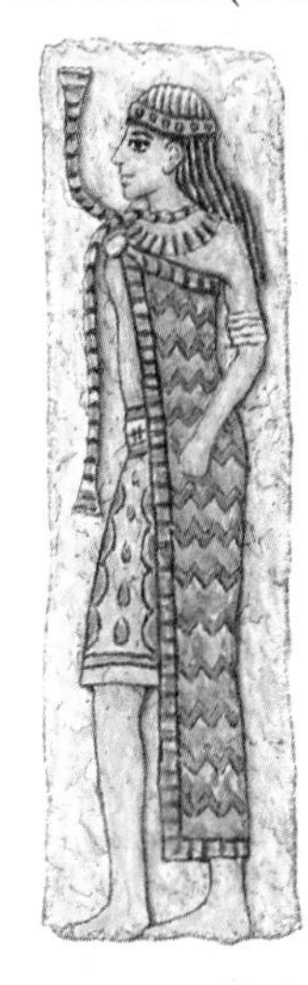

A prisoner wearing the elegant attire of a Syrian or Palestinian noble under Rameses III

Symbols

The star of David is one of the most important symbols of Judaism. The six points represent the elements, inter-twined to form a united whole.

The authors of the Old Testament often used symbols: numbers or words, which were images in themselves with particular associations.

Numbers with a symbolic meaning

Four was a symbol of universality or completion. Four rivers flowed out of the garden of Eden; The four letters YHWH spelled Yahweh.

Seven symbolised fulfilment and perfection. Was not the world made in 7 days? The number had an almost magic power. Joshua marched 7 times round the city of Jericho before the walls fell (**Josh 6.15-20**). Elisha told Naaman to bathe 7 times in the Jordan before he was healed (**2 Kgs 5.14**).

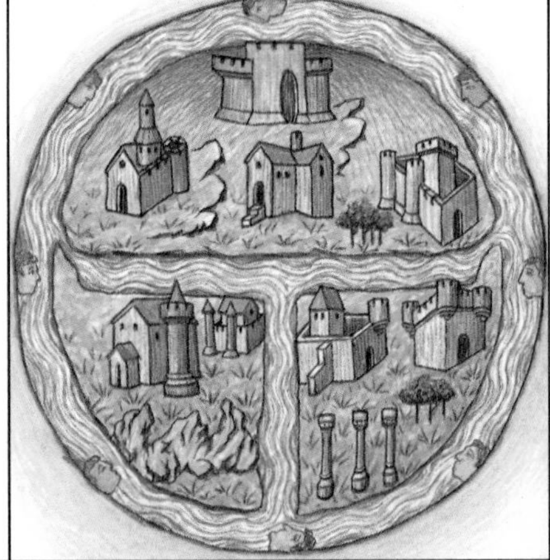

This artist's impression of the earth is more mystical than scientific. It is divided into three – the perfect number. The East, with Jerusalem at its centre, occupies the top half, Africa and the West the lower half.

Twelve was the sign of God's elect. The sons of Jacob were 12 in number; 12 precious stones on the High Priest's breastplate commemorated the 12 tribes of Israel.

Symbolic places

The sky is the domain of God who rules supreme over earth and mankind.

The sea represents death and destruction for mankind.

The desert represents a time of testing, of cleansing, of reconciliation with God.

Mountains, half-way between heaven and earth, are places where God and mankind meet.

The Bible contains many descriptions of weird and monstrous beasts, which are all symbols of one sort or another.
The four beasts in Daniel's vision were symbols of the power of oppression exercised by four great nations in succession.

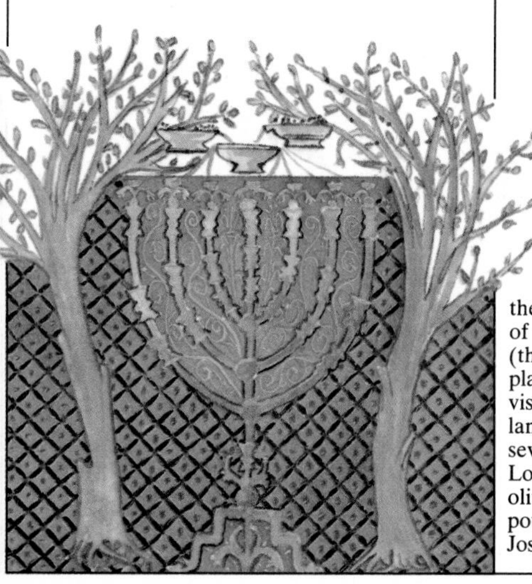

The *menorah*, a seven-branched candelabrum representing the light of the world (the sun and six planets). In Zechariah's vision, the seven lamps were the seven eyes of the Lord and the two olive trees pouring oil represented Joshua and Zerubbabel.

COLLINS BIBLE HANDBOOK

New Testament

The Good News in 27 books

Book of Kells (Irish)

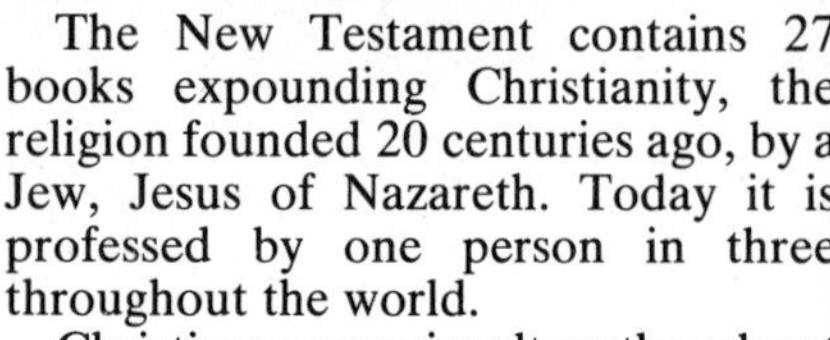

The New Testament contains 27 books expounding Christianity, the religion founded 20 centuries ago, by a Jew, Jesus of Nazareth. Today it is professed by one person in three throughout the world.

Christians recognise altogether about 70 books which make up the Christian Bible. These are:

– the holy books of the Jewish religion. Christians call these the 'Old Testament', by which they mean the first covenant made by God with the Jewish people.

– the books written by the first Christians about the founder of their religion and about the life of the first Christian communities. This collection of books is known as the 'New Testament', after the covenant established by God in Jesus with all human beings. Its message is often called 'Gospel' or 'Good News'.

Synoptic (comparative) table of the gospels of Matthew, Mark and Luke (11th c.).

The books of the New Testament:

The four gospels of
- Matthew
- Mark
- Luke
- John

Acts of the Apostles

The letters (epistles) of
- Paul (14)
- James (1)
- Peter (2)
- John (3)
- Jude (1)

Apocalypse of John

How the New Testament has come to us

A fragment of the *Codex Sinaiticus*, written in Greek capitals known as biblical uncials. This manuscript was found in the 19th c. in the monastery of St Catherine, built on Mount Sinai in the 6th c.

The manuscripts

All these books were written in Greek between 51 and 100 A.D. We no longer possess the originals (as is the case with other ancient texts), but we do have more than 5,000 very early copies. The most ancient fragment of manuscript dates from before 150, and was discovered in Egypt. The earliest complete manuscripts of the New Testament date from the 4th c. They are the *Codex Vaticanus*, preserved in the Vatican Library, and the *Codex Sinaiticus*, discovered at the monastery of St Catherine on Mount Sinai and preserved in the British Museum in London. During the Middle Ages, before the invention of printing, the Bible was copied by hand in monasteries. In 1456 Gutenberg produced the first printed copy.

The translations

Translations began to appear in the 2nd c.: in Latin and Syriac (2nd c.), in Coptic (3rd c.), in Gothic, Georgian and Ethiopian (4th c.), in Armenian

I passed on to you what I received.
1 Cor 15.3

(5th c.), in Arabic, Chinese and Anglo-Saxon (8th c.), in German, Slavonic and Frankish (9th c.). Today, the New Testament has been translated into 495 languages; about 15 million copies are sold or distributed each year. It is bought and read more than any other book in the world.

How do I look up a passage in the New Testament?

Chapters and verses are numbered. When we quote passages from the New Testament we give an abbreviation of the name of the book, then the chapter number and finally the verse numbers. So **Mk 3.2-6** means the gospel according to Mark, chapter 3, verses 2 to 6.

Throughout the Middle Ages, monks copied the Bible by hand. Bound together, the pages formed a Codex. This was sometimes bound with leather.

The Turin Shroud, which has inspired many portraits of Christ

10th c. Christ (carved ivory plaque)

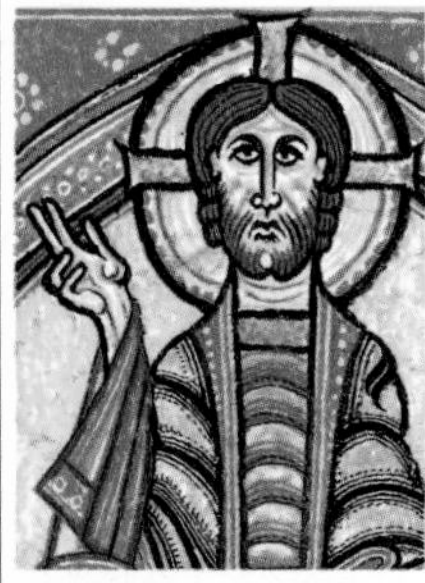
Catalan Christ (12th c.)

13th c. window

Jesus is the central character of the Gospel. He was born in Bethlehem in Palestine, which was occupied by the Romans. This was in the time of Augustus and the last years of Herod the Great, King of the Jews. He spent his youth in Nazareth, a little town in Galilee, in northern Palestine.

When he was about thirty, during the reign of the Emperor Tiberius, he went to Judaea to join the group led by John the Baptist, on the banks of the Jordan.

Then, leaving John, Jesus began to proclaim the coming of the Kingdom of God, first in Galilee, then throughout Palestine and even beyond its borders.

His message both perpetuated and radically altered the Jewish religion. In a few months he fired the enthusiasm of

Jesus and King David, after a miniature in the Albenga psalter.

Jesus

the crowds, who recognised him as a prophet. Gradually however, they abandoned him, as he failed to meet their expectations by restoring a political kingdom in Palestine. He also had to withstand the attacks of the Jewish leaders.

During his last visit to Jerusalem, his

Crucified Christ represented by a lamb (6th c. Byzantine ciborium).

enemies, with the help of one of his disciples, had him arrested and handed him over to the Roman authorities. They accused him of plotting against the Emperor.

The Roman procurator, Pilate, tried to save him, but in the end he yielded to pressure. Jesus was crucified, perhaps on 30 April, 30 A.D.

Some time later, his disciples proclaimed that God had raised Jesus from the dead, and they in their turn began to proclaim his message. Within fifty years, Christian communities had sprung up throughout the Roman Empire.

Russian icon (2nd half of 13th c.)

Ethiopian Christ

By Georges Rouault

Christianity

63 B.C. The Roman general Pompey captures Jerusalem

40 B.C. Romans recognise Herod as King of the Jews
27 B.C. Accession of the Roman Emperor Augustus

20 B.C. Herod begins reconstruction of the temple in Jerusalem

4 B of J Na

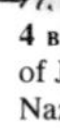

April 30 Crucifixion of Jesus

Pentecost 30-31 First Christian community

36 Conversion of Paul. Stephen first Christian martyr

48-49 First cour at Jerusalem

61-63 Imprisonment of Paul in Rome. He writes his first letters

62 Stoning of James, the 'brother of Jesus'

64 Nero sets fire to Rome. Persecution of Christians and martyrdom of Peter in Rome

66 Beginnir Jewish upris in Jerusalem

c. 70 Gospel according to Mark

70 Siege and destruction of Jerusalem by Rome

73 Siege of the citadel of Masada

79 Eruption of vius. Destructic Herculaneum a Pompeii

is born in history

6-15 A.D. Annas is Jewish High Priest
14 Death of Augustus. Tiberius succeeds

26-36 Pontius Pilate is Roman procurator in Judaea

27-30 Jesus preaches in Galilee and Judaea

49 Claudius expels Jews from Rome

54 Claudius poisoned. Nero emperor. Time of the philosopher Seneca and the author Petronius

Pentecost 58 Paul arrested in Jerusalem. Appears before the procurator Felix. Detention in Caesarea

60 Paul's journey to Rome. Shipwreck off Malta

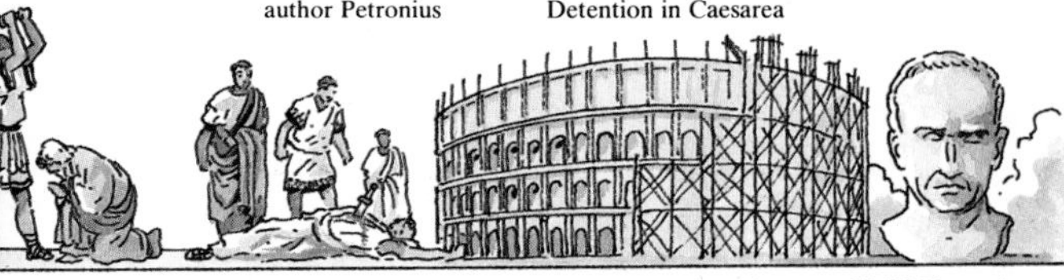

Paul beheaded in
me

68 Suicide of Nero

69 Construction of the Coliseum

68-79 Vespasian emperor

79-81 Titus emperor

c. 80 Gospels according to Matthew and Luke; Acts of the Apostles

81-96 Domitian emperor
96-98 Nerva emperor

c. 100 Gospel according to John

The country they inhabit
is bordered to the East by Arabia,
and to the South by Egypt;
to the West there are the Phoenicians
and the sea;
the North emerges in the distance,
in the direction of Syria. . . .
Most of the Jews live scattered in villages;
they also have towns.
Jerusalem is the capital of their nation;
you can see there a temple of immense splendour.

Tacitus, *History*, Book 5

THE PLACES

Rome and the world

It was Rome's ambition to conquer the *orbis terrarum*, the whole world. A winged goddess (this one comes from Syria) was the symbol of Rome's presence.

The major cities of the Empire

Alexandria: almost one million inhabitants.

Antioch: capital of the Roman province of Syria, third most important city of the Empire.

Tarsus: about 500,000 inhabitants.

Corinth: a cosmopolitan city of some 500,000 inhabitants, capital of the Roman province of Achaia.

Ephesus: capital of the Roman province of Asia, celebrated for its temple dedicated to Diana.

Jerusalem: 50,000 inhabitants at normal times, 250,000 during festivals.

Barbarian prisoners captured by Roman legionaries

Means of communication

Paving a road

By land

The Roman Empire was covered by a vast network of roads, 80,000 km (50,000 miles) in all, built from the 2nd c. onwards. These were the famous Roman roads. They linked districts and provinces to Rome, the capital of the Empire. The roads made possible the swift delivery of imperial despatches and they enabled the Roman legions to intervene in unruly provinces. They

Journeys were made on horseback (about 50 miles a day), in a carriage (25 miles) and on foot (16 to 20 miles). The Roman mile was 1000 paces (1620 yards or 1472 metres) long. The statute mile is 1760 yards.

were also useful for transporting supplies (especially when the sea routes were paralysed by bad weather) and for cultural exchanges.

The building and upkeep of these roads was the responsibility of the Roman governors. They used prisoners of war and local people, supervised by legionaries, as a workforce.

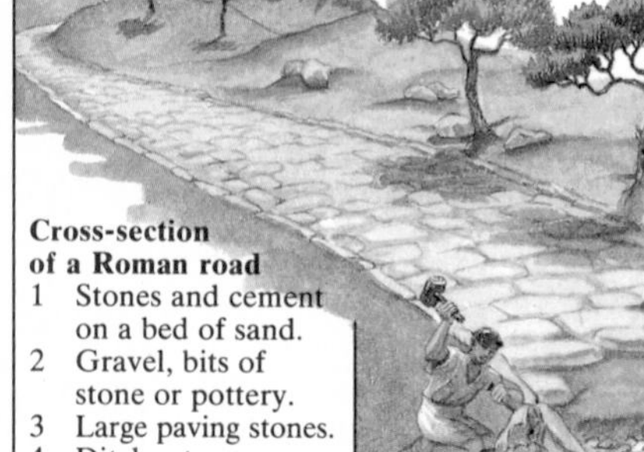

Cross-section of a Roman road
1 Stones and cement on a bed of sand.
2 Gravel, bits of stone or pottery.
3 Large paving stones.
4 Ditches to ensure drainage of water.

Unloading merchant ships

By sea

Shipping was very busy throughout the Mediterranean; called *mare nostrum*, 'our sea', by the Romans. War ships, trading ships and passenger ships cut across the open seas or plied along the coasts. A regular service from Alexandria to Rome transported Egyptian wheat. This was vitally important if Italy was to have enough food and so the wheat trade was a state monopoly.

Many private companies brought to Rome the wealth of Africa and Asia: gold, ivory, papyrus, linen, glass, beer, oil, incense, myrrh, wool, hemp, pearls, cotton, bitumen, wood, silk, horses and slaves.

Because of the weather, journeys by ship in the Mediterranean were considered safe only between 26 May and 14 September (summertime). Even then you had to reckon with the winds: the journey from Puteoli to Alexandria could take anything from eight to fifty days.

A Roman lighthouse

Different types of ship on the Mediterranean

– light-weight ships with oars, 170 oarsmen (essentially war ships).

– ships with sails, used to transport goods and people (the *oneraria* or *frumentaria*); these were quite large and could carry 600 people.

On the prow was sculpted the ship's figurehead: a god or symbolic animal. The Jews of the diaspora used to hire ships to take them to Jerusalem for the great festivals.

Marseilles
Taragon
Rome
Carthage

The economy of the Empire

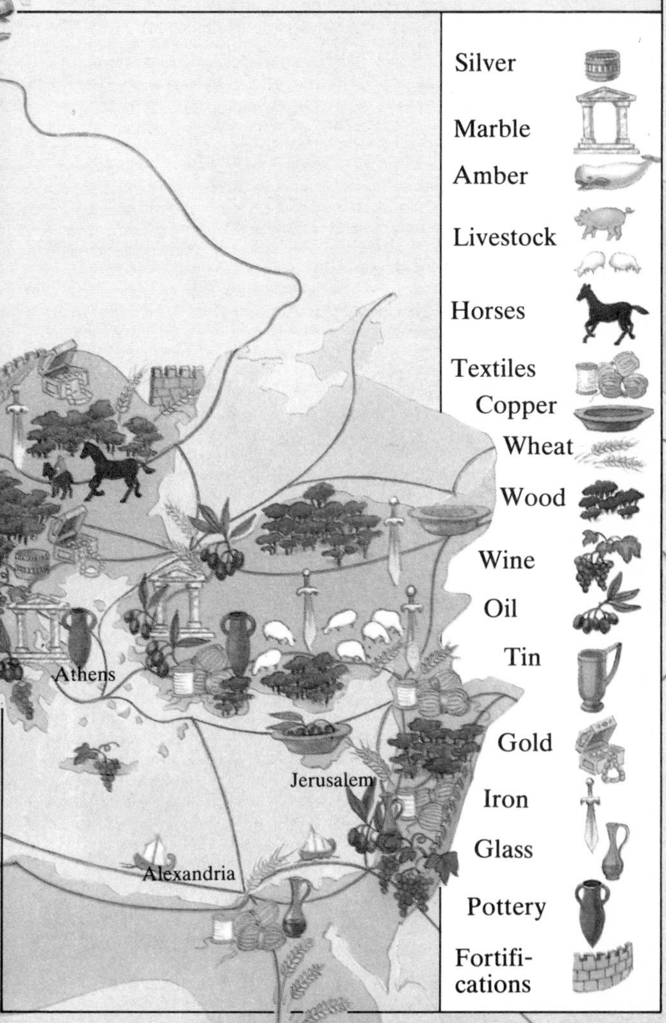

The city of Rome

Rome at the height of the Empire

1 Temple of Aescula-pius
2 Temple of Jupiter Capitolinus
3 Temple of Mars
4 Curia (Senate House)
5 Temple of Venus and of Rome

In Jesus' time, Rome, the capital of the Empire, had a population of about one million. It stood on the banks of the Tiber and was built on seven hills. The emperors built their palaces and their gardens on the Palatine (hill), on the Capitoline, Rome's religious centre, rose the Temple of Jupiter; the Aventine was the working class quarter.

Between the Capitoline and the

The Forum today

Aventine lay the Forum, the city's political centre.

The poor were crammed into *insulae*, buildings with several storeys. The only heating came from braziers and all water had to be fetched from the nearest fountain. The streets were labyrinthine. Only the main roads were paved, the rest were dirty, running with used water and rubbish.

6 Temple of Jupiter Victor
7 Coliseum
8 Temple of Claudius
9 Aqueduct of Nero
10 Circus Maximus

The Roman Forum

Roman courts under the Empire
Civil and criminal justice were dealt with by officials appointed by the Emperor.

Punishments:
These varied according to whether the culprit was a citizen or a non-citizen (freed man or slave), rich or poor.
The death sentence for citizens was by beheading, hanging, or strangulation.
The death sentence for slaves meant crucifixion.

Direct appeal to the Emperor was always possible for a citizen, even one from the provinces.

The Forum was the heart of the city, the centre of business and of the political and religious life of Rome.

On the ancient *comitium* (public square), the people gathered for official assemblies or meetings. Orators spoke from a speaker's platform, known as 'the rostrum' because it was decorated with ships' prows (*rostra* in Latin) captured from the enemy. There was also a golden column 3 m (10 ft) high (the golden milestone) from which all Roman roads set out across the Empire.

The Emperor Augustus and his successors had four new squares built: the imperial forums of Augustus, Nerva, Vespasian and Trajan, each more grandiose than the last.

The Curia was the normal meeting place of the Senate (six hundred members appointed by the Emperor). This made laws and appointed magistrates.

The basilicas (great covered halls with columns) were used as courts,

Bas-relief from the speaker's platform in the Forum. This shows scribes carrying tax records to be burnt at the order of the Emperor: a demonstration of clemency towards the citizens.

markets and meeting places, and for strolling about. The most famous was the Julian basilica. The main road (the *via sacra*) was narrow. It was lined with many different stalls and banks.

There were many temples. The oldest were that of Janus – open in times of war, closed in times of peace – and that of Saturn, which housed the public treasury. The new ones were those of Caesar, of Minerva, built by Domitian, and of Augustus, built by Tiberius.

The Regia was the home of the high priest of Rome. Close by was the house of the vestal virgins, priestesses of the round Temple of Vesta.

The Tullianum was the prison. Near this were the *Gemoniae.* These were steps cut into the rock on which the bodies of executed criminals were exposed.

1 Temple of Caesar
2 Speaker's platform decorated with prows from the ships of Antony and Cleopatra
3 Arch of Augustus
4 Temple of the Dioscures
5 Speaker's platform
6 Statue of Constantine
7 Columns of Domitian
8 Coliseum of Diocletian
9 Julian basilica

6 7 8 9

The circus and the amphitheatre

The stadium drew the most crowds when it was transformed into a lake and used for naval battles, or *naumachia*.

The Roman circus was a long rectangle, rounded at both ends. It was very popular on account of its chariot races. The oldest and most famous was the Circus Maximus in Rome. Competing chariots with two horses (*bigae*) or four (*quadrigae*) had to go round the track seven times, keeping close to the 214 m (700 ft) long *spina* (central wall).

Architecturally, the Roman **circus** was inspired by the Greek hippodrome. The great circus in Rome could hold 200,000 spectators. It was used mainly for chariot races, on which bets were placed. The chariots were pulled by slaves or by professionals (*aurigae*). Eight to ten chariots competed in each race of seven laps; a total of 8.4 km (5¼ miles). There were sometimes as many as a hundred races in a single day.

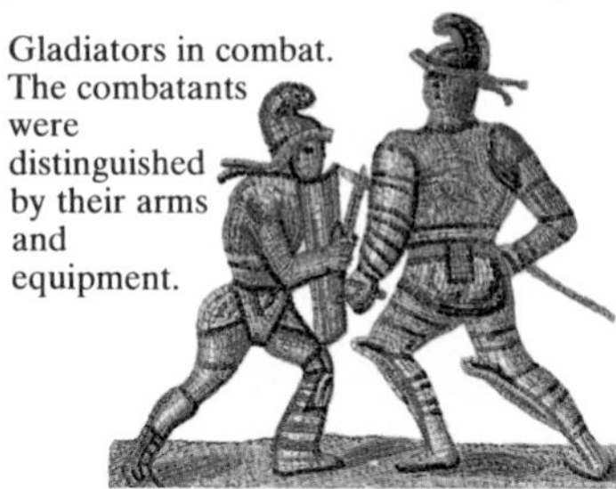

Gladiators in combat. The combatants were distinguished by their arms and equipment.

The **amphitheatre** was a typically Roman creation. The most famous was the Colosseum, which could hold up to 100,000 spectators. It was here that the gladiator contests took place. The combatants, trained in a special school, were slaves or men condemned to death

Gladiator's bronze helmet, found at Herculaneum

The amphitheatre was also used for animal fights. They either killed one another, or were given as prey men condemned to death. Many of the first Christians met their death in this way.

for whom this was a last chance. On the day of the show, the entire troupe (up to 10,000 men) would parade into the arena. The combatants were drawn by lot. When a gladiator was wounded, the public cried: *habet* (he has it). If the Emperor or his representative raised his thumb, the loser's life was saved; if he lowered his thumb, the man was put to death.

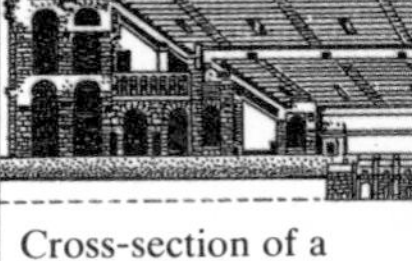

Cross-section of a reconstruction of the Coliseum

Theatres and baths

Dress of a patrician lady from Pompeii

A man's tunic, or toga, was a long piece of material which could be wrapped round the body in different ways. The lower classes wore a short tunic.

There were many **theatres** in the Empire, most of them made of wood. The first stone theatre was built in

55 B.C. One of the best preserved theatres is at Orange, in Roman Gaul.

Farces were very popular as were lavishly-staged shows.

The Romans regarded the **baths** as a normal feature of daily life and there were several hundred of them in Rome. While the richer members of society had private baths with warm water (an invention which pre-dated 70 B.C.), most people went to the public baths. There was a moderate charge for this, but on certain occasions entrance was free. These baths, in which men and women were segregated, were open daily from sunrise to sunset, except on days of national mourning and religious festivals.

They included dressing rooms (*apodyteria*), a cool room for the cold bath (*frigidarium*), a warm room (*tepidarium*) where people rested and were massaged with oil, and a very hot room (*caldarium*) for the steam bath.

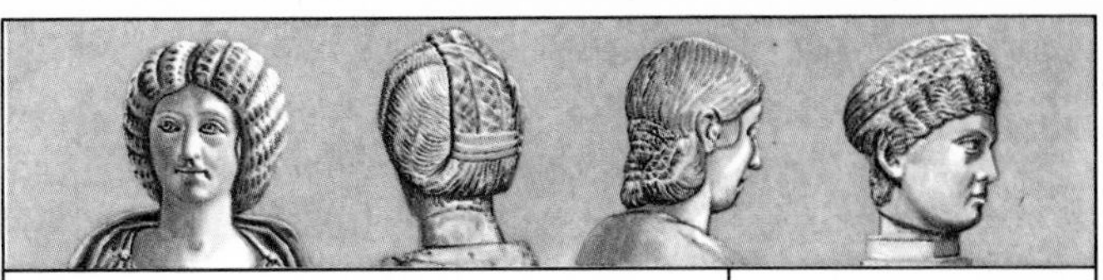

First, people washed with soda ash and a lubricant, or else they used a pumice stone. Then they rubbed themselves down with a sort of scraper called a *strigilis.*

A highly-sophisticated heating system enabled warm air to circulate under the stone floor. Drains (*cloaca*) got rid of the dirty water.

Warm baths came into common usage among the Jews in the 1st c. A.D.

Women's hairstyles, fashionable in Rome: 1st to 3rd c.

1 Men's entrance
2 Women's entrance
3 Slaves' entrance
4 *Apodyterium*
5 *Frigidarium*
6 *Tepidarium* 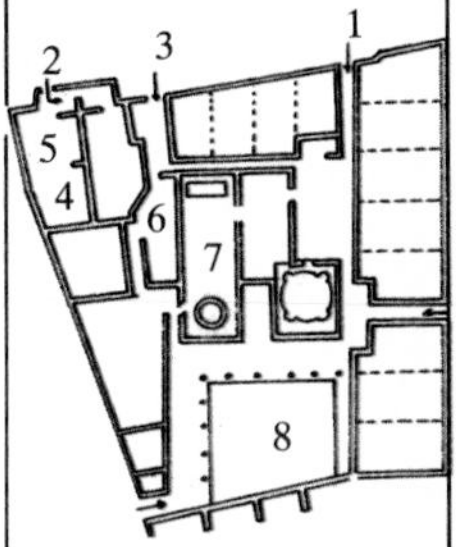
7 *Caldarium*
8 *Palaestra* (exercise room)

Roman baths

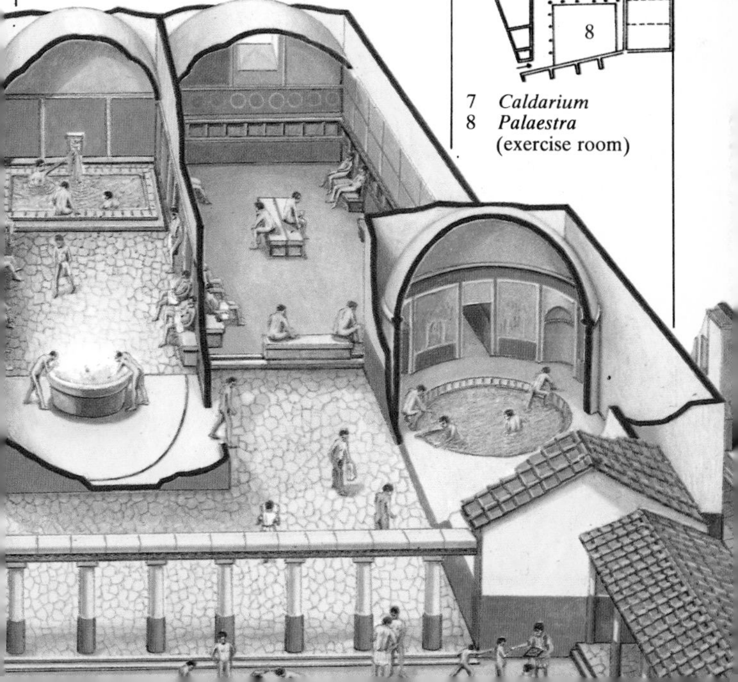

The Roman house

In order to house the population of Rome, architects built upwards. In the poor quarters people were crowded into *insulae* (flats), which sometimes

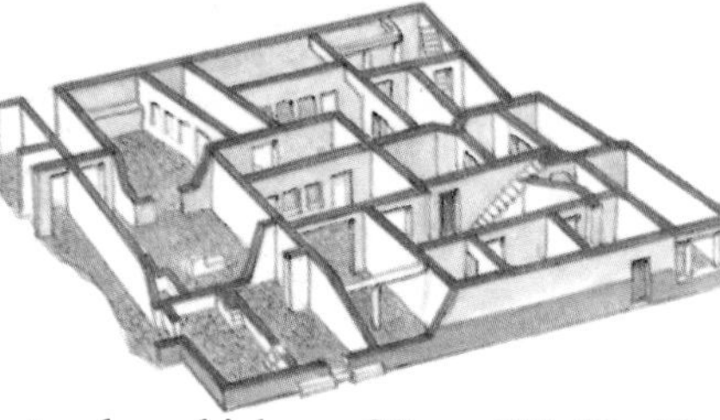

Insula in Capernaum, probably built in the reign of Herod the Great

stood as high as 20 m (65 ft). The different floors were reached by narrow, ladder-like staircases. The windows were small and looked out on narrow streets.

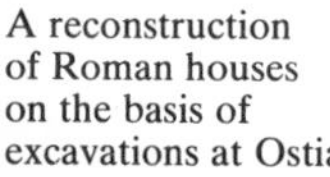

A reconstruction of Roman houses on the basis of excavations at Ostia

Interior of a rich person's house. First floor: the *atrium* (hall).

Comfort was precarious. People lived in constant fear of fire. When there was a fire, the firemen often found it difficult to reach the scene of the disaster because the streets were so congested, and their access to water was restricted.

Wealthier citizens owned town houses, or *villae*, in the country, in spa towns or in towns well above sea level. These houses were highly decorated – with frescoes, marble, mosaics and oriental carpets.

A street in Pompeii. The blocks of stone on the road provided a path for pedestrians.

A typical Roman *villa*. Includes the owner's house, farm, storehouses and barns, as well as the surrounding land.

The temples

Round temple from the Forum Boarium: a relatively rare architectural style.

More often, Roman temples were rectangular in plan, inspired by Greek buildings like the temple at Paestum (6th c. B.C.).

Temples dedicated to the gods of Rome multiplied under the Emperor Augustus and his successors. More than eighty-four of them were restored, embellished or constructed by Augustus himself.

A walled sanctuary (the *cella*) housed the statue of the god. In front was a covered portico and a staircase. This had an uneven number of steps so that the priest and the people, having started with their right foot (lucky side) would arrive at the top on the same foot. Ceremonies took place in the open, around an altar placed on the portico.

Among the Roman temples best preserved today is the Pantheon in Rome. Built by Agrippa, Augustus' son-in-law, it was dedicated first to the guardian deities of the imperial family (Venus, Apollo and Mars) and later to all the gods of heaven. Outside Rome, there is the Maison Carrée at Nîmes in France, which was built

during the reign of Augustus in memory of the Emperor's grandsons.

Pediment from the temple of Jupiter Capitolinus

The priests

The *pontiffs*: this college, led by the supreme pontiff, had overall responsibility for worship. It drew up the calendar.

The *flamines*: each was dedicated to the service of a particular god; from Augustus' time onwards they were also attached to the cult of the Emperor,

The vestals had to submit to a strict discipline. Those who broke the rule of chastity were walled-up alive.

deified by order of the Senate.

The *fetiales*: they were responsible for the rituals that accompanied declarations of war.

The *vestals*: they maintained the sacred fire of Rome in the temple of Vesta.

The *haruspices* or soothsayers: they interpreted the will of the gods from the entrails of animals.

Fastus, nefastus: these two notions, which regulated much of the Romans' way of life, referred to what pleased or offended the gods.

Roman and Jewish burial customs

Interior (above) and entrance (below) of the necropolis at Beth-Shearim in Galilee

Among the Jews, no corpse was supposed to remain unburied. The body of the dead person was washed, rubbed with perfumes and wrapped in a shroud. A cloth was placed over the face and the hands were tied with bandages.

Burial took place eight hours after death. The corpse was carried on a stretcher, to the accompaniment of loud lamentations. It was placed in a tomb, usually carved out of the rock, and covered with spices. Each year the tomb was whitened with chalk.

Among the Romans, the body of the dead person was carefully washed and perfumed. It was then reclothed in a toga. A branch of pine or cypress (trees symbolising immortality because they are evergreen) was hung on the dead person's door. The funeral took place between two and ten days after death.

Sarcophagus of a Roman child

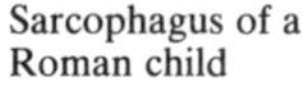

Poor people were buried in a common grave. Richer people were taken to the tomb at night. The torchlight procession was accompanied by flute players and weeping women.

Cremation was a common practice. Mourning lasted for ten months.

The three Jews dance in the fiery furnace (catacomb of Priscilla, Rome)

Roman mausoleum at Haïdra in Tunisia

The catacombs

These were underground cemeteries in which the first Christians buried their dead. The Roman catacombs formed a labyrinth 600 km (370 miles) long.

Some chambers were decorated with frescoes portraying symbols of Christ and the resurrection.

The most elaborate tomb in the necropolis of Beth-Shearim

Left: ossuary of a 1st c. Jewish tomb near Jerusalem

Palestine in the time of Jesus

The Philistines gave Palestine its name when they invaded the region – the land of Canaan – in the 12th c. B.C.

Palestine – 200 km (140 miles) long and 50-100 km (30-60 miles) wide – had a dry season in summer; the rainy season lasted from October to April. Fertile plains stretched to the west. The Jordan valley, hemmed in by mountains (and below sea level), was almost a desert. There were two chains of mountains, one on either side of the river, reaching heights between 600 and 1200 m (1,970–3,940 ft).

Herod the Great came from the province of Idumea.

The provinces

Idumea: the ancient kingdom of Edom, conquered in 126 B.C.

Judaea: included Jerusalem.

Samaria: country of the Samaritans, people of Jewish and Assyrian descent.

The Jews of Jerusalem regarded the Samaritans as heretics – people, that is, whose faith was not pure. Even now they form a separate group within Judaism.

Galilee: a border region, inhabited by Jews and non-Jews.

Perea: conquered in the 1st c. B.C.

Decapolis: a group of ten towns with non-Jewish populations, attached to the Roman pro-consul of Syria.

Iturea, Gaulanitis, Batanea and Trachonitis: conquered by Herod the Great.

Free cities on the Mediterranean coast: Ascalon and Gaza.

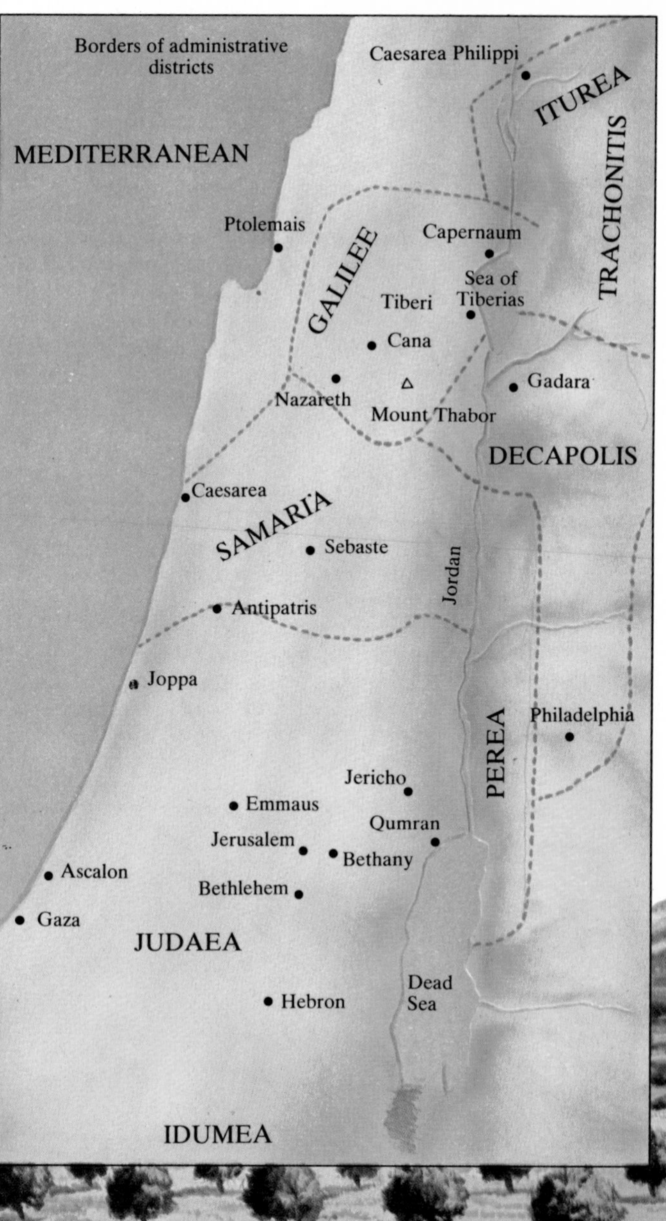
Borders of administrative districts
Caesarea Philippi
ITUREA
MEDITERRANEAN
TRACHONITIS
Ptolemais
GALILEE
Capernaum
Sea of Tiberias
Tiberi
Cana
Nazareth
Mount Thabor
Gadara
DECAPOLIS
Caesarea
SAMARIA
Sebaste
Jordan
Antipatris
Joppa
Philadelphia
PEREA
Jericho
Emmaus
Qumran
Jerusalem
Bethany
Ascalon
Bethlehem
Gaza
JUDAEA
Dead Sea
Hebron
IDUMEA

The natural resources of Palestine

Basic crops: figs

olives

Fish was eaten fresh, or else preserved in salt or by smoking.

Agriculture and cattle-rearing

As in Old Testament times, the Jews of Jesus' time tilled the soil and raised domestic animals. Wheat and barley were the basic crops, along with figs, olives and vines. Goats provided milk and sheep wool. Donkeys and camels were used for transporting heavy burdens and for drawing the plough and driving the mill.

Fishing

This happened on the shores of the Mediterranean, but above all on the Sea of Galilee (the Sea of Tiberius), which was very rich in fish. The Jews distinguished two sorts of fish: the clean and the unclean. The clean or edible ones had fins and scales: tench, carp, gudgeon, perch, pike. The rest, with neither fins nor scales, were thrown back into the lake: silurid, eel, ray, lamprey.

Camel driving the heavy stone of a mill

Scenes of rustic life: cattle farming, goats,

sheep, oxen;

cultivation of grapes, wheat and olives;

hunting and fishing.

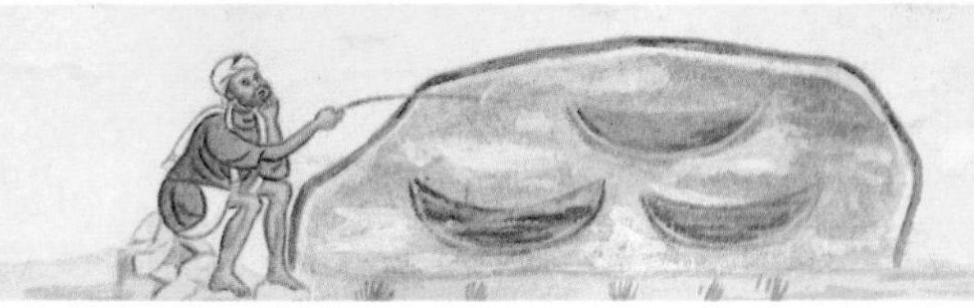

(After an 11th c. manuscript.)

The new towns of Palestine

The most important tool in Roman construction techniques was the windlass, usually operated by slaves

Herod the Great, King of the Jews, who reigned from 37 to 4 B.C., undertook many large-scale building works and founded new towns. Caesarea was built on the Mediterranean and it had a very busy port. Phasaëlis was built in memory of Herod's brother and Antipatris in honour of his father.

He restored the city of Samaria and renamed it Sebaste. He built a chain of fortresses in the south to protect himself against Arab invaders and to maintain order in the country. Among the most famous were Herodion, near Bethlehem (where he was buried), Macheronte, east of the Dead Sea, and Masada, to the west of the Dead Sea.

Finally, Herod undertook the restoration of the temple in Jerusalem (see p. 310), as well as the construction of the Antonia tower, attached to the temple. He also built a vast palace, a hippodrome and a theatre.

Herod erected a number of temples and public buildings outside Palestine, notably at Antioch, Athens and Rhodes.

Ploughing the first furrow to define the area of a new town.

Herod Antipas, son of Herod the Great, who reigned from 4 B.C. to 39 A.D., built Tiberias on the shores of the Sea of Galilee – as a non-Jewish city filled with the spirit of Greece. He also fortified the cities of Sephoris and Julia.

Herod Philip, son of Herod the Great, who reigned from 4 B.C. to 34 A.D., restored the city of Panias and renamed it Caesarea Philippi.

He did the same for Bethsaida (near the Sea of Galilee), giving it the name Julia.

Agrippa I, grandson of Herod the Great (34–44 A.D.), enlarged the ramparts of Jerusalem by 3½ km (2.2 miles).

Pontius Pilate, Roman procurator (26–36 A.D.), built a new aqueduct in Jerusalem.

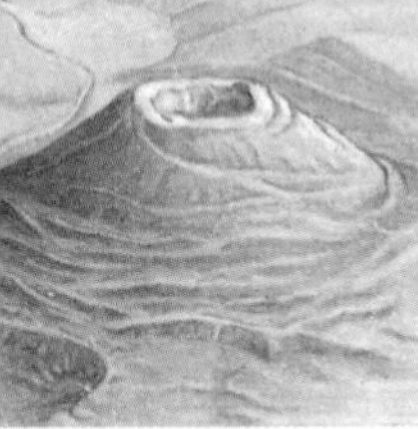

The Herodion, one of the most important fortresses built by Herod the Great, in which he is buried.

Port of Caesarea and triumphal arch of Palmyra

Jerusalem in the time of Jesus

1 Temple
2 Antonia fortress
3 Golgotha
4 Herod's Palace
5 Cenacle: the room in which the Last Supper took place
6 Palace of the Hasmoneans
7 Amphitheatre
8 Hippodrome
9 Valley of Gehenna
10 Valley of Kidron
11 Mount of Olives
12 Garden of Gethsemane
13 Agrippa's keep
14 Herod's keep

When Pompey captured Jerusalem in 63 B.C., the walls were again demolished. Following Rome's great victory and the installation in power of Pompey's 'friend and ally', Herod the Great, the city entered a period of profound change. Within twenty years, the capital of Judaea assumed the appearance of a Greek city. It had theatres, amphitheatres and even a hippodrome where games were organised every five years in honour of Augustus. These games were fully comparable to those which took place in Rome, with gladiators, athletes and animal fights.

The wall of Herod's palace seen from outside the city

Herod was an astute politician: in order to make sure of the good will of the people he decided to rebuild the House of God. The new temple, opened in 9 B.C., was considered at the time to be one of the wonders of the Mediterranean world.

Panorama of the old city from the Mount of Olives

Jerusalem as imagined by a medieval artist (15th c. illumination)

The Temple of Herod

Weighing the shekel, a tax imposed to pay for the first and second temples.

The Romans used the Antonia tower to keep watch over the temple courts.

1 Court of the Gentiles, reserved for non-Jews
2 Wall separating Jews from non-Jews
3 Court of the Women
4 Court of Israel, reserved for men
5 Court of the Priests
6 Altar of sacrifice
7 Entry portico
8 The Holy
9 The Holy of Holies, for Jews the place of God's presence

The temple in Jerusalem was the centre of Jewish religious life. When Jesus was born it had just been rebuilt by Herod the Great, though the work was not quite finished. It was begun in 20 B.C., opened in 9 B.C. and completed in 64 A.D. However, it was destroyed by the Romans in 70 A.D.

The first temple, built by Solomon in 950 B.C., had been destroyed by the Babylonians (in 586 B.C.). A second,

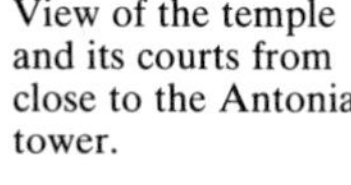

View of the temple and its courts from close to the Antonia tower.

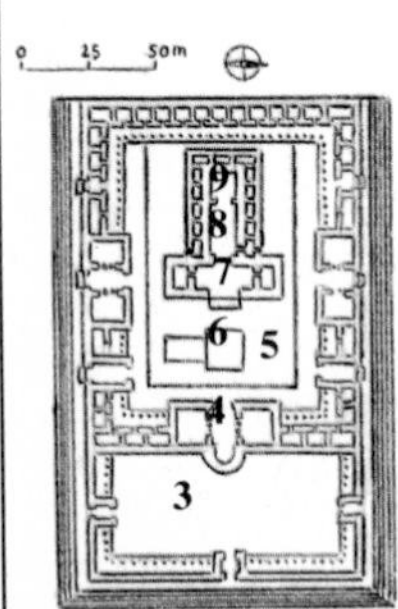

smaller one, was built (520-516 B.C.) after the Babylonian exile.

In 20 B.C., wishing to win favour with the people, Herod decided to enlarge it and restore it to the splendour it had in Solomon's day.

This temple was built on a grand scale following the plans of the first temple. Made of white stone enhanced with gold panels, it stood at the centre of a court 480 m by 300 m (1,570 ft by 980 ft). The court was paved with coloured stones and from its high vantage point the temple dominated the city. It was surrounded by a carved marble balustrade, through which non-Jews were not allowed to pass.

With its porticoes and superb marble columns, it filled Jesus' contemporaries with admiration.

Coin from the 2nd c. showing the façade of the temple

Called by Christians the 'Wailing Wall' (in Hebrew *Kotel*), this fragment of the western wall, built under Herod, is the only part of the temple that remains. For Jews it is therefore the holiest place of all.

The synagogue

Parchment decorated with candelabrum and psalms, hanging from the synagogue wall.

Jews in Jesus' time used the word synagogue, which was Greek in origin, to signify both the house set aside for study of the Bible and for prayer, and the community which gathered there.

The synagogue probably dates back to the time of the Babylonian exile (586–536 B.C.). Deprived of the temple, the Jews came together to study the Bible and to pray. After the exile, synagogues spread throughout the Jewish communities of the diaspora and even amongst the Jews in Jerusalem.

Inside of a synagogue: when the reading of the Torah was over, the scroll was replaced in the Ark.

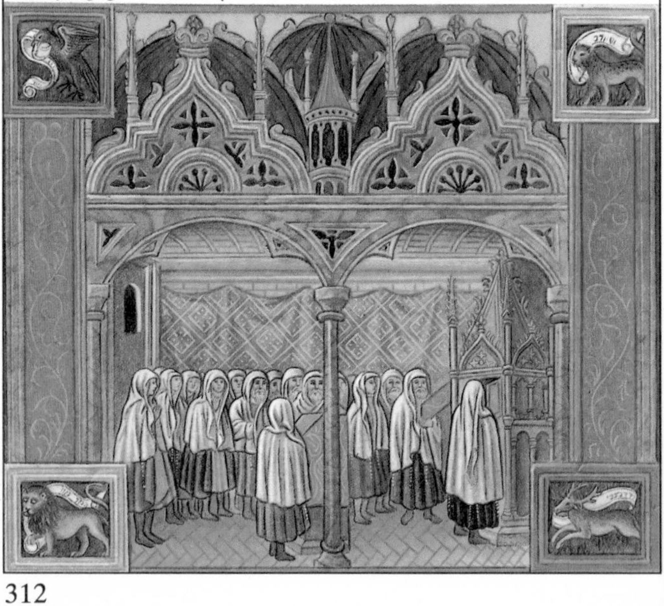

The synagogue was often built at the highest point in the town or on the banks of a river. It was rectangular and faced Jerusalem. Inside, at the far end, was a sacred chest – the Ark. Lamps

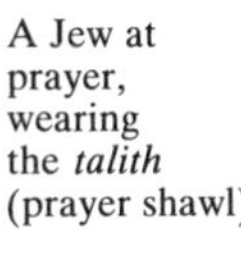

A Jew at prayer, wearing the *talith* (prayer shawl).

burnt constantly in front of the Ark, and inside it were the rolls of the Torah (the Law).

A college of elders elected a leader, whose task it was to preside over and organise the service. He decided who was to recite the prayer and who was to read and comment on the Scriptures. An assistant looked after the synagogue, presented the text to the reader and taught the children.

The main service took place on the morning of the Sabbath (Saturday). This included prayer and readings, first from the Law and then from one of the prophets. There followed a sermon on the texts and then the blessing. The texts were read first in Hebrew but were then translated into Aramaic, since Hebrew had become a dead language.

Ruins of Capernaum (right, the synagogue, and above, an impression of it). Jesus lived there for a while, and some of his disciples were born there.

18th or 19th c. copper lamp for Hannukah (Festival of Lights).

In the synagogue,

the seat 'of Moses' was reserved for the teachers.

The Jewish house

Jewish oil lamp. This was often a house's only source of light. To keep the house cool and discourage burglars, there were few windows.

The people lived mainly in villages or hamlets.

The modest houses were built of wattle and daub or of bricks made of a mixture of clay and straw, which was trodden together and then baked. The walls were whitened with lime.

The houses were shaped like a large square box. They had a single room which was divided into two different levels: the raised part served as the kitchen, dining room and bedroom; the lower part was used as a stable, becoming a playroom or a workroom when the animals were out in the fields.

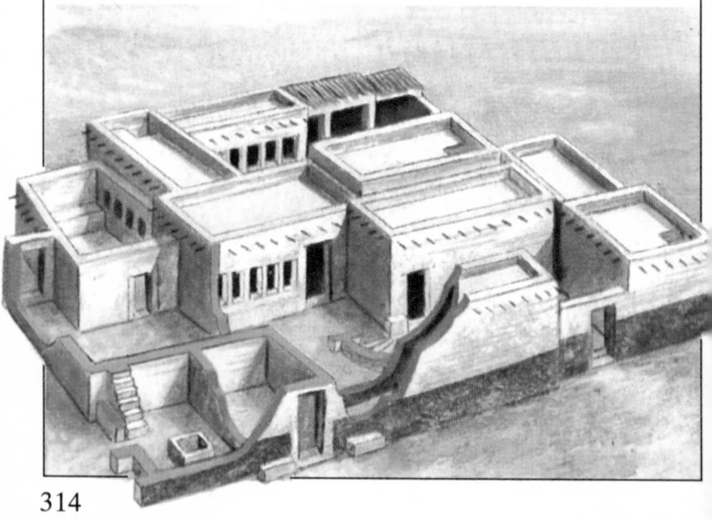

Wealthier people built their houses from stone or mortar based on lime. The rooms were arranged round a central courtyard. There was sometimes

another storey: the 'upper room' was reserved for passing guests. Such houses would also have a cistern and a bathroom.

The roof was flat. It was made of beams intertwined with branches and coated with thick mud. The whole thing had to be strengthened each year before the rainy season. It was surrounded by a parapet, and was reached by an external staircase. People used their roofs for taking the air, sleeping, drying vegetables, ripening fruits and praying.

There was no fireplace. People put their embers into a cavity in the middle of the room, or else they used a brazier.

Richer people had central heating: a system of pipes, carrying either water or warm air, led off from a furnace and travelled round the walls or under the floor.

On the feast of *Succoth*, the Jews built huts out of branches either in front of their homes or on the terraces. This was to commemorate the people's journey in the desert before God settled them in the land promised to Abraham.

Paschal meal or *seder*. According to an ancient rite, the house was marked with the blood of a sacrificial lamb to protect the inhabitants.

Above the door hung the *mezuzah*, a small casket containing a passage from the Torah.

I looked,
and there was an enormous crowd –
no one could count all the people!
They were from every race,
tribe, nation, and language.

Rev 7.9

THE PEOPLE

The expansion of the Empire

Having become a republic, Rome set about conquering the area round the Mediterranean. Until the 2nd c. A.D. it maintained the so-called *pax romana* – a state of relative social and political stability – in the territories it had annexed.

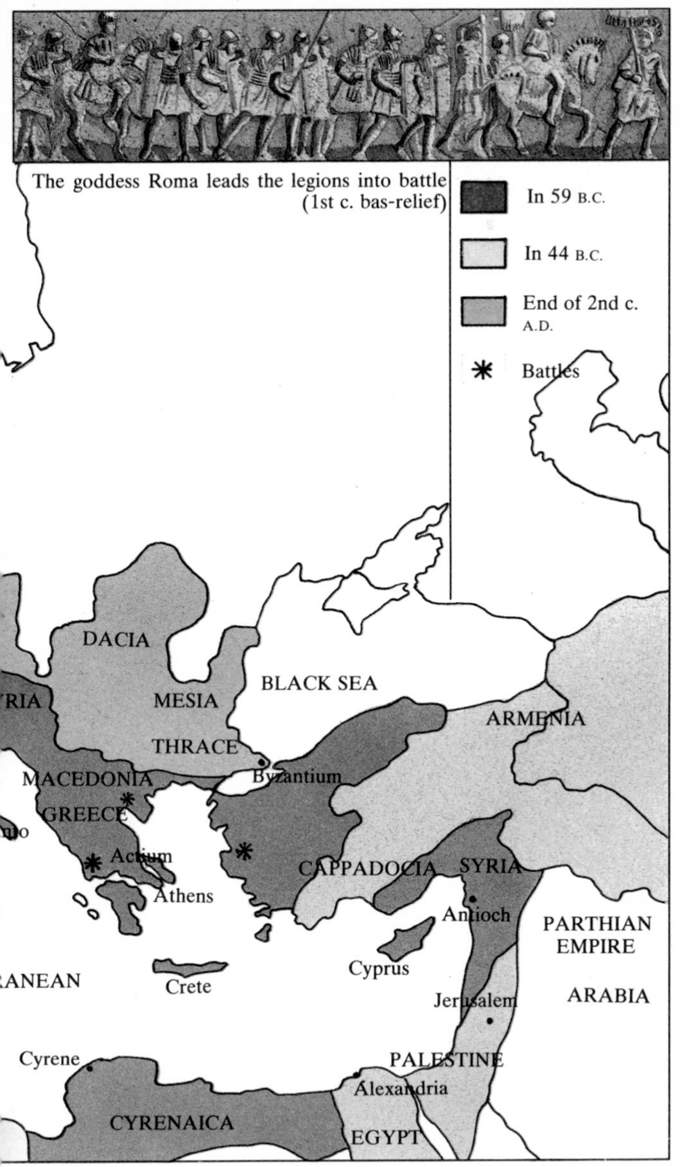

The goddess Roma leads the legions into battle (1st c. bas-relief)

The Roman administration

Voting ceremony: access to the status and the rights of a Roman citizen became gradually easier as the Empire spread.

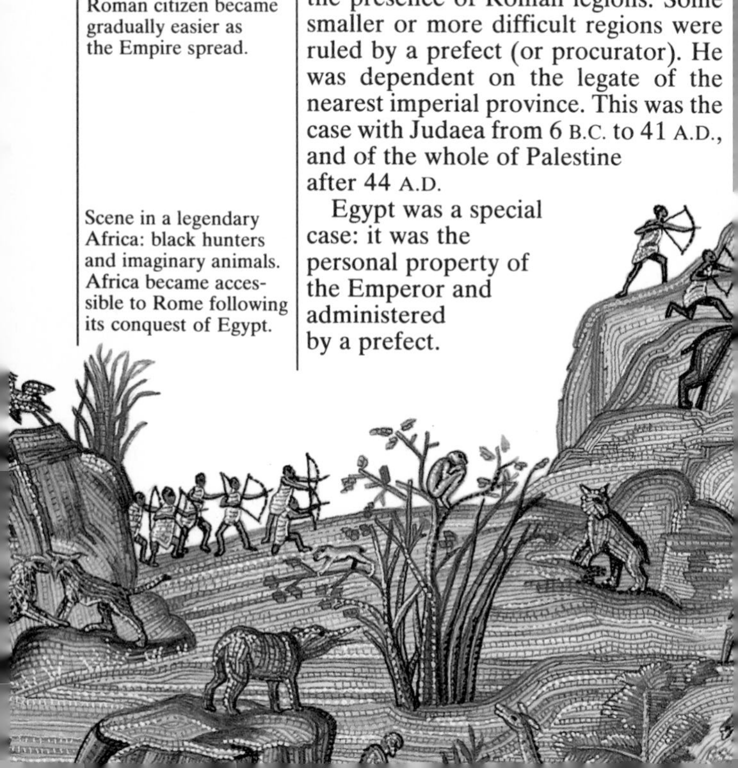

Scene in a legendary Africa: black hunters and imaginary animals. Africa became accessible to Rome following its conquest of Egypt.

Rome administered the territories it conquered in various ways.

Provinces

Senatorial provinces, under the control of the Senate, were distinguished from imperial provinces, under the direct control of the Emperor. The senatorial provinces were quite peaceful, unlike the recently conquered imperial provinces. These were entrusted to legates and required the presence of Roman legions. Some smaller or more difficult regions were ruled by a prefect (or procurator). He was dependent on the legate of the nearest imperial province. This was the case with Judaea from 6 B.C. to 41 A.D., and of the whole of Palestine after 44 A.D.

Egypt was a special case: it was the personal property of the Emperor and administered by a prefect.

It is not just people but territories, nations, that we have tried to fuse together under the name of Rome.
Tacitus, *Annals*, bk XI

While respecting the laws and customs of its subjects, Rome reserved the right to put a person to death.

Subject kingdoms

These were allowed considerable internal autonomy. In return, they had to submit to Rome in external political matters and pay a tax. Their kings were 'friends of the Roman people', and their children were brought up at the Emperor's court.

Above:
an eastern goddess.

Left:
three Gallo-Roman deities. Even the gods of conquered regions acquired Roman characteristics.

Greek cities

Certain cities of the Empire, populated by former legionaries, were treated like cities in Italy. Their inhabitants were Roman citizens, paid no taxes and came within the jurisdiction of the Roman courts.

Other Greek cities were self-governing under the sovereignty of Rome. In Palestine, Decapolis was a federation of ten Greek cities established in 63 B.C.

The peoples of the Empire

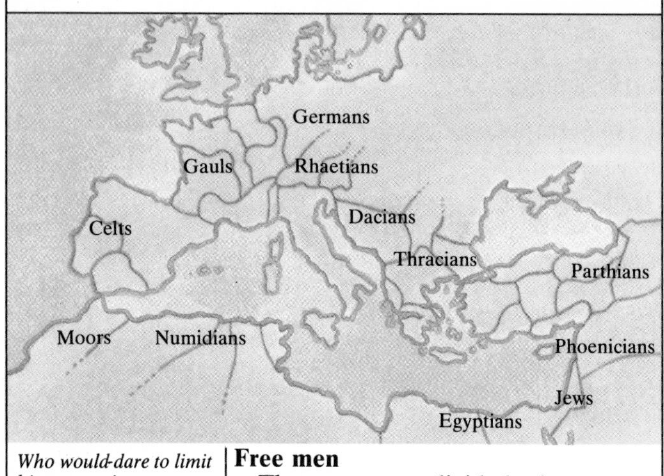

Who would-dare to limit his generosity to those who wear the Roman toga? Seneca, Roman Stoic philosopher, 1st c. A.D.

Free men

These were divided into two categories: Roman citizens, and *peregrini*, e.g. visitors to a Roman city. They were subject to the laws of their own city or people. The number of

Phoenician woman Dacian Parthian Egyptian

A landscape in ancient Germania, a territory which was conquered with great difficulty.

citizens increased as the Empire spread, for the Edict of Caracalla in 212 A.D. granted the title to all its inhabitants. A Roman citizen had the right to vote, to be a magistrate and a legionary, and to appeal to the imperial tribune.

Slaves

There were many slaves: one for every free man in Rome. They were normally prisoners, captured in war and sold at a low price in the slave market. They had no civil or religious rights, although, under the influence of Stoicism in particular, Roman law gradually became less harsh and the most serious forms of ill treatment were banned. Once freed in exchange for the service they had given, slaves became free men and even Roman citizens.

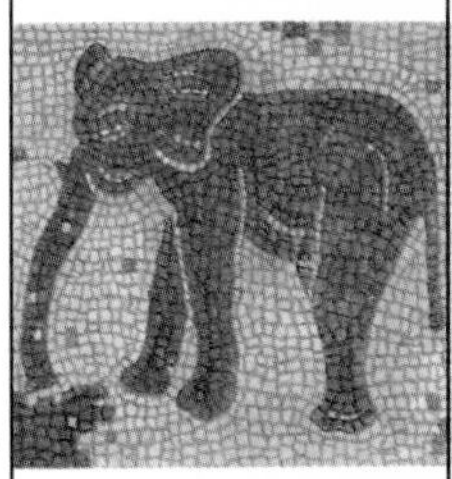

The elephants of the Carthaginian Hannibal had impressed the Romans: but Rome in the end held this part of Africa.

Communication in the Empire

A political inscription on a wall in Pompeii

The languages

Latin was spoken only in the western part of the Empire: Italy, Gaul, Spain.

Greek was essential throughout the Empire as the international language of business, government and cultivated society. For this reason it was known as the 'common language'. All of the New Testament was written in Greek.

Aramaic, which originated in Syria and had been used in the countries of the Middle East since the 7th century B.C., was also spoken. In Palestine in the 1st century B.C. it finally took the place of Hebrew, which the Jewish population no longer understood.

Postal services

The official imperial mail was carried along the Roman roads by a public postal service. Private correspondence, however, did not benefit from this public service.

The public postal service set up by the Emperor Augustus benefited from a system of staging posts and inns.

Books

In the absence of printing, the author would dictate his text to scribes and secretaries. The originals were lent or hired out to be recopied . . . which explains the frequent errors found in the copies.

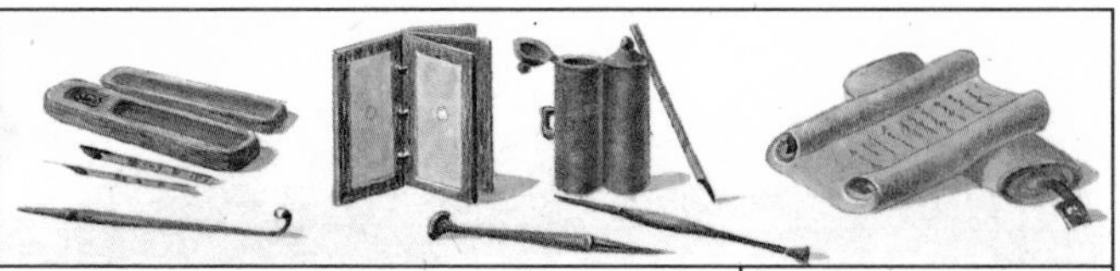

From left to right: inkwell and styluses; wax tablets; boxes for parchment scrolls. Inks were made of soot, mixed with glue or vinegar. People wrote with a metal stylus or a sharpened reed – the *calamus* – on wooden tablets covered with a thin layer of wax. In order to rub out what had been written they had only to warm the wax – hence the expression *tabula rasa* (clean tablet).

There were some sizable public libraries, for example the one in Alexandria in Egypt. Some fortunate individuals had their own private library.

The young Roman woman in this Pompeiian fresco is holding a *codex* or bound collection of these wooden tablets.

Information

News was passed on in various ways: there was a public crier; placards were fixed up in the main square for public notices; wall signs were used to advertise merchandise.

Legionaries' helmets

1st c. swords and dagger

Lead missiles hurled by slings

Soldier carrying his kit

It was the business of the Roman army to keep guard over the frontiers of the Empire, make sure that order was maintained in the provinces and quell rebellions when these occurred. It also made sure that travel was safe on the Roman roads.

It was a professional army, recruiting from among both Roman citizens and non-citizens. The latter were granted citizenship at the end of their period of service, which was legally fixed at 20 years. Payment was one denarius a day. At the end of his time, a Roman soldier

1 army = 22 legions
1 legion = 10 cohorts
1 cohort = 2 manipules
1 manipule = 3 centuries
(1 century = 100 men)

got either 3000 denarii, or a plot of land to cultivate in Italy or in one of the provinces of the Empire.

Composition of the army

The regular army was divided into 22 legions of infantry. Each legion was a unit of 6000 men, made up of ten cohorts of 600 men. Each cohort had two companies (manipules), which were subdivided into three centuries of 100 men each.

The Roman army

The legions were commanded by legates, the cohorts by tribunes, the centuries by centurions. Legates and tribunes were appointed by the Emperor.

Each legion had a cavalry detachment of 120 horses attached to it.

The legions were accompanied by auxiliary forces made up of non-citizens. They provided the foot soldiers, cavalrymen, archers, sappers, slingers and men in charge of the siege engines.

There was also a medical service for the soldiers and a veterinary service for the animals.

The Praetorian Guard was a special detachment responsible for the personal protection of the Emperor.

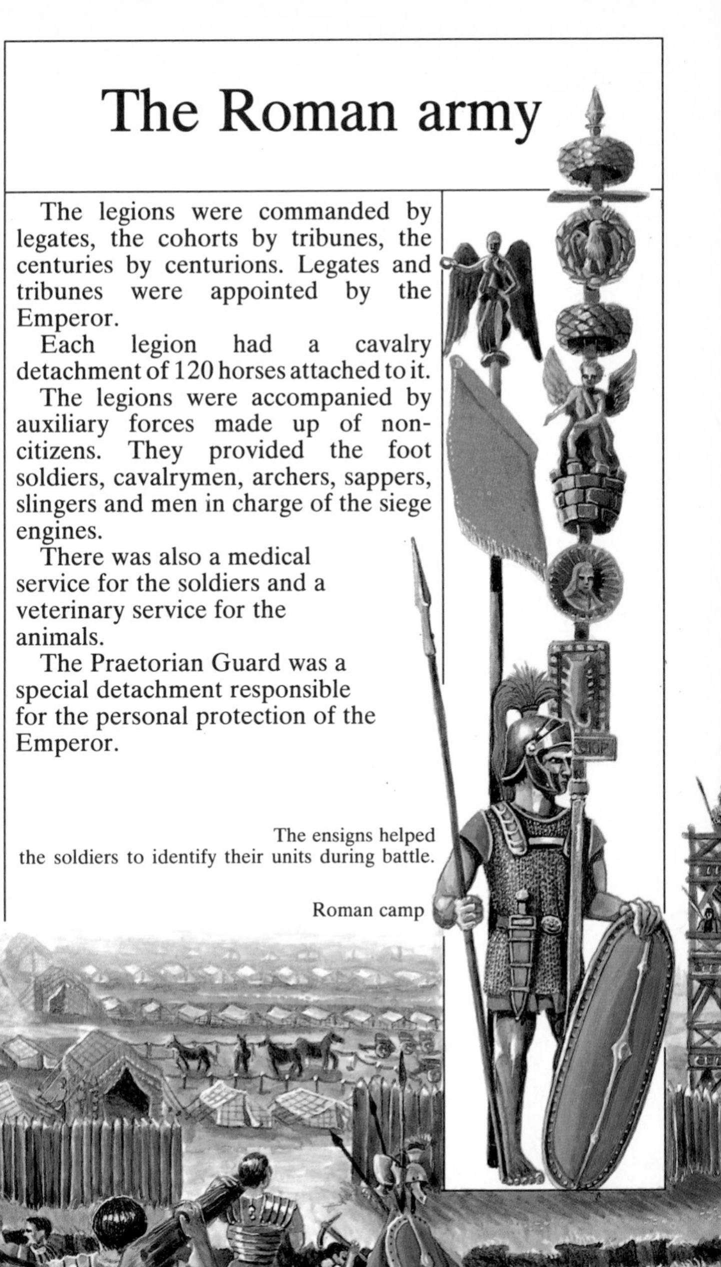

The ensigns helped the soldiers to identify their units during battle.

Roman camp

The Emperor-god

Augustus 27 B.C.- 14 A.D.

Tiberius 14-37 A.D.

Caligula 37-41 A.D.

Claudius 41-54 A.D.

Nero 54-68 A.D.

Galba 68-69 A.D.

In the time of Jesus and the first Christians, the Roman Empire was governed by the Emperor, who enjoyed full political, military and religious power. At the political level, he appointed and strictly supervised the governors of the imperial provinces.

At the military level, he commanded the 300,000 soldiers of the legions which maintained order in the provinces and protected the frontiers of the Empire.

At the religious level, he was the high priest (*pontifex maximus*) of the Roman religion, and more importantly he became the object of a cult to which all his subjects had to submit.

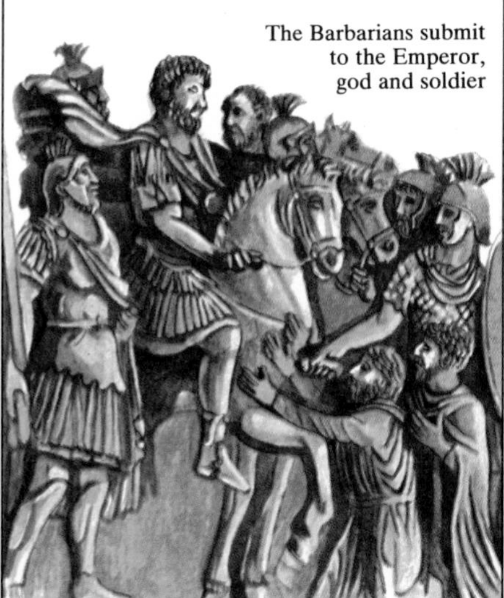
The Barbarians submit to the Emperor, god and soldier

Having left the world which he governed,
Augustus will ascend to heaven
and answer the prayers of mortals.
Ovid, *Metamorphoses*, 15.870

The cult of the Emperor

When Octavius became the first Roman Emperor, he allowed the Senate to give him the title Augustus (majestic, holy), reserved until then for the gods. He was soon hailed as the saviour and liberator of the human race, and his birth was celebrated as a gift from the gods. Temples were dedicated to him in the cities of the Empire. When he died

he was given a place among the gods and a cult was set up in his memory.

This imperial cult and adoration of the sovereign had an important political function: they made it possible to unite many different peoples in a single Empire. Only one people was dispensed from worshipping the Emperor: the Jewish people, which jealously guarded its monotheism. Jews had only to offer a daily sacrifice for the Emperor in the temple in Jerusalem. As long as they were classed with the Jews, the early Christians also enjoyed this privilege.

Seal of the Emperor Augustus

When Augustus came to power in 27 B.C., Rome had just lived through many difficult years of civil war. Augustus helped to re-establish a much longed-for peace, and this was one of the reasons for the cult that grew up around him from then on. His apotheosis (transformation into a god) was accepted from the 1st c. of the Empire. It is represented on this cameo (left), symbolised by an eagle and a crown. The decision to deify certain emperors after their death was taken by the Senate.

Gods of Rome and elsewhere

Above: the Egyptian goddess Isis.
Right: two Syrian priestesses.
The eastern gods owed part of their popularity in Rome in the early days of the Empire to the fact that there was an element of mystery in the ceremonies performed in their honour: this secrecy added to their attraction.

Unlike the Christians and the Jews, whose religion was monotheistic – that is to say, they recognised only one God – the Romans were polytheists: their pantheon included dozens of gods. As the Empire expanded, they added to their number foreign cults imported from the countries they conquered.

The gods imported from the east became increasingly popular from the 1st c. onwards. This was because they promised resurrection in a better world.

The Roman pantheon

The principal gods were: Jupiter (Zeus in Greek), the supreme god, lord of thunder and lightning; his wife Juno (Hera in Greek); Mars (Ares), god of war; Apollo, god of the sun and of the arts; Pluto (Hades), god of the underworld; Neptune (Poseidon), god of the sea; Venus (Aphrodite) goddess of love; Bacchus (Dionysus), god of the vine and the cycle of nature; Ceres

(Demeter), goddess of the harvest; Mercury (Hermes), messenger of the gods and god of travellers; Vulcan (Hephaestus), god of fire; Diana (Artemis), goddess of the moon and the hunt; Minerva (Athena), goddess of wisdom.

Philosophical beliefs

It was from Athens that Rome borrowed its most important philosophical doctrines: Epicureanism and Stoicism.

The Epicureans thought happiness was to be found in physical and intellectual pleasures. The Stoics, disregarding suffering, held submission to reason to be the highest good.

Rome built temples throughout the lands it conquered. In return, it introduced at home cults like that of the Iranian god Mithras, shown here during the ritual sacrifice of the bull.

Domestic altar, in front of which the father of the family recited prayers each day and offered food and wine.

Top of page: instruments used for the sacrifice and insignia of the pontiff (priest of the cult): axe, sprinkler, tripod with offerings, divining rod, knife, peg, water jug.

High priest

Domestic worship

Directed to the gods of the earth (*lares*) and the gods that protected the family (*penates*), this took place within the home.

Worship of the official gods

– Prayers: the worshipper touched the altar or the knees of the statue and repeated aloud the formulas recited by the priests.

– Sacrifices: these mainly involved the ritual killing of animals, whose flesh had to be consumed by the fire. An unblemished animal was adorned with ribbons and flowers. Before the sacrifice, a cake made of honey and salted flour and sprinkled with wine, was placed on its head.

The reading of omens or divination

The Romans interpreted the will of the gods through signs and omens.

The soothsayer took the auspices,

Worship in Rome

that is, he looked for certain signs, favourable or otherwise.

The *haruspex* or soothsayer examined the entrails of sacrificial victims. A lesion in the lungs, for example, meant that one should avoid any new undertaking.

The Sibylline books (the Sibyl was a famous prophetess) foretold Rome's future. They were consulted when circumstances were really grave.

The cult of the Emperor (see p. 328)

Games

Processions, races, fights involving wild animals, combats and so on were dedicated to one or other of the gods. Their number increased until they took up 175 days a year.

Sacred chickens in a cage. Their good appetite was interpreted as a favourable sign by soothsayers.

During the sacrifices a particular animal was assigned to each god: a pig to Ceres, a heifer to Minerva, a white bull to Jupiter.

The soothsayer also watched the flight of birds. If he saw one to his right this was an unfavourable omen.

The temple candelabrum, taken as a trophy to Rome by Titus

From the 6th century until the 2nd century B.C., the Jewish people lived under foreign domination, first Babylonian, then Persian, Greek, Egyptian, and finally Syrian. In 164 B.C., the Jews rose up against Antiochus IV of Syria, who wanted to suppress their religion and impose pagan beliefs. Under the leadership of Judas Maccabeus and his brothers, they regained their independence (pp. 260-261). Judas' brother Simon and his descendants became kings and high priests, creating the Hasmonean dynasty.

In 64 B.C., two of Simon's grandsons – Hyrcanus II and his brother, Aristobulus – were fighting one another for power. Each sent a delegation to Damascus, to the Roman general Pompey, who had just conquered Syria. And each asked for the support of the Roman army.

The *cornicen* or horn-blower. He announced manoeuvres to the troops.

A coin showing captive Judaea

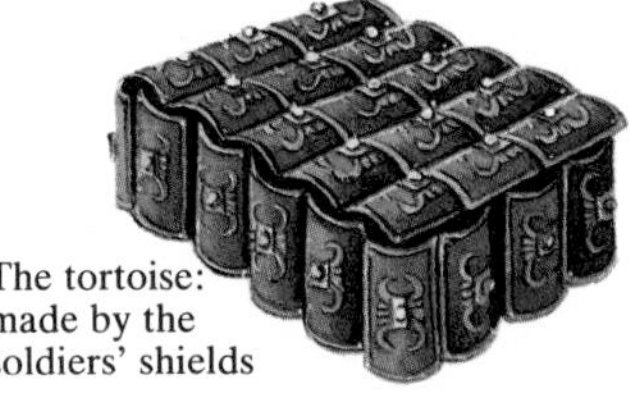

The tortoise: made by the soldiers' shields

Siege techniques used by the Romans. The access ramp: the legionaries filled in the ditch which separated them from the enemy city.

Pompey took Hyrcanus' side and marched on Jerusalem, where Aristobulus and his supporters had barricaded themselves in. After a three-month siege the city was taken. Palestine lost its political independence for ever, becoming a Roman pro-

Rome's conquest of Palestine

tectorate obliged to pay tribute. Hyrcanus was appointed high priest and ethnarch (provincial ruler) by the Romans. Aristobulus, his brother, was taken captive to Rome, along with his two sons, Alexander and Antigonus. They soon escaped, and their return to Palestine started a civil war.

Unable to resist Aristobulus and his sons, Hyrcanus delegated his power to Antipater, governor of Idumea, who took the opportunity to appoint his two sons, Phasael and Herod, to important positions – one as ruler of Jerusalem, the other as ruler of Galilee.

The assault tower: a wooden tower on wheels, which was brought to the wall of the besieged city.

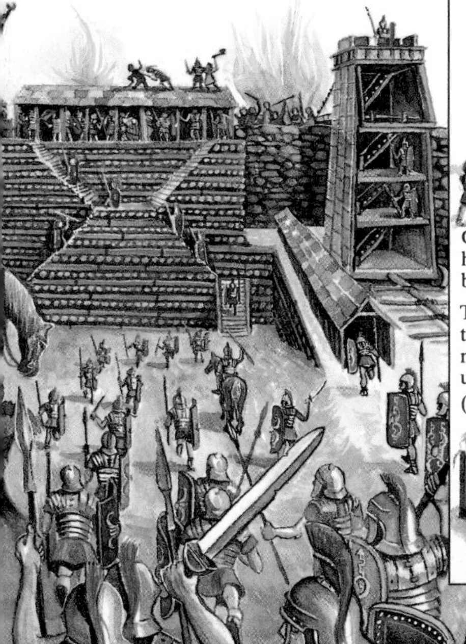

Catapults were used to hurl arrows, stones or burning objects.

The onager: a sling that hurled stone or metal missiles for up to 450 m (1500 ft).

Herod the Great
King of the Jews

His succession
When he died his kingdom was divided between his three surviving sons:
– Archelaus became ethnarch of Judaea, Idumea and Samaria in 6 A.D.
– Herod Antipas was named tetrarch of Galilee and Perea.
– Herod Philip was named tetrarch of Batanea, Auranitis and Trachonitis.
– Agrippa I (his grandson) ruled the kingdom for four years.
– Agrippa II (his great-grandson) was appointed governor of the temple in 49 A.D.

Faithful ally of Rome

Thanks to the support of the Romans, whose faithful ally he was, Herod ruled as undisputed master of Palestine from 37 to 4 B.C. In 32 B.C. he won the confidence of Octavius, the new master of Rome, who in 27 B.C. became the Emperor Augustus.

Herod watching the massacre of the innocents (14th c., after Giotto)

Hated by the Jews

Because he was of non-Jewish origin and appointed by Rome, he was despised by the Jews. The Pharisees called him 'the Idumean slave'.

A good administrator

Herod tried to curry favour with the Jewish people by marrying Mariamne,

Jesus was born in Bethlehem in Judaea during the time when Herod was king.
Mt 2.1

who was of the Hasmonean dynasty, and by rebuilding the temple. He also developed foreign trade through the creation of the port of Caesarea, maintained order within the kingdom and helped when the country fell victim to a famine (25 B.C.), reduced taxes (20-14 B.C.), and protected the country against invasion through the construction of fortresses.

A repressive and cruel sovereign

At the same time, he showed no mercy to his opponents. He cruelly suppressed an uprising of Pharisees. He did not even spare those closest to him: suspecting that his wife Mariamne and several of his sons were plotting against him, he had them executed. Shortly before his own death he had some young men who removed the golden eagle he had set up over the main door of the temple put to death.

Herod Antipas, son of Herod the Great, had John the Baptist beheaded. John had condemned his behaviour.

The palace of Herod the Great, in Jerusalem

Judaism in the time of Jesus

Objects used during worship, arranged round the altar of holocausts. The tree, standing on the Mount of Olives, is where the Messiah would appear at the end of time. (From a 14th c. Catalan illumination.)

The Jewish faith

The Jews believed in a single god. They did not dare to speak his name, Yahweh (YHWH), revealed earlier to Moses (pp. 166-167). The holy books of the Jewish religion (about 50 in all), written between the 10th and 1st centuries B.C, form the Jewish Bible.

The pillars of the Jewish faith

– **The Law** (in Hebrew *Torah*) explained what God expected of his people. The written Law – the first five books of the Bible – was read, and commented on in the synagogue each Sabbath (the weekly day of rest consecrated to God). Its essentials are contained in the Ten Commandments.

The oral Law (in Hebrew *Mishna*) is known as the tradition of the Elders. Over the centuries, the elders interpreted the written Law to adapt it to the circumstances of life. This oral tradition

Every day, morning and evening, the priests offered sacrifices in the temple. (From the *Mishneh Torah* of Maimonides, 15th c. illumination.)

was written down in the 2nd c. A.D., and, along with other writings, came to form the Talmud.

– **The temple**: there was only one temple, the one in Jerusalem. For Jews it represented the centre of the world.

Greek inscription forbidding non-Jews to enter the temple, on pain of death (7)

– **Circumcision** involved cutting off a boy's foreskin. It dated back to the exile in Babylon and was the sign that the person belonged to the people of God.

Altar of Holocausts (2)

1 Sanctuary
3 Court of the priests
4 Court of the men
5 Deposit for food for sacrifices

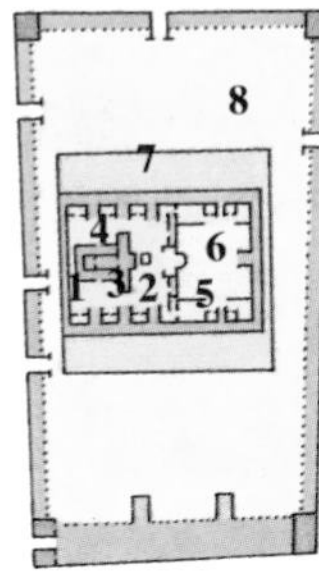

6 Court of the women
8 Court of the Gentiles (non-Jews)

The Jewish clergy

Ivory vase shaped like a pomegranate with six petals. 8th c. B.C., probably from the temple of Solomon.

Circumcision was carried out by the priests.

The High Priest

The High Priest was the head of the clergy; he was responsible for the temple and he presided over meetings of the Sanhedrin. From the time of Herod the Great he was appointed and dismissed by the King and then by the Roman procurators. He was very rich. So as not to lose his position he co-operated with the Romans.

The chief priests

They usually belonged to the family of the High Priest, or were his friends.

The temple commandant

He saw that worship was properly performed and the temple policed.

The leaders of the 24 weekly teams organised the priests who took it in turns to offer sacrifices in the temple.

The 7 temple overseers were responsible for the temple's upkeep.

The 3 treasurers managed the finances of the temple.

The priests

Were all descended from Moses' brother Aaron. They usually had another job as well, but even so they were generally poor. Many of them were sympathisers of the Zealots. Their office was hereditary.

The levites (assistants to the priests)

They, like the priests, were divided into 24 weekly teams. And they too were badly paid and lived poorly from their profession.

The Jewish authorities in Jerusalem sent some priests and levites to John, to ask him 'Who are you?'

Jn 1.19

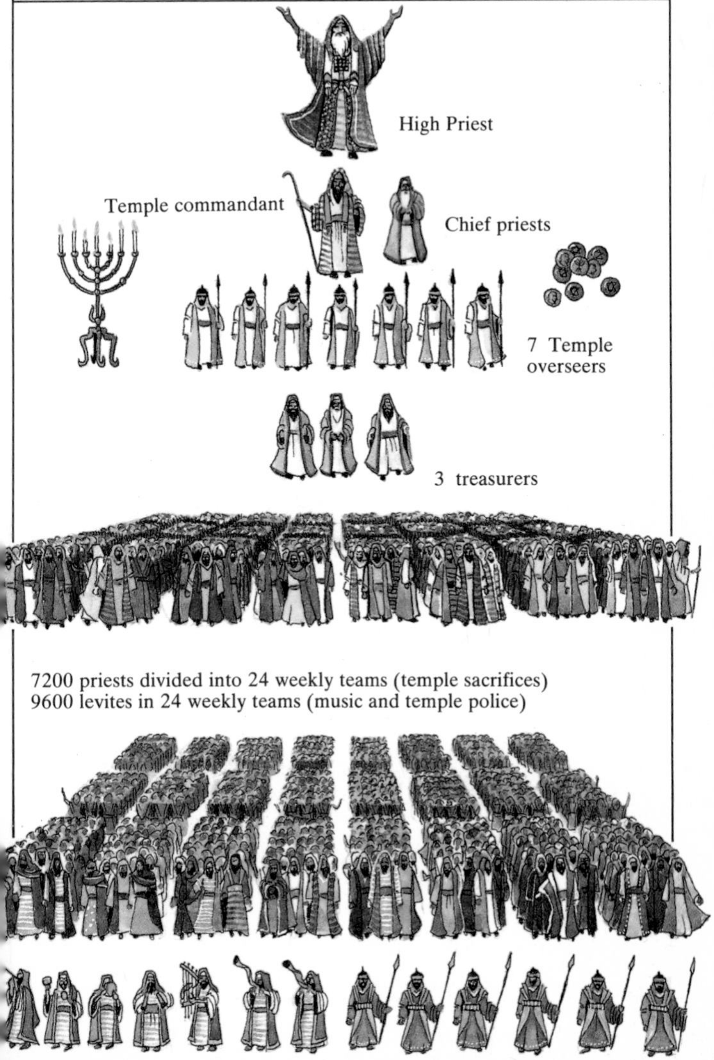

High Priest

Temple commandant

Chief priests

7 Temple overseers

3 treasurers

7200 priests divided into 24 weekly teams (temple sacrifices)
9600 levites in 24 weekly teams (music and temple police)

The Scribes

One of the scribes' tasks was to make copies of the *Torah.*

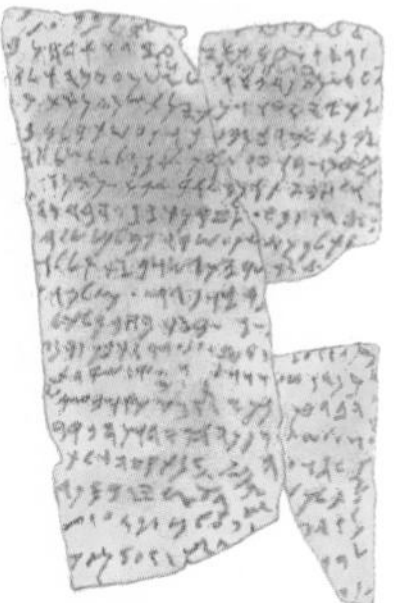

Right: A scribe teaching the *Torah*, the Jewish Law.

Bench and writing

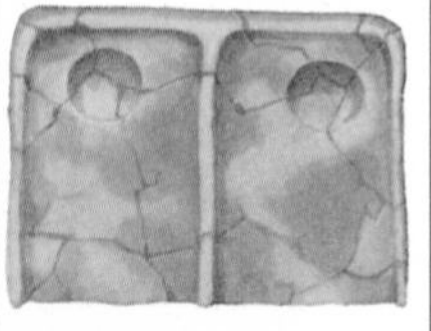

palette found in the scriptorium at Qumran.

As specialists in the written and oral Law, the scribes were responsible for passing it on and interpreting it. As the Law governed every aspect of life in the Jewish community, the scribes had great power and influence.

Their functions

They taught the Law of Moses (written Law) and the tradition of the Elders (oral Law), adding their own interpretations. In Jesus' time there were several schools of scribes and their

interpretations of the Law differed.

Another of the scribes' functions was to administer justice in the courts. They also had a seat in the Sanhedrin – the assembly which dealt with the internal affairs of Judaism and so played a part in government.

Their training

This was very intense. Each pupil spent several years studying under a famous teacher, who taught him the

They preserve the stories of famous men, and draw morals from them.
Ben Sirach, scribe, c. 200 B.C.

Law and passed on to him a hidden and secret knowledge about God, creation and the end of time. When he was forty, he was ordained a scribe with the laying on of hands. He then had a right to the titles sage, doctor of the Law, and master (*rabbi*). He wore the dress of the scribes and in the synagogue he was accorded a place of honour.

Their prestige

This was considerable, and sprang from knowledge of which they had a monopoly. From every corner of the diaspora, Jewish youth streamed into Jerusalem to follow the teachings of the masters. (St Paul came from Tarsus to sit at the feet of Gamaliel.) At their death, tombs were built for them near those of the patriarchs and prophets.

Their way of life

The scribes were usually poor because they had to do their teaching for nothing. They therefore had to work at a trade for their living. They also received gifts from their pupils and assistance from the temple.

After the destruction of the temple at Jerusalem (70 A.D.) and the disappearance of the priests, the scribes, along with the Pharisees, became the most important figures in Jewish society and in the Jewish religion.

The Pharisees

These were fervent Jews who knew the Law, both written and oral, perfectly. They formed communities in which they could live faithfully following the commandments. Each Friday evening they gathered to share a meal. They were uncompromising, and avoided associating with people who

did not know or did not keep the Law. They accused the Sadducees of betraying God by collaborating with the Romans. They themselves would have no contact with sinners, for fear of becoming unclean (Lk 15.2).

The Pharisees were waiting impatiently for the coming of the reign of God and his Messiah. For them, only detailed observance of the Law would hasten that coming.

In Hebrew and Aramaic pharisee means 'separated'.

They followed scrupulously the rules about food and worship, as well as those relating to fasting. That is why a Pharisee would only buy from another Pharisee. Jesus was often angry with them: *How terrible for you, teachers of the Law and pharisees! You hypocrites! You give to God a tenth even of the seasoning herbs . . . but you neglect to obey the really important teachings of the Law, such as justice and mercy and honesty. These you should practice without neglecting the others.* **Mt 23.23**

Pharisees and a student commenting on the *Torah.*

Why do you look at the speck in your brother's eye and pay no attention to the log in your own eye? **Mt 7.3**

The Sadducees

There were relatively few of them, but they formed a powerful group, composed of the priestly aristocracy (the chief priests, former high priests and the reigning high priest) and of well-known rich and cultivated Jews from Jerusalem.

They fulfilled the most important priestly and administrative functions in the temple. For a long time they had a majority in the Sanhedrin. Their power was based on money. But they had a limited influence on the people, from whom they were remote, and whom they despised.

They were conservatives. They only recognised the written Law, rejecting the oral traditions and the new beliefs – such as the resurrection of the dead – put about by the Pharisees. Sadducees and Pharisees were often in conflict with one another.

To preserve their position, their power and their interests, they collaborated with the Romans and tried to lessen the people's hostility towards Rome. After the destruction of Jerusalem and the temple in 70 A.D., they disappeared from history.

Moses receiving the tablets of the Law from God on Mount Sinai (from a 14th c. German manuscript).

Closed to all new doctrines and mistrustful of commentaries, the Sadducees had time only for the written Law.

The Sanhedrin

A stoning:
this punishment was meted out for the most serious offences.

A High Priest tearing his garments as a sign of anger.
The garments were sewn loosely so as to make this dramatic gesture possible.

The great Sanhedrin

Sanhedrin comes from the Greek word *synedrion*, meaning 'assembly, council'. The Sanhedrin ruled the

Jewish people religiously, administratively and juridically. Its power, limited by King Herod the Great, was acquired by the Romans when he died.

The high priest presided over it. There were seventy-one members, divided between the Sadducee faction (distinguished people called elders, former high priests, the current High Priest, and priests) and the Pharisee faction (scribes).

Its power covered every aspect of Jewish life at home and abroad.

– *religious power*: it controlled doctrine, the liturgical calendar and religious life.

– *administrative power*: it made the

Rabbinic court: one of the Sanhedrin's tasks was to judge crimes against the Law of Moses (after a 15th c. Italian miniature).

laws, employed a police force, controlled relations with the Romans.

– *juridical power*: it was the highest tribunal, judging the most serious crimes against the Law. To condemn someone to death it apparently had to obtain the agreement of the Romans.

After the destruction of Jerusalem in 70 A.D, the Great Sanhedrin was set up at Jamnia as a religious institution, run by the pharisaic scribes.

The local sanhedrins

These were local courts, whose role was to pass judgement in ordinary matters.

The Essenes

Of the many manuscripts found at Qumran, only one, a scroll of Isaiah dating from about 100 B.C., is complete.

The Essenes put the manuscripts in jars, which they placed deep in the caves.

Their origin

Towards 150 B.C., some fervent Jews decided to break away from their corrupt religious leaders. Under the leadership of a priest, the master of justice, they retired to the desert. Here, on the shores of the Dead Sea, they lived as a community.

There were about four thousand of them, scattered in various monasteries. The most important of these was undoubtedly Qumran, to the north-west of the Dead Sea, which was discovered in 1947.

Their principles

Regarding the Law: they kept the Jewish Law uncompromisingly, setting

great store by ritual purity. They insisted on God's hatred of sinners and waited for the moment when the sons of light (themselves) would triumph in their struggle against the sons of darkness (Jewish sinners, pagans, the Romans).

Regarding the temple: they refused to go to the temple in Jerusalem, believing that the ceremonies carried out there by irreligious high priests – who had also changed the traditional calendar – were invalid.

Their way of life

When they met in council, the priests exercised absolute authority and discipline was strict. The emphasis was on prayer, manual work, common ownership of goods, sacred meals, study of the Holy Books and the rules of the community, and ritual baths. Most Essenes were celibate.

Their disappearance

Between 66 and 70 B.C., the community of Qumran was destroyed by the Romans. Before dispersing and being massacred, the members of the community hid their precious library in some nearby caves.

It was near these steep cliffs, hollowed out with caves and overlooking the Dead Sea, that the Essenes established their monastery.

No one may come into the assembly of God if he is marked by any human impurity. Whoever suffers in his flesh (leprosy), has paralysed feet and hands, or is blind, deaf, or affected by any other weakness of the body, or even an old man who cannot stand up in the assembled community – such people may not enter.

Extract from the rule of Qumran

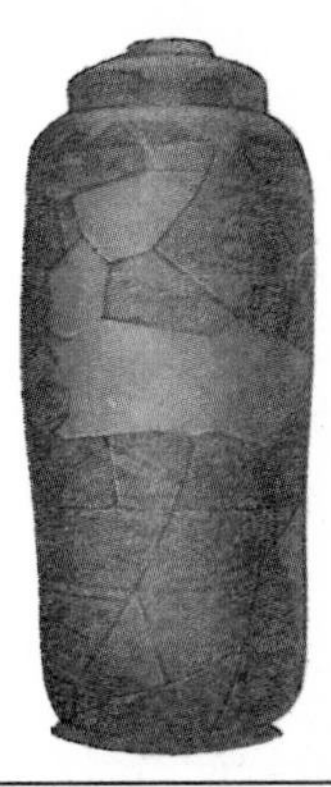

The zealots

GALILEE
SAMARIA
Jordan
JUDAEA
Jerusalem
Dead Sea
Masada

Evidence of the way of life of the last Jewish resisters has been found at Masada.

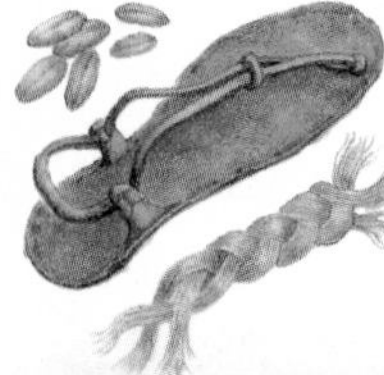

The word zealot comes from the Greek and means 'he who is zealous for' the Law. It referred to fervent Jews, often poor, who were unhappy about the Roman occupation of their country and wished to put an end to it.

Their teaching

They considered it a sacrilege to call the Emperor 'king' or 'lord' (since God alone is king and lord), and they thought it idolatrous to pay taxes or take part in the census. As they saw it, 'holy war' had to be waged against Rome. Once liberated, the people of God would have to live by an ideal of justice: abolishing large landholdings, freeing slaves and sharing the goods of the earth.

Their actions

In 6 A.D., Herod the Great's son Archelaus was banished. Judaea became a Roman province and a census of the population was carried out for tax purposes. At this point, Judas the Galilean led a rebellion in Galilee. This was put down in a bloody manner by the Romans.

The fortress of Masada, last bastion of Zealot resistance.

The baptists

The baptists performed baptisms (hence their name) and were very popular with the ordinary people.

They differed from:

– the Pharisees: they did not believe that minute observance of the Law was essential; life in God comes from conversion of the heart.

– the Sadducees: they did not place so much value on the temple and on blood sacrifices.

– the Essenes: they did not multiply ritual washings, but immersed people in the water only once (baptism), since this symbolised trust in God who alone brings about conversion of heart.

In the 1st century, the two best known groups were those of John, called 'the Baptist', and of Jesus, his disciple. These groups were despised by other religious groups.

A source of life and regeneration, water is associated with many Jewish purification rituals.

The Jordan, which flows for 300 kms (190 m) from Mount Hermon in Lebanon to the Dead Sea, is the river of rivers. Jesus was baptised in it.

Many of the people were waiting for a messiah-king of the family of David.

The word comes from the Hebrew *meshiah* which means 'anointed with oil' and so 'consecrated'. In Greek it is *christ.* It was used with reference to kings and high priests.

The prophets looked forward to a kingdom of justice and peace over which a messiah of God would reign.

This expectation only increased during the many crises the Jewish people experienced: deportations, domination by a succession of foreign powers,

Ascension of the prophet Elijah in his fiery chariot (15th c. Russian icon). According to biblical tradition, he did not die but was raised up to heaven. The Jews awaited his return, which was to coincide with the coming of the Messiah.

persecution in the 2nd century B.C., Roman occupation from 63 B.C. onwards, etc. From the 2nd century B.C., many writings claimed to announce the coming of the Kingdom of God. They are described as 'apocalyptic' (from the Greek *apocalupsis*, 'revelation'), since they professed to reveal the hidden meaning of events.

Top of page: one aspect of the awaited messiah: the warrior who would be able to triumph over the occupying Romans.

The messiahs

This is how they described the various stages in the coming of the Kingdom of God to be established by his messiah:

— every kind of tribulation: earthquakes, plagues . . .

— return of the prophet Elijah

— coming of the messiah, accompanied by wonders similar to those once worked by Moses in the desert

— struggle and victory against the forces of evil (sinners, foreigners, occupying peoples)

— establishment of the Kingdom of God (purification of Jerusalem and of the temple, Jewish domination of other nations, political reign of the messiah, redistribution of goods to the poor)

— resurrection of the dead

— judgement of God, bringing the just to eternal happiness and the wicked to eternal fire.

The gospels have as a background anticipation of the coming of the kingdom of God and his messiah.

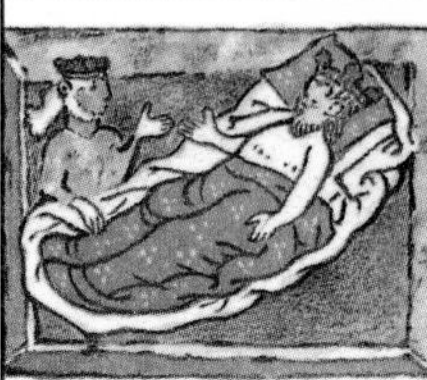

Almost no one imagined a messiah like the Suffering Servant of the Old Testament.

The image of the messiah-prophet was often linked with that of the messiah-king.

THE STORY
1 Jesus the Messiah

Abbreviations

Matthew	Mt
Mark	Mk
Luke	Lk
John	Jn
Acts	Acts
Romans	Rom
1 Corinthians	1 Cor
2 Corinthians	2 Cor
Galatians	Gal
Ephesians	Eph
Philippians	Phil
Colossians	Col
1 Thessalonians	1 Thes
2 Thessalonians	2 Thes
1 Timothy	1 Tim
2 Timothy	2 Tim
Titus	Tit
Philemon	Phlm
Hebrews	Heb
James	Jms
1 Peter	1 Pet
2 Peter	2 Pet
1 John	1 Jn
2 John	2 Jn
3 John	3 Jn
Jude	Jude
Revelation	Rev

Many people have done their best to write a report of the things that have taken place among us. . . . Because I have carefully studied all these matters from their beginning, I thought it would be good to write an orderly account for you. I do this so that you will know the full truth about everything which you have been taught.

Beginning of Luke's Gospel

Now, there are many other things that Jesus did. If they were all written down one by one, I suppose that the whole world could not hold the books that would be written.

End of John's Gospel

Tacitus,
the Roman historian,
early 2nd c.

Learned Jew
studying the Talmud

Jesus died in about the year 30 of our era. He left no writings: we only know him through what others have written about him. Four groups of documents are the source of our knowledge of Jesus.

The Christian documents

The most important documents are the four books we call gospels. They were written by the first Christians in the second half of the 1st century. They are not biographies of Jesus of Nazareth but the testimony of believers.

So, in the final section of this book, we are going to present not a biography of Jesus, but the significant moments of his life based on what the four gospels have to say about them.

There are other, unofficial documents. These are called *apocrypha*, that is, hidden. They were written from the 2nd century onwards. The best known are the gospels of Peter, Thomas and James.

The pagan documents

– In his *Annals*, written in 116-117, the Roman historian Tacitus mentions Jesus, calling him Christ, in connection with Nero's persecution of the Christians in 64: *Their name comes from Christ who was put to death, while Tiberius was on the throne, by the procurator Pontius Pilate.*

– In about 110, Pliny the Younger (legate of the Emperor Trajan in the province of Bithynia in Asia Minor)

How do we know Jesus?

wrote a letter about the presence of Christians in his territory.

The Jewish documents

– Flavius Josephus, a Jewish historian (37-100), refers to Jesus twice in his *Jewish Antiquities.*

– The Talmud, a collection of ancient oral traditions set down in writing in the 5th and 6th centuries A.D, also mentions Christ.

The Muslim documents

The Koran, which was written in Arabia in the 7th century, mentions Jesus. What it says seems to have been inspired by the apocryphal gospels.

Top left: Christ teaching (from a fresco in the catacomb of Domitilla).

At this time there was a wise man named Jesus whose way of life was good; his virtues were acknowledged. Perhaps he was the Messiah, in whose connection the prophets had spoken of wonders.

Flavius Josephus

The Koran presents Jesus as a prophet who announced the coming of Mahomet, the founder of Islam. *Yes, the Messiah, Jesus, son of Mary, is the prophet of God, his Word, whom he cast into Mary, a Spirit emanating from himself.*

Koran IV, 171

In the Islamic tradition, Jesus will return at the end of time (16th c. Turkish miniature).

The origin of the gospels

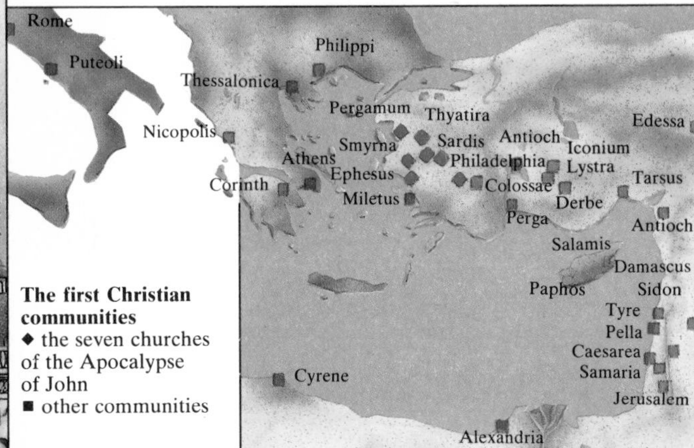

The first Christian communities
◆ the seven churches of the Apocalypse of John
■ other communities

Each of the four gospels bears the imprint of its author. It is also strongly influenced by the community from which it emerged or for which it was destined. Throughout history there have been repeated, although unimportant, attempts to reduce the four gospels to one. One of the most systematic was that of the 2nd c. Greek apologist Tatian.

Each of the gospels is attributed to one person: Matthew, Mark, Luke, John. In fact, they are the work of a number of people.

Written for the first Christians

The early Christians did not set out to write books about Jesus. However, in order to nourish their own faith as well as to share it, they told others about the deeds and words of Jesus. To convince the pagans, they described certain miracles. At each eucharistic meal they repeated the words Jesus had spoken at the Last Supper.

Authentic texts

Gradually, these words and deeds were set down in writing. It was with the help of such texts that the gospel of Mark was finished in 65 or 70, those of

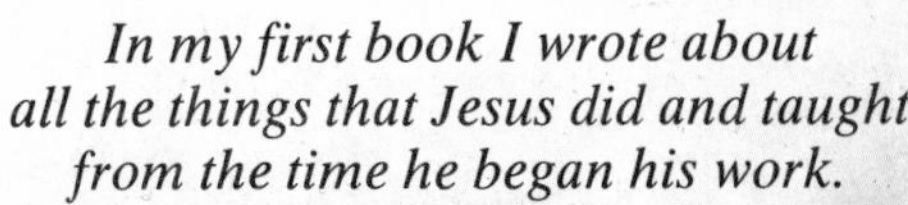

In my first book I wrote about all the things that Jesus did and taught from the time he began his work.

Acts 1.1

Matthew and Luke between 75 and 80, and that of John in about 95.

John's gospel and the synoptics

Three of the four gospels have many passages in common. They are known as the synoptic gospels because it is possible to place their texts in parallel columns to make comparison easier. This form of presentation is sometimes used in the next section of this book.

The gospel of John stands apart. Although it shares some passages with the synoptics, it contains many developments that are entirely its own.

The Gospel and the gospels

The word gospel, which comes orginally from Greek, means a joyful message. For Jesus it meant the coming of the Kingdom of God: good news of liberation for all men and women.

For the first Christians, the Gospel was not just what Jesus said and did, but Jesus himself. The four gospels were four ways of proclaiming the Gospel of Jesus.

Matthew's gospel

His symbol: an angel or a man. This was because he traced the genealogy of Jesus.

According to a 2nd century tradition, Matthew was the tax-collector from Capernaum whom Jesus called to be his disciple.

Matthew's community

Consisted of Christians of Jewish origin living in Syria-Palestine. Matthew's gospel is the most Jewish of the four.

These Christians were proud of their tradition: Matthew presented Jesus to them as the new Moses, who came not to abolish the Jewish Law but to fulfil it (Mt 5.17).

They were rejected by official Judaism and, in about 80, were excluded from the synagogue. This explains Matthew's harsh attitude towards the Pharisees and the importance he gives to Galilee, for him a symbol of the pagan nations.

Matthew insisted on the universality of the gospel: *Go then, to all peoples everywhere and make them my disciples.* **Mt 28.19**

Mark's gospel

Towards the beginning of the 2nd century, people began to mention a certain Mark, the interpreter of Peter, 'who wrote down exactly all he remembered of the words and actions of the Lord'. For this reason the gospel Mark is identified with the John Mark mentioned in the Acts of the Apostles.

The house of Mark's mother, Mary, was a meeting place for Christians in Jerusalem. He accompanied the apostle Paul for a time on Paul's first missionary journey. Then he was to be found with Barnabas in Cyprus. In Rome, where he settled, he attached himself to the apostle Peter.

According to an ancient tradition, Mark wrote his gospel on the basis of Peter's memories.

Mark's community

These were Christians of pagan origin. They were probably based in Rome, and threatened by the persecutions.

Mark explained Jewish customs to them (Mk 7.3-4). He liked to emphasise that God loved them as much as the Jews.

His gospel is the oldest of the four.

His symbol: the lion
Mark's gospel begins by recalling John the Baptist in the desert:
Someone is shouting in the desert:
Get the road ready for the Lord.
(**Mk 1.3**) According to popular belief at the time, the desert was full of wild animals. This is what the lion, always associated with the evangelist, refers to.

Luke's gospel

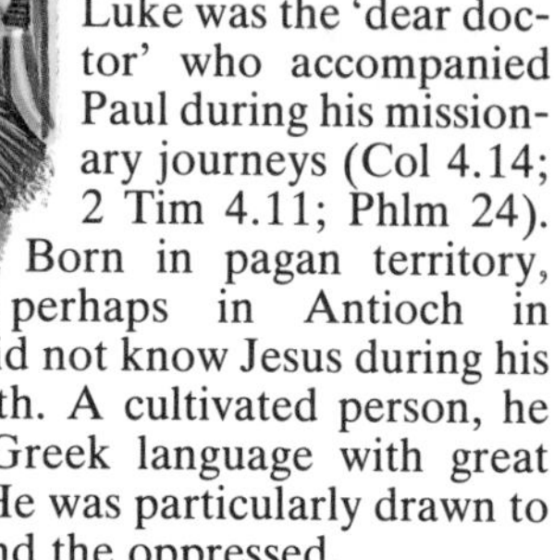

It is very likely that Luke was the 'dear doctor' who accompanied Paul during his missionary journeys (Col 4.14; 2 Tim 4.11; Phlm 24). Born in pagan territory, perhaps in Antioch in Syria, he did not know Jesus during his life on earth. A cultivated person, he used the Greek language with great elegance. He was particularly drawn to the poor and the oppressed.

Luke's community

This was made up of Christians of pagan origin living outside Palestine and influenced by Greek culture. Some were poor and rejected by those among whom they lived, Jewish and pagan.

Luke insisted on the reality of Jesus' resurrection, an idea that was quite unfamiliar to the Greeks. He called Jesus 'saviour', a more specific title than that of 'messiah'. Going against the widespread practice in pagan circles, he emphasised that the only Lord was Jesus – not the Emperor.

In order to buoy up the hope of these despised Christians, Luke stressed the liberation brought by the Gospel (Lk 4.18). In the Acts of the Apostles (which he also wrote) he describes how the Christian faith spread throughout the Empire.

John's gospel

According to tradition, the author of the fourth gospel was the apostle John, the son of Zebedee.

John's community

This is usually thought to have been in Ephesus, in Asia Minor. It was influenced by:

– the celebrated philosophy of the Greeks, in which God the unknowable makes himself known through his word. That is why John presents Jesus as the Word (Jn 1);

– gnosticism (from the Greek word *gnosis*, meaning knowledge). John presents Jesus as the one who reveals God's secret: a boundless love which is quite undeserved;

– Judaism.

John's symbol: the eagle
Unique in being able to gaze at the sun, the eagle symbolises contemplation.
This explains its connection with John, the most reflective of the evangelists.
The eagle is associated not only with various gods and heroes but also with Christ.
Hence its connection with John, who is often called 'the disciple whom Jesus loved'.

John dictating his gospel to a scribe (from a 16th c. Russian icon).

Luke's symbol: the ox
Facing page: Luke, after a 15th c. manuscript, *Les Heures de Rohan.*

Jesus' infancy and childhood

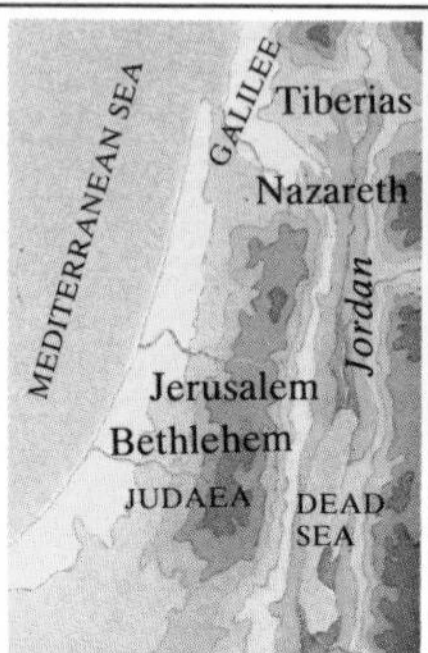

When Jesus began to speak publicly, he was about thirty years old. Where did he come from and what had he been doing up until then?

The gospels are extremely discreet about this period. They agree that Jesus came from Nazareth, a small village in Galilee which was little known and rather despised by the citizens of Jerusalem. In fact, Galileans were suspected of failing to observe the Jewish Law in all its purity.

Jesus' mother was called Mary and his father, Joseph, was a carpenter.

The gospels make several references to Jesus' brothers and sisters (Mk 6.3). As the word for brother in both Hebrew and Greek meant cousin as well as brother, we cannot say for certain whether or not Jesus had brothers and sisters in our sense of the words.

Only the gospels of Matthew and Luke mention – in different ways – the infancy of Jesus. These gospels of the infancy were written a long time after the event. They resemble accounts

of the childhood of famous men in the Bible (Isaac, Moses, Samuel, Samson), written after the event to show that these heroes of the Jewish people had been raised up by the almighty power of God.

Luke's gospel of the infancy

This is set out in such a way as to establish a parallel between John the Baptist and Jesus: both are great in the eyes of God but Jesus is the greater.

Jesus and John the Baptist playing

Matthew's gospel of the infancy

After the genealogy of Jesus there are five short stories, each containing a quotation from the Bible introduced by the formula: *in order to make what the Lord said through the prophets come true.* Three of these stories focus on Joseph, the other two on Herod.

The genealogies of Jesus in Matthew and Luke are different for they are not historical but symbolic. Matthew looks for Jesus' roots among the Jewish people of whom he is the culmination; Luke goes back to Adam: Jesus came for all people.

Luke's gospel of the infancy (1)

The virgin birth of Jesus – that is, without the intervention of a man – was the first Christians' way of saying that Jesus, whom they recognised as the Messiah and the son of God, was God's greatest gift of all.

Luke follows the pattern of other annunciations in the Bible:
– presentation of the people involved, with emphasis on a difficulty (for example, the sterility of the mother)
– appearance of an angel (messenger of God)
– distress
– announcement of a child, his name and his mission
– objection and request for a sign
– reply, naming the sign
– coming of the sign and birth of the promised child.

The annunciation

God sent the angel Gabriel to a town in Galilee named Nazareth. He had a message for a girl promised in marriage to a man named Joseph, who was a descendant of King David. The girl's name was Mary. . . . The angel said to her, . . . 'You will become pregnant and give birth to a son, and you will name him Jesus. He will be great and will be called the Son of the Most High God. The Lord God will make him a king, as his ancestor David was . . . his kingdom will never end!' Mary said to the angel, 'I am a virgin. How then, can this be?' The angel answered, 'The Holy Spirit will come on you. . . . For this reason the holy child will be called the Son of God. Remember your relative Elizabeth . . . she herself is now six months pregnant, even though she is very old.'

Lk 1.26-36

'I am the Lord's servant,' said Mary;
'may it happen to me as you have said.'
Lk 1.38

The visitation

Mary went to visit her cousin Elizabeth who was soon to give birth to John the Baptist. Elizabeth cried out:

'As soon as I heard your greeting, the baby within me jumped with gladness.'. . .

Mary said, 'My heart praises the Lord; my soul is glad because of God my Saviour, for he has remembered me, his lowly servant! From now on all people will call me happy, because of the great things the Mighty God has done for me. His name is holy; from one generation to another he shows mercy to those who honour him. He has stretched out his mighty arm and scattered the proud with all their plans. He has brought down mighty kings from their thrones, and lifted up the lowly. He has filled the hungry with good things.' **Lk 1.42-53**

Mary's words, now known as the Magnificat (the first word of the Latin translation) were mostly inspired by the song of Anna, the mother of Samuel (**1 Sam 2.1-10**) in the Old Testament. The Magnificat expresses, in a few words, at the beginning of Luke's gospel, the heart of the Christian faith, which is illustrated by the words and actions of Jesus.

Annunciation and visitation, after Fra Angelico (15th c.)

Luke's gospel of the infancy (2)

Year 1 of our era: In the 15th c., it became usual in the West to count the years from the birth of Jesus. But a mistake was made in the calculation: Jesus' birth took place between 6 and 4 B.C.

Was he born in a cave? The Gospel does not say so. The first person to suggest it was Justin (2nd c.).

Between ox and ass: this tradition dates back to Origen, a famous Christian scholar from North Africa (3rd c.).

Jesus' birth in Bethlehem

At that time the Emperor Augustus ordered a census to be taken throughout the Roman Empire. . . . Everyone, then, went to register himself, each to his own town.

Joseph went from the town of Nazareth in Galilee to the town of Bethlehem in Judaea, the birthplace of King David. Joseph went there because he was a descendant of David. He went to register with Mary, who was promised in marriage to him. She was pregnant, and while they were in Bethlehem, the time came for her to have her baby. She gave birth to her first son, wrapped him in strips of cloth and laid him in a manger – there was no room for them to stay in the inn.

Lk 2.1-7

*Glory to God in the highest heaven,
and peace on earth to those
with whom he is pleased.* **Lk 2.14**

The announcement to the shepherds

There were some shepherds in that part of the country who were spending the night in the fields, taking care of their

flocks. An angel of the Lord appeared to them, and the glory of the Lord shone over them. They were terribly afraid but the angel said to them, 'Don't be afraid! I am here with good news for you, which will bring great joy to all the people. This very day in David's town your Saviour was born – Christ the Lord! And this is what will prove it to you: you will find a baby wrapped in strips of cloth and lying in a manger.'

Suddenly a great army of heaven's angels appeared with the angel, singing praises to God. . . .

The shepherds *hurried off and found Mary and Joseph and saw the baby lying in the manger. When the shepherds saw him, they told them what the angel had said . . . Mary remembered all these things and thought deeply about them.* **Lk 2.8-19**

December 25: this date is not given in the gospels. It was fixed in Rome in the 4th c. to supplant the pagan feast of the Unconquered Sun.

The custom of making a crib in churches and homes dates back to St Francis of Assisi in 1223.

For Jews in the time of Jesus, shepherds were a despised and distrusted group, because they did not respect the Jewish Law. In this gospel account, they represent the humble, the poor, and the outcasts towards whom Jesus will be particularly attentive.

The infancy according to Matthew

The wise men's gifts came from Arabia. The Bible often mentions them as gifts brought by the pagan nations to the expected Messiah. **(Is 60.6)** This exotic gesture is brought out by this mosaic in Ravenna.

Jesus was born in Bethlehem in Judaea, during the time when Herod was king. Soon afterwards, some men who studied the stars came from the east to Jerusalem and asked, 'Where is the baby born to be the king of the Jews? We saw his star when it came up in the east, and we have come to worship him.'

Herod was troubled and asked the chief priests where the Christ was to be born.

'In the town of Bethlehem in Judaea,' . . . For this is what the prophet wrote: . . . 'From you will come a leader who will guide my people Israel.'

Herod then summoned the wise men and said: *'Go and make a careful search for the child, and when you find him, let me know, so that I too may go and worship him.'*

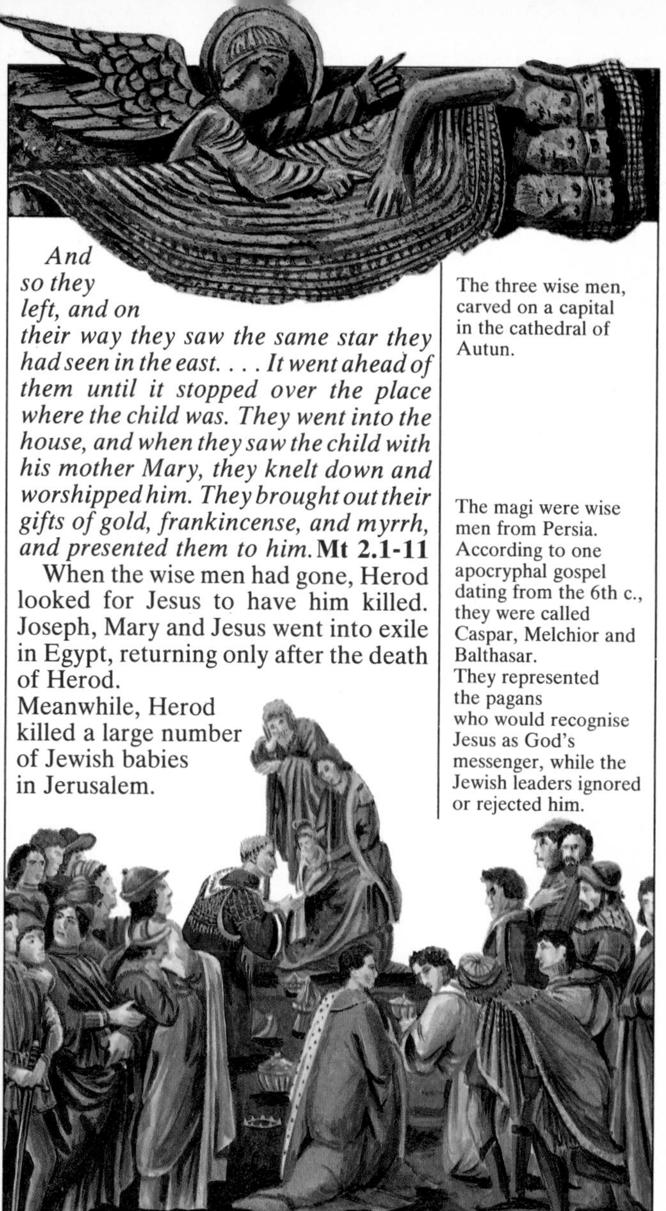

And so they left, and on their way they saw the same star they had seen in the east. . . . It went ahead of them until it stopped over the place where the child was. They went into the house, and when they saw the child with his mother Mary, they knelt down and worshipped him. They brought out their gifts of gold, frankincense, and myrrh, and presented them to him. **Mt 2.1-11**

When the wise men had gone, Herod looked for Jesus to have him killed. Joseph, Mary and Jesus went into exile in Egypt, returning only after the death of Herod.
Meanwhile, Herod killed a large number of Jewish babies in Jerusalem.

The three wise men, carved on a capital in the cathedral of Autun.

The magi were wise men from Persia. According to one apocryphal gospel dating from the 6th c., they were called Caspar, Melchior and Balthasar.
They represented the pagans who would recognise Jesus as God's messenger, while the Jewish leaders ignored or rejected him.

Jesus, disciple of John the Baptist

The baptism given by John the Baptist
Those who chose to be converted, that is to change their lives by being faithful to the Law of God, were immersed by John in the waters of the Jordan. For them it was a new beginning.

Until he was thirty, Jesus lived in Nazareth. One day he left his village. He went down to Judaea to meet a strange prophet who was proclaiming his message on the banks of the Jordan. The crowds gathered round to be baptised. This was John the Baptist.

At that time John the Baptist came to . . . Judaea and started preaching. 'Turn away from your sins,' he said, 'because the Kingdom of heaven is near!'

John was the man the prophet Isaiah was talking about when he said, 'Someone is shouting in the desert, "Prepare a road for the Lord; make a straight path for him to travel!"'

John's clothes were made of camel's hair; he wore a leather belt round his waist, and his food was locusts and wild honey. People came to him from Jerusalem, from the whole province of Judaea. . . . They confessed their sins, and he baptised them in the Jordan. **Mt 3.1-6**

After a few weeks – or perhaps months – Jesus asked John to baptise him.

. . . Jesus also was baptised. While he was praying, heaven was opened, and the Holy Spirit came down upon him in bodily form like a dove. And a voice

I assure you that John the Baptist is greater than any man who has ever lived. But he who is least in the Kingdom of heaven is greater than John. **Mt 11.11**

came from heaven, 'You are my own dear Son. I am pleased with you.' **Lk 3.21-22**

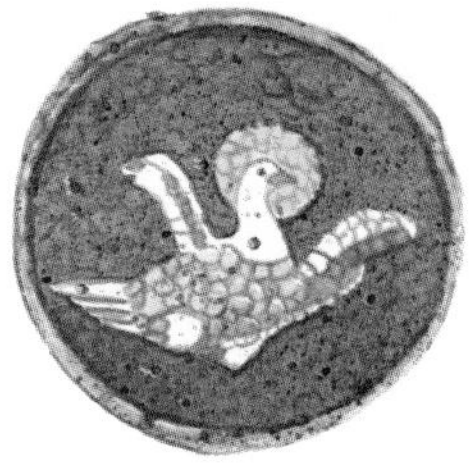

Then, having spent time alone in the desert, Jesus began to preach and baptise like John, a little way off, by the Jordan. He gathered his first disciples round him. John encouraged people to go and listen to Jesus.

. . . 'You yourselves are my witnesses that I said, "I am not the Messiah, but I have been sent ahead of him." . . . He must become more important while I become less important.' **Jn 3.28-30**

The death of John the Baptist
John was to be imprisoned and then killed by Herod Antipas, whom he reproached for marrying his brother's wife.

Jesus is baptised by John the Baptist, after a Russian icon (15th-16th c.)

Jesus in the desert

(Lk 4.1; Mk 1.13; Mt 4.1)

The three synoptic gospels tell how, after his baptism by John the Baptist, Jesus withdrew to the desert, where he was tempted by the devil.

Then the Spirit led Jesus into the desert to be tempted by the Devil. After spending forty days and nights without food, Jesus was hungry. Then the Devil came to him and said, 'If you are God's Son, order these stones to turn into bread.' But Jesus answered, 'The scripture says, "Man cannot live on bread alone, but needs every word that God speaks."'

This account of Jesus' temptations at the beginning of the gospels sums up those he was to face during his life: the temptation to be a temporal messiah, who would bring abundance and prosperity to his people, who would impose his will on all nations. Jesus resisted the temptations to which the people of the Bible had succumbed. After God had sent them food: manna and

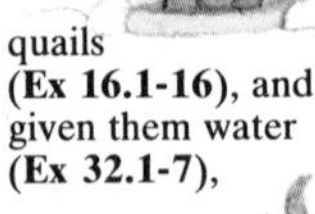

quails (**Ex 16.1-16**), and given them water (**Ex 32.1-7**),

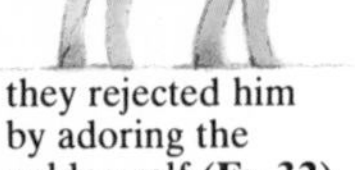

they rejected him by adoring the golden calf (**Ex 32**).

Then the Spirit led Jesus into the desert to be tempted by the devil.
Mt 4.1

Then the Devil took Jesus to Jerusalem, the Holy City, set him on the highest point of the Temple, and said to him: 'If you are God's Son, throw yourself down . . . "God will give orders to his angels . . . not even your feet will be hurt on the stones."'

Jesus answered, 'But the scripture also says, "Do not put the Lord your God to the test."'

Then the Devil took Jesus to a very high mountain and showed him all the kingdoms of the world in all their greatness. 'All this I will give you,' the Devil said, 'if you kneel down and worship me.'

Then Jesus answered, 'Go away, Satan! The scripture says, "Worship the Lord your God and serve only him!"'

Then the Devil left Jesus; and angels came and helped him. **Mt 4.1-11**

Jesus stayed in the desert for forty days. The figure forty is symbolic. It signifies the time needed to mature through an experience.

The desert
In the Bible, it is the place where a person comes face to face with God alone, to be tested. The Jewish people experienced this after their liberation from Egypt. So did Moses and Elijah, two great figures of the Old Testament.

Devil or Satan
The two words mean the same. Devil comes from the Greek and means divider, accuser, calumniator.

Satan comes from the Hebrew and means adversary. These words (and also demons, whose leader is Beelzebub) are used to signify the enemy of Jesus who opposes the coming of the Kingdom of God.

Jesus proclaims the Good News

Now God's salvation has come. Now God has shown his power as King. **Rev 12.10**

Reign and kingdom of God: *reign* signifies the intervention of God, *kingdom* the new world which would result from this intervention.

Jesus did not stay long in Judaea. When Herod arrested John the Baptist he went back to Galilee, his own part of the country. There, in all the towns and villages, he proclaimed the Good News.

The right time has come, . . . and the Kingdom of God is near! Turn away from your sins and believe the Good News! **Mk 1.15**

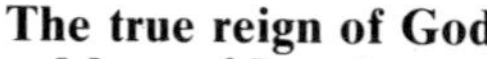

The true reign of God

Many of Jesus' contemporaries were waiting for the coming of God. The majority hoped it would be a dramatic intervention to drive the Romans from Palestine, or to annihilate those who did not observe the Law.

But Jesus proclaimed the coming of the reign of God in terms that disconcerted more than one listener.

Jesus went to Nazareth, where he had been brought up, and on the Sabbath he went as usual to the synagogue. He stood up to read the Scriptures and was handed the book of the prophet Isaiah. He unrolled the scroll and found the place where it is written, 'The Spirit of the Lord is upon me, because he has chosen me to bring good news to the

Jesus went round visiting all the towns and villages. He taught in the synagogues, preached the Good News about the Kingdom.
Mt 9.35

poor. He has sent me to proclaim liberty to the captives and recovery of sight to the blind; to set free the oppressed and announce that the time has come when the Lord will save his people.'

Jesus rolled up the scroll, gave it back to the attendant, and sat down. All the people in the synagogue had their eyes fixed on him, as he said to them, 'This passage of scripture has come true today, as you heard it being read.'

They all . . . marvelled at the eloquent words that he spoke.'

Then Jesus went to Capernaum, . . . where he taught the people on the Sabbath. They were all amazed at the way he taught, because he spoke with authority. **Lk 4.16-21, 31-32**

In Jesus' time, some, like the Pharisees, the Zealots and the Essenes, hoped the reign of God would bring about the restoration of the Law. The baptists emphasised conversion of heart.

A word that gives life

(Lk 4.38; Mk 1.29; Mt 8.14)

Jesus' miracles fall into four groups:
- cures
- exorcisms
- resurrections
- miracles worked on the elements.

Jesus was neither the first nor the only person to work miracles in Jewish and non-Jewish circles.
- in Jewish circles some scribes did so in Jesus' time **(Mt 12.27)**
- in non-Jewish circles belief in healing gods was widespread. The sick flocked to the sanctuary of Aesculapius at Epidaurus in Greece; eighty accounts of cures are recorded.

Jesus was in Capernaum – a town on the shores of Lake Tiberias, alive with people and activity. There one would meet fishermen like Simon and Andrew, and the merchants who supplied the caravans for trade abroad. There, too, lived officials like Matthew the customs officer, who collected the taxes. And there was also a detachment of Roman soldiers, commanded by a centurion.

Growing fame

Jesus was welcomed into the family of Simon and Andrew, who had become his friends. On the Sabbath he would go to the synagogue to teach.

The people who heard him were amazed at the way he taught, for he wasn't like the teachers of the Law; instead, he taught with authority.

Just then a man with an evil spirit in him came into the synagogue and screamed, 'What do you want with us, Jesus of Nazareth? Are you here to destroy us? I know who you are – you are God's holy messenger!' Jesus ordered the spirit, 'Be quiet, and come out of the man!' The evil spirit shook the man hard, gave a loud scream, and

God loved the world so much that he gave his only son, so that everyone who believes in him may not die but have eternal life.

Jn 3.16

came out of him. The people were all so amazed that they started saying to one another, 'What is this? Is it some kind of new teaching? This man has authority to give orders to the evil spirits, and they obey him!'

And so the news about Jesus spread quickly . . . in . . . Galilee.

Jesus and his disciples, including James and John, left the synagogue and went straight to the home of Simon and Andrew. Simon's mother-in-law was sick in bed with a fever, and as soon as Jesus arrived, he was told about her. He went to her, took her by the hand, and helped her up. The fever left her, and she began to wait on them.

After sunset . . . , people brought to Jesus all the sick and those who had demons. . . . Jesus healed many who were sick with all kinds of diseases.

Mk 1.21-34

Capernaum was one of the towns cursed by Jesus because it rejected his teaching: *And as for you, Capernaum! Did you want to lift yourself up to heaven? You will be thrown down to hell! . . . You can be sure that on the Judgement Day God will show more mercy to Sodom than to you.*

Mt 11.23-24

The healing of Peter's mother-in-law

Get up and walk!

(Lk 5.17; Mk 2.1; Mt 9.2)

For Jesus, the cures announced the reign of God. They showed forth in action the liberation proclaimed by the Good News. He was to pass on his healing power to the Twelve and to the 72 disciples.

There are about 25 accounts of cures in the gospels, among them:
- leprosy (**Mk 1.40-44**)
- paralysis (**Mk 8.5-13**)
- epilepsy (**Mt 17.14-21**)
- haemorrhage (**Mk 5.25-34**)

In Jesus' time, illnesses were attributed to the powers of evil (demons, impure spirits) or to the sins of the sick person.

Jesus travelled all over Galilee to proclaim the reign of God. It comes, he said, when people are truly living, when they stop suffering in body and in spirit. He used actions to show what he meant.

On one of the religious festivals, he went to Jerusalem.

. . . *Near the Sheep Gate in Jerusalem there is a pool with five porches; in Hebrew it is called Bethzatha. A large crowd of sick people were lying in the porches – the blind, the lame, and the paralysed. A man was there who had been ill for thirty-eight*

years. Jesus saw him lying there, and he knew that the man had been ill for such a long time; so he asked him, 'Do you want to get well?' The sick man answered, 'Sir, I have no one here to put me in the pool when the water is stirred up; while I am trying to get in, somebody else gets there first.' Jesus said to him, 'Get up, pick up your mat, and walk.' Immediately the man got well; he picked up his mat and started walking.

The day this happened was a Sabbath, so the Jewish authorities told the man who had been healed, 'This is a Sabbath, and it is against our Law for you to carry your mat.' He answered, 'The man who made me well told me to pick up my mat and walk.' They asked him, 'Who is the man who told you to do this?' But the man who had been healed did not know who Jesus was, for there was a crowd in that place, and Jesus had slipped away. **Jn 5.1-13**

Healing of a paralysed person (from a Byzantine manuscript)

Jesus claimed that he had cured the man in the name of God his Father; and what is more, he worked the miracle on a Sabbath day: two things which drew down on him the hatred of certain Jews, who plotted to kill him.

The sick appeal for help (after Rembrandt)

The blind see, the deaf hear

(Mk 9.27; Mk 8.22; 10.46; Lk 7.21; Jn 5.3)

Heal the sick, bring the dead back to life, heal those with dreaded skin diseases. You have received without paying so give without being paid. **Mt 10.8**

The gospels report frequent healings of blind and deaf-and-dumb people.

They came to Jericho, and as Jesus was leaving with his disciples and a large crowd, a blind beggar named Bartimaeus son of Timaeus was sitting by the road. When he heard that it was Jesus of Nazareth, he began to shout, 'Jesus! Son of David! Take pity on me!'

Mk 10.46-47

He was told to keep quiet, but in vain. Jesus then called him. *He threw off his cloak, jumped up, and came to Jesus. 'What do you want me to do for you?' Jesus asked him. 'Teacher,' the blind man answered, 'I want to see again.' 'Go,' Jesus told him, 'your faith has made you well.' At once he was able to see and followed Jesus on the road.*

Mk 10.50-52

Open up!

Jesus then left the neighbourhood of Tyre and went on through Sidon to Lake Galilee. . . . Some people brought him a man who was deaf and could hardly speak, and they begged Jesus to place his hands on him. So Jesus took him off alone, away from the crowd, put his fingers in the man's ears, spat, and touched the man's tongue. Then Jesus looked up to heaven, gave a deep groan, and said to the man, 'Ephphatha,' which means, 'Open up!'

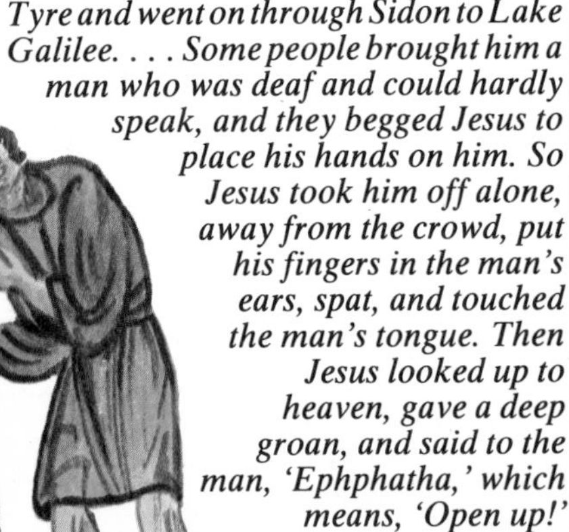

I came into this world to judge,
so that the blind should see
and those who see should become blind.

Jn 9.39

There were many blind and deaf-and-dumb people in Palestine in Jesus' time. Their disability was thought to be God's punishment for their own sins or the sins of their parents. Generally despised, they were often reduced to begging.

'Are you the one John said was going to come, or should we expect someone else?' Jesus answered, 'Go back and tell John what you are hearing and seeing: the blind can see, the lame can walk, those who suffer from dreaded skin diseases are made clean, the deaf hear, the dead are brought back to life and the Good News is preached to the poor.'

Mt 11.3-5

At once the man was able to hear, . . . and he began to talk without any trouble. . . . And all who heard were completely amazed. 'How well he does everything!' they exclaimed. 'He even causes the deaf to hear and the dumb to speak!' **Mk 7.31-37**

Jesus touched their eyes and said, 'Let it happen, then, just as you believe!' – and their sight was restored. **Mt 9.29**

No one is excluded

(Lk 5.27; Mt 9.9; Mk 2.13)

I know my sheep and they know me.
Jn 10.14

'The Kingdom of Heaven is approaching,' Jesus proclaimed. But were not sinners – those, that is, who publicly flaunted the Law of God – excluded? The Pharisees and scribes thought so and avoided meeting them. That is why they were so scandalised by Jesus' behaviour when he associated with them and even ate with them. One of them was even to become his companion.

As he walked along, Jesus saw a tax collector, named Matthew, sitting in his office. He said to him, 'Follow me.' Matthew got up and followed him. While Jesus was having a meal in Matthew's house, many tax collectors and other outcasts came and joined Jesus and his disciples at the table. Some Pharisees saw this and asked his disciples, 'Why does your teacher eat with such people?' Jesus heard them and answered, 'People who are well do not need a doctor, but only those who

The good shepherd

Matthew, the tax-collector, called by Jesus (from a painting by Carpaccio, 15th c.)

are sick. Go and find out what is meant by the scripture that says: "It is kindness that I want, not animal sacrifices." I have not come to call respectable people, but outcasts.' **Mt 9.9-13**

Zacchaeus the just

Jesus went on into Jericho and was passing through. There was a chief tax collector there named Zacchaeus, who was rich. He was trying to see who Jesus was, but he was a little man and could not . . . because of the crowd. So he ran ahead . . . and climbed a sycamore tree to see Jesus. . . . When Jesus came to that place, he looked up and said to Zacchaeus, 'Hurry down, Zacchaeus, because I must stay in your house today.' Zacchaeus hurried down and welcomed him with great joy. All the people who saw it started grumbling. 'This man has gone as a guest to the home of a sinner!' Zacchaeus stood up and said to the Lord, 'Listen, sir! I will give half my belongings to the poor, and if I have cheated anyone, I will pay him back four times as much.' Jesus said to him, 'Salvation has come to this house today, for this man, also, is a descendant of Abraham. The Son of Man came to seek and to save the lost.' **Lk 19.1-9**

The only people excluded in the end would be those who refused to respond to Jesus' invitation.

When it was time for the feast, he sent his servant to tell his guests, 'Come, everything is ready!' But they all began to make excuses. **Lk 14.17**

The two tax collectors, Matthew and Zacchaeus, were publicans, responsible for the business of the public Treasury; the greed of such people was legendary. In Luke's gospel one tax-collector accuses himself: *'God, have pity on me, a sinner!'* **Lk 18.13**

'I tell you, the tax-collectors and the prostitutes are going into the Kingdom of God ahead of you.' **Mt 21.31**

The beatitudes

Buddhism preaches withdrawal from the world to achieve serenity.
The disinherited faithful to the gospel – like the poor and the mourners evoked by the beatitudes – face up to the hardships of existence, thanks to their certainty of being liberated by God.

The gospels of Matthew and Luke report, each in its own way, Jesus' prescriptions for happiness. These are known as 'the beatitudes'.

As Matthew presents them, the beatitudes offer the ideal of life to be achieved by the disciple of Christ. The poverty and hunger mentioned here refer to dispositions of the heart.

Happy are those who know they are spiritually poor; the Kingdom of Heaven belongs to them!

Happy are those who mourn; God will comfort them!

Happy are those who are humble; they will receive what God has promised!

Happy are those whose greatest desire is to do what God requires; God will satisfy them fully!

Jesus spoke to the Pharisees again.
'I am the light of the world.
Whoever follows me will have the light of life
and will never walk in darkness.' **Jn 8.12**

Happy are those who are merciful to others; God will be merciful to them!

Happy are the pure in heart; they will see God!

Happy are those who work for peace; God will call them his children!

Happy are those who are persecuted because they do what God requires; the Kingdom of Heaven belongs to them!

Happy are you when people insult you and persecute you and tell all kinds of evil lies against you because you are my followers. Be happy and glad, for a great reward is kept for you in heaven. This is how the prophets who lived before you were persecuted. **Mt 5.3-12**

For Luke, the beatitudes did not represent an ideal: they announced the reversal of the situation of the poor and despised Christians, for whom God was opening up a way of liberation.

Happy are you poor; the Kingdom of God is yours!

Happy are you who are hungry now; you will be filled!

Happy are you who weep now; you will laugh!

But how terrible for you who are rich now; you have had your easy life!

How terrible for you who are full now; you will go hungry!

How terrible for you who laugh now; you will mourn and weep!

How terrible when all people speak well of you; their ancestors said the very same things about the false prophets.
Lk 6.20-26

Saint Sebastian, a 3rd c. Roman soldier, died a martyr's death because he helped Christians.
He was first pierced with arrows — which is how he is represented in many works of art — and then flogged to death.

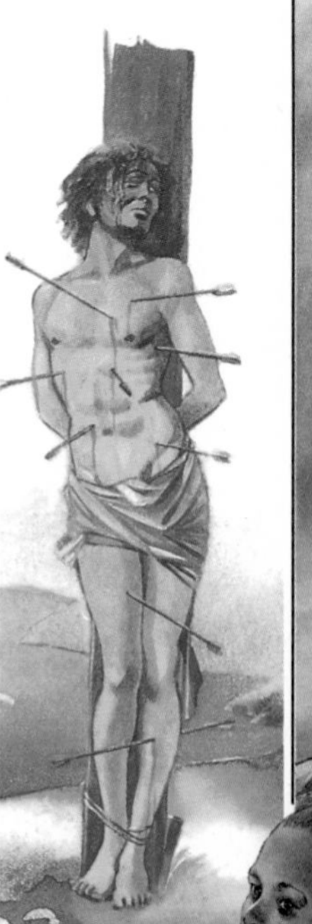

Good News in parables

(Lk 8.4; Mk 4.3; Mt 13.3)

Jesus was not the first person to use parables; several examples can be found in the Old Testament (eg, **2 Sam 12.1-4**)

Jesus was a great storyteller. To make his teaching understood, he used short stories – what we know as the parables (from the Greek for 'comparison').

To the crowd which gathered on the shore of the lake, he said this:

Once there was a man who went out to sow corn. As he scattered the seed in the field, some of it fell along the path, and the birds came and ate it up. Some of it fell on rocky ground, where there was little soil. The seeds soon sprouted, because the soil wasn't deep. Then, when the sun came up, it burnt the young plants; and because the roots had not grown deep enough, the plants soon dried up. Some of the seed fell among thorn bushes, which grew up and choked the plants, and they didn't produce any corn. But some seeds fell in good soil, and the plants sprouted, grew, and produced corn: some had thirty grains . . . others a hundred.

In Jesus' time and later, the rabbis (scribes) made up their own parables to illustrate their teaching of the Law. This is one told by Rabbi Yohanan ben Zakkai (1st c. A.D): a king invited his servants to a feast without stating the time. Only those who got ready immediately and set off at once could enter: the incredulous who went off to work first were not admitted.

The reason I use parables in talking to them is that they look, but do not see, and they listen but do not hear or understand.
Mt 13.13

The disciples then asked for an explanation. Jesus told them:

The sower sows God's message. Some people are like the seeds that fall along the path; as soon as they hear the message, Satan comes and takes it away. . . . Other people are like the seeds sown among the thorn bushes. These are the ones who hear the message, but the worries about this life, the love for riches, and all other kinds of desires crowd in and choke the message, and they don't bear fruit. But other people are like the seeds sown in good soil. They hear the message, accept it, and bear fruit: some thirty, some sixty, and some a hundred. **Mk 4.4-9; 14-20**

Parable of the weeds and the good seed

The kingdom of heaven is like a man who sowed good seed; while he was not looking his enemy sowed weeds as well. The owner of the field allowed the grain and the weeds to grow together. Only when harvest time came did he sort out the good from the bad. **Mt 13.24-30**

The parables of the Kingdom

(Lk 13.18; Mk 4.30; Mt 13.31)

Jesus frequently made use of parables to explain the Kingdom of God.

Parable of the mustard seed

What shall we say the Kingdom of God is like? What parable shall we use to explain it? It is like this. A man takes a mustard seed, the smallest seed in the world, and plants it in the ground. After a while it grows up and becomes the biggest of all plants. It puts out such large branches that the birds come and

make their nests in its shade. . . .

Mk 4.30-32

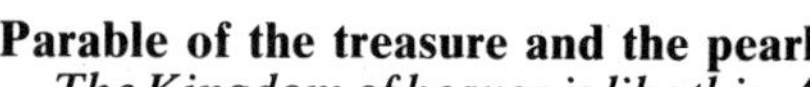

Parable of the treasure and the pearl

The Kingdom of heaven is like this. A man happens to find a treasure hidden in a field. He covers it up again, and is so happy that he goes and sells everything he has, and then goes back and buys that field. **Mt 13.44**

Parable of the growing seed

The Kingdom of God is like this. A man scatters seed in his field. He sleeps at night, is up and about during the day, and all the while the seeds are sprouting and growing. Yet he does not know how it happens. The soil itself makes the plants grow and bear fruit; first the tender stalk appears, then the ear, and finally the ear full of corn. When the corn is ripe, the man starts cutting it with his sickle, because harvest time has come. **Mk 4.26-29**

The use of parables in the gospels has a twofold purpose: these vivid and down-to-earth stories help us to understand Jesus' message. They can, however, contain a hidden meaning: so they are only fully accessible to attentive minds and hearts prepared to receive them.

Parable of the net

Also, the Kingdom of Heaven is like this. Some fishermen throw their net out in the lake and catch all kinds of fish. When the net is full, they pull it to shore and sit down to divide the fish: the good ones go into their buckets, the worthless ones are thrown away. It will be like this at the end of the age: the angels will go out and gather up the evil people from among the good and will throw them into the fiery furnace, where they will cry and grind their teeth. **Mt 13.47-50**

Parable of the yeast

Again Jesus asked, 'What shall I compare the Kingdom of God with? It is like this. A woman takes some yeast and mixes it with forty litres of flour until the whole batch of dough rises.'

Lk 13.20-21

The workers in the vineyard

Jesus first proclaimed the Good News of the Kingdom of God to the Jews, but many of them refused to listen. To those who turned a deaf ear he addressed two parables.

The first compared the reign of God to the master of a house who went out at dawn to hire workers for his vineyard. He sent them to work promising them one denarius. At the third, sixth, ninth and eleventh hour he did the same, always promising one denarius. At the end of the day the workers who had been hired at the eleventh hour were the first to be paid, and they received one denarius; the others who came up next received the same. To the workers hired in the morning, who protested that they had worked longer than the others, the master replied: *Listen, friend, I have not cheated you. After all, you agreed to do a day's work for one silver coin. Now take your pay and go home. I want to give this man as much as I have given you. . . . Those who are last will be first, and those who are first will be last.*

Mt 20.1-16

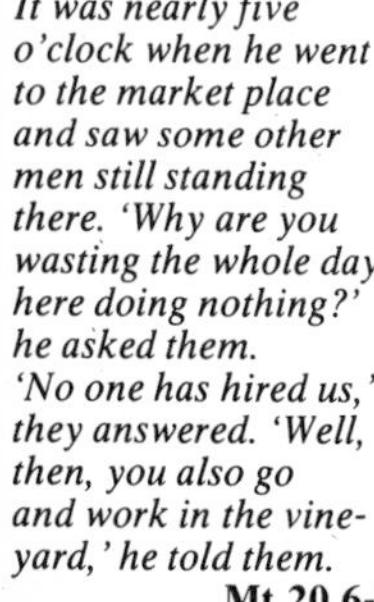

It was nearly five o'clock when he went to the market place and saw some other men still standing there. 'Why are you wasting the whole day here doing nothing?' he asked them. 'No one has hired us,' they answered. 'Well, then, you also go and work in the vine-yard,' he told them.

Mt 20.6-7

The guests at the feast

A man had invited guests to a great feast. When the time came, they all made excuses. The first told him: *'I have bought a field and must go to look at it.'* Another said: *'I have bought five pairs of oxen and am on my way to try them out.'* And a third said: *'I have just got married, and for that reason I cannot come.'* The master was angry, and said to his servant: *'Hurry out to the streets and alleys of the town, and bring back the poor, the crippled, the blind, and the lame.' Soon the servant said, 'Your order has been carried out, sir, but there is room for more.' So the master said to the servant, 'Go out to the country roads and lanes and make people come in, so that my house will be full. I tell you all that none of those men who were invited will taste my dinner!'* **Lk 14.16-24**

The man who sent out the invitations is God. The feast is the Kingdom of God. The servant is Jesus. The first guests are the Jewish people. The second guests are the poor, the sick, Jewish sinners and the pagans.

'Be on your guard'

(Mt 25.13; Lk 12.35; Mk 13.34)

In another parable called 'the talents' (**Mt 25.14-30**), the good servant is the one who makes a profit by investing his master's money in his absence. The bad servant is the one who only saves it unchanged.

A talent was worth six thousand denarii.

The virgins with the lamps, inspired by a mosaic in Ravenna.

To recognise the Kingdom of God, which will come unexpectedly, Jesus urged his followers to be watchful.

At that time the Kingdom of heaven will be like this. Once there were ten girls who took their oil lamps and went out to meet the bridegroom. Five of them were foolish, and the other five were wise. The foolish ones took their lamps but did not take any extra oil with them, while the wise ones took containers full of oil for their lamps.
Mt 25.1-4

A lamp from Jesus' time

Woken during the night by the arrival of the husband, the girls dressed their lamps with oil. Those who had none had to go and buy some, while the girls who remained went into the wedding. When the others arrived, the husband said to them: *'I don't know you.'* **Mt 25.12**

The dead are raised to life

(Lk 7.12; Mk 5.41; Mt 9.25; Jn 11.1)

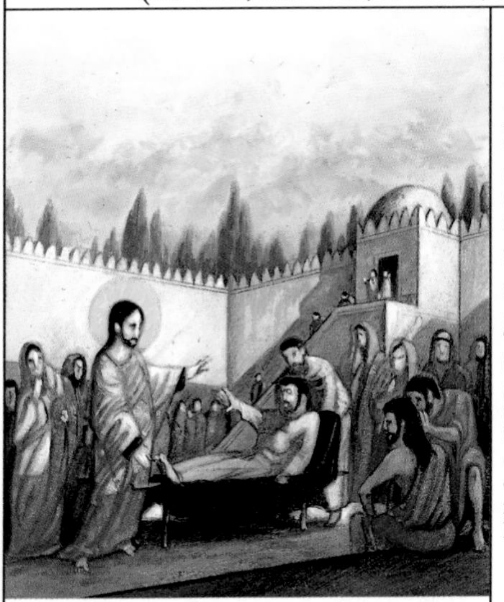

As he arrived at the gate of the town, a funeral procession was coming out. The dead man was the only son of . . . a widow. . . . The Lord walked over and touched the coffin, and the men carrying it stopped. Jesus said, 'Young man! Get up I tell you!' The dead man sat up and began to talk, and Jesus gave him back to his mother. **Lk 7.12-16**

Like the great prophets of the Old Testament Elijah and Elisha, Jesus raised people from the dead.
The two others he raised were Lazarus (**Jn 11.1-41**) and the daughter of Jairus (**Mt 9.18-26**).
What is involved here is really a simple return to life.
The term resurrection is only applied in the gospels to the passage to full and eternal life with God, beyond death (the resurrection of Jesus and that of all men and women at the last day).

The gospels paint a picture of a nomadic Jesus, travelling tirelessly throughout Galilee and the neighbouring regions, Samaria, Judaea, Decapolis . . . He travelled about mostly on foot (walking even on the water) and less frequently by boat, or exceptionally on a donkey. The popular legend of St Christopher carrying Christ on his back signifies that today Jesus has no other legs but ours to move about the world, and no other hands but ours with which to do things.

Different accounts

It is impossible to reconstruct very precisely the journeys undertaken by Jesus, since the gospels do not agree on this point.

The synoptics follow the same scheme (Mark's being the original), which distinguishes three periods in Jesus' public life:

– he announced the Good News in Galilee and the surrounding pagan regions

– he then went to Jerusalem

– he stayed in Jerusalem, where he preached and where he died.

In this scheme of things, Jesus went only once to Jerusalem. The gospel of John however is quite different. Here Jesus made several visits to Jerusalem, for the religious festivals.

These differences show that the evangelists were not trying to retrace Jesus steps from day to day. Wishing to bear witness to his faith, each Gospel writer wrote according to the aspect of Christ he wished to emphasise.

Jesus' movements

The Holy Family fleeing to Egypt to escape the massacre ordered by Herod. From his childhood onwards, travel was a way of life for Jesus.

GALILEE
Capernaum
Sea of Galilee
Tiberias
Cana
Nazareth

Some things are certain

All the same, we can take some things for certain:

– in order to proclaim the Kingdom of God, Jesus moved about a lot; his way of life was simple

– on several occasions he crossed the Jewish frontier into pagan territory, in Decapolis (Mk 5.1) or the region of Tyre and Sidon (Mk 7.24-31), or else the villages near Caesarea Philippi (Mk 8.27)

– from time to time he withdrew into the desert to reflect and to pray (Mk 1.34-45)

– he made several journeys into Judaea: here scholars agree that John's gospel comes closer to the historical reality than do the other three.

Legend has it that St Christopher (from the Greek 'Christ-bearer') carried across a river a child who revealed that he was the Christ.

Jesus and his disciples

While the disciples of the scribes received from their master teaching on the Law, written and oral, the text of which they learnt by heart, Jesus' disciples watched their master speak and act with authority.

During a storm the desperate disciples woke Jesus, who calmed the winds. *What kind of man is this? Even the winds . . . obey him.* **Mt 8.27**

Wherever Jesus went, men and women attached themselves to him. The gospels call them 'disciples'.

Some, like Martha, Mary and Lazarus, stayed where they were to proclaim what Jesus said and did; others went with him.

Jesus chose twelve of these disciples as *apostles*, that is 'messengers'.

Simon (whom he named Peter) and his brother Andrew; James and John, Philip and Bartholomew, Matthew and Thomas, James son of Alphaeus, and Simon (who was called the Patriot), Judas son of James, and Judas Iscariot, who became the traitor. **Lk 6.14-16**

His disciples asked him many questions since they did not always understand what he said and did. His teaching was new, it broke with everything they were familiar with. Jesus was always ready with a patient reply. Listening to him and watching what he did day after day, they gradually discovered what the Good News he was announcing was about, and what it involved. *If one of you wants to be first he must be the slave of all.* **Mk 10.44-45**

Whoever believes in me will do what I do – yes, he will do even greater things because I am going to the Father.
Jn 14.12

Jesus called his apostles to him:

Then he sent them out to preach the Kingdom of God and to heal the sick, after saying to them, 'Take nothing with you for the journey: no stick, no beggar's bag, no food, no money, not even an extra shirt.' **Lk 9.2-3**

He then appointed seventy-two other disciples:

'Go! I am sending you like lambs among wolves.'
Lk 10.3

He said to them, '. . . Go! . . .'

The seventy-two men came back in great joy. 'Lord,' they said, 'even the demons obeyed us when we gave them a command in your name!' Jesus answered them, . . . 'Listen! I have given you authority, so that you can walk on snakes and scorpions and overcome all the power of the Enemy, and nothing will hurt you. But don't be glad because the evil spirits obey you; rather be glad because your names are written in heaven.' **Lk 10.3-20**

The enemies of Jesus: Pharisees and scribes

You snakes and sons of snakes! How do you expect to escape from being condemned to hell? **Mt 23.33**

'How terrible for you, teachers of the Law and Pharisees! You hypocrites! You are like whitewashed tombs, which look fine on the outside but are full of bones and decaying corpses on the inside.' **Mt 23.27**

Jesus said to them, 'Take care; be on your guard against the yeast of the Pharisees and Sadducees.' **Mt 16.6**

Then the disciples understood that he was not warning them to guard themselves from the yeast used in bread but from the teaching of the Pharisees and Sadducees. **Mt 16.12**

These were the men of the Law. Calling on the authority of God, they accused Jesus of not respecting it. For them he was a blasphemer, whose behaviour offended God.

Their accusations

— What? He eats with tax-collectors and sinners! (**Mk 2.16**)

— Look at the way his disciples behave on the Sabbath! They pick ears of wheat for food. That is not allowed. (**Mk 2.24**)

— Why does he feel free to heal on the Sabbath? It's forbidden! (**Mt 12.10**)

— Why do his disciples eat their meals with unwashed hands? (**Mk 7.5**)

Jesus' replies

At once Jesus knew what they were thinking, so he said to them, 'Why do you think such things?' (**Mk 2.8**)

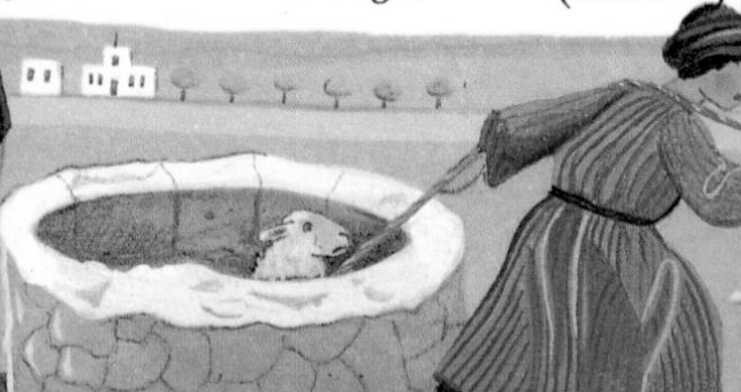

Is it easier to say to this paralysed man, 'Your sins are forgiven', or to say 'Get up, pick up your mat, and walk'?
Mk 2.9

'I will prove to you, then, that the Son of Man has authority on earth to forgive sins.' So he said to the paralysed man, 'I tell you, get up, pick up your mat, and go home!' **(Mk 2.10-11)**

People who are well do not need a doctor, but only those who are sick. I have not come to call respectable people, but outcasts. **(Mk 2.17)**

The Sabbath was made for the good of man; man was not made for the Sabbath. So the Son of Man is Lord even of the Sabbath. **(Mk 2.27)**

What if one of you has a sheep and it falls into a deep hole on the Sabbath? Will he not take hold of it and lift it out? And a man is worth much more than a sheep. **(Mt 12.11)**

The Law to which the scribes and Pharisees referred contained very precise rules. Those relating to the Sabbath, for example, forbade all work. You could care for a sick person only if he or she was in danger of death. Ritual purifications before meals were enforced equally strictly.

Jesus cures a paralysed man; sometimes the crowd was so thick in front of the house that the sick person had to be let down through a hole in the roof. **(Mk 2.4)**

The enemies of Jesus:

Jesus himself went to the temple and took part in worship there. But he condemned religious practices that were not accompanied by justice and mercy. Jesus encouraged respect for the temple, yet he foretold its destruction (shown here in a medieval miniature).

The Saddducees

The chief priests accused Jesus of being an agitator and, worse, of having blasphemed by decrying the temple: *Not a single stone here will be left in its place.* **Mk 13.2**

Jesus' words were quoted during his trial. **(Mk 14.55-59)**

The Herodians

They were partisans of Herod Antipas and they collaborated with the Romans. They were on their guard against anything that disturbed public order or threatened the authority of their master. They hunted down prophets. Herod had already beheaded John the Baptist. At one stage, Jesus was forced to flee into Galilee, because Herod wanted to kill him.

Herodians and Saddducees

The Pharisees went off and made a plan to trap Jesus with questions. Then they sent to him some of their disciples and some members of Herod's party. 'Teacher,' they said, 'we know that you . . . teach the truth about God's will for man. . . . Tell us, then, what do you think? Is it against our Law to pay taxes to the Roman Emperor, or not?'

Jesus . . . said, 'You hypocrites! Why are you trying to trap me? Show me the coin for paying the tax!' They brought him the coin, and he asked them, 'Whose face and name are these?' 'The Emperor's,' they answered. So Jesus said to them, 'Well, then, pay the Emperor what belongs to the Emperor, and pay God what belongs to God.' When they heard this, they were amazed; and they left him and went away. **Mt 22.15-22**

A coin with Caesar's head on it.

Pay the Emperor what belongs to the Emperor, and pay God what belongs to God. **Mt. 22.21**

Jesus went to the temple and began to drive out all those who were buying and selling. He overturned the tables of the moneychangers and the stools of those who sold pigeons. **Mk 11.15**

Love your enemies

(Mt 5.43; Lk 6.27)

Some Samaritans refused to accept Jesus. James and John reacted violently: *'Lord, do you want us to call fire down from heaven to destroy them?' Jesus turned and rebuked them.*
Lk 9.54-55

Jesus often preached this surprising precept, which was badly understood and badly received by those around him.

What he said

'But I tell you who hear me: Love your enemies, do good to those who hate you. . . . If anyone hits you on one cheek, let him hit the other one too; if someone takes your coat, let him have your shirt as well. Give to everyone who asks you for something, and when someone takes what is yours, do not ask for it back. Do for others just what you want them to do for you.

If you love only the people who love you, why should you receive a blessing? Even sinners love those who love them! And if you do good only to those who do good to you, why should you receive a blessing? Even sinners do that! And if you lend only to those from whom you hope to get it back, why should you receive a blessing? Even sinners lend to sinners, to get back the same

Bless those who curse
and pray for those who ill-treat you.
Lk 6.28

Christ being insulted (after Fra Angelico, 15th c.)

amount! No! Love your enemies and do good to them; lend and expect nothing back. You will then have a great reward, and you will be sons of the Most High God. For he is good to the ungrateful and the wicked. Be merciful just as your Father is merciful.' **Lk 6.27-35**

Peter asked him:

'Lord, if my brother keeps on sinning against me, how many times do I have to forgive him? Seven times?' 'No, not seven times,' answered Jesus, 'but seventy times seven.' **Mt 18.21-22**

Mercy in action

When they came to the place called 'The Skull,' they crucified Jesus and two criminals, one on his right and the other on his left. Jesus said, 'Forgive them, Father! They don't know what they are doing.' **Lk 23.33-34**

Jesus' words: *'If anyone hits you on one cheek, let him hit the other too'* are often wrongly interpreted. This attitude is neither cowardly nor passive: it reflects true inner strength. To refuse to respond to violence with violence can change the behaviour of one's opponent and prevent the brutality from escalating. The gospels show how Jesus used this non-violent kind of opposition.

Babylon destroyed (after a 13th c. manuscript)

Jesus and children

A Jewish child under the age of twelve (the age of religious majority for a boy) was put in the same category as the deaf, the dumb, the blind, pagans, women and slaves – all regarded as incompetent under the Law.

The Essenes ruled that: 'Stupid people, mad people, under-age children, none of these may enter the assembly.'

Against the tradition that children were not important, Jesus welcomed them. The disciples were astonished.

Some people brought children to Jesus for him to place his hands on them, but the disciples scolded the people. When Jesus noticed this, he was angry and said to his disciples, 'Let the children come to me, and do not stop them, because the Kingdom of God belongs to such as these. I assure you that whoever does not receive the Kingdom of God like a child will never enter it.' **Mk 10.13-16**

Jesus even went so far as to hold children up as an example to adults.

At that time the disciples came to Jesus, asking, 'Who is the greatest in the Kingdom of heaven?' So Jesus called a child . . . and said, 'I assure you that unless you change and become like children, you will never enter the Kingdom of Heaven. The greatest in the Kingdom of Heaven is the

Whoever welcomes this child in my name, welcomes me. **Lk 9.48**

A mother playing with her child – after a drawing by Leonardo da Vinci. This reflects a different age and a different culture: several centuries earlier, a rabbi would have considered that chatting with children hastened a person's downfall, in the same way as sleep in the morning and wine at midday.

one who humbles himself and becomes like this child. And whoever welcomes in my name one such child as this, welcomes me.' **Mt 18.1-5**

The sleeping child

Among Jesus' many miracles, the gospels tell how he brought a little girl of twelve back to life.

. . . *A Jewish official came* to Jesus, *knelt down before him, and said, 'My daughter has just died; but come and place your hands on her, and she will live.' So Jesus got up and followed him, and his disciples went along with him. Then Jesus went into the official's house. When he saw . . . the people all stirred up, he said, 'Get out, everybody! The little girl is not dead – she is only sleeping!' Then they all laughed at him. But as soon as the people had been put out, Jesus went into the girl's room and took hold of her hand, and she got up.* **Mt 9.18-25**

Jesus told the parents to say nothing, but the news soon spread.

Even in western Europe, children were not really recognised as entirely separate beings until the 18th c.

Jesus and women

She kissed his feet and poured perfume on them. **Lk 7.38**
The repentant Magdalene, after Giovanni da Milano

Jesus showed a woman with a bad reputation in a new light

A Pharisee invited Jesus to have dinner with him. . . . In that town was a woman who lived a sinful life. She heard

that Jesus was eating in the Pharisee's house, so she . . . stood behind Jesus, . . . wetting his feet with her tears. Then she dried his feet with her hair. . . . When the Pharisee saw this, he said to himself, 'If this man really were a prophet, he would know . . . what kind of sinful life she lives!' Jesus . . . said to him, 'Simon, I have something to tell you. There were two men who owed money to a money-lender. . . . One

In the Latin tradition, Mary of Bethany, sister of Lazarus, Mary of Magdala (Mary Magdalene) and the sinful woman are the same person. Many churches have been dedicated to her.

The great love she has shown proves that her many sins have been forgiven. Whoever has been forgiven little shows only a little love. **Lk 7.47**

owed him five hundred silver coins, and the other owed him fifty. Neither of them could pay him back, so he cancelled the debts of both. Which one, then, will love him more?' 'I suppose,' answered Simon, '. . . the one who was forgiven more.' 'You are right,' said Jesus. Then he said to the woman, 'Your faith has saved you; go in peace.'
Lk 7.36 . . . 50

Martha and Mary, the sisters of Lazarus, represent for Christians two ways of honouring Christ: action and contemplation.

Jesus and women

Jesus saves the life of a condemned woman
The teachers of the Law and the Pharisees brought in a woman who had been caught committing adultery . . . 'Master, Moses commanded that such a woman must be stoned to death. Now, what do you say?' 'Whichever one of you has committed no sin may cast the first stone.' When they heard this, they all left, one by one. Jesus said to her: 'Go, but do not sin again.' **Jn 8.3-11**

Jesus protected women from men
Some Pharisees came to him and tried to trap him. 'Tell us,' they asked, 'does our Law allow a man to divorce his wife?' Jesus answered with a question, 'What law did Moses give you?' Their answer was, 'Moses gave permission for a man to write a divorce notice and send his wife away.' Jesus said to them, 'Moses wrote this law for you because you are so hard to teach. But in the beginning, at the time of creation, "God made them male and female . . . and the two will become one." So they are no longer two, but one. Man must not separate, then, what God has joined together.' **Mk 10.2-9**

His disciples returned,
and they were greatly surprised to find him
talking with a woman.

Jn 4.27

Jesus broke taboos: he dared to speak to a foreign woman

... In Samaria Jesus came to a town. ... Jacob's well was there. ...

A Samaritan woman came to draw some water, and Jesus said to her, 'Give me a drink of water.' ... The woman answered, 'You are a Jew, and I am a Samaritan – so how can you ask me for a drink?' ... Jesus answered, 'If only you knew what God gives and who it is that is asking you for a drink, you would ask him, and he would give you life-giving water.' 'Sir,' the woman said, 'give me that water! Then I will never be thirsty again.' Then the woman left her water jar, went back to the town, and said to the people there, 'Come and see the man who told me everything I have ever done. Could he be the Messiah?' ...

Jn 4.5 ... 29

Mary Magdalene according to the eastern tradition (icon).

Top left: the adulterous woman (after a 16th c. ceramic).

Far left: Christ and the Samaritan woman (Ravenna, 6th c.).

Jesus and his family

(Lk 8.19; Mk 3.31; Mt 12.46)

The wedding at Cana, to which Jesus and Mary his mother were invited. When the wine ran out, Mary pointed this out to Jesus. He then performed his first miracle (or sign) by turning water into wine.

Jesus was not always understood by his family. Surely he was going too far? He led a demanding life, creating problems and enemies for himself. His close relatives were upset.

But Jesus refused to become trapped within his family circle.

A crowd was sitting round Jesus, and they said to him, 'Look, your mother and your brothers and sisters are outside, and they want you.' Jesus answered, 'Who is my mother? Who are my brothers?' He looked at the people sitting round him and said, 'Look! Here are my mother and my brothers! . . .' **Mk 3.31-34**

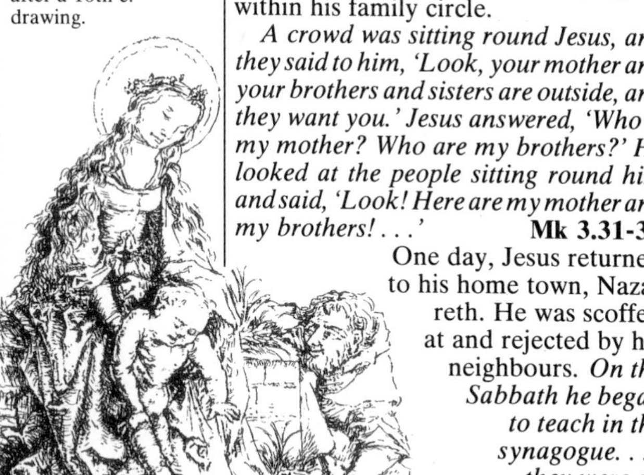

Joseph playing with the child Jesus, after a 16th c. drawing.

One day, Jesus returned to his home town, Nazareth. He was scoffed at and rejected by his neighbours. *On the Sabbath he began to teach in the synagogue. . . . they were all amazed. . . . 'What*

Procession of the elect: *Whoever does what God wants him to do is my brother, my sister, my mother.* **Mk 3.35**

wisdom is this that has been given him? How does he perform miracles? Isn't he the carpenter, the son of Mary, and the brother of James, Joseph, Judas and Simon? Aren't his sisters living here?' And so they rejected him. **Mk 6.2-3**

Jesus' family is not mentioned again until the day of his death.

Standing close to Jesus' cross were his mother, his mother's sister, Mary the wife of Clopas, and Mary Magdalene. Jesus saw his mother and the disciple he loved standing there; so he said to his mother, 'He is your son.' Then he said to the disciple, 'She is your mother.' **Jn 19.25-27**

After Jesus' resurrection, his brothers and sisters joined the first Christian community in Jerusalem. James was its leader.

Jesus and the pagans

(Mk 5.1; 7.6; Lk 7.2)

Roman centurion (after a 2nd c. bas-relief)

Jesus never stopped proclaiming that God loves everyone, pagan or Jew, without distinction. This was truly revolutionary in the Judaism of the time. What is more, he proved it through his actions.

The centurion's servant

A Roman centurion had a sick servant – a servant whom he loved and respected. He sent some Jewish leaders to plead with Jesus, so that he would heal the sick man. When Jesus came to his house he said:

'Sir, don't trouble yourself. I do not deserve to have you come into my house, neither do I consider myself worthy to come to you in person. Just give the order, and my servant will get well. . . .' Jesus was surprised when he heard this . . . and said to the crowd following him, 'I tell you, I have never found faith

Pagan
The word comes from the Latin for countryman.

Jesus did not condemn the pagans (as the Essenes did), he did not ask them to become converts (as the Pharisees did), or to be baptised (as the baptists demanded). He simply called them to faith, affirming that God loved them.

like this, not even in Israel!' The messengers went back to the officer's house and found his servant well.

Lk 7.6 . . . 10

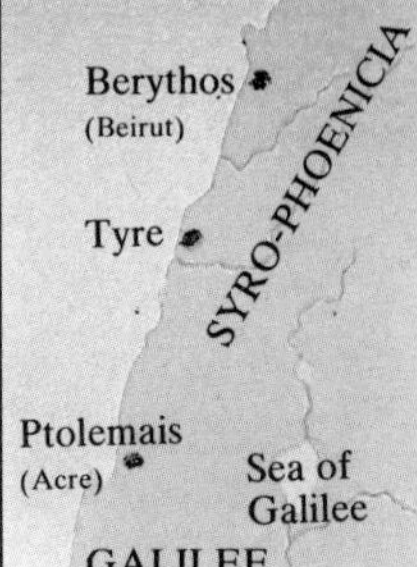

A Greek woman's prayer

In the course of a visit to Tyre, Jesus was asked by a Greek woman of Syro-Phoenician origin to cure her daughter. The child was possessed by a demon.

To this request, Jesus replied:

'Let us first feed the children. It isn't right to take the children's food and throw it to the dogs.' 'Sir,' she answered, 'even the dogs under the table eat the children's leftovers!' So Jesus said to her, 'Because of that answer, go back home, where you will find that the demon has gone out of your daughter!' She went home and found her child lying on the bed; the demon had indeed gone out of her. **Mk 7.27-30**

Jesus and the Greek woman (from a 12th c. stained glass window). In this episode the children and the little dogs symbolised Jews and non-Jews respectively – a rather contemptuous comparison that was current in Jesus' time.

The possessed man of Gerasa

(Mt 8.28; Mk 5.1; Lk 8.26)

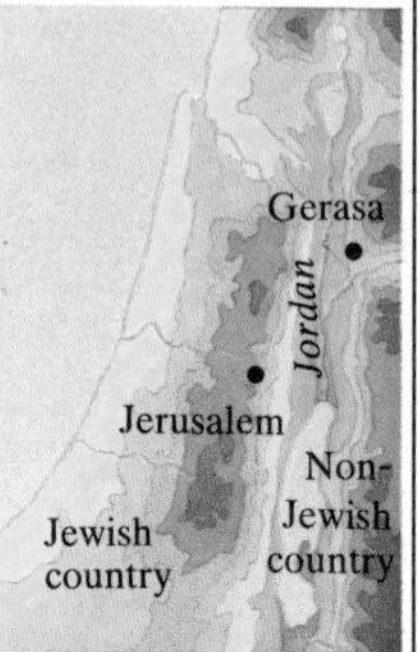

The release of the possessed reveals in action the victory of God, who frees people from all that binds them.

The exorcism of the possessed man of Gerasa, recalled in a Byzantine manuscript.

In Decapolis Jesus came across a possessed man.

This man had an evil spirit in him and lived among the tombs. Nobody could keep him chained up any more. . . . He was too strong for anyone to control him. Day and night he wandered among the tombs and through the hills, screaming and cutting himself.

He was some distance away when he saw Jesus; so he ran, fell on his knees before him, and screamed in a loud voice, 'Jesus, Son of the Most High God! What do you want with me? For God's sake, I beg you, don't punish me!' (He said this because Jesus was saying, 'Evil spirit, come out of this man!') So Jesus asked him, 'What is your name?' The man answered, 'My name is "Mob" – there are so many of us!' And he kept begging Jesus not to send the evil spirits out of that region.

It is by means of God's power that I drive out demons, and this proves that the Kingdom of God has already come to you. **Lk 11.20**

There was a large herd of pigs near by. . . . So the spirits begged Jesus, 'Send us to the pigs, and let us go into them.' He let them go, and the evil spirits went out of the man and entered the pigs. The whole herd . . . rushed down the side of the cliff into the lake and was drowned.

The swineherds ran *and spread the news. . . . People went out to see what had happened, and when they came to Jesus, they saw the man . . . sitting there, clothed and in his right mind; and they were all afraid.* **Mk 5.3-15**

When the possessed man, now healed, wanted to join Jesus, Jesus asked him to stay at home (and therefore in non-Jewish territory) and tell people there what he had done for him.

The tombs
These were dug out of the rock and could be used as a place of refuge.

Pigs
For Jews they were the most impure of all animals.

The lake
In the Bible, this was the home of the forces of evil and of death.

Bread for all

(Mk 6.32; 7.31; Mt 14.16; Lk 9.12; Jn 6.5)

The first multiplication took place in Galilee. The twelve baskets mentioned by the evangelist recall the twelve tribes of Israel. In this account, Jesus brings his teaching to the Jewish people.

Mark's gospel gives us two accounts of the multiplication of the loaves. They seem very similar when you first read them, but contain important differences.

First account

In Galilee, a crowd of about five thousand people gathered round to listen to Jesus. When night fell the disciples advised him to let the people go home to their evening meal. But he wanted to feed them himself.

They asked, 'Do you want us to go and spend two hundred silver coins on bread in order to feed them?' So Jesus asked them, 'How much bread have you got? Go and see.' When they found out, they told him, 'Five loaves and also two fish.' **Mk 6.37-38**

Having blessed and broken the five loaves and then done the same with the two fishes, Jesus had the food distributed.

In this picture of the miracle (after a mosaic in Ravenna) there are seven baskets of bread. The number seven symbolises universality: the crowd fed by this miracle is therefore the whole world, to whom the Gospel is addressed.

Everyone ate and had enough. Then the disciples took up twelve baskets full of what was left of the bread and the fish. **Mk 6.42-43**

This mosaic decorates the floor of a church which was built in the 4th or 5th c. over what was thought to be the site of the first multiplication of the loaves at Tabga, not far from Capernaum.

Second account

On this occasion, Jesus was in the region of Decapolis. The circumstances were the same, and the same miracle took place. But this time, Mark tells us, there were seven loaves and a few fish.

Everybody ate and had enough. Then the disciples took up seven baskets full of pieces left over. **Mk 8.8**

The first multiplication took place in Jewish territory, the second in pagan territory. So the Gospel – symbolised by the food – is offered to all, Jews and non-Jews.

The figure seven, which here replaces the twelve of the previous account, is a biblical symbol for completion.

Baking the unleavened bread which was eaten in the time of Christ.

Who is my neighbour?

(Lk 10.25; Mt 25.31)

The hero of the parable praised by Jesus is a Samaritan – traditionally a false friend, a heretic – while the Jewish priest and levite, who should have been setting an example do nothing of the sort.

The good Samaritan (after Rembrandt)

The Jewish Law reminded people that they had to love even foreigners living in Palestine. But just how far did the Law apply?

Jesus answered, 'There was once a man who was going down from Jerusalem to Jericho when robbers attacked him . . . and beat him up, leaving him half dead. It so happened that a priest was going down that road; but when he saw the man, he walked on by, on the other side. . . . A Levite also . . . walked on by, on the other side. But a Samaritan who was travelling that way came upon the man, and when he saw him, his heart was filled with pity. He went over to him, poured oil and wine on his wounds and bandaged them; then he . . . took him to an inn, where he took care of him. . . .'

Jesus concluded, . . . 'which one of these three acted like a neighbour towards the man attacked by the robbers?' The teacher of the Law answered, 'The one who was kind to him.' Jesus replied, 'You go, then, and do the same.'

Lk 10.30-37

Do for others
what you want them to do for you.
Mt 7.12

At the end of the day, people would be judged on the way in which they had loved the poorest, weakest and most needy of their fellow human beings.

. . . Then the King will say to the people on his right, 'Come, you that are blessed by my Father! Come and possess the kingdom which has been prepared for you ever since the creation of the world. I was hungry and you fed me, thirsty and you gave me a drink; I was a stranger and you received me in your homes, naked and you clothed me; I was sick and you took care of me, in prison and you visited me.'

'The righteous will then answer him, "When, Lord, did we ever see you hungry and feed you, or thirsty and give you a drink? When did we ever see you a stranger and welcome you in our homes, or naked and clothe you?" . . . The King will reply, "I tell you, whenever you did this for one of the least important of these brothers of mine, you did it for me!"' **Mt 25.34-40**

When the Son of Man comes as King and all the angels with him, he will sit on his throne, and the people of all the nations will be gathered before him. Then he will divide them into two groups, just as a shepherd separates the sheep from the goats. He will put the righteous people on his right and the others on his left. **Mt 25.31-33**

Jesus' humour
Jesus turned the question round. The lawyer (scribe) asked: 'Who is my neighbour?' Jesus told him the parable, and then asked: 'Which one behaved like a neighbour to the man who fell into the hands of the bandits?'

Jesus and the rich

(Lk 16.13; Mt 6.24)

In some translations of this story, the rich man wears a purple robe. For the Romans purple was a sign of wealth: it was an expensive dye, extracted from a mollusc – the murex – and produced mainly in Tyre, in Phoenica (modern Lebanon).

As far as Jesus was concerned, the rich were not excluded from the Kingdom of God and did not have to give up everything to become his disciples.

All the same, it is difficult for rich people to enter the Kingdom of God since they run the risk of becoming avaricious, uncaring and closed to the needs of the poor.

'There was once a rich man who dressed in the most expensive clothes and lived in great luxury every day. There was also a poor man named Lazarus, covered with sores, who used to be brought to the rich man's door, hoping to eat the bits of food that fell from the rich man's table. Even the dogs would come and lick his sores.

Look at the birds: they do not sow seeds, gather a harvest and put it into barns; yet your Father in heaven takes care of them. Aren't you worth much more? **Mt 6-26**

The poor man died and was carried by the angels to sit beside Abraham at the feast in heaven. The rich man died and was buried, and in Hades, where he was in great pain, he looked up and saw

Abraham, far away, with Lazarus at his side. So he called out, "Father Abraham! Take pity on me, and send Lazarus to dip his finger in some water and cool my tongue, because I am in great pain in this fire!" But Abraham said, "Remember, my son, that in your lifetime you were given all the good things, while Lazarus got all the bad things. But now he is enjoying himself here, while you are in pain."'

Lk 16.19-25

Jesus appealed to those who were rich not to forget the essential:

Store up riches for yourselves in heaven, where moths and rust cannot destroy and robbers cannot break in and steal. **Mt 6.20**

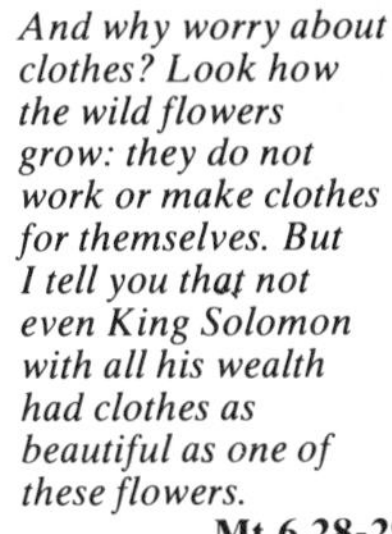

And why worry about clothes? Look how the wild flowers grow: they do not work or make clothes for themselves. But I tell you that not even King Solomon with all his wealth had clothes as beautiful as one of these flowers.

Mt 6.28-29

I repeat: it is much harder for a rich person to enter the Kingdom of God than for a camel to go through the eye of a needle.

Mt 19.24

The God of Jesus

Other parables about the tenderness of God:
– the parable of the lost sheep
(Lk 14.4-7)
– the parable of the lost coin
(Lk 15.8-10)

The most moving things Jesus had to say about God are perhaps to be found in the parable of the prodigal son.

. . . *'There was once a man who had two sons. The younger said, "Father, give me my share of the property now." So the man divided his property. . . . After a few days the younger son . . . left home with the money. . . .He spent everything he had.* He went abroad but there was a severe famine – he survived by looking after pigs on a farm. *At last he came to his senses and said, "All my father's hired workers have more than they can eat, and here I am about to starve! I will get up and go to my father and say, "Father, I have sinned against God and against you. I am no longer fit to be called your son. . . ." He was still a long way from home when his father saw him; his heart was filled with pity, and he ran, threw his arms round his son, and kissed him. . . . The father called his servants. . . . "Go and get the*

He went to a country far away, where he wasted his money in reckless living.
Lk 15.13

Whoever believes in me
believes not only in me
but also in him who sent me.
Jn 12.44-45

prize calf and kill it, and let us celebrate with a feast! . . ."

The elder son was out in the field. . . . He was angry . . . "Look, all these years I have worked for you. What have you given me? Not even a goat for me to have a feast with my friends! But this son of yours . . . when he comes back home, you kill the prize calf for him!" "My son," the father answered, "you are always here with me, and everything I have is yours. But we had to celebrate . . .; because your brother was dead, but now he is alive; he was lost, but now he has been found."' **Lk 15.11-32**

He wished he could fill himself with the bean pods the pigs ate, but no one gave him anything to eat . . . **Lk 15.16**

The father called his servants: 'Hurry! Bring the best robe and put it on him. Put a ring on his finger and shoes on his feet.'
Lk 15.22

When Jesus spoke about God he said: my Father, the Father, your Father who is in heaven.

Prayer

In his own prayer, Jesus called God 'Abba' (an Aramaic word meaning 'papa' or 'dad'). No one before had ever spoken to God in such a familiar way.

The gospels tell how Jesus used to go off alone to pray — as he did when the disciples returned from a mission full of joy because they had driven out demons in his name:

. . . Jesus was filled with joy by the Holy Spirit and said, 'Father, Lord of heaven and earth! I thank you because you have shown to the unlearned what you have hidden from the wise and learned.' **Lk 10.21**

He prayed before he was arrested: *'My Father! All things are possible for you. Take this cup of suffering from me. Yet not what I want, but what you want.'* **Mk 14.36** The gospels also tell of his prayer on the cross: *'Father forgive them. They don't know what they are doing.'* **Lk 23.34** *'Father! In your hands I place my spirit!'* **Lk 23.46**

Jesus taught his disciples to pray

Matthew's gospel

Our Father in heaven:

May your holy name be honoured;

may your Kingdom come;

may your will be done on earth as it is in heaven.

Give us today the food we need.

Forgive us the wrongs we have done, as we forgive the wrongs that others have done to us.

Do not bring us to hard testing,
but keep us safe from the Evil One.

Mt 6.9-13

Luke's gospel

Father:

May your holy name be honoured;

may your Kingdom come.

Give us day by day the food we need.

Forgive us our sins, for we forgive everyone who does us wrong.

And do not bring us to hard testing.

Lk 11.1-4

When you pray,
go to your room,
close the door,
and pray to
your Father,
who is unseen.
And your Father,
who sees what you
do in private,
will reward you.
When you pray,
do not use a lot of
meaningless words,
as the pagans do,
who think that God
will hear them
because their
prayers are long.
Do not be like
them. Your Father
already knows
what you need
before you ask him.

Mt 6.6-8

Who is he?

John the Baptist, whose disciple Jesus was to become, had his own moment of doubt.

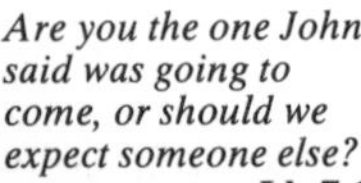

Are you the one John said was going to come, or should we expect someone else?
Lk 7.19

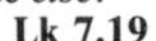

Contradictory opinions

Some of Jesus' contemporaries were unstinting in their praise of him:

They were all completely amazed and praised God, saying, 'We have never seen anything like this!' **Mk 2.12**

Others did not trust him – Jesus challenged their ideas, their interests and their authority. Pharisees, scribes, chief priests and Herodians were virulently opposed to him: *Look at this man! He is a glutton and a drinker, a friend of tax collectors and other outcasts.* **Lk 7.34** *We caught this man misleading our people, telling them not to pay taxes to the Emperor and claiming that he himself is the Messiah, a king.* **Lk 23.2**

Finally there were those who were not sure. Even Jesus' disciples were sometimes puzzled. *Teacher! Don't you care that we are about to die?* **Mk 4.38**

Jesus' reactions

Jesus maintained his independence.

Seeing this miracle that Jesus had performed, the people there said, 'Surely this is the Prophet who was to come into the world!' Jesus knew that they were about to . . . make him king

'Who is this man?
Even the wind and the waves obey him!'
Mk 4.41

by force; so he went off again to the hills by himself. **Jn 6.14-15**

The account of his temptations (**Mt 4.11; Lk 4.1**) is a symbolic illustration of his refusal to be used.

On the other hand, he allowed his apostles to call him the Messiah. *'What about you?' he asked them. 'Who do you say I am?' Peter answered, 'You are the Messiah.' Then Jesus ordered them, 'Do not tell anyone about me.'* **Mk 8.29-30**

In response to John the Baptist's doubts or the Pharisees' false accusations, Jesus let his actions speak:

'Go back and tell John what you have seen and heard: the blind can see, the lame can walk . . . the deaf can hear, the dead are raised to life, and the Good News is preached to the poor.'
Lk 7.22

Seeing this miracle that Jesus performed, the people there said, 'Surely this is the prophet who was to come into the world!' Jesus knew that they were about to come and seize him in order to make him king by force; so he went off again to the hills by himself. **Jn 6.14-15**

Elijah in the desert (after a Russian icon): some people thought Jesus was the reincarnation of this great prophet. Others said, *'He is Elijah.'* Others said, *'He is a prophet like one of the prophets of long ago.'*
Mk 6.15

Mount Thabor is the traditional site of the transfiguration.

In the gospels, the event known as the ‘transfiguration’ revealed to Jesus’ followers his true identity.

Jesus took with him Peter and the brothers James and John and led them up a high mountain where they were alone. As they looked on, a change came over Jesus: his face was shining like the sun, and his clothes were dazzling white. Then the three disciples saw

Moses and Elijah, the two greatest figures of the Old Testament, representing the Law and the prophets.

The secret revealed

(Mt 17.1; Mc 9.2; Lk 9.28; 2 Pet 1.17)

Moses and Elijah talking with Jesus. So Peter spoke up and said to Jesus, 'Lord, how good it is that we are here! If you wish, I will make three tents here, one for you, one for Moses, and one for Elijah.'

While he was talking, a shining cloud came over them, and a voice from the cloud said, 'This is my own dear Son, with whom I am pleased — listen to him!'

When the disciples heard the voice, they were so terrified that they threw themselves face downwards on the

ground. Jesus came to them and touched them. 'Get up,' he said. 'Don't be afraid!' So they looked up and saw no one there but Jesus.

As they came down the mountain, Jesus ordered them, 'Don't tell anyone about this vision you have seen until the Son of Man has been raised from death.'

Mt 17.1-9

For the first Christians, this was a good summary of their faith: Jesus is the beloved Son of God, the Messiah announced by the prophets.

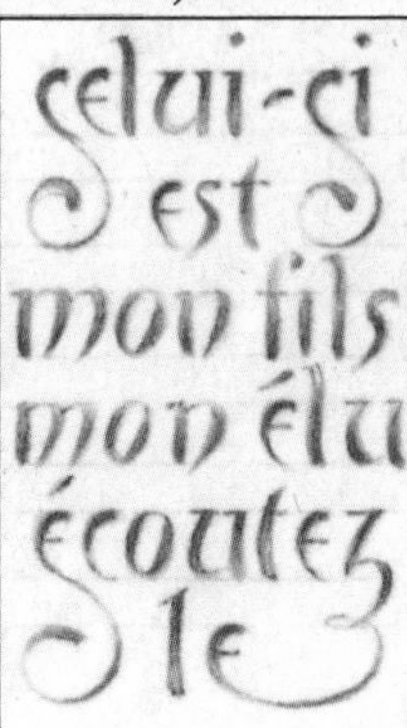

The mountain: a place of encounter between God and human beings.

The shining cloud, the voice: signs of God's presence.

Falling with one's face to the ground: an attitude of adoration.

The conspiracy

(Lk 22.1; Mk 14.1; Mt 26.1; Jn 11.47)

The miracle of the raising of Lazarus (**Jn 11.1-11**) rallied a crowd of people behind Jesus: to his enemies, the situation seemed more dangerous than ever. Judas' treachery (shown here in a 14th c. fresco) enabled the plot to go ahead.

The way in which Jesus proclaimed the Kingdom of Heaven made his enemies furious. Pharisees, scribes, chief priests and Herodians agreed to get rid of him by having him put to death. They were continually on the watch for a favourable moment.

In Capernaum, Jesus cured a man in the synagogue on the Sabbath. It was not the first time he had broken the law of the Sabbath like this. The Pharisees who were present: *left the synagogue and met at once with some members of Herod's party, and they made plans to kill Jesus.* **Mt 3.6**

In Nazareth, his home town, Jesus announced the Good News. His words surprised, shocked and scandalised.

'I have done many good deeds in your presence which the Father gave me to do; for which one of these do you want to stone me?'
Jn 10.31

Table ready for the Seder (Jewish paschal meal) with ritual food: bitter herbs and salt water (recalling the slavery in Egypt); hard boiled eggs (a reminder of temple offerings); vegetables; fruit.

When the people . . . heard this, they were filled with anger. They rose up, dragged Jesus out of the town.
Lk 4.28-29

The decision

It was now two days before the Festival of Passover. . . . The chief priests and the teachers of the Law were looking for a way to arrest Jesus secretly and put him to death. . . . **Mk 14.1-2**

Then they got their chance: *Judas Iscariot, one of the twelve disciples, went off to the chief priests in order to betray Jesus to them. They were pleased to hear what he had to say, and promised to give him money. So Judas started looking for a good chance to hand Jesus over to them.* **Mk 14.10-11**

Jesus foretells his death

(Mt 21.33; Mk 12.1; Lk 20.9; Jn 12.33)

The prophet Jeremiah, sent by God, met with nothing but hostility and loneliness. (From an 18th c. Catalan Bible.)

The theme of the good person or prophet who is persecuted is common in the Old Testament:
— Jeremiah, the most persecuted prophet of all
— innocent sufferers recalled in **Ps 22, 31, 66**
— the suffering servant **Is 53**.

Jesus was not a seer, he did not claim to know in advance what was going to happen to him. But he gradually realised that his life was in danger. Every day his enemies spied on him, keeping watch to catch him out and accuse him. Several times Jesus foretold his death to his disciples.

. . . *'The Son of Man must suffer much and be rejected by the elders, the chief priests and the teachers of the Law. He will be put to death, but three days later he will rise to life.'* **Mk 8.31**

But they did not understand what this . . . meant, and they were afraid to ask him. **Mk 9.32**

One day Jesus spoke directly to his enemies, telling them a parable: per-

The parable of the murderous vineyard workers, (from a 10th c. book of the gospels from Ethternach).

haps they would realise what a crime they were going to commit and abandon the idea.

. . . *Once there was a man who planted a vineyard, put a fence round it, dug a hole for the winepress, and built a watch-tower. Then he let out the vineyard to tenants and left home on a journey. . . . He sent a slave to the tenants to receive from them his share of the harvest. The tenants seized the slave, beat him, and sent him back without a thing. Then the owner sent another slave; the tenants beat him over the head and treated him shamefully. . . . They treated many others the same way. . . . Last of all, then, he sent his son to the tenants. 'I am sure they will respect my son,' he said. But those tenants said to one another, 'This is the owner's son. Come on, let's kill him, and his property will be ours!' So they seized the son and killed him and threw his body out of the vineyard.*

'What, then, will the owner of the vineyards do?' asked Jesus. 'He will come and kill those men and hand the vineyard over to other tenants. . . . '

The Jewish leaders tried to arrest Jesus, because they knew that he had told this parable against them. But they were afraid of the crowd, so they left him and went away. **Mk 12.1 . . . 12**

I am telling you the truth: a grain of wheat remains no more than a single grain unless it falls into the ground and dies. If it does die, then it produces many grains. **Jn 12.24**

Jerusalem, Jerusalem! You kill the prophets and stone the messengers God has sent you! How many times have I wanted to put my arms round all your people, just as a hen gathers her chicks under her wings, but you would not let me. **Mt 23.37**

The entry of Jesus into Jerusalem. Above: from a Byzantine manuscript. Below: after Giotto (15th c.).

Why a donkey? Whereas the horse, which was used to pull chariots and military equipment, is a symbol of brute force, the donkey, a homely animal, is a symbol of peace.

Jesus went up to Jerusalem for the last time. His fame had preceded him: many people waited to welcome him.

As Jesus and his disciples approached Jerusalem, they came to Bethphage . . . There Jesus sent two of the disciples on ahead . . . 'Go to the village there ahead of you, and at once you will find a donkey tied up with her colt beside her. Untie them and bring them to me. And if anyone says anything, tell him, "The Master needs them"; and then he will let them go at once.'

This happened to make what the prophet had said come true: 'Tell the city of Zion, "Look, your king is coming to you! He is humble and rides on a donkey and on a colt, the foal of a donkey."

So the disciples . . . brought the donkey and the colt, threw their cloaks over them, and Jesus got on. A large crowd of people spread

Look, your king is coming to you!
He comes triumphant and
victorious, but humble and
riding a donkey.
Zechariah (4th c. B.C.)

The triumphal entry into Jerusalem

(Mt 21.1; Mk 11.1; Lk 19.28; Jn 12.12)

their cloaks on the road while others cut branches from the trees and spread them on the road. The crowds . . . began to shout, 'Praise to David's Son! God bless him who comes in the name of the Lord! Praise God!'

When Jesus entered Jerusalem, the whole city was thrown into an uproar. 'Who is he?' the people asked. 'This is the prophet Jesus, from Nazareth in Galilee,' the crowds answered.

Mt 21.1-11

The Last Supper

(Mt 26.17; Mk 14.12; Lk 22.7; Jn 13.1)

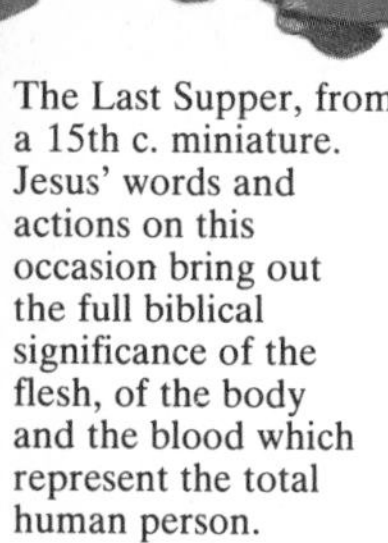

The Last Supper, from a 15th c. miniature. Jesus' words and actions on this occasion bring out the full biblical significance of the flesh, of the body and the blood which represent the total human person.

Christians regularly re-enact what Jesus did, in memory of him. This celebration is known as the Eucharist, or the Divine Liturgy, or the Mass or the Lord's Supper.

Jesus was in Jerusalem with the Twelve for the feast of the Passover. He knew that his enemies had sworn to kill him, and were trying to arrest him. He had little time left to spend with his friends.

His last meal – known as the Last Supper – was the traditional meal Jewish families took together in order to remind themselves how God had rescued their ancestors from Egypt, where they were living in slavery.

When the hour came, Jesus took his place at the table with the apostles. He said to them, 'I have wanted so much to eat this Passover meal with you before I suffer! For I tell you, I will never eat it until it is given its full meaning in the Kingdom of God.'

'I am the bread of life,' Jesus told them. 'He who comes to me will never be hungry; he who believes in me will never be thirsty.'

Jn 6.35

Then Jesus took a cup, gave thanks to God, and said, 'Take this and share it among yourselves. I tell you that from now on I will not drink this wine until the Kingdom of God comes.'

Then he took a piece of bread, gave thanks to God, broke it, and gave it to them saying, 'This is my body, which is given for you. Do this in memory of me.' In the same way, he gave them the cup after the supper, saying, 'This cup is God's new covenant sealed with my blood, which is poured out for you.'

Lk 22.14-20

According to John's gospel, Jesus washed his disciples feet at the Last Supper – a task usually performed by slaves or domestic servants. Afterwards he said to them:

. . . I, your Lord and Teacher, have just washed your feet. You, then, should wash one another's feet. I have set an example, for you so that you will do just what I have done for you. . . .

Jn 13.14-15

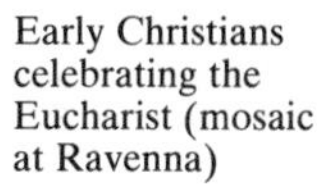

Early Christians celebrating the Eucharist (mosaic at Ravenna)

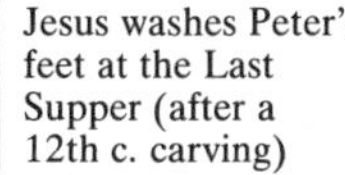

Jesus washes Peter's feet at the Last Supper (after a 12th c. carving)

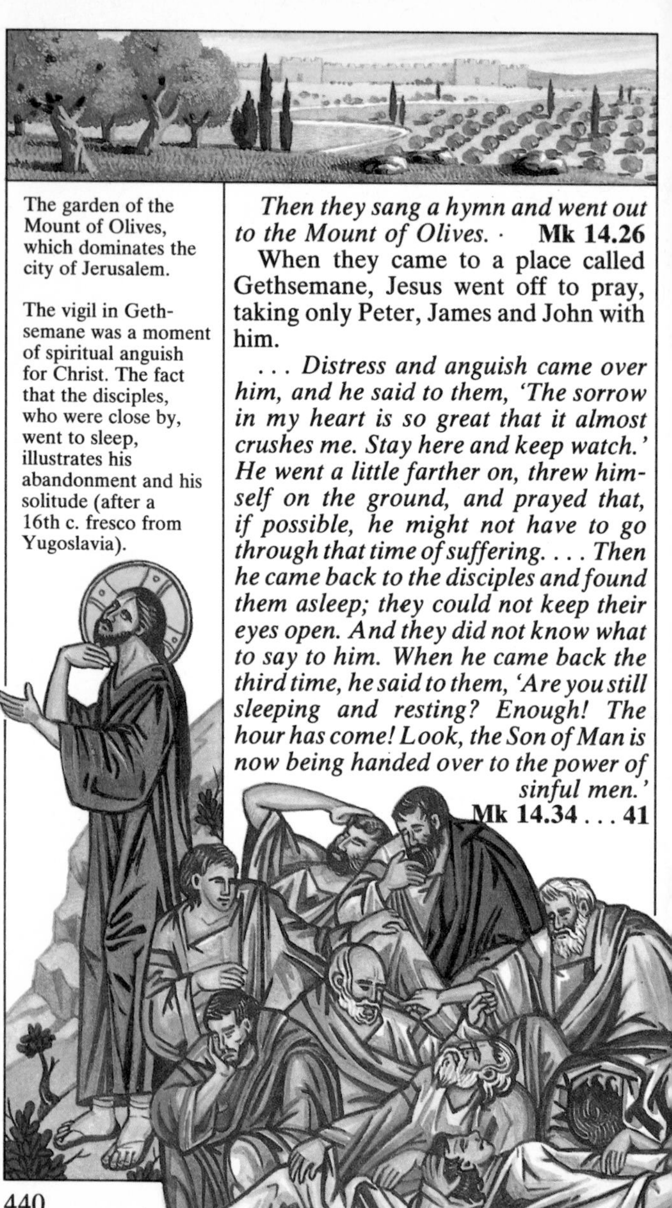

The garden of the Mount of Olives, which dominates the city of Jerusalem.

The vigil in Gethsemane was a moment of spiritual anguish for Christ. The fact that the disciples, who were close by, went to sleep, illustrates his abandonment and his solitude (after a 16th c. fresco from Yugoslavia).

Then they sang a hymn and went out to the Mount of Olives. · **Mk 14.26**

When they came to a place called Gethsemane, Jesus went off to pray, taking only Peter, James and John with him.

. . . Distress and anguish came over him, and he said to them, 'The sorrow in my heart is so great that it almost crushes me. Stay here and keep watch.' He went a little farther on, threw himself on the ground, and prayed that, if possible, he might not have to go through that time of suffering. . . . Then he came back to the disciples and found them asleep; they could not keep their eyes open. And they did not know what to say to him. When he came back the third time, he said to them, 'Are you still sleeping and resting? Enough! The hour has come! Look, the Son of Man is now being handed over to the power of sinful men.'

Mk 14.34 . . . 41

The vigil at Gethsemane

(Lk 22.39; Mk 14.26; Mt 26.30; Jn 18.1)

During his long, lonely vigil, Christ accepted the will of his Father: *My Father! All things are possible for you. Take this cup of suffering away from me. Yet not what I want, but what you want.* **Mk 14.36**

The arrest

Judas, one of the Twelve, arrived with a crowd of people armed with swords and clubs. He had agreed to show which man was to be arrested by kissing him.

As soon as Judas arrived, he went up to Jesus and said, 'Teacher!' and kissed him. So they arrested Jesus and held him tight. But one of those standing there drew his sword and struck at the High Priest's slave, cutting off his ear. Then Jesus spoke up and said to them, 'Did you have to come with swords and clubs to capture me, as though I were an outlaw? Day after day I was with you teaching in the temple, and you did not arrest me. But the Scriptures must come true.' Then all the disciples left him and ran away. **Mk 14.45-50**

And when one of his companions – Simon according to John's gospel – tried to defend him by striking the High Priest's servant, Jesus showed the same acceptance: *Put your sword back in its place. Don't you know that I could call on my Father for help, and at once he would send me more than twelve armies of angels? But in that case, how could the Scriptures come true which say that this is what must happen?* **Mt 26.52-54**

The trial

(Mt 26.57; Mk 14.53; Lk 22.54; Jn 18.24)

King Herod

The chief priests, scribes and Pharisees, who for a long time had been bent on destroying Jesus, brought him before the Sanhedrin. *They all said, 'Are you then the Son of God?' He answered them, 'You say that I am.'*

Lk 22.70

On the strength of that admission, Jesus was taken next to the Roman prefect Pilate. Pilate saw no reason to condemn Jesus, but on the insistence of his accusers sent him to Herod – under whose jurisdiction Jesus came.

Standing before Herod, Jesus remained silent. *Herod and his soldiers mocked Jesus and treated him with contempt; then they put a fine robe on him and sent him back to Pilate.*

Lk 23.11

The Roman prefect then summoned the people and suggested that he free the accused, who seemed innocent to

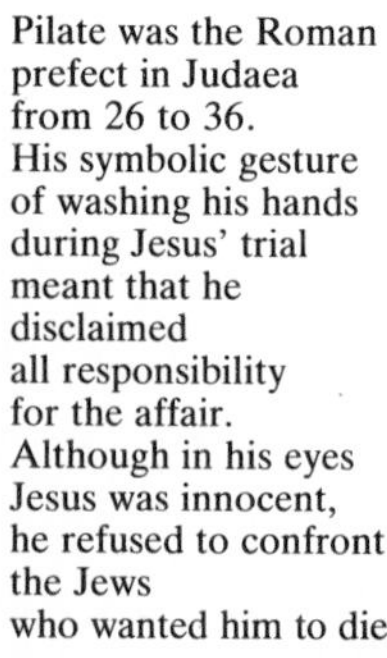
Pilate was the Roman prefect in Judaea from 26 to 36. His symbolic gesture of washing his hands during Jesus' trial meant that he disclaimed all responsibility for the affair. Although in his eyes Jesus was innocent, he refused to confront the Jews who wanted him to die.

So Pilate went outside to them and asked, 'What do you accuse this man of?'
Jn 18.29

him. Also, it was customary during the festival to release one prisoner. *The whole crowd cried out, 'Kill him! Set Barabbas free for us!'* **Lk 23.18** (Barabbas was a recently-imprisoned criminal.) *They kept on shouting . . . that Jesus should be crucified, and finally their shouting succeeded. So Pilate passed the sentence on Jesus that they were asking for.* **Lk 23.23-24**

Peter followed from a distance as Jesus was led away. It was then that a woman recognised him and accused him of being a disciple of the condemned man. *But Peter denied it, 'Woman, I don't even know him!'*
Lk 22.57

Peter denied Jesus two more times; at daybreak, desperate at his own weakness, he *wept bitterly.* **Lk 22.62**

Christ is insulted

The men who were guarding Jesus mocked him and beat him. They blindfolded him and asked him, 'Who hit you? Prophesy!' They said many other insulting things to him.
Lk 22.63-65

Before dawn on the day when Christ was scourged and then crucified, Peter denied him three times. In this way he fulfilled the prophecy Jesus himself had made the evening before, during the Last Supper (**Lk 22.34**).

The road to Calvary

(Lk 23.26; Mk 15.20; Mt 27.31; Jn 19.16)

Crucifixion
The condemned person was stretched out on a beam, to which his wrists were nailed; then he was hoisted onto the fixed, upright, part of the cross. His feet were nailed, and his legs broken, so that he could not use them as support. He died of asphyxiation.

According to an 11th c. tradition, a woman called Veronica took pity on Jesus and wiped his face. The towel retained the imprint of his face. 'Veronica's veil' is in St Peter's in Rome.

On the way to Golgotha

. . . As they were going, they met a man from Cyrene named Simon who was coming . . . from the country. They seized him, put the cross on him, and made him carry it behind Jesus.

A large crowd of people followed him; among them were some women who were weeping and wailing for him. Jesus turned to them and said, 'Women of Jerusalem! Don't cry for me, but for yourselves and your children. For the days are coming when people will say, 'How lucky are the women who never had children. . . .' **Lk 23.26-29**

Jesus is nailed to the cross

Two . . . criminals, were also led out to be put to death with Jesus. When they came to the place called 'The Skull', they crucified Jesus there, and the two criminals, one on his right and the other on his left. Jesus said, 'Forgive them, Father! They don't know what they are doing.' They divided his clothes among themselves by throwing dice. . . .

The way of the cross, inspired by Peter Brueghel the Elder.

The greatest love a person can have for his friends is to give his life for them.
Jn 15.13

As the people watched, the Jewish leaders jeered at him. *The soldiers also mocked him: they came up to him and offered him cheap wine, and said, 'Save yourself if you are the king of the Jews!' Above him were written these words: 'This is the King of the Jews.'*
Lk 23.32-38

The repentant thief

One of the criminals hanging there

hurled insults at him: 'Aren't you the Messiah? Save yourself and us!'

The other one, however, rebuked him, saying 'Don't you fear God? You received the same sentence he did. Ours, however, is only right, because we are getting what we deserve for what we did; but he has done no wrong.' And he said to Jesus, 'Remember me, Jesus, when you come as King!' Jesus said to him, 'I promise you that today you will be in Paradise with me.' **Lk 23.39-43**

That was at the sixth hour. Suddenly the sky darkened. At the ninth hour – three o'clock – the moment when Jesus died on the cross, the veil of the Temple was torn in two. The evangelists give us four very similar accounts.

Golgotha (Hebrew for skull) is a hill outside Jerusalem. It was a place many people passed and the authorities relied on the sight of a crucifixion as a deterrent to others.

The four accounts of Jesus' death

The lance used to pierce his side and the sponge dipped in cheap wine, the last instruments used to torment Jesus.

Luke

It was about twelve o'clock when the sun stopped shining and darkness covered the whole country until three o'clock; and the curtain hanging in the temple was torn in two. Jesus cried out in a loud voice, 'Father! In your hands I place my spirit!' He said this and died.

Lk 23.44-46

John

Jesus knew that [all] *had been completed; and in order to make the scripture come true, he said, 'I am thirsty.' A bowl was there, full of cheap wine; so a sponge was soaked in the wine, put on a stalk of hyssop, and lifted up to his lips. Jesus drank the wine and said, 'It is finished!'*

Jn 19.28-30

Darkness, earthquakes, splitting rocks: symbolic language indicating the defeat of the forces of evil and the coming of a new world willed by God.

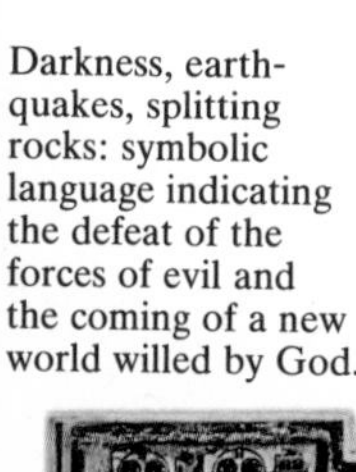

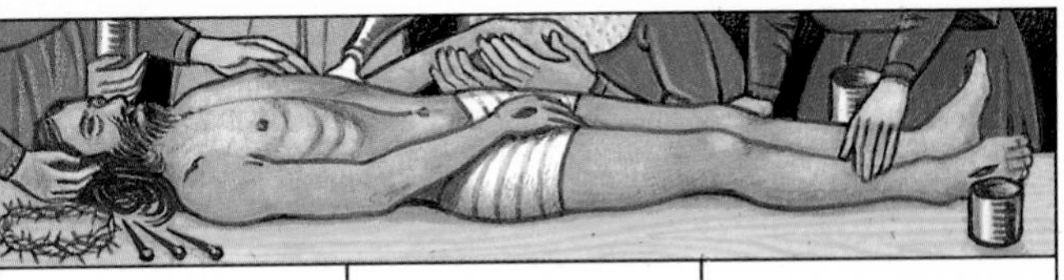

Mark

At three o'clock Jesus cried out with a loud shout, 'Eloi, Eloi, lema sabachthani?' *which means, 'My God, my God, why did you abandon me?' . . . One of them ran up with a sponge, soaked it in cheap wine, and put it on the end of a stick. Then he held it up to Jesus' lips and said, 'Wait! Let us see if Elijah is coming to bring him down from the cross!'*

With a loud cry Jesus died.

The curtain hanging in the temple was torn in two, from top to bottom.

Mk 15.34-38

Christ victorious, in a 12th c. Italian painting

Matthew

At about three o'clock Jesus cried out with a loud shout, 'Eli, Eli, lema sabachthani?' *which means, 'My God, my God, why did you abandon me?'*

Someone . . . ran up at once, took a sponge, soaked it in cheap wine, put it on the end of a stick, and tried to make him drink it. . . .

Jesus again gave a loud cry and breathed his last.

Then the curtain hanging in the temple was torn in two from top to bottom. The earth shook, the rocks split apart.

Mt 27.46-53

A man named Joseph from Arimathea . . . asked for the body of Jesus. Then he took the body down, wrapped it in a linen sheet. **Lk 23.50-53**

Mary supported by Mary Magdalene

He is risen!

(Lk 24.1; Mt 28.1; Jn 20.1 and 21.1)

In Jesus' time it was common in the East to anoint the bodies of dead people with vegetable substances like myrrh and aloes, in order to preserve them as long as possible.

After the Sabbath was over, Mary Magdalene, Mary the mother of James, and Salome bought spices to go and anoint the body of Jesus. Very early on Sunday morning, at sunrise, they went to the tomb. On the way they said to one another, 'Who will roll away the stone

for us from the entrance to the tomb?' . . . Then they looked up and saw that the stone had already been rolled back. So they entered the tomb, where they saw a young man sitting on the right, wearing a white robe – and they were alarmed.

'Don't be alarmed,' he said. 'I know you are looking for Jesus of Nazareth, who was crucified. He is not here – he has been raised! Look, here is the place where they put him. Now go and give this message to his disciples, including Peter: "He is going to Galilee ahead of you; there you will see him, just as he told you." '

So they went out and ran from the tomb, distressed and terrified. . . .

Mk 16.1-8

Some time after Jesus' death, his disciples proclaimed the astonishing news: Jesus, who was crucified, has been raised by God from the dead. He is now living with God. He is truly God's messenger, his messiah, who brings a new world to birth.

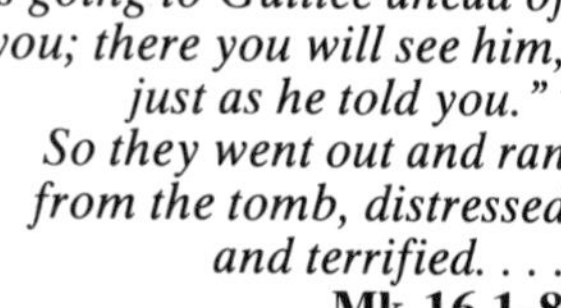

Whoever follows me will have the light of life and will never walk in darkness.
Jn 8.12

Keys to the text

The young man dressed in white
In the Bible, white is the divine colour. The young man is a messenger from God. His role is to announce to men and women the good news God has for them.

He is risen
Literally: he has awakened from the dead. Another expression used is: he has been raised from the dead.

He is not here
The empty tomb does not prove Jesus' resurrection. It was on the word of the messenger from God that the women accepted the news.

What happened?

None of the gospels describes Jesus' resurrection. This account, like those that follow, tries to express in images the disciples' experience of faith in the resurrection of Jesus.

Jewish tombs, like the one in which Jesus was buried, consisted of a cavity, often dug out of the rock. A round stone was rolled in front of this to act as a seal.
It was not until the Middle Ages that people began to represent Christ's tomb as a stone coffin.

An angel of the Lord came down from heaven, rolled the stone away and sat on it. . . .
The guards were so afraid that they trembled and became like dead men.
Mt 28.2-4

The risen Lord appears to Mary Magdalene

The presence of angels, here as at the birth of Jesus, is a reminder that in moments like this God is made manifest on earth.

At the end of each gospel there are accounts of the appearances of the risen Jesus. He showed himself to women, to men, to simple disciples, to the Eleven (Judas, the traitor, having died).

All these accounts are constructed in the same way:

– The risen Jesus takes the initiative to get himself recognised.

– The disciples, overcoming their difficulties, their doubts and their despair, recognise him.

– The risen Jesus gives the disciples the mission to share the Good News with others.

Early on Sunday morning, while it was still dark, Mary Magdalene went to the tomb and saw that the stone had been taken away from the entrance.

Mary stood crying outside the tomb. While she was still crying, she bent over and looked in the tomb and saw two angels there dressed in white, sitting where the body of Jesus had been, one at the head and the other at the feet. 'Woman, why are you crying?' they asked her. She answered, 'They have taken my Lord away, and I do not know where they have put him!'

After Jesus rose from death early on Sunday, he appeared first to Mary Magdalene, from whom he had driven out seven demons.
Mk 16.9

Then she turned . . . and saw Jesus . . . but she did not know that it was Jesus. 'Woman, why are you crying?' Jesus asked her. . . . She thought he was the gardener, so she said to him, 'If you took him away, sir, tell me where you have put him, and I will go and get him.'

Jesus said to her, 'Mary!' She turned towards him and said in Hebrew, 'Rabboni!' (This means 'Teacher'.) 'Do not hold on to me,' Jesus told her, 'because I have not yet gone back up to the Father. But go to my brothers and tell them that I am returning to him who is my Father and their Father, my God and their God.'

So Mary Magdalene went and told the disciples that she had seen the Lord and related to them what he had told her.
Jn 20.1, 11-18

An astonishing turn of events

– *At first*: Mary Magdalene stands motionless by the tomb, weeping. She is disappointed. She came to venerate the body of Jesus her master, and it has disappeared. Who will give it back to her?

– *In the end*: Mary Magdalene runs off to share her good news: I have seen the Lord. Why the change? Jesus said to her: *go to my brothers and tell them. . . .* Mary understands that Jesus is not her property, that she is only the messenger of the resurrection.

The way to Emmaus

Luke's gospel sites Emmaus about 60 *stadia* north of Jerusalem – about 10 km or 6 miles (the *stadium*, a Greek measure, was equivalent to about 170 m/560 ft).

A few days after Jesus' death, two of his disciples were walking together towards Emmaus. On the way they discussed recent events: it was at this point that Jesus joined them. *They saw him, but somehow did not recognise him. Jesus said to them, 'What are you talking about to each other, as you walk along?'*

They stood still, with sad faces. One of them, named Cleopas, asked him, 'Are you the only visitor in Jerusalem

The exact position of Emmaus has been much discussed: some agree with the position given by Luke, but others put the village at the site of present-day Amouas, 30 km (19 miles) from Jerusalem. Emmaus is visible at the back of this evocation of the scene, (inspired by a mosaic in Ravenna).

who doesn't know the things that have been happening there these last few days?'

Then they described how Jesus had been put to death, adding:

'We had hoped that he would be the one who was going to set Israel free! Besides all that, this is now the third day since it happened. Some of the women of

our group surprised us; they went at dawn to the tomb, but could not find his body. They came back saying they had seen a vision of angels who told them that he is alive. Some of our group went to the tomb and found it exactly as the women had said, but they did not see him.'

Then Jesus said to them, 'How foolish you are, how slow you are to believe everything the prophets said! Was it not necessary for the Messiah to suffer these things and then to enter his glory?'

Lk 24.16-26

The revelation

When they reached Emmaus, the two disciples – still blind to the truth – begged their companion to share their meal with them. *He sat down to eat with them, took the bread, and said the blessing; then he broke the bread and gave it to them. Then their eyes were opened and they recognised him, but he disappeared from their sight.*

Lk 24.30-31

Jesus' two companions on the road to Emmaus were ordinary disciples. Despite their fervour, they had not yet understood exactly who this Jesus was, whom they had taken to be the messiah who was to deliver Israel. The explanations Jesus gave on the way and his revelation during the meal were needed before they understood the full spiritual significance of his death.

The pilgrims at Emmaus (after a drawing by Rembrandt).

Jesus appears to the Eleven

Thomas recognised Jesus from the wounds he received on the cross. A medieval artist arranged on a cross all the instruments used in this form of punishment.

The four gospels give very different accounts of the appearances of the risen Jesus to the Eleven. Places, times, words and actions vary. For the evangelists it was a matter less of describing the event than of expressing in symbolic terms what they believed.

In John's gospel

It was late that Sunday evening, and the disciples were gathered together behind locked doors, because they were afraid of the Jewish authorities. Then Jesus came and stood among them. 'Peace be with you,' he said. After saying this, he showed them his hands and his side. The disciples were filled

with joy at seeing the Lord. Jesus said to them again, 'Peace be with you. As the Father sent me, so I send you.' Then he breathed on them and said, 'Receive the Holy Spirit. If you forgive people's sins, they are forgiven; if you do not forgive them, they are not forgiven.'

One of the twelve disciples, Thomas (called the Twin), was not with them when Jesus came. So the other disciples

Put your finger here, and look at my hands; then stretch out your hand and put it in my side. Stop your doubting and believe.

Jn 20.27

told him, 'We have seen the Lord!'

Thomas said to them, 'Unless I see . . . I will not believe.'

Jn 20.19-25

In Matthew's gospel

The eleven disciples went to the hill in Galilee where Jesus had told them to go. When they saw him, they worshipped him, even though some of them doubted. Jesus drew near and said to them, 'I have been given all authority in heaven and on earth. Go, then, to all peoples everywhere and make them my disciples: baptise them in the name of the Father, the Son, and the Holy Spirit, and teach them to obey everything I have commanded you.' **Mt 28.16-20**

He said to them, 'Why are you alarmed? Why are these doubts coming up in your minds?' **Lk 24.38**

The appearance to the Eleven (after a mosaic in Ravenna).

THE STORY

All the believers continued together
in close fellowship
and shared their belongings with one another.
They would sell their property and possessions,
and distribute the money among all,
according to what each one needed.

Acts 2.44-45

2 The first Christians

New Testament books about the first Christians

– The **Acts of the Apostles**, written by Luke between 80 and 90. They show how Jesus' teaching, which was rejected by most Jewish people, spread from Jerusalem to Judaea, Samaria, Asia Minor and even Rome, thanks to Peter, John, James, Philip, Barnabas and, above all, Paul.

– the **letters (epistles)** are to Christian communities and offer wise counsel. They were written by Paul, or some of his disciples, and by James, Peter, John and Jude.

– the **Apocalypse of John**, addressed to persecuted Christians, proclaimed the victory of God.

The ascension of Jesus

(Lk 24.50; Mk 16.19; Acts 1.9)

The men in white garments are messengers of God.

The Holy Spirit: breath in Hebrew. The same word is used for the wind, human breath, and the power of God, who changes people's hearts and gives them the power of God. To be baptised in the Holy Spirit is to be immersed in the power of God.

In the Bible, a cloud symbolises the presence of God.

The Acts of the Apostles begins by describing the end of the appearances of the risen Jesus.

And when they came together, he gave them this order: 'Do not leave Jerusalem, but wait for the gift . . . my Father promised. John baptised with water, but in a few days you will be baptised with the Holy Spirit.'

When the apostles met together with Jesus, they asked him, 'Lord, will you at this time give the Kingdom back to Israel?' Jesus said to them, 'The times and occasions are set by my Father's own authority, and it is not for you to know when they will be. But when the Holy Spirit comes upon you, you will be filled with power, and you will be witnesses to me in Jerusalem . . . and to the ends of the earth.' After saying this, he was taken up to heaven as they watched him, and a cloud hid him from their sight.

They still had their eyes fixed on the sky, . . . when two men dressed in white . . . stood beside them and said, 'Galileans why are you . . . looking up

The election of Matthias

at the sky? This Jesus, who was taken from you into heaven, will come back in the same way that you saw him go to heaven.' **Acts 1.4-11**

Peter suggested that they should elect someone to take the place of Judas, who had committed suicide.

'Someone must join us as a witness to the resurrection of the Lord Jesus. He must be one of the men who were in our group . . . from the time John preached his message of baptism until the day Jesus was taken up from us to heaven.'

So they proposed two men: Joseph, who was called Barsabbas (also known as Justus), and Matthias. Then they prayed, 'Lord, you know the thoughts of everyone, so show us which of these two you have chosen to serve as an apostle in the place of Judas.' . . . Then they drew lots . . . and the one chosen was Matthias. . . . **Acts 1.21-26**

Filled with remorse, Judas *went off and hanged himself.* **Mt 27.5**

Pentecost

Pentecost is a Greek word which signifies the *fiftieth* day after Easter.

The Jewish feast of Shavouth, seven weeks after Passover, recalled the gift of the Law, made by God to Moses on Mount Sinai, and God's covenant with the people.

It was on this day that the Holy Spirit was given to Jesus' disciples: God's new covenant with the human race was to be based henceforth on the gift of the Spirit of Jesus.

In the Bible, violent noises, gusts of wind and fire are manifestations of the power of God. The dove, symbol of peace in the Old Testament, now becomes a symbol of the Holy Spirit. *They saw what looked like tongues of fire which spread out and touched each person there.*
Acts 2.3

When the day of Pentecost came, all the believers were gathered together. . . . Suddenly there was a noise . . . like a strong wind blowing, and it filled the whole house. . . . They were all filled with the Holy Spirit and began to talk in other languages. . . .

There were Jews living in Jerusalem, religious men who had come from every country in the world. When they heard this noise, a large crowd gathered. They were all excited, because each one of them heard the believers speaking in his own language. . . . About three thousand people were added to the group that day. **Acts 2.1-6, 41**

Right: Pentecost, from a 12th c. Romanesque illumination.

The first community in Jerusalem

On the day of Pentecost Peter addressed the crowd: *All the people of Israel are to know for sure that this Jesus, whom you crucified, is the one that God has made Lord and Messiah!*
Acts 2.36

All those who were converted joined the disciples and the first Christian community was born.

Peter teaching, after Fra Angelico (15th c.)

They spent their time in learning from the apostles, taking part in the fellowship, and sharing in the fellowship meals and the prayers.

Many miracles and wonders were being done through the apostles, and everyone was filled with awe. All the believers continued together in close fellowship and shared their belongings with one another. They would sell their property and possessions and distribute the money among all, according to what each one needed. Day after day they met as a group in the temple, and they had their meals together in their homes, eating with glad and humble hearts, praising God, and enjoying the good will of all the people. And every day the Lord added to their group those who were being saved. **Acts 2.42-47**

The first community, centred in Jerusalem, observed the rules of life known as 'the four pillars'. The disciples concentrated on:

– the teaching of the apostles (what Jesus did and said, and how they had to live to remain in the spirit of Jesus).

– life in community. This was the bond of fellowship characterised by unity and the sharing of possessions. (Luke seems to idealise the situation, since the rest of his account brings out a number of difficulties.)

– the breaking of bread. This was a re-enactment of Jesus' last meal.

– prayer. The first Christians

composed the prayers. Thus Luke was the author of Mary's song, the *Magnificat* (**Lk 1.46-55**) and of the song of Zechariah, the father of John the Baptist (**Lk 1.68-79**).

Over the years, the first Christians in Jerusalem, who were Jewish by birth, continued to go to the temple. It was only gradually that they were expelled from Judaism as heretics.

They had their meals together in their homes, eating with glad and humble hearts. **Acts 2.46**

The Holy of Holies, the sacred part of the temple. This sheltered the Ark which contained the tablets of the Law.
The first Christians, who came from Judaism, continued to take part in the temple worship.

Left: an example of the charity the disciples tried to practise (after the 16th c. Bugnon reredos).

The first clashes with authority

The Beautiful Gate separated the Court of the Gentiles from that of the Jewish women.

Miracles in the Acts of the Apostles
A certain number of cures, exorcisms and resurrections were carried out by Jesus' apostles in his name (**5.15; 9.32-43** . . .). They have the same significance as Jesus' miracles: the Kingdom of Heaven comes when people are free from all that weighs them down physically or spiritually.

One day Peter and John went to the Temple at three o'clock in the afternoon, the hour for prayer. There at the Beautiful Gate, as it was called, was a man who had been lame all his life. . . . When he saw Peter and John going in, he begged them to give him something.
Acts 3.1-3

Peter said to him:

'I have no money at all, but I give you what I have: in the name of Jesus Christ of Nazareth I order you to get up and walk!'

The lame man immediately got up and followed them. Peter and John then explained to the crowd that they had worked this miracle in Jesus' name. At that moment the priests and Sadducees arrived and arrested them. Next day, John and Peter appeared before the Sanhedrin, who asked them to explain:

'How did you do this? What power have you got or whose name did you use?' Peter, full of the Holy Spirit, answered them, *'Leaders of the people and elders: if we are being questioned today about the good deed done to the lame man and how he was healed, then you . . . and all the people of Israel*

The stone that you the builders despised turned out to be the most important of all.
Acts 4.11

should know that this man stands here before you completely well through the power of the name of Jesus Christ of Nazareth – whom you crucified and whom God raised from death.'
Acts 4.7-10

The Sanhedrin ordered them to stop teaching.

Attempt at intimidation

Once freed, Peter and John did not obey; they went on proclaiming the gospel in the temple and doing cures and exorcisms.

There followed a test of strength: Peter and John were arrested again. But an angel set them free and urged them to continue their teaching in the Temple. There they found the officers who had been told to bring them before the authorities. When the High Priest accused them of disobeying his command, Peter replied: *'We must obey God not men.'*
Acts 5.29

In the face of the Sadducees' intransigence, Gamaliel, a Pharisee and teacher of the Law, pleaded for the release of the apostles.
(Acts 5.34-39)

Faith is offered, instead of the expected money (after a 15th c. Italian fresco).

The choice of the Seven

Why seven?
This symbolic number stands for fullness, totality, perfection.

The daily service
was a service of solidarity (food, gifts) in favour of the poorest in the community.

The Hellenists
were Christians of Jewish origin who had contacts with the Greek world, and had adopted its language, culture and customs. They had their own synagogues and were allowed to read the Bible in Greek.

The Hebrews
were Christians from a strict Jewish background. They obeyed the Law scrupulously and distrusted anything that was not Jewish.

Some time later . . . the Greek-speaking Jews claimed that their widows were being neglected in the daily distribution of funds. So the twelve apostles called the whole group of believers together and said, 'It is not right for us to neglect the preaching of God's word in order to handle finances.

So then, brothers, choose seven men among you who are known to be full . . . of wisdom, and we will put them in charge of this matter. We ourselves, then, will give our full time to prayer and the work of preaching.' The whole group was pleased with the apostles' proposal, so they chose Stephen, . . . and Philip, Prochorus, Nicanor, Timon, Parmenas, and Nicolaus.

Acts 6.1-6

At first their job was to care for the poor. Later, called deacons (ones who serve), they concentrated on the service of the Word.

Stephen, the first martyr

Stephen . . . performed great miracles and wonders among the people. But he was opposed by some . . . members of the synagogue. . . . They . . . started arguing with Stephen. But the Spirit gave Stephen such wisdom that when he spoke, they could not refute him. So they bribed some men to say, 'We heard him speaking . . . against God!' In this way they stirred up the people. . . . They seized Stephen and took him before the Council. **Acts 6.8-12**

Stephen spoke for a long time to his 'brothers and fathers', reminding them of the great events in Jewish history.

Stephen was stoned to death in the sight of Saul – the future Paul.

That day the church in Jerusalem began to suffer cruel persecution. All the believers, except the apostles, were scattered throughout the provinces of Judaea and Samaria. **Acts 8.1**

Stephen before the Sanhedrin.

He knelt down and cried out in a loud voice, 'Lord do not remember this sin against them.' He said this and died. **Acts 7.59-60**

The Gospel in Samaria

Evil spirits came out from many people with a loud cry.
Acts 8.7

Philip preached in Samaria, doing many cures. One day he met a magician called Simon.

Simon himself also believed; and after being baptised, he stayed close to Philip and was astounded when he saw the . . . miracles that were being performed.

The apostles in Jerusalem heard that the people of Samaria had received the word of God, so they sent Peter and John to them. . . . Simon saw that the Spirit had been given to the believers when the apostles placed their hands on them. So he offered money to Peter and John, and said, 'Give this power to me too.' . . . But Peter answered him, 'May you and your money go to hell, for thinking that you can buy God's gift with money! . . . Repent. . . .'

Simon said, . . . 'Please pray to the Lord for me. . . .' After they had given their testimony . . . Peter and John went back to Jerusalem. **Acts 8.6 . . . 25**

Many paralysed and lame people were healed. **Acts 8.7**

Money-lending (after a medieval Jewish manuscript).

The conversion of an Ethiopian

This episode describes the stages of Christian baptism: desire to know, reading the Bible in the light of the Gospel, request for baptism, profession of faith, baptism.

An angel of the Lord said to Philip, 'Get ready and go south to the road that goes from Jerusalem to Gaza.' . . . So Philip . . . went. Now an Ethiopian eunuch . . . had been to Jerusalem to worship God and was going back home in his carriage. As he rode along, he was reading from the book of the prophet Isaiah. The Holy Spirit said to Philip, 'Go over to that carriage and stay close to it.' Philip ran over and . . . asked him, 'Do you understand what you are reading?' . . . The passage of scripture which he was reading was this: 'Like a sheep that is taken to be slaughtered, . . . he was humiliated and justice was denied him.'

The official asked Philip, 'Tell me, of whom is the prophet saying this? Of himself or of someone else?' Then Philip . . . told him the Good News about Jesus. . . . They came to a place where there was some water, and the official said, 'Here is some water. What is to keep me from being baptised?' . . .

Acts 8.26 . . . 38

The passage the Ethiopian was reading (**Is 53**) was about the Suffering Servant, who symbolised the persecuted Jewish people bringing salvation. For Christians he became a figure of Christ.

14th c. Ethiopian miniature illustrating a gospel text. Christianity was introduced into Ethiopia in the 4th c. There it established a long tradition to which many wall paintings and miniatures bear witness.

Paul is thrown to the ground at the gates of Damascus (after an illumination in the Bible of Charles the Bald, 9th c.)

Saul (from his Roman name, Paul) came from Tarsus in Cilicia. He was a fervent Jew who persecuted the Christians. It was for this purpose that he was going to Damascus.

. . . *suddenly a light from the sky flashed round him. He fell to the ground and heard a voice saying to him, 'Saul, Saul! Why do you persecute me?' 'Who are you, Lord?' he asked. 'I am Jesus, whom you persecute,' the voice said. 'But get up and go into the city, where you will be told what you must do.'*

A disciple, Ananias, was warned in a dream about Paul's conversion.
He restored his sight and baptised him.

The blind Paul recovering his sight symbolises the passage from non-belief to belief. This was already the meaning behind certain cures of blind people in the gospels.

The men who were travelling with Saul . . . heard the voice but could not see anyone. Saul got up from the ground and opened his eyes, but could not see a thing. So they . . . led him into Damascus. For three days he was not able to see, and . . . did not eat or drink anything. **Acts 9.3-9**

The Lord appeared in a dream to the disciple Ananias, who replied: *'Lord, many people have told me about this man and about all the terrible things he has done to your people in Jerusalem. And he has come to Damascus with authority from the chief priests to arrest all who worship you.'*

Paul on the road to Damascus

The Lord then revealed Paul's mission to Ananias.

So Ananias went . . . and placed his hands on him. 'Brother Saul,' he said, 'the Lord has sent me – Jesus . . . who appeared to you . . . as you were coming here. He sent me so that you might see again and be filled with the Holy Spirit.' At once something like fish scales fell from Saul's eyes. **Acts 9.17-18**

Having spent three years in the Arabian desert (**Gal 1.17-18**), Saul began to proclaim that Jesus was the Messiah. The Jews were hostile and wanted to kill him. He narrowly escaped and fled to Jerusalem. The Christians were suspicious of him because of his past. Barnabas, a Hellenist, got him accepted.

The circumstances of Paul's conversion recall the manifestations of God in the Old Testament: intense light, witnesses blinded and thrown to the ground. These images attempt to describe God's meeting with a human being.

Having spent several days in Damascus, Paul *went to the synagogues and began to preach that Jesus was the Son of God.*
Acts 9.20

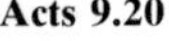

Peter among the pagans

Peter's vision according to a 16th c. miniature, *Les Heures d'Henri II*: God was asking him to eat animals regarded as unclean. When Peter refused a voice from heaven said: *Do not consider anything unclean that God has declared clean.*
Acts 11.9

Peter moved about a lot. In Lydda he healed a paralysed man, in Joppa he restored Tabitha to life (**Acts 9.32-43**).

One day he had a strange vision:

He saw heaven opened and something coming down that looked like a large sheet being lowered by its four corners to the earth. In it were all kinds of animals, reptiles, and wild birds.
Acts 10.9-10

God told him he would be visited by two men, whom he would have to follow. The two men were messengers from a Roman centurion, Cornelius, who urged him to come and talk to him about the Gospel. Peter went to Cornelius' house. As a stranger and a representative of the occupying power, Cornelius would have been doubly unclean for the Jews.

God has given to the Gentiles also the opportunity to repent and live!
Acts 11.18

While Peter was still speaking, the Holy Spirit came down on all those who were listening to his message. The Jewish believers . . . were amazed that God had poured out his gift of the Holy Spirit on the Gentiles also. . . . Peter spoke up: 'These people have received the Holy Spirit, just as we also did. Can anyone, then, stop them from being baptised with water?' So he ordered them to be baptised in the name of Jesus Christ. **Acts 10.44-48**

Back in Jerusalem, Peter answered criticisms by Jewish Christians:

God gave those Gentiles the same gift that he gave us when we believed in the Lord Jesus Christ; who was I, then, to try to stop God!'

When they heard this, they stopped their criticism and praised God.
Acts 11.16-18

Christians of strict Jewish origin (whom Luke calls Hebrews and amongst whom were Jesus' family) believed it was wrong to associate with the uncircumcised, and that a pagan could not become Christian without being circumcised.
For the Hellenists this was unnecessary. Peter, who disregarded this taboo, caused a scandal.

Peter baptising the Roman centurion Cornelius (after a 15th c. tapestry).

Foundation of the Church at Antioch

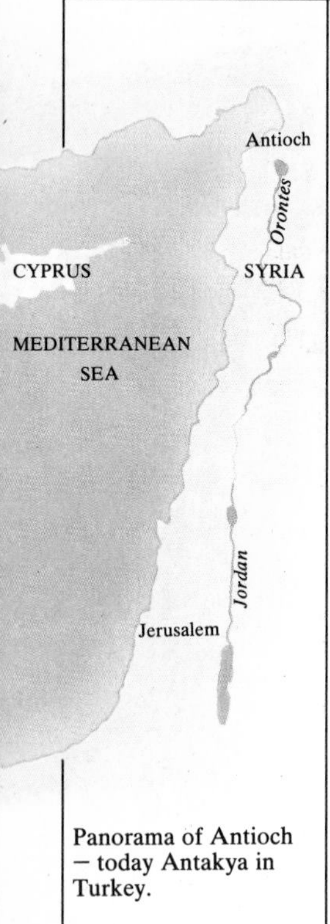

Panorama of Antioch – today Antakya in Turkey.

Persecutions around the time of Stephen's death drove some of the Christians from Jerusalem. Some went to Phoenicia, Cyprus or Antioch, where they preached the Gospel to the Jews.

Other believers, men from Cyprus and Cyrene, went to Antioch and proclaimed the message to Gentiles also, telling them the Good News about the Lord Jesus. The Lord's power was with them, and a great number of people believed and turned to the Lord.

The news about this reached the church in Jerusalem, so they sent Barnabas to Antioch. When he arrived and saw how God had blessed the people, he was glad and urged them all to be faithful and true to the Lord. . . . Barnabas was a good man, full of the Holy Spirit and faith, and many people were brought to the Lord.

Acts 11.20-24

Paul and Barnabas

It was Barnabas who, when they got to Jerusalem, introduced Paul (Saul) to the somewhat distrustful disciples.

Saul went to Jerusalem and tried to join the disciples. But they would not believe that he was a disciple. . . . Then Barnabas . . . explained to them how Saul had seen the Lord on the road and that the Lord had spoken to him. He also told them how boldly Saul had preached in the name of Jesus in Damascus. And so Saul stayed with them and went all over Jerusalem. **Acts 9.26-28**

In the church at Antioch there were some prophets and teachers.
Acts 13.1

It was also Barnabas who brought Paul to Antioch.

Then Barnabas went to Tarsus to look for Saul. When he found him, he took him to Antioch, and for a whole year the two met with the people of the church and taught a large group. It was at Antioch that the believers were first called Christians. **Acts 11.25-26**

Warning of a famine

About that time some prophets went from Jerusalem to Antioch. One of them, named Agabus, stood up and by the power of the Spirit predicted that a severe famine was about to come over all the earth. . . . The disciples decided that each of them would send as much as he could to help their fellow believers . . . in Judaea. They did this . . . and sent the money to the church elders.
Acts 11.27-30

Antioch – with Rome and Alexandria one of the three capitals of the Empire – became the centre from which Christianity spread to the East.

Prophets: the name given to those who, in the early churches, helped Christians discern which actions were faithful to the Spirit of Christ.

Elders: At first, together with the Twelve, they led the church in Jerusalem. This arrangement spread later to other churches.

Church: the English word for the Greek *ekklesia* (assembly). It appears here for the first time in the Acts, as does the word Christian.

The famine under the Emperor Claudius lasted from 46 to 48.

James is martyred

James the Greater, apostle, son of Zebedee and brother of John, was honoured during the Middle Ages by an important pilgrimage to Compostela in Spain. He should not be confused with James the Less, son of Alphaeus and one of the Twelve, who is often identified with James, the brother of Jesus and leader of the community in Jerusalem.

Round about 43 or 44, Herod decided to get rid of certain members of the Christian Church.

He had James, the brother of John, put to death by the sword. When he saw that this pleased the Jews, he went on to arrest Peter. **Acts 12.2-3**

Peter would be executed, Herod decided, after the feast of the Passover. He was therefore kept in prison.

The night before Herod was going to bring him out to the people, Peter was sleeping between two guards. He was tied with two chains, and there were guards on duty at the prison gate. Suddenly an angel of the Lord stood there, and a light shone in the cell. The angel shook Peter by the shoulder, woke him up, and said, 'Hurry! Get up!' At once the chains fell off Peter's hands. . . . They passed by the first guard post and then the second, and came at last to the iron gate leading into the city. The gate opened for them by

The martyrdom of James, after an 11th c. Greek manuscript.

Peter's escape

itself, and they went out. They walked down a street, and suddenly the angel left Peter. **Acts 12.6-7, 10**

His companions' surprise

. . . He went to the home of Mary, the mother of John Mark, where many people had gathered and were praying. Peter knocked at the outside door, and a servant-girl named Rhoda came to answer it. She recognised Peter's voice and was so happy that she ran back in without opening the door, and announced that Peter was standing outside. 'You are mad!' they told her. But she insisted that it was true. So they answered, 'It is his angel.' Meanwhile Peter kept on knocking. At last they opened the door, and when they saw him, they were amazed. He motioned with his hand for them to be quiet, and he explained to them how the Lord had brought him out of prison. . . .

When morning came, there was a tremendous confusion among the guards – what had happened to Peter? Herod gave orders to search for him, but they could not find him. So he had the guards . . . put to death. **Acts 12.12-19**

The King Herod mentioned here is Herod Agrippa I. He succeeded Herod Antipas, who put John the Baptist to death and was one of the judges who judged Jesus (who called him 'that fox'). Herod Antipas was himself the son of Herod the Great, who massacred the innocents (p. 370).

Peter's astonishment, but also his trust, is expressed in this 15th c. Florentine fresco.

Paul's first journey

When Paul worked a miracle the crowd took him for one of their gods. *They gave Barnabas the name Zeus and Paul the name Hermes because he was the chief speaker.* **Acts 14.12**

In the church at Antioch there were some prophets and teachers. . . . The Holy Spirit said to them, 'Set apart for me Barnabas and Saul, to do the work to which I have called them.' They fasted and prayed, placed their hands on them, and sent them off. **Acts 13.1-3**

In Cyprus, the island's proconsul was converted. In Antioch in Pisidia, Paul and Barnabas were well received, but then were driven out by hostile Jews. (**Acts 13.4-52; 14.1-7**).

In Lystra there was a man who had been lame from birth. . . . Paul saw that he believed . . . and said, . . . 'Stand up straight on your feet!' The man jumped up. . . . When the crowds saw what Paul had done, they started shouting. . . . 'The gods . . . have come down to us!' . . . The priest of the god Zeus . . . wanted to offer sacrifice to the apostles.

When Barnabas and Paul heard what they were about to do, they . . . ran into the middle of the crowd, shouting, 'Why are you doing this? We ourselves are only human beings like you! We are

Bas-relief discovered in the ruins of the Roman theatre at Philippi (Macedonia): a bull is decorated with garlands, ready for immolation.

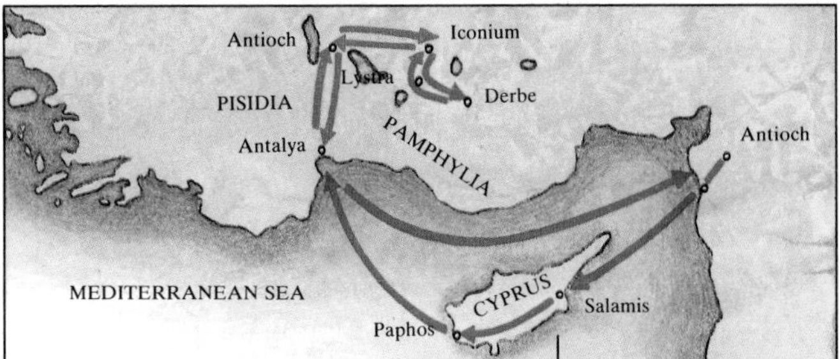

Antioch
Iconium
Lystra
Derbe
PISIDIA
PAMPHYLIA
Antalya
Antioch
MEDITERRANEAN SEA
CYPRUS
Salamis
Paphos
Jerusalem

here to announce the Good News, to turn you . . . to the living God. . . .'

Some Jews came from Antioch in Pisidia and from Iconium; they won the crowd over to their side, stoned Paul and dragged him out of the town, thinking that he was dead. But when the believers gathered round him, he got up and went back into the town. The next day he and Barnabas went to Derbe.

Acts 14.8 . . . 20

4th c. bronze lamp. The ship represents the Church; Paul, at the prow, scans the horizon, while Peter controls the rudder.

Paul and Barnabas returned to Lystra, Iconium and Antioch. Then they travelled round Pisidia and on to Pamphylia, passed through Perge, went down to Antalya and set sail for Antioch. Their journey lasted from 45 to 49.

Once he began to speak more particularly to the pagans, Saul adopted for good the name that was his as a Roman citizen: Paul.

The council of Jerusalem

Paul and Peter (who, before Jesus called him was known as Simon or Simeon) played a major role in relations between Jewish and non-Jewish converts.

Right: Peter and Paul on a 4th c. bas-relief.

14th c. Spanish representation of Paul.

The Christians who came from Judaea said that Christians had to be circumcised, else they would not be saved. Paul and Barnabas strongly objected to this and suggested that it be put to the apostles and elders in Jerusalem.

The apostles and the elders met together to consider this question. After a long debate Peter stood up and said, 'My brothers, you know that a long time ago God chose me from among you to preach the Good News to the Gentiles, so that they could hear and believe. And God, who knows the thoughts of everyone, showed his approval of the Gentiles by giving the Holy Spirit to them, just as he had to us. He made no difference between us and them; he forgave their sins because they believed. So then, why do you now want to put God to the test by laying a load on the backs of the believers which neither our ancestors nor we ourselves were able to carry? No! We believe and are saved by

I will return, says the Lord,
and restore the kingdom of David.
I will rebuild its ruins
and make it strong again. **Acts 15.16**

the grace of the Lord Jesus, just as they are.'

James spoke in his turn.

It is my opinion . . . that we should not trouble the Gentiles who are turning to God. Instead, we should write a letter telling them not to eat any food that is ritually unclean . . . to keep themselves from sexual immorality; and not to eat any animal that has been strangled, or any blood. . . .

Then the apostles and the elders, together with the whole church, decided to choose some men from the group and

send them to Antioch with Paul and Barnabas. They chose . . . Judas, called Barsabbas, and Silas.

Acts 15.1 . . . 29

Four rules were adopted: not to eat meat that had been sacrificed to idols; to abstain from unions that were wrong in the eyes of the Law (prostitution, **Lv 18.6-18**); not to eat the meat of animals that had been strangled (**Lv 17.10-14**), or blood, which is life (**Gn 9.4**).

After the council of Jerusalem (48-49), circumcised and uncircumcised Christians could meet together, thanks to prohibitions accepted by both. (The operation is shown here in a medieval Jewish manuscript.)

James (14th c. Gothic statue)

Paul's second journey

The python was the snake that watched over the prophetess in the famous Greek sanctuary at Delphi. The pythian spirit was a spirit of divination (foretelling the future).

From 50 to 52, Paul travelled with Silas. At Philippi they were imprisoned.

One day as we were going to the place of prayer, we were met by a slave-girl who had an evil spirit that enabled her to predict the future. She earned a lot of money for her owners by telling fortunes. She followed Paul and us, shouting, 'These men are servants of the Most High God! They announce to you how you can be saved!' She did this for many days, until Paul became so upset that he turned round and said to the

Paul and Silas were given a beating: *The crowd joined in the attack. Then the officials tore the clothes off Paul and Silas and ordered them to be whipped. After a severe beating they were thrown in gaol.* **Acts 16.22-23**

spirit, 'In the name of Jesus Christ I order you to come out of her!' The spirit went out of her that very moment.

When her owners realised that their chance of making money was gone, they . . . brought them before the Roman officials and said, 'These men are Jews, and they are causing trouble in our city. They are teaching customs that are against our law. . . .'

Acts 16.16-21

The author uses the first person plural. He is one of Paul's companions.

Paul and Silas were imprisoned. Suddenly the doors opened and their chains fell off, but they did not make their escape. The astonished gaoler was converted. Alarmed to find that these men were Romans, the authorities asked them to leave the city.

Magistrates administered justice: lictors walked before them carrying a bundle of sticks and an axe – signs of judicial power.

Paul in Athens

Paul tried to talk to the Athenian philosophers in terms they would find familiar. But the misunderstanding remained total, since Jesus and the resurrection merely made them think again of idols.

The Areopagus, on the west of the Acropolis, was a public square as well as the meeting place of the wise men of Athens.

In Athens, Paul was upset by the sight of the idols and discussed them with passers-by in the main square. Philosophers, mocking or curious, asked him to explain his teaching. So Paul spoke in the Areopagus:

'I see that in every way you Athenians are very religious. For as I walked through your city and looked at the places where you worship, I found an altar on which is written, "To an Unknown God". That which you worship, then, even though you do not know it, is what I now proclaim to you. God, who made the world and everything in it, is Lord of heaven and earth. . . .

"In him we live and move and exist." It is as some of your poets have said, "We too are his children."'

Acts 17.22-24.28

Paul explained that since human beings belong to the family of God, the divine being does not resemble an idol. Then he announced that the reign of God was near at hand and that Jesus had risen from the dead.

When they heard Paul speak about a raising from death, some . . . made fun of him, but others said, 'We want to hear you speak about this again.'

Acts 17.32

Paul in Corinth

Paul left Athens for Corinth. There he stayed with Aquila and Priscilla, Jews recently driven out of Italy. They were tent makers and Paul worked with them. Every Sabbath, in the synagogue, he spoke to the Jews.

When they opposed him . . . he protested by shaking the dust from his clothes and saying, . . . 'If you are lost, you yourselves must take the blame for it! . . . From now on I will go to the Gentiles.' . . . Crispus, who was the leader of the synagogue, believed in the Lord, together with all his family; and many other people in Corinth heard the message, believed, and were baptised.

One night Paul had a vision in which the Lord said to him, 'Do not be afraid, but keep on speaking and do not give up, for I am with you. No one will be able to harm you, for many in this city are my people.' **Acts 18.6, 8-10**

Paul did nevertheless have to face further outbursts of hostility from the Jews in Corinth. At the end of his stay, which lasted about two years, he set sail for Syria.

Poseidon

Corinth, on the isthmus of the Peloponnese, was a great political and maritime power; it regularly organised games in honour of Poseidon, god of the sea. It was also famous for its great temple of Apollo.

Aquila and Priscilla must have left Italy when the Emperor Claudius published a decree expelling the Jews from Rome.

Paul's letters to the Thessalonians

Thessalonica was the capital of the Roman province of Macedonia. In 168 B.C. it was conquered by the Romans, becoming a free city in 42 B.C. It was administered by a council elected by the people.

In Paul's time it was an expanding centre for trade, thanks to its intense

Among the many religions practised was the cult of Dionysus, the god of wine and of the rebirth of nature, who offered his devotees moments of ecstasy.

activity as a port.

Its population was cosmopolitan: native Macedonians, Greeks, Romans, and a significant Jewish community with its own synagogue.

In Thessalonica Paul became a tent-maker, *working day and night so as not to be an expense to any of you.* **2 Thes 3.8**

Paul preached the gospel at Thessalonica during his second missionary journey. He got a better reception from the pagans than from the Jews, who drove him out and started to persecute the new Christians.

Some months after he left the city, in 51, Paul wrote to the young church, encouraging it to persevere in the Christian faith.

May our God and Father himself and our Lord Jesus prepare the way for us to come to you! May the Lord make your

love for one another and for all people grow more and more and become as great as our love for you. **1 Thes 3.11**

. . . You, brothers, must not get tired of doing good. It may be that someone . . . will not obey the message we send you. . . . If so, take note of him and have nothing to do with him, so that he will be ashamed. But do not treat him as an enemy; instead, warn him as a brother. **2 Thes 3.13-15**

When he comes on that day to receive glory from all his people. **2 Thes 1.10**

The Last Judgement (after a miniature from the 13th c. Hildesheim Psalter)
. . . when the Lord Jesus appears from heaven with his mighty angels.
2 Thes 1.7

Paul's third journey

Paul spent two years and three months in Ephesus (from 54 to 57). Very soon problems arose.

A silversmith named Demetrius who had a profitable business making models of the temple of the goddess Artemis, called together his workers and similar workers to warn them that Paul's message was threatening their prosperity. Paul had spoken out against man-made idols and Demetrius feared that their business would get a bad name and that Artemis might be forgotten.

As the crowd heard these words, they became furious and started shouting, 'Great is Artemis of Ephesus!' The uproar spread throughout the whole city. The mob seized Gaius and Aristarchus, two Macedonians who were travelling with Paul. . . .

At last the town clerk was able to calm the crowd. 'Fellow-Ephesians!' he said,

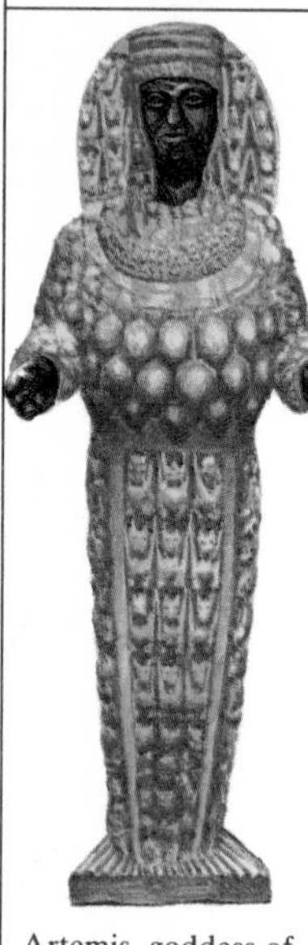

Artemis, goddess of fruitfulness and fertility (symbolised by her many breasts) drew large crowds on pilgrimage. Her temple, with its 127 columns, was one of the wonders of the ancient world.

Temple of Artemis at Ephesus

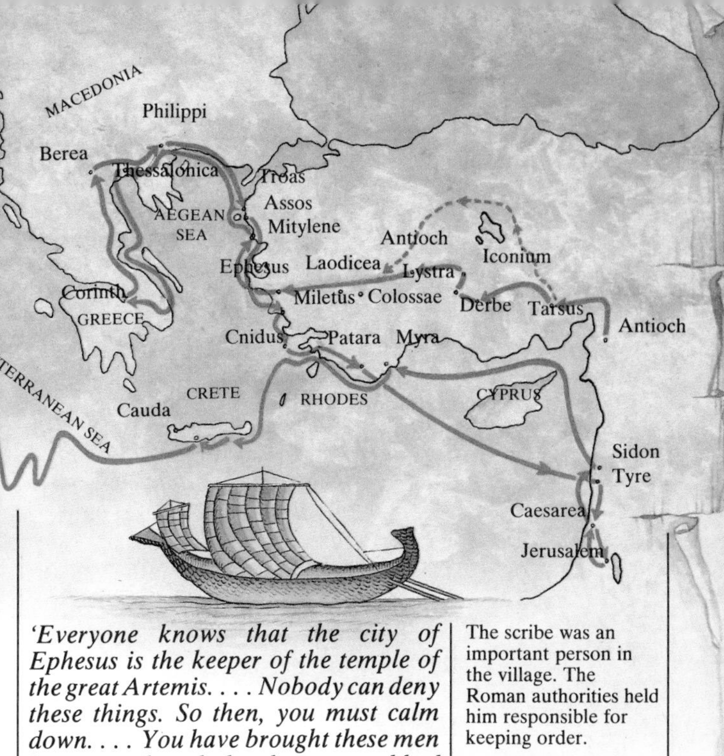

'Everyone knows that the city of Ephesus is the keeper of the temple of the great Artemis. . . . Nobody can deny these things. So then, you must calm down. . . . You have brought these men here even though they have not robbed temples or said evil things about our goddess. If Demetrius and his workers have an accusation against anyone, we have the authorities and the regular days for court; charges can be made there. But if there is something more that you want, it will have to be settled in a legal meeting of citizens. . . .'

Acts 19.23 . . . 39

During his stay in Ephesus, Paul wrote two letters to the Corinthians, his letter to the Galatians, and, probably, the one to the Christians at Philippi.

The scribe was an important person in the village. The Roman authorities held him responsible for keeping order.

Paul's letters to the Corinthians

A praying figure of the kind often represented by the early Christians (2nd c. bas-relief)

The church in Corinth and its problems

Paul founded it between 50 and 52. Apollos and perhaps Peter followed him there, and this led to cliques.

Against cliques

I appeal to all of you. . . . Be completely united, with only one purpose. . . . Each one of you says something different. One says, 'I follow Paul'; another, 'I follow Apollos'; another, 'I follow Peter'; and another, 'I follow Christ.' Christ has been divided into groups! Was it Paul who died on the cross for you? Were you baptised as Paul's disciples?

1 Cor 1.10, 12-13

. . . Who is Apollos? And who is Paul? We are simply God's servants, by whom you were led to believe. . . . I sowed the seed, Apollos watered the plant, but it was God who made the plant grow.

1 Cor 3.5-6

The young community was made up of Jews and many Latins, Greeks and Orientals, rich and many poor, slaves and freed men. This diversity led to

Greek bas-relief showing a sacrifice: disputes about eating this meat caused sharp divisions among the Christians.

If anyone eats the Lord's bread or drinks from his cup in a way that dishonours him, he is guilty of sin against the Lord's body and blood.
1 Cor 11.27

conflict and there was a tendency to forget the less fortunate.

Against factions

. . . *All of us, whether Jews or Gentiles, whether slaves or free, have been baptised into the one body by the same Spirit, and we have all been given the one Spirit to drink.* **1 Cor 12.13**

The Christians of pagan origin found it very hard to give up their old customs.

They had difficulty in accepting resurrection from the dead. As for the Christians of Jewish origin, they were shocked to see their Christian brothers happily eating meat that had been sacrificed to idols.

Against forgetting their fellowship

. . . *I do not praise you, because your meetings for worship actually do more harm than good. . . . When you meet together . . . it is not the Lord's Supper that you eat. For as you eat, each one goes ahead with his own meal, so that some are hungry while others get drunk.*
1 Cor 11.17, 20-21

The Christians of Corinth asked Paul to resolve their hesitations about meals taken in common or the clothes worn by women during prayer.

Her long hair has been given to her to serve as a covering.
1 Cor 11.15

Paul's letter to the Galatians

Galatia, in Asia Minor, gets its name from the Gauls, who came and settled in the region towards the 4th c. B.C.

Paul introduced the Galatians to the gospel during his second and third missionary journeys (**Acts 16.6** and **18.23**). But Christian teachers of Jewish origin caused trouble in the new communities by exhorting them to observe the Law.

'You cannot be saved unless you are circumcised as the Law of Moses requires.' **Acts 15.1**

The Galatians, impressed by this, rallied round the newcomers and abandoned the teaching of Paul, who had taught that it is not the Law that saves but faith in Jesus. So Paul wrote to them:

I am surprised at you! In no time at all you are deserting the one who called you by the grace of Christ, and are accepting another gospel. Actually, there is no 'other gospel,' but . . . there are some

The Old and New Covenants of God with mankind. Left: Moses receives from God instructions for building the Ark, symbol of the Covenant, and its furnishings – in particular the seven-branched candelabrum. Right: the rites of the New Covenant, presided over by Christ (after a 14th c. miniature).

Christ has set us free!
Stand, then, as free people,
and do not allow yourselves
to become slaves again. **Gal 5.1**

people who are upsetting you and trying to change the gospel of Christ.

Gal 1.6-7

I, Paul, tell you that if you allow yourselves to be circumcised, it means that Christ is of no use to you at all. . . . For when we are in union with Christ Jesus, neither circumcision nor the lack of it makes any difference at all. . . . For the whole Law is summed up in one commandment: 'Love your neighbour as you love yourself.' But if you act like wild animals . . . watch out, or you will completely destroy one another.

Gal 5.2 . . . 15

The dying Galatian: a marble statue representing one of the warriors of Gallic origin who settled in Asia Minor. He wears a *torquis*, the metal collar characteristic of the Gauls.

Paul's letter to the Philippians

It was from Rome, during his captivity (61-63), that Paul wrote this letter to the young Christian community at Philippi in Macedonia. Paul had stayed there in 50. But he was beaten-up by the authorities and had

I run straight towards the goal in order to win the prize, which is God's call through Christ Jesus to the life above. **Phil 3.14**

(after a 2nd c. Roman fresco)

had to leave the town. However, the Christian community there remained faithful to him. So his letter to the Philippians was one of gratitude.

I thank my God for you every time I think of you; and every time I pray for you all, I pray with joy . . . **Phil 1.3-4**

He urged them to persevere in their faith:

Your way of life should be as the gospel of Christ requires, so that, whether or not I am able to go and see you, I will hear that you are standing firm . . . fighting together for the faith of the gospel. Don't be afraid of your

For what is life? To me it is Christ.
Death, then, will bring more.
Phil 1.21

enemies; always be courageous, and this will prove to them that . . . you will win, because it is God who gives you the victory. For you have been given the privilege of serving Christ, not only by believing in him, but also by suffering for him. Now you can take part with me in the battle. It is the same battle you saw me fighting in the past, and . . . the one I am fighting still.
Phil 1.27-30

Then he encouraged them to rejoice continuously, the truth being that joy is the mark of our union with God:

May you always be joyful in your union with the Lord. I say it again: rejoice! . . . in all your prayers ask God for what you need, always asking him with a thankful heart. And God's peace, which is far beyond human understanding, will keep your hearts and minds safe in union with Christ Jesus. **Phil 4.4, 6-7**

Finally, concerned about the fate of his friends, Paul told them that a companion, Timothy, was on his way.

The closing words of this letter show that the faith had penetrated even into the Emperor's household: *All God's people here send greetings, especially those who belong to the Emperor's palace.* **Phil 4.22**

Paul and one of his companions (from a 12th c. fresco). The companion may be Timothy, who was possibly bishop of Ephesus.

Paul's letter to the Romans

In the spring of 58, Paul wrote to the Romans to prepare for his coming: his mission in Macedonia, Asia Minor and Achaia seemed to be over.

I am eager to preach the Good News to you also who live in Rome. I have complete confidence in the gospel; it is God's power to save all who believe.
Rom 1.15-16

Paul wringing the neck of an evil bird (initial letter in an 11th c. illuminated Bible).

To introduce himself, he set out his thinking on the great questions the churches were debating, especially the relationship between the Law and faith.

God has shown us how much he loves us – it was while we were still sinners that Christ died for us.
Rom 5.8

I am certain that nothing can separate us from his love: neither death nor life, neither angels nor other heavenly rulers or powers, neither the present nor the future, neither the world above nor the world below – there is nothing in all creation that will ever be able to separate us from the love of God which is ours through Christ Jesus our Lord. **Rom 8.38-39**

The church in Rome was probably founded in the 40's. Its members came from the large Jewish community (20,000 to 50,000 members) and from former pagans.

In 49, an edict issued by Claudius expelled all Jews from Rome. On their

return, once the edict had been repealed, Christians of Jewish origin were badly received by their fellow Christians of pagan birth, who looked down on them.

Paul insisted on the reasons and the need for a spirit of fellowship.

We have many parts in the one body, and all these parts have different functions. In the same way, though we are many, we are one body in union with Christ. . . . So we are to use our different gifts in accordance with the grace that God has given us. . . . Love one another warmly as Christian brothers, and be eager to show respect for one another. Work hard and do not be lazy. Serve the Lord with a heart full of devotion. Let your hope keep you joyful, be patient in your troubles, and pray at all times. . . .

Ask God to bless those who persecute you — yes, ask him to bless, not to curse. Be happy with those who are happy, weep with those who weep. Have the same concern for everyone. Do not be proud, but accept humble duties. . . .

Rom 12.4 . . . 16

Many of the Roman Christians were of Jewish origin, and very attached to the Law.

Above: the scales of justice and the tree of life, symbolising the Torah, guarded by two lions.

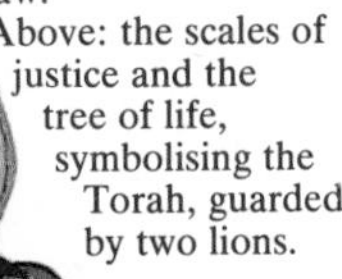

Paul drew comparisons between the sacrifice of Abraham and that of Christ.

Paul and solidarity between the churches

Suppose there are brothers or sisters who need clothes and don't have enough to eat. What good is there in your saying to them, 'God bless you! Keep warm and eat well!'? . . . Show me how anyone can have faith without actions.
I will show you my faith by my actions.
Jms 2.15-18

Paul returned to Jerusalem with funds for the church there. During the council of Jerusalem, in 48 or 49, he had promised to help local Christians. In the course of his second missionary journey, he went to the churches of Macedonia (Philippi) and Achaia (Corinth) and encouraged them to show solidarity with their poorer fellow-Christians in Jerusalem.

The church in Philippi was generous. Paul sang its praises to the Corinthians.

They have been severely tested by the troubles they went through; but their joy was so great that they were extremely generous in their giving, even though they are very poor. **2 Cor 8.2**

Corinth was less forthcoming, so Paul sent Titus to encourage them.

Remember that . . . one who sows many seeds will have a large crop. Each one should give, then, as he has decided, not with regret or out of a sense of duty; for God loves the one who gives gladly. **2 Cor 9.6-7**

To put the charity on a proper footing, Paul appointed collectors.

We are taking care not to stir up any complaints about the way we handle

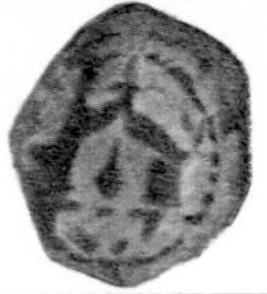

this generous gift. Our purpose is to do what is right, not only in the sight of the Lord, but also in the sight of man.

2 Cor 8.20-21

Nine years later the money was in, and Paul took it to Jerusalem.

Macedonia and Achaia have freely decided to give an offering to help the poor among God's people in Jerusalem. That decision was their own; but, as a

matter of fact, they have an obligation to help them. Since the Jews shared their spiritual blessings with the Gentiles, the Gentiles ought to use their material blessings to help the Jews. . . .

Rom 15.26-27

And so, what Luke found in the first community in Jerusalem spread throughout the young Christian Church: *All the believers continued together in close fellowship and shared their belongings with one another.*

Acts 2.44

Since you have plenty at this time, it is only fair that you should help those who are in need. Then when you are in need and they have plenty, they will help you. In this way both are treated equally. As the Scripture says, 'The one who gathered much did not have too much, and the one who gathered

little did not have too little.' **2 Cor 8.14**

Paul is arrested and tried

Paul (from a 6th c. mosaic). His father passed on to him his title to Roman citizenship: this status was a protection against punishments like scourging. So the procurator Felix had to abandon the idea of having Paul scourged once he learned from him that he was a Roman citizen.

After an absence of nine years, Paul returned to Jerusalem for Pentecost. James and the elders warned him that the Jews were seeking his life.

They have been told that you have been teaching all the Jews who live in Gentile countries to abandon the Law of Moses, telling them not to circumcise their children or follow the Jewish customs. **Acts 21.21**

The anger of the crowd

All the same, Paul did not hesitate to go to the temple during the feast.

Some Jews from the province of Asia saw Paul in the temple. They stirred up the whole crowd and seized Paul. . . .

Confusion spread through the whole city. . . . **Acts 21, 27, 30**

Paul's arrest (after a bas-relief in St Peter's, Rome)

The mob was trying to kill Paul, when a report was sent up to the commander of the Roman troops that all Jerusalem was rioting.
Acts 21.31

Alerted to this disturbance, the tribune Lysias had Paul transferred to Caesarea, to the procurator Felix. Felix brought him face to face with his Jewish accusers; to their dismay, Paul replied by describing his conversion and explaining his gospel mission. The furious crowd demanded his death. Felix decided to keep him in prison.

The Roman procurator wanted to hand Paul over to Roman jurisdiction, but to learn first from the confrontation between Paul and his accusers (after a 12th c. enamel).

Paul was to stay in prison for two years before he appeared before King Herod Agrippa I, Princess Bernice and the governor Festus. He pleaded his cause so eloquently that his judges were inclined to release him.

Then the king, the governor, Bernice, and all the others got up, and after leaving they said to each other, 'This man has not done anything for which he should die or be put in prison.' And Agrippa said to Festus, 'This man could have been released if he had not appealed to the Emperor.'
Acts 26.30-32

Paul went to Rome to stand trial.

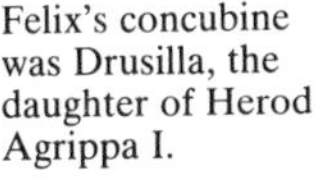

Felix's concubine was Drusilla, the daughter of Herod Agrippa I.

Shipwreck off Malta

Statuette from the island of Malta, evidence of a very ancient civilisation (8000-3000 B.C.)

As a prisoner, and guarded by a centurion, Paul was taken by ship to Italy. To avoid storms, they sailed as close as possible to the coasts. Shortly after they passed Crete however, a hurricane blew up in the area. It was a storm of unprecedented violence.

For many days we could not see the sun or the stars, and the wind kept on blowing very hard. We finally gave up all hope of being saved. **Acts 27.20**

Then Paul intervened:

But now I beg you, take heart! Not one of you will lose his life; only the ship will be lost. For last night an angel of the God to whom I belong and whom I

Paul encouraging his companions during the storm (bas-relief on a tomb, 3rd c.)

worship came to me and said, 'Don't be afraid, Paul! . . . God in his goodness to you has spared the lives of all those who are sailing with you.'

Acts 27.22 . . . 26

Finally, on the fourth day, they saw land. The approach was difficult and the boat seemed about to break up. To stop the prisoners escaping by

swimming away, the soldiers made a plan to kill them.

But the army officer wanted to save Paul, so he stopped them from doing this. **Acts 27.43**

A warm welcome

At last, safe and sound, they all reached land.

When we were safely ashore, we learnt that the island was called Malta. The natives there were very friendly to us. . . .

Not far from that place were some fields that belonged to Publius, the chief official of the island. He welcomed us kindly and for three days we were his guests. Publius' father was in bed, sick with fever and dysentry. Paul went into his room, prayed, placed his hands on him, and healed him. When this happened, all the other sick people on the island came and were healed. They gave us many gifts, and when we sailed, they put on board what we needed for the voyage. **Acts 28.1-2, 7-10**

The castaways spent three months on the island, then took to the sea again, disembarking at Puteoli in Italy. Paul was then taken by stages to Rome, where he lived under house arrest.

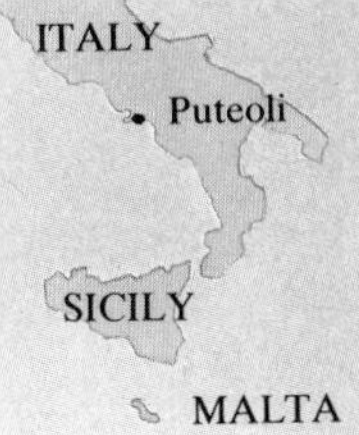

Paul suffered many tribulations during his journeys: blows, stoning, shipwreck, attacks by robbers. **(2 Cor 11.24-28)**

Paul's first imprisonment in Rome

This ancient ivory depicts a serene picture of imperial authority.

Three days after his arrival in Rome, Paul called the Jewish leaders together and said to them:

'My fellow Israelites, even though I did nothing against our people or the customs that we received from our ancestors, I was made a prisoner in Jerusalem and handed over . . . the Romans wanted to release me, because they found that I had done nothing for which I deserved to die. But when the Jews opposed this, I was forced to appeal to the Emperor, even though I had no accusation to make against my own people. That is why I asked to see you and talk with you.' **Acts 28.17-20**

Closed hearts

A little later, at Paul's request, the Jews went in large numbers to his house to listen to him. Paul spoke to them at length about Christ, beginning with the Law of Moses and the prophets.

Some of them were convinced by his words, but others would not believe. So they left . . . after Paul had said this one thing: 'How well the Holy Spirit spoke through the prophet Isaiah to your ancestors! For he said, "Go and say to this people: You will listen and listen, but not understand; . . . because this people's minds are dull, and they have stopped up their ears and closed their eyes. Otherwise, their eyes would see, their ears would hear, their minds would understand, and they would turn to me, says God, and I would heal them."'

Paul concluded: '. . . Know, then, that God's message of salvation has been sent to the Gentiles. They will listen!' **Acts 28.24-28**

It may seem surprising that a prisoner could issue invitations and organise meetings at his house. In fact, Paul's captivity put him not in prison, but under house arrest. The 'captive' had a

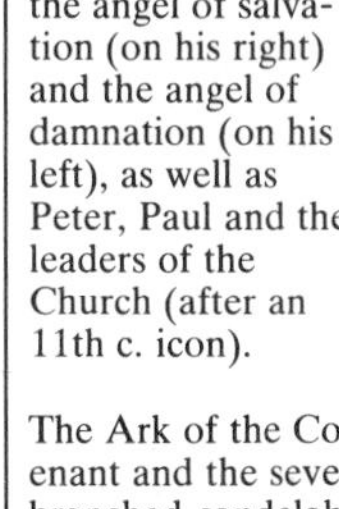

house where he could receive the many people who came to see him.

From morning till night he explained . . . his message about the Kingdom of God. **Acts 28.23**

But Paul lived and moved under the constantly watchful eyes of the soldiers attached to him. In this way, he managed to teach in Rome for two years before he was set free.

For two years Paul lived in a place he rented . . . he welcomed all who came to see him. He preached about the Kingdom of God and taught about the Lord Jesus Christ, speaking with all boldness and freedom. **Acts 28.30**

Christ's return at the end of time, with the angel of salvation (on his right) and the angel of damnation (on his left), as well as Peter, Paul and the leaders of the Church (after an 11th c. icon).

The Ark of the Covenant and the seven-branched candelabrum on a fragment of glass: evidence of Jewish life in Rome in the first centuries.

Roman centurion

To the Colossians and the Ephesians

Against violence, a reminder of the gospel message: *you must clothe yourselves with compassion, kindness, humility.* **Col 3.12**

Masters, be fair and just in the way you treat your slaves. Remember that you too have a Master in heaven. **Col 4.1**

The church at Colossae in Asia Minor seems to have been led astray by its preachers: the Gospel, they said, needed to be complemented by practices such as circumcision, by a special calendar, or by food rituals.

Paul, in captivity in Rome, was warned about this by his disciple Epaphras. It was to correct these deviations that he wrote to the Christians of Colossae: the Gospel, he reminded them, frees us from anything that binds us unnecessarily.

You have died with Christ and are set free from the ruling spirits of the universe. Why, then, do you live as though you belonged to this world? Why do you obey such rules as 'Don't handle this,' 'Don't taste that,' . . . all these refer to things which become useless once they are used; they are only man-made rules and teachings.
Col 2.20-22

The baptised are free; the only thing

Put on God's armour now! . . .
Accept salvation as a helmet,
and the word of God as the sword
which the Spirit gives you. **Eph 6.13,17**

Roman bas-relief

Husbands, love your wives just as Christ loved the Church and gave his life for it. . . . Men ought to love their wives just as they love their own bodies.
Eph 5.25-28

that binds them is mutual love.

Be tolerant with one another . . . and to all these qualities add love, which binds all things together in perfect unity.
Col 3.13-14

Shortly after writing this letter, Paul wrote, so it is believed, to the church at Ephesus. Like the letter to the Colossians, it draws attention to the virtues a Christian should possess.

I urge you, then — I who am a prisoner because I serve the Lord: live a life that measures up to the standard God set when he called you. Be always humble, gentle, and patient. . . . Do your best to preserve the unity which the Spirit gives by means of the peace that binds you together. There is one body and one Spirit, just as there is one hope to which God has called you. **Eph 4.1-4**

From the last lines of this letter to the Ephesians, we learn that Paul sent another friend, Tychicus, to them, *so that you may know how all of us are getting on, and to encourage you. . . .*

Mary, Christ's mother, may have lived in Ephesus, with John. It was on the site of John's tomb that this church was built in the 6th c.

Paul's letter to Philemon

Paul's shortest letter was written to Philemon, a member of the church at Colossae.

Philemon's slave, Onesimus, had run away to Rome. He joined Paul, who converted and baptised him. Paul grew very fond of him and made him one of his collaborators during his captivity.

But the situation was critical: runaway slaves and their accomplices were punished very severely under Roman law. Paul sent Onesimus back to his master, Philemon, but he asked the latter to receive his slave like a brother in Christ and as if he were Paul himself.

I am Paul, the ambassador of Christ Jesus, and at present also a prisoner for his sake. So I make a request to you on behalf of Onesimus, who is my own son in Christ. It may be that Onesimus was away from you for a short time so that you might have him back for all time. And now he is not just a slave, but . . . a dear brother in Christ. How much he means to me! And how much more he will mean to you, both as a slave and as a brother in the Lord! So, if you think of me as your partner, welcome him back just as you would welcome me. If he has done you any wrong or owes you anything, charge it to my account.

Phlm 9-10, 15-18

Timothy

Having become a Christian, Timothy, who came from Lystra, accompanied Paul on all his journeys. Appointed leader

A slave is set free

Paul and slavery
Paul did not question the institution, perhaps for fear that bloodshed would follow any revolt, perhaps because he believed inner slavery to be more serious. On the other hand, he kept repeating that in Christ differences no longer exist, and he would have wanted Christian masters to free their slaves.

Paul's last years

of the church at Ephesus, he received two letters from Paul reminding him of his duties.

Once he was set free, Paul seems to have paid one last visit to some of the churches he had founded. At Ephesus, he put Timothy in charge of the community. In Crete, he left the task of watching over the church to Titus.

He stopped at Troas in Macedonia, and wintered at Nicopolis in Dalmatia.

However, he was then denounced to the authorities by Alexander, a metalworker who had been expelled from the church. Paul was again transferred to Rome. His second period of captivity, in the Mamertine prison, was much harder than the first. *I suffer but I am still full of confidence, because I know whom I have trusted.* **2 Tim 1.12**

Paul was executed in 67, during the persecution of Nero.

As a Roman citizen, Paul had the right to be beheaded – a 'noble' punishment.

Peter's first letter

Peter wrote this letter in 64, shortly before the persecution of Nero, during which he died. He addressed it to the various Christian communities of Asia Minor (Pontus, Galatia, Cappadocia, Bithynia). His aim was to strengthen their faith, which had been tried by the ill will and persecutions of the pagans.

My dear friends, do not be surprised at the painful test you are suffering. . . . Rather be glad that you are sharing Christ's sufferings, so that you may be full of joy when his glory is revealed. Happy are you if you are insulted because you are Christ's followers.

1 Pet 4.12-14

Massacre of Christians (after Dürer). Persecution of Christians continued until 313, when the Edict of Constantine allowed freedom of worship.

According to tradition, Peter spent the last years of his life in Rome, where he was crucified.

Letter to the Hebrews

The identity of the author is unclear but he was certainly a companion of Paul. The letter was addressed to Jewish Christians. Once the enthusiasm of conversion was over, they were tired and tempted to lose heart. Their Jewish customs had been brushed aside and they were beginning to miss the past. The author mentions the ceremonies of the Old Covenant, for which he senses these Christians are feeling nostalgic, in order to compare and contrast them with Christ and the New Covenant.

When Christ went through the tent and entered once and for all into the Most Holy Place, he did not take the blood of goats and bulls to offer as a sacrifice; rather, he took his own blood and obtained eternal salvation for us. . . . For this reason Christ is the one who arranges a new covenant, so that those who have been called by God may receive the eternal blessings that God has promised. **Heb 9.12, 15**

A Hebrew marriage (after a 14th c. Jewish manuscript)

The mystic mill (on a capital at Vézelay in France): this allegory has Isaiah pouring in the Law, which Paul receives once it has been refined. A symbol of the continuity of the Old and New Testaments.

Letters of John,

These letters, traditionally from John the Evangelist, were written to a church in crisis, perhaps that at Ephesus, towards the end of the 1st c.

Preachers there were putting forward a doctrine that contradicted the Gospel. They claimed that one could be in communion with God without bothering to act justly and love one's

God is light
1 Jn 1.5

fellow human beings.

John reacted vigorously against those whom he called anti-christs, false prophets, liars. He reminded them that the sign of communion with the God of Jesus was that one based one's life on faith in Jesus, the Son of God, and obeyed the commandment of love.

The message you heard from the very beginning is this: we must love one

The letter of Jude who may have been a brother of Jesus and of James, was written about 70. It was addressed to Jewish circles: *Even though you know all this I want to remind you of how the Lord once rescued the people of Israel from Egypt, but afterwards destroyed those who did not believe.* **Jude 5**

Roman graffiti with the intentionally blasphemous representation of a crucified man with an ass's head (2nd c.)

James and Jude

another. We must not be like Cain; he . . . murdered his own brother Abel. Why did Cain murder him? Because the things he himself did were wrong, but the things his brother did were right.

So do not be surprised, my brothers, if the people of the world hate you. We know that we have left death and come over into life; we know it because we love our brothers. Whoever does not love is still under the power of death. Whoever hates his brother is a murderer, and . . . a murderer has not got eternal life in him. This is how we know what love is: Christ gave his life for us. We too, then, ought to give our lives for our brothers! If a rich person sees his brother in need, yet closes his heart against his brother, how can he claim that he loves God? My children, our love should not be just words and talk; it must be true love, which shows itself in action. **1 Jn 3.11-18**

If anyone declares that Jesus is the Son of God, he lives in union with God and God lives in union with him. . . . God is love, and whoever lives in love lives in union with God and God lives in union with him. **1 Jn 4.15-16**

We love because God first loved us. If someone says he loves God, but hates his brother, he is a liar. For he cannot love God, whom he has not seen, if he does not love his brother, whom he has seen. The command that Christ has given us is this: whoever loves God must love his brother also. **1 Jn 4.19-21**

The letter of James, written between 80 and 90 by a disciple of James (who may have been the Lord's brother), is addressed to Christians in a large commercial city of the Empire. It condemns inequalities between rich and poor. *My brothers . . . you must never treat people in different ways. . . . Suppose a rich man wearing a gold ring and fine clothes comes to your meeting, and a poor man in ragged clothes also comes. . . . God chose the poor people of this world.* **Jam 2.1-5**

The Apocalypse of John the Divine

The colours

black: idolatry, death

green: death, corruption

red: violence, murder

white: victory, colour of God

The numbers

7 totality, perfection
6 (7-1): imperfection
4 world
3.5 (half 7): imperfection, suffering, trial
12 people of Israel, Church
24 (12 × 2): unanimity
144 (12 × 12): perfection
1000 multitude

A text to sustain the hope of sorely tried believers

The word apocalypse comes from the Greek *apocalupsis.* It means ‘unveiling’, ‘revelation’. The aim of an apocalypse was to reveal to believers the hidden meaning of events by passing on to them visions and words received from God.

In the Old Testament, the best known apocalypse is the book of Daniel. Between the 2nd c. B.C. and the 2nd c. A.D., apocalypses were widespread in Jewish circles. When believers were going through difficult times, the authors of apocalypses assured them that a day would come, very soon, when God would re-establish justice and destroy the forces of evil.

Written in cryptic terms

This was to deflect the attention of persecutors and to highlight the invisible realities revealed by God.

This is Patmos, a small island in the Aegean. John was a prisoner here when he wrote his Apocalypse or Revelation. *‘I am John . . . I was put on the island of Patmos because I had proclaimed God’s word and the truth that Jesus revealed.’* **Rev 1.9**

Happy is the one who reads this book, and happy are those who listen to the words of this prophetic message and obey what is written . . . for the time is near. **Rev 1.3**

The images

robe: dignity of the priest

horn: power

golden girdle: royal power

lamb: Christ

woman: people of God, Church

The Apocalypse of John

This was written at the end of the 1st c. (in about 90 or 95), during the reign of Domitian, who persecuted the Christians. It was addressed to the seven churches of Asia Minor and, beyond them, to the Church as a whole.

Vision of Christ

I turned round to see who was talking to me, and I saw seven gold lampstands, and among them . . . what looked like a human being, wearing a robe that reached to his feet, and a gold belt round his chest. His hair was white as . . . snow, and his eyes blazed like fire; . . . and his voice sounded like a roaring waterfall. He held seven stars in his right hand, and a sharp two-edged sword came out of his mouth. His face was as bright as the midday sun. **Rev 1.12-16**

The apostle John, who is believed to have been the author of the Apocalypse.

The woman and the dragon

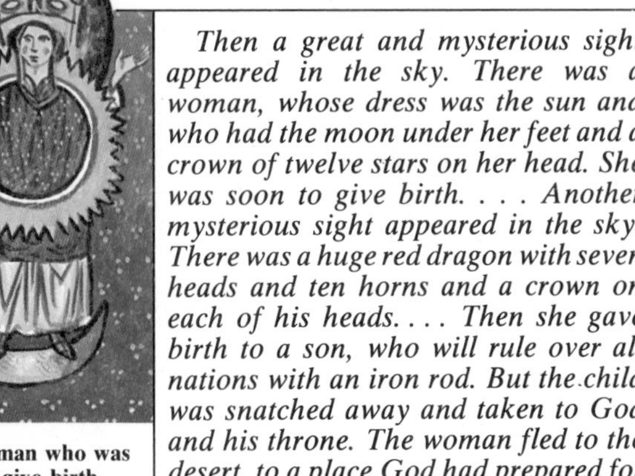

Then a great and mysterious sight appeared in the sky. There was a woman, whose dress was the sun and who had the moon under her feet and a crown of twelve stars on her head. She was soon to give birth. . . . Another mysterious sight appeared in the sky. There was a huge red dragon with seven heads and ten horns and a crown on each of his heads. . . . Then she gave birth to a son, who will rule over all nations with an iron rod. But the child was snatched away and taken to God and his throne. The woman fled to the desert, to a place God had prepared for her, where she will be taken care of for 1,260 days. Then war broke out in heaven. . . . The huge dragon was . . . thrown down to earth.
Rev 12.1 . . . 9

The woman who was soon to give birth is the Church. The pains and suffering of childbirth are persecution and the difficulty of remaining faithful.

The dragon is the serpent of Genesis, the devil.

The male child is Jesus Christ. The iron rod symbolises his power over the nations. His being taken to God is his resurrection.

The 1260 days (three and a half years) are the time of trial.

The triumph of the two beasts

Then I saw a beast coming up out of the sea. It had ten horns and seven heads; on each of its horns there was a crown, and on each of its heads there was a name that was insulting to God. The beast looked like a leopard, with feet like a bear's feet and a mouth like a lion's mouth. The dragon gave the beast his own power, his throne, and his vast authority. . . . It began to curse God, his name, the place where he lives, and all those who live in heaven. . . .

Then I saw another beast, which came up out of the earth. It had two horns like a lamb's horns, and it spoke like a dragon. It used the vast authority of the first beast in its presence. It forced the earth and all who live on it to worship the first beast, whose wound had healed. **Rev 13.1 . . . 12**

The beast represents the divinised Roman imperial power, persecutor of Christians. Its six horns represent its immense power; its seven heads are the seven emperors since Augustus. The Emperor is the sworn enemy of God, Christians and the Church.

The other beast represents the ministers of the imperial cult, which it was their task to impose.

The two beasts shown in the jaws of hell, according to a miniature of the Apocalypse from Cambrai, 12th c.

God's victory over the beast

There were seven angels with seven plagues. . . .

Then I heard a loud voice speaking from the temple to the seven angels: 'Go and pour out the seven bowls of God's anger on the earth!' The first angel went and poured out his bowl on the earth. Terrible and painful sores appeared. The second angel poured out his bowl on the sea. The water became like blood. . . .

The third angel poured out his bowl on the rivers . . . and they turned into blood.

Then the fourth angel poured out his bowl on the sun, and it was allowed to burn people with its fiery heat. . . .

Then the fifth angel poured out his bowl on the throne of the beast. Darkness fell over the beast's kingdom. . . . Then the sixth angel

The seventh trumpet announces the coming of God and of Christ (from the Apocalypse of St Severus, 11th c.)

The bowls recall the plagues sent down on the Egyptian pharaoh, who persecuted the Hebrew people. Some of them reappear here: ulcers, water turned into blood, darkness, frogs, thunder, hail.

The seven angels unleash the plagues over the earth (from a 15th c. miniature)

poured out his bowl on the great river Euphrates. The river dried up. . . .

Then the seventh angel poured out his bowl in the air. A loud voice came from the throne in the temple, saying, 'It is done!' . . . God remembered great Babylon and made her drink the wine from his cup — the wine of his furious anger. . . . **Rev 15.1; 16.1 . . . 21**

Then I saw a new heaven and a new earth. . . . There will be no more death, no more grief or crying or pain. The old things have disappeared. **Rev 21.1-4**

The victory of the lamb

The new Jerusalem is the Church, gathering in human beings at the end of time.

The throne is the throne of God. The image suggests the power of God who rules over the world.

Paradise regained, with the tree and the river of life. *Nothing that is under God's curse will be found in the city.* **Rev 22.17**

Everyone who hears this must also say, 'Come!' Come whoever is thirsty; accept the water of life as a gift, whoever wants it. **Rev 22.17**

Illustrators

Old Testament

Christine Adam, Nicole Baron,
Yves Besnier, Dominique Briffaut,
Christian Broutin, Élisabeth Dirat,
Dorothée Duntze, Nicole Hanoune,
Gilbert Houbre, Pierre de Hugo,
Christian Jégou, Jean-Jacques Larrière,
Nicolas Lesnikowski, René Mettler,
Isabelle Molinard, Jean-Pierre Moreau,
Brigitte Paris, Sylvaine Pérols,
François Pichon, François Place,
Aline Riquier, Christian Rivière,
Dominique Thibault, Pierre-Marie Valat,
Nataële Vogel, Pierre Weitzel.

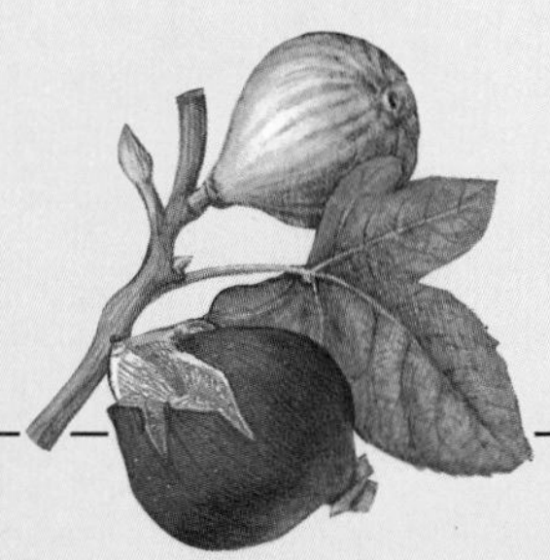

New Testament

Christine Adam, Nicole Baron,
Paul Bontemps, Laura Bour,
Henri Galeron, Donald Grant,
Gilbert Houbre, Pierre de Hugo,
Georges Lemoine, Florence Lequette,
Nicolas Lesnikowski, Manne,
Philippe Munch, Daniel Moignot,
Jean-Marc Pariselle, Sylvaine Pérols,
François Pichon, François Place,
Bruno Poiré, Jean-Marie Poissenot,
James Prunier, Agnès Regnault,
Christian Rivière, Jean-Claude Sénée,
Etienne Souppart, Dominique Thibault,
Nataële Vogel, Pierre Weitzel.

Index of Principal Characters in the Old Testament

Index of Principal Characters in the Old Testament

Index of Principal Characters in the New Testament